Cruise Ships
A Design Voyage
Bruce Peter

Cover: The giant *Norwegian Epic* emerges from a baptism of fire-fighting jet sprays at the commencement of her career in the summer of 2010. The vessel's 'piled up' superstructure typifies 'economy of scale' design approaches in contemporary mass market cruise ships.

Title page: A busy scene at Nassau in the Bahamas with large cruise ships from the Royal Caribbean, Disney Cruise Line, Costa Cruises, Carnival Cruise Line and MSC Cruises fleets tied up at the quays; they are the *Oasis of the Seas*, *Costa Atlantica*, *Disney Wonder*, *Carnival Sensation* and *MSC Poesia*.

Frontispiece: Celebrity Cruises' 2011-built *Celebrity Silhouette* catches morning light as she arrives off Newhaven in the River Forth in the summer of 2016. The vessel's streamlined forward aspect and many decks of cabin balconies typify recent design approaches to cruise tonnage.

Copyright © 2017 Ferry Publications.
All rights reserved.
ISBN 978-1-911268-08-6
The rights of Bruce Peter to be identified as the author of this work have been asserted in accordance with the Copyright Act 1991.
No part of this publication may be reproduced, stored in a retrieval system or transmitted in any form or by any means, electronic, mechanical, photocopying, recording or otherwise, without prior permission in writing from the publisher.
Produced in the Isle of Man by Ferry Publications (a trading name of Lily Publications Ltd).

Contents

Introduction 4

Chapter 1: The origins of cruising 14

Chapter 2: Cruising in the wake of the Wall Street Crash 23

Chapter 3: The post-war shift from liner to cruise 30

Chapter 4: Small and specialized 51

Chapter 5: The Caribbean Mass Market 53

Chapter 6: New cruise ships for world-wide itineraries 69

Chapter 7: Under Mediterranean flags 72

Chapter 8: The Oil Crisis and after 76

Chapter 9: West Germany's new cruise fleet 80

Chapter 10: The 1980s cruise ship generation in North America 83

Chapter 11: The Wärtsilä concept ships and their derivations 95

Chapter 12: Expansion and consolidation 102

Chapter 13: The mid-1990s generation 120

Chapter 14: Post-Panamax cruise ships 140

Chapter 15: A globalising cruise market 155

End notes 188

Bibliography 197

Index 203

ACKNOWLEDGEMENTS

The author wishes to offer his especial thanks to Miles Cowsill of Ferry Publications for producing this book, Roz Stimpson for copy-editing the manuscript, Matthew Sudders and Kalle Id for acting as 'critical friends' in advising on the manuscript content, Mick Lindsay and Mike Louagie for generously supplying many photographs from their collections and Ann Glen, John Peter and Elspeth Hough for their love and support throughout the project. The author also wishes to thank Knud Erik Bengtsen, Alan Blackwood, Jonathan Boonzaier, David Buri, Duncan Chappell, Anthony Cooke, Jim Davis, Philip Dawson, Ann Haynes, Albert Hinckley, Trevor Jones, Allan Jordan, Ian Johnston, Hans Kjærgaard, Peter Knego, Hans Otto Kristensen, John Kristiansen, Vuokko Laakso, Christian Landtman, Kai Levander, Bill Mayes, John McNeece, Catherine Moriarty, Peter Newall, Bruce Nierenberg, Nicholas Oddy, Stephen Payne, Paolo Piccione, Peter Quartermaine, Martin Saarikangas, Joel Schalit, Ian Schiffman, Ted Scull, Sarah Smith, Johan Snellman, Heikki Sorvali, Costis Stamboulelis, Holger Terpet, Rich Turnwald, Jan Erik Wahl, Tage Wandborg.

A panoramic view of Genoa with MSC Cruises' *MSC Opera* illuminated in the foreground; the popular image of a pristine while passenger ship with lights twinkling in the windows continues to have great popular appeal.

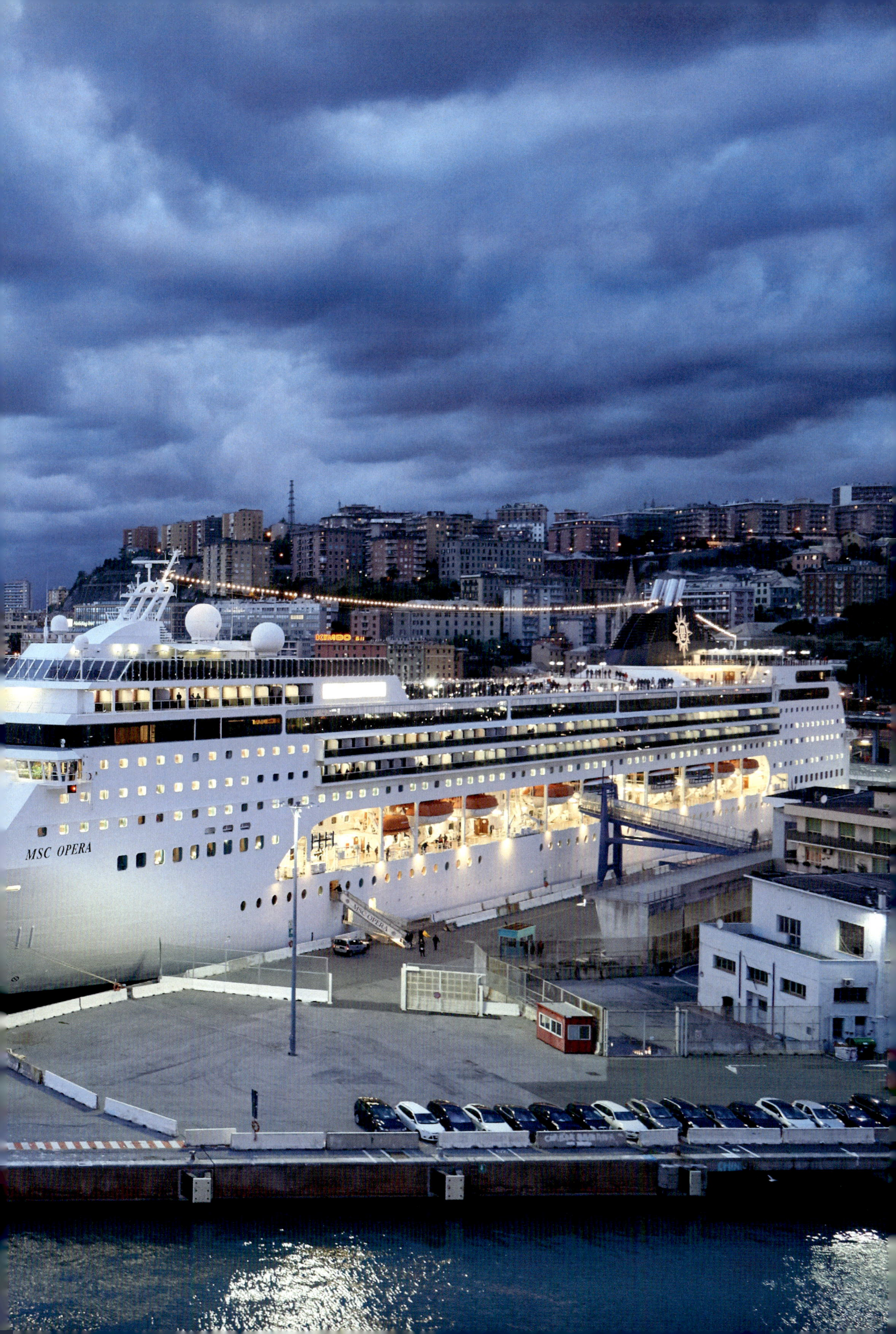
MSC OPERA

6 | Cruise Ships: A Design History

Today's largest cruise ships are essentially floating entertainment resorts, yet each one represents an extraordinary technological and commercial accomplishment. On Royal Caribbean's *Oasis of the Seas*, *Allure of the Seas* and *Harmony of the Seas*, there is an indoor mall, an outdoor 'Central Park', numerous deck activities, an ice rink and even a 'Boardwalk' amusement park, inspired by Coney Island.

Introduction

The rapid and seemingly exponential growth of the global cruise industry has been one of the defining leisure phenomena of our era. According to the industry's trade body, the Cruise Lines International Association, which collates an annual 'State of the Cruise Industry Outlook', in the past decade, global demand for cruises has increased by 68%. In 2009, there were 17.8 million global cruise passengers but by 2015, the number had shot up to over 23 million, a third of whom took Caribbean cruises, followed by 18% who cruised in the Mediterranean.[1] Presently, there are 57 new ocean-going cruise ships on order with over 120,700 additional berths to be filled.[2] In recent years, in the USA, the growth of cruise travel has outpaced general leisure travel by 22% and, in 2014, around 11.2 million American passengers chose a cruise vacation, each one spending an average of $127 on board every day, the highest sum of any cruising nation. Britain came second with 1.77 million cruise passengers, followed by 1.6 million Germans and one million Australians. The Chinese market presently stands at 700,000 though, as with everything in China, growth is rapid. Globally, the cruise industry accounts for almost one million jobs and its total economic impact is estimated to be worth $119.9 billion dollars per annum.[3]

In the mid-1980s, the biggest purpose-built cruise ship was Carnival Cruise Line's 46,052gt the *Holiday*, which had a capacity for 1,452 passengers. The only bigger passenger ships at that time were former trans-Atlantic liner the *Norway* (ex-*France*), which had recently been converted for cruising purposes, and the *Queen Elizabeth 2*, which had also been designed primarily for scheduled liner service. Today, the largest cruise ships are Royal Caribbean's trio of behemoths: the *Oasis of the Seas*, *Allure of the Seas* and *Harmony of the Seas*, delivered between 2009 and 2016, measuring over 225,000gt and with a capacity for 5,400 passengers each. Carnival, too, has a number of very large new cruise ships on order with passenger capacities estimated at 6,000 per ship. Among the Royal Caribbean vessels' attractions are a theatre accommodating 1,380 in which Broadway musicals are performed, a New York-style 'Central Park', containing over 50 trees and 10,000 assorted plants, an ice rink, an aqua theatre, a bionic bar in which drinks are mixed by robotic arms, a rock-climbing wall, zip lines, a surf simulator and the 'Ultimate Abyss', which is a helter-skelter with a 100-foot plunge. More conventional facilities include 16 restaurants, a shopping mall, a huge casino and numerous bars. The aim of such diversions seems to be to delay the onset of boredom and, hence, dissatisfaction in clienteles whose attention spans appear to be gradually decreasing – an ironic situation, given that for much of cruising's history, spending days at sea doing very little was the main point.

The advent of giant cruise ships such as these in so large numbers clearly demonstrates the expansion of wealth and of leisure culture in the past three decades. Since the mid-1980s, the cruise industry's leading operators have successfully applied the mass-standardisation principles of Henry Ford and the workplace efficiency theories of Frederick Taylor, both of which were first codified in the early twentieth century in the context of American manufacturing industry. The globalised economy also plays an important role in enabling cruise lines to raise capital from world-wide markets (just one of Royal Caribbean's new ships costs 800 million dollars) and to recruit low-wage crew members from third world nations (a crew of 2,394 serves aboard each of them). Nowadays, it is not uncommon to see week-long cruises with flights included being advertised in travel agents' shop windows for under £500 – about the same figure as a week on a much smaller cruise ship with far fewer facilities would have cost 40 years ago. A couple of decades beforehand, in the 1960s, when commercial jet planes swept away ocean liners as the primary means of travelling overseas, many predicted that 'deep sea' passenger shipping was doomed and numerous vessels were sent prematurely to the breakers. A liner voyage and a cruise are, however, very different phenomena; the former is any scheduled passage by sea carrying goods and/or passengers from A to B, primarily as a practical means of transport and therefore to be accomplished as quickly as possible. As with air travel, liners were strictly class-divided according to the price of ticket paid, meaning that those in each class only had access to a part of the ship. A cruise, by contrast, is carried out purely for leisure purposes and is usually a relatively slow-paced circuit of some attractive tourist region from A to B to C to D to E… and back to A again. Although some redundant liners have in the past been converted into cruise ships to be economically viable, the cruise industry nowadays depends upon purpose-designed and -built tonnage. Modern cruise ships are among the biggest and most technically complex man-made objects ever conceived. Aesthetically, they are rich in iconography and therefore surely deserving of a design historical analysis. The growth of the cruise industry also relates to wider socio-economic and political factors, for example America's changing status as a superpower, the rise of so-called neo-liberal capitalism and associated forces of 'globalisation.'

The design of a modern cruise ship is a complex process and involves focused creative enterprise involving naval architects, structural, mechanical and service engineers, plus interior, industrial and graphic designers. Every cruise ship

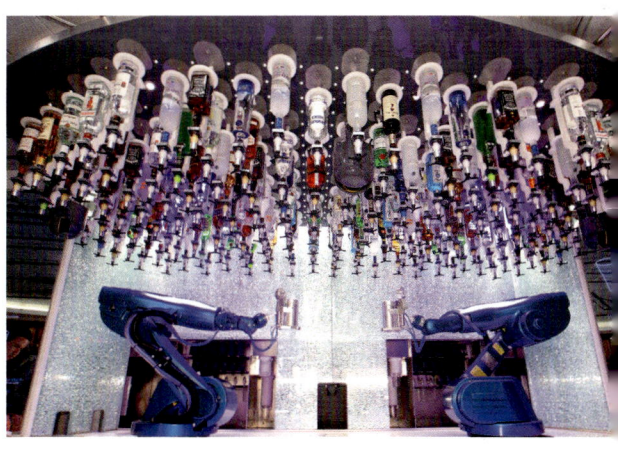

Above: Back in the 1950s, cruising was merely about relaxing and watching the sea drift by, as the two upper images show. Nowadays, mass market vessels feature numerous attention-grabbing distractions, including on Royal Caribbean's latest vessels a bionic bar with robot arms to mix drinks, pictured above.

Right: On Royal Caribbean's *Quantum of the Seas* of 2014 and her sisters, one can experience the sensation of 'sky-diving' in a vertical wind tunnel; this produces a strong upward draft to support a person in mid-air.

Below: The 'Freefall' illuminated waterslide, located ahead of the funnel on Norwegian Cruise Line's 2014-built *Norwegian Getaway*. Such family-friendly attractions make present-day cruise ships attractive to passengers of all ages.

begins as a concept derived from a commercial requirement to attract a particular passenger demographic for a certain type of cruise operation. The amount they are thought willing to pay will affect the vessel's size and the types of facilities to be provided for their recreation. How often the vessel will be bunkered and provisioned, the average and maximum speeds needed to carry out typical cruise itineraries and the navigating constraints of the waterways and harbours to be used are other issues to be resolved during the earliest planning stages. A project's development will be based upon a finely balanced mix of existing knowledge and careful predictions of future conditions – after all, every cruise ship represents a considerable financial risk and may take years to design and build.

The passenger and crew accommodation, machinery spaces, auxiliary services, fuel and ballast tanks, stores areas, safety equipment such as lifeboats, external decks and deck machinery positions all make up what is collectively known as the general arrangement or GA drawing. The circulation 'flows' of passengers, crew and provisions and the so-called 'adjacency' (or locations of revenue-generating facilities relative to each other) are important considerations when developing a cruise ship GA. This, along with the lines plan and transverse sectional drawings, provide the 'recipe' for building a ship and therefore form the centrepiece of the design. In addition, thousands of detailed construction drawings are necessary to show how individual aspects will be built.

In designing the hull lines, the principles of hydrodynamics are applied to minimise resistance and drag. The aim is to achieve a satisfactory compromise between the optimum sea-keeping characteristics and the restrictions of size, payload and fuel economy. Detailed stability calculations are needed and the international safety regulations and conventions governing shipping must be interpreted and applied for the ship to be registered by the classification societies. The design must take into account the vessel's precise performance when damaged by fire, collision or other mishap, such as sinking. The naval architect's work includes detailed planning to meet specific criteria for a safe and timely evacuation.

Yet, to explain the design process for cruise ships in terms of strict commercial and engineering rationalism is to ignore cruising's established and emerging social conventions to which vessels' visual identities are directly related. The idea of a cruise conjures images of luxury, romance, escapism, social advancement and – possibly – nostalgia. The types of atmosphere and experiences passengers expect to enjoy on board therefore align with the wider theories and practices of post-modernism in architecture, design and visual culture.[4]

While Europe drained its resources by fighting two World Wars, America emerged as the twentieth century's dominant cultural and economic power. It was thus American design values that came to define the leisure and hospitality industries from the mid-century onward, including the styling of cruise ships. Indeed, since the 1920s, approximately half of all cruise passengers have been American, even although the vessels themselves are much more likely to have been designed and built in Finnish, French, German or Italian shipyards for European owners and to be navigated and managed by European officers. The idea of taking a cruise, however, aligns very well with a libertarian ethos of meritocracy, tempered with strong social and cultural aspirations towards a life of leisure – surely the perfect fulfilment of 'the American Dream.'

In mid-twentieth century America, a vibrant commercial leisure culture emerged in large, self-contained indoor shopping malls, the theme parks of Disney World and the gaming resorts of Reno, Atlantic City and, especially, Las Vegas. In parallel, the chain hotels and resorts of Hilton, Radisson, Marriott and Holiday Inn – with their system-built modernist accommodation towers, large reception halls with banks of elevators, *en suite* rooms, air conditioning, and fabulous interior décor – came to define popular conceptions of modern luxury hospitality provision. From the latter-1960s onward, similar aesthetics began to be applied to the branding, exterior and interior design of cruise ships.

The need for such great expansion of leisure provision arose as a consequence of the exponential growth of the middle classes. Throughout the twentieth century, they benefitted from wider access to education, an increase in office-based work, commensurately higher wages and more leisure time. This led to a 'massification' of activities that previously had been the preserve of small elites. The size and technical sophistication of passenger ships used for cruises grew in parallel.

The French sociologist Pierre Bourdieu in his major work *Distinction: A Social Critique of the Judgement of Taste* (1979) demonstrated how relative wealth and differences in education are demonstrated in consumers' taste, which is complex and operates at multiple levels. As Bourdieu famously states 'taste classifies and it classifies the classifier' – in other words, people judge each other's taste individually and as members of wider social groups. A related concept is that of 'habitus' – Bourdieu's term for people's complete physical and social contexts, the long-term experience of which constrains where they feel most comfortable and encourages the replication of familiar cultural mores from one generation to the next. Bourdieu sees the multitudinous facets of each individual's background and everyday experience of living as both conditioning and reflecting their tastes and expectations. As he puts it, 'Taste functions as a sort of social orientation, a 'sense of one's place', guiding the occupants of a given… social space towards the social positions adjusted to their properties, and towards the practices or goods which befit the occupants of that position.'[5] Selecting a type of holiday – such as a cruise – and, once aboard, choosing what clothing and jewellery to wear, what food to eat, which shore excursions to join and which fellow passengers to consort with for the duration all provide opportunities for the demonstration of taste. Indeed, a cruise ship – with its highly defined spatial and operational hierarchy – is arguably an ideal setting for hyper-normalised forms of cultural signification and social interaction to occur.

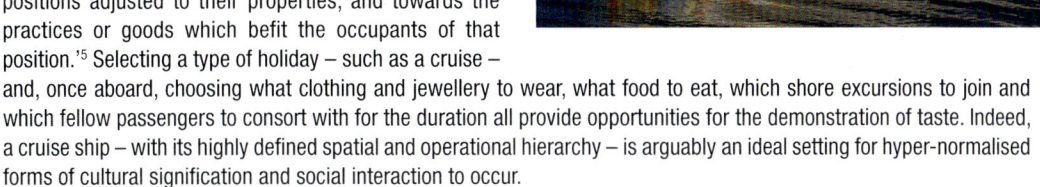

In order to appeal to wide diversities of consumers, commercial leisure environments of all kinds have sought to be relatively pluralistic in their stylistic references, often featuring conglomerations of wildly diverse imagery, usually far removed from its historical contexts. After all, younger or older generations prefer different types of music, dancing, comedy, food, drink, clothes, furniture and so on. Furthermore, it was vitally important to ensure a clear differentiation from either users' home or work environments – a situation explained by the concept of 'third place.' Whereas the typical home is decorated with items of personal significance and the office is primarily intended for serious activity, reflected in its standardised furnishings, a 'third place' can be flamboyantly themed in a variety of historicist styles, or, conversely, it might attempt to assert a futuristic 'sci-fi' identity. When promotional literature is produced to sell such environments to consumers, it is usual to find them described with vague, but suitably aspirational, terminology – 'classic', 'contemporary', 'traditional', 'modern', 'luxurious' and 'iconic' being the words most commonly used, sometimes in combination with one another.

Such commercial pragmatism often runs contrary to intellectualised ideas of what constitutes 'good design' – which has usually tended towards the aesthetic purity sought by followers of the Modern Movement. In the 1920s and 30s, several prominent modernist architects and designers had contended that the exteriors of trans-Atlantic and colonial ocean liners were exemplars of functional beauty, coupled with the useful application of up-to-date technologies. The idea that a ship – or any other design object – should be visually coherent has for long had a deep appeal for those educated in aesthetic matters, their (highly dubious) logic being that aesthetic purity and moral purity are somehow interlinked. However, it is arguable that this proposition masked a wider concern that the downward percolation of wealth would undermine the privileged positions of those who considered themselves to have superior taste. Indeed, much existing writing about cruise ships and the culture of cruising is riddled with snobbery.

Writing in the mid-1980s at the high point of 'Reaganomics' and the related advent of a boom in the construction of large, purpose-built cruise ships, designed specifically for the American market, the New York-based passenger liner historian John Maxtone-Graham (1929-2015) observed of recent Caribbean cruise ship interior designs:

> 'There is a prevailing school of lounge decorators that favours yellow and orange highlighted with Miami gold and rust. More recently, one finds the spectrum's mauve bands exploited for effect – magenta, plum and violet predominate, sometimes leavened with pink, that most dangerous choice. Lacking sorely in dignity.
>
> These efflorescences spring from attempts to pander to an archetypal passenger/customer. Though foreign-built and foreign-owned, cruise ships sail with American passenger loads… In consequence, owners encourage their designers to adhere closely to what they, the owners, perceive as America's decorative ideal. At stake is the approval of a particular passenger composite that I once found delineated in a Wärtsilä [Finnish shipbuilding company] memorandum: a middle-aged, middle-western American housewife. (Presumably, in line with her other centrist characteristics, she is middle class as well, though socioeconomic value judgements of this kind are rare in Scandinavia.) She is the cruise lines' mythic client-at-large, queen of America's demographic Reno-Trenton heartland, the prototypical passenger to please. And it is in an attempt to define the elusive parameters of her taste that today's public rooms are awash with sunbelt glitz.'[6]

During this period, Maxtone-Graham was admired as one of the leading – and certainly the most incisive – of a small number of specialist commentators addressing cruise ship design and cruising as a leisure activity. A former Broadway theatre manager, he was urbane in manner, an erudite writer and lecturer and, as with many New York sophisticates, he seemed to aspire more to the tastes of a 'traditional' English gentleman than to those of his go-getting fellow citizens. By Maxtone-Graham's own admission, he was 'Old School' in his preference for 'traditional' cruise ships with the design and decorative characteristics of past generations of trans-Atlantic liners and with a capacity of between 500 and 1,000 'seasoned' passengers for whom being at sea was the ultimate aim. Although he found the newer purpose-built 'mass market' cruise ships – with their emphases on increased passenger capacity and onboard revenue generation – both intrinsically interesting and an understandable development, for him, they were clearly inferior to the older, grander, more exclusive and expensive examples of previous generations. Although far too polite to say so directly, Maxtone-Graham appears disdainful of what the British sociologist Dick Hebdige referred to as 'the spectre of Americanisation' haunting

Above: The *Norwegian Getaway*, which features hull art to create a colourful and more distinctive image, indicating an informal shipboard atmosphere; built by Meyer Werft in Germany, the vessel typifies the unique expertise of a few European shipbuilders in quickly building complex vessels of this type.

10 | Cruise Ships: A Design History

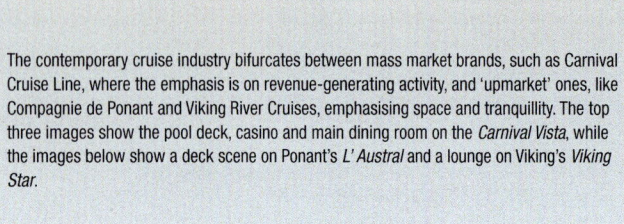

The contemporary cruise industry bifurcates between mass market brands, such as Carnival Cruise Line, where the emphasis is on revenue-generating activity, and 'upmarket' ones, like Compagnie de Ponant and Viking River Cruises, emphasising space and tranquillity. The top three images show the pool deck, casino and main dining room on the *Carnival Vista*, while the images below show a deck scene on Ponant's *L' Austral* and a lounge on Viking's *Viking Star*.

popular culture' ('popular' often being used as a polite pseudonym for 'coarse' or 'inferior').[7]

Although cruise ships are designed and promoted to appeal to the tastes and budgets of a fairly broad range of potential users, these map very precisely onto the segmented structure of the middle classes. Relatively few genuine aristocrats have ever taken cruises – even if cruise companies' promotional language would have one believe otherwise. Thus, cruise ship design and cruising as an activity may be related to the concept of 'The Middlebrow' – which is a culturally loaded and historically disreputable term, first used by the satirical magazine *Punch* in December 1925, according to which 'it consists of people who are hoping that someday they will get used to the stuff they ought to like.'[8] In other words, 'the Middlebrow' refers to people, objects, places and texts which aspire to superior cultural status and which, in line with critical representations of bourgeois culture, seek enhancement by the easy means of spending money (as opposed to the comparatively difficult means of education to achieve more profound knowledge and insights). 'The Middlebrow' therefore occupies an uncomfortable and insufficiently 'anchored' position in cultural debates between the plateau of 'high culture' and the supposed 'depths' of popular culture. Indeed, 'the Middlebrow' usually represents popular culture aspiring towards some of the more superficially alluring characteristics of high culture. However, in commercial contexts such as cruise ship interiors, imperatives of speed and economy tend to cause imagery originating in high culture to be re-rendered as kitsch simulacra – in other words, it is decontextualised and often manufactured using inferior materials.

A further issue raised – though uncommented upon – by Maxtone-Graham is that of gender in the design of cruise ships, particularly of their interiors. As he observes, the cruise industry's own image of its typical passenger – or at least the one getting to choose the vacation – is female. For the transport and hospitality industries, even in the latter nineteenth century, this was perceived to be the case. As both shipping and the railway industries had image problems due to their potential for discomfort and danger, managements sought to focus on easing the concerns of female travellers through the elegant and 'respectable' interior design of First Class carriages, ships' saloons and cabins, it being assumed that men would travel in any case out of necessity (or that the macho surrounding culture would prevent them from revealing doubts). In upmarket ladies' magazines such as *The Queen* (the forerunner to *Harpers & Queen*), well-travelled female writers wrote trenchant critiques of the decoration and standards of hospitality found aboard passenger ships as much as hotels and other sites of modern 'luxury.'

To achieve the correct shipboard atmosphere, it was not uncommon for shipping company's directors' wives to help choose the décor, thereby appealing to like-minded ladies whose husbands would be paying for liner voyages. In the 1950s, leading trans-Atlantic liner companies, such as Cunard, French Line and United States Line all employed female professional interior designers for these same reasons and, a generation later, the modern cruise industry continued to follow similarly 'feminised' – or even somewhat camp – approaches when selecting interior decorative treatments for its new generations of purpose-built vessels. In the architecture, design and engineering worlds, dominated by heterosexual men, the feminised characteristics of cruise ship interior design have often been unfairly denigrated. Such interiors have been criticised for appearing too 'comfortable', 'bland' and 'safe' on the one hand, or for being too superficially flamboyant and 'theatrical' on the other, whereas it is arguable that instead they ought to have been celebrated for their ability to please broad social cross-sections, providing glamorous backgrounds for collective *bon vivant*. To use social sciences jargon, cruise ship interiors may indeed be thought of as 'stages' for the 'experience' and 'performance' of modernity through their provision of highly stylised forms of hospitality, food and beverage service and social activity.

As the illustrations in this book will prove, with the benefit of hindsight, many cruise ship interiors of the past were superb examples of the design values and material culture of their respective eras and even the 1970s and 80s examples criticised by Maxtone-Graham nowadays would be perceived by many as possessing a certain 'retro chic.' Such environments – relying so heavily on upholstery, drapes and lighting for their effects – are, however, very ephemeral and frequently refitted to reflect subsequent trends, meaning that few survive for any length of time in pristine condition. Indeed, it is arguable that – in common with other types of leisure and entertainment attraction, such as fairgrounds, theme parks and shopping malls – passenger ship interiors exist in a constant state of flux with major modifications carried out during bi-annual refits and minor changes enacted by shipboard maintenance crews on an ongoing basis.

Just as in the casino resorts of Las Vegas and in large Mid-Western shopping malls, wide varieties of design themes are nowadays juxtaposed together, often in ways that those who consider themselves design literate find excessive, illogical or in poor taste. Yet, cruise ship interiors exist to please their users, to give them a sense of escapism from the mundanities of work or home life, as well as a feeling of being in receipt of 'good value for money.' Frequently, elements of alluring design styles from the past are mixed with contemporary aesthetics, this Janus-like (simultaneously backward- and forward-looking) approach often reflecting cruising's romantic and nostalgic allusions to a lost 'golden age' of liner travel, coupled with the assurance of the latest comfort-giving innovations.

In contrast to their cocooning, hotel-like interiors, cruise ship exteriors connote different sets of values, which arguably tend towards a more assertively masculine interest in technological modernity. The earliest purpose-built cruise ships in the *fin de siècle* 1900s sought to emulate the appearance of large, privately-owned steam yachts. For those who were very rich – but insufficiently so actually to own a yacht – taking a cruise on such a vessel was the next best option. During the mid-twentieth century, by contrast, the external design of large trans-Atlantic and colonial liners became highly

Above: In recent time, extensive spa and 'wellness' facilities, offering 'pampering', therapies and holistic treatments have become common facilities on cruise ships of all types. The Nordic Spa on *Viking Star* is a good example of the tranquil design approach preferred for such spaces.

culturally influential, not least in the design of leisure buildings ashore, the 'streamline moderne' stylings of which sought to reflect such vessels' whiteness and curving lines. By the 1960s, passenger liners and their architectural imitations had become passé, usurped by the new, futuristic imageries of the jet age and of the space age and these were emulated in other transport forms, including cars and yachts. So when the first purpose-built Caribbean cruise ships appeared at the end of the decade, their design inspiration came once again from the most up-to-date motor yachts. As cruise ships grew bigger from the 1980s onward and modular construction techniques were introduced by shipyards, meaning the elimination of hull sheer and rounded stern lines, a great deal of effort continued to be expended in lending these vessels suitably impressive silhouettes, making extensive use of tinted glazing and with curves imposed to soften the potentially bulky forms of their superstructures. The world's current biggest cruise ships, Royal Caribbean's Oasis-class, clearly demonstrate the results of this design effort – even if these vessels' fundamentally elephantine proportions overwhelm most of the imposed styling. As with clothing on people, the judicious application of paint on vessels' exteriors can also help to disguise their mass.

As the cruise industry has expanded, large, purpose-built 'mass market' ships have come to provide types of service and cuisine previously only found on the more expensive and exclusive vessels. Furthermore, behind the scenes, nearly all cruise ships are designed around similar service-flow strategies and are equipped with mostly generic fixtures and fittings. To maintain their privileged position, therefore, 'luxury' cruise brands have tended to seek to distinguish themselves partly through offering more space per passenger and including elements in the cruise ticket price that on mass market lines would be optional extras, purchased at the point of consumption. Above all, the 'upmarket' lines nowadays emphasise in promotional material what might be considered as metaphors for 'luxury' and 'exclusivity' – such as having white-gloved stewards to serve afternoon tea or the use of 'fine bone china' rather than plastic tableware in the buffet. These supposedly 'superior' details of service provision – which in reality cost relatively little extra to provide – are also taken by professional cruise industry critics and promoters – such as the writers of the Berlitz Guides – as signifiers of quality. The 'upmarket' lines' passengers – who have, after all, invested more money in believing that they are receiving a superior cruise 'experience' – also recognise and comment upon the fulfilment of such details, or their sudden disappearance due to cost-cutting measures. To a large extent, this approach to creating perceptions of qualitative hierarchies reflects the ways in which hotels are allocated star ratings, based on their ranges of facilities and the details of their service presentation.

So far as staffing is concerned, however, large passenger ships are upstairs/downstairs worlds; just like the stately homes and grand hotels from which their interior design inspiration often was taken, hospitality provision depends on hidden infrastructures of rather spartan and cramped crew accommodation and circulation systems to move baggage, laundry and food and beverage supplies. Occasionally, the opening of a door marked 'Crew Only' in a carpeted cabin corridor enables passengers to have the briefest glimpse into this hidden realm of hard painted steel surfaces, unfinished deck heads and bare fluorescent lighting that is the crew's domain. In order to allow passengers the maximum daylight, cruise ships' crew accommodation is in the centre of the hulls' lower decks and therefore often entirely lacking in natural illumination. The most upmarket cruise ships have passenger-to-crew ratios of approximately 1:1 while around 1:2.5 is otherwise standard.

Until the early 1980s, approaches to the staffing of cruise ships split between those almost entirely crewed from the flag nation (such as the vessels of the upmarket and expensive Norwegian-owned Royal Viking Line, whose entire staffs came from Norway) and those of the emerging 'mass market' cruise operators, such as Carnival, whose vessels were Panamanian-registered with Italian officers and crew from Honduras and elsewhere. In the ensuing years, the former model disappeared due to its inherent costliness, coupled with an inability to recruit enough suitable Western employees willing to work long hours as cabin or restaurant stewards for relatively little pay. Almost invariably, present day cruise ships' officers continue to be European with hotel staff drawn from a wide diversity of third world nations. This perpetuates a tradition first established in the nineteenth century on many colonial liners. Britain's East India Company and, subsequently, the Peninsular and Oriental Steam Navigation Company found that employing seafarers from nations on the Horn of Africa and the Indian sub-continent was highly advantageous as, not only they could be paid less than Britons but also, for religious reasons, they did not resort to alcohol – which was regarded by ship owners and officers as the scourge of shipboard discipline. Thus, the power hierarchies of the imperial world order were replicated on board ship.

On contemporary cruise ships, similar hierarchies reflect the differences between nations with high levels of education and low levels of corruption – and those where the opposite situations prevail. Today, the highest proportions of cruise ship deck and hotel staff come from the Philippines and Indonesia, both countries with exceptionally large, youthful populations in which opportunities for constructive and remunerative employment are sadly too few and far between. Their typical basic pay might be as little as 500 U.S. dollars per month – a paltry sum – but this is augmented by the mandatory service charges added to passengers' bills at the ends of their cruises. Only with these extras added can salaries that are quite adequate by the typical earning levels of the employees' nations of origin be obtained. Yet, for many young men and women from such backgrounds, gaining a job on a cruise ship is seen as a springboard to greater opportunities. Although cruise ships' hotel staff are worked hard, seven days a week, typical contracts are for shorter terms and with greater remuneration overall than for hotel work ashore in the Middle East, for example, and there are opportunities to learn foreign languages and to gain hospitality industry skills of a high international standard that could be put to use later on in starting a hotel or restaurant business ashore.

On the larger mass-market cruise ships with several thousand employees, it can be hard to engender a sense of camaraderie among the crew as many shipmates inevitably remain strangers – and this is a big change from earlier eras when crew were numbered in hundreds and most knew one another. A majority of cruise passengers being treated to very attentive cabin and restaurant services on a daily basis, even having paid less than £100 per day for their cruise, will be unlikely to consider the living conditions and terms of employment of those serving them. It is surely this aspect of the cruise industry, more than its supposed lapses of decorative taste, that renders it truly kitsch.

Furthermore, each large cruise ship's ability to deposit between 3,000 and 6,000 passengers on Caribbean islands raises issues about the ethics of mass cruise travel when viewed from cultural-geographical perspectives, as well as those of political economy. John Urry's 1990 study *The Tourist Gaze* uses the concept of 'the gaze' as an ideologically-charged way of looking upon other peoples and cultures with an implicit and unequal power relationship between the observer and that which is observed. When we travel, we bring with us certain amounts of wealth and particular assemblages of educational and cultural capital. We then look upon the environments and lives of others whom we visit through a prism of that with which we are already familiar, judging the objects of our gazes by our own standards of what is considered 'normal' and, conversely, what is 'strange' or 'exotic.' Urry notes that, whereas in the past, tourism was primarily educational, in more recent time, its definition has become blurred as it has been mixed with shopping, sport and other highly diverse activities (all found on large cruise ships). He also observes hierarchies associated with the definition of tourists, whom he suggests are usually considered to be less admirable in status and aims than explorers or travellers – hence the implicit caché of 'adventure' cruise ships over the mass market variety. Yet, cruise passengers undoubtedly bring wealth and prosperity to the destinations vessels serve and, arguably, the more remote or undeveloped the destination, the more significant the impact. The cruise industry, however, demands security, service and leisure infrastructures that change cruise destinations both for better and for worse. Pollution caused by diesel auxiliary engines running while in port to provide power for onboard services and garbage disposal are other problems to be resolved – though, in recent years, the industry has become increasingly environmentally-conscious. The growing use of liquid natural gas for fuel and the fitment of exhaust gas 'scrubbers' to remove pollutants is reflective both of toughening legislation and some passengers' increasing expectations. Many observers of the cruise industry would, however, point out that such measures largely constitute what has come to be known as 'green washing' – in other words, giving an appearance of environmental consciousness while continuing to cause pollution and degradation. As water is resistant, moving any hull volume through it needs large amounts of energy and so it may be questionable as to whether this is well-spent when the purposes are mainly entertainment and consumerism.

The last major published work on cruise ship design was Philip Dawson's *Cruise Ships: An Evolution in Design*, produced in 2000 and now out of print. At that time, only the first of the so-called 'mega ships', measuring over 100,000gt, had appeared – these being Carnival Cruise Line's 101,353gt, 3,400-passenger the *Carnival Destiny* (1996) and P&O Princess Cruises' 108,806gt, 3,300-passenger the *Grand Princess* (1998). During the decade-and-a-half since, there have been major developments in the sizes and facilities of subsequent new buildings and, in China a major new cruise market has begun to emerge. This volume seeks to provide a wider range of perspectives and contexts through which cruise ship design and the cruise industry may be better understood. Whereas Dawson concentrated solely on the production of cruise ship design, here, there is in addition a focus on how vessels have been consumed and experienced, locating the cruise industry within wider economic, political and cultural contexts.

To give an idea of the size of each vessel, gross tonnages and passenger capacities are quoted. Neither statistic is ideal however. Gross tonnage is a measure of internal volume, the regulations for the calculation of which have changed periodically, meaning that one could not make a direct comparison between a 1950s tonnage figure and one from the 1990s. Passenger capacity gives an even less precise impression of size as the more exclusive cruise ships have lower passenger densities – though, when set against gross tonnage, it does reveal a vessel's relative spaciousness. Generally, the figures quoted throughout should give readers an idea of just how greatly cruise ships have grown in scale, particularly since the 1980s.

Below: Departure time for cruise ships at Marseille, with *MSC Preziosa* and *Costa Serena* catching early evening sunlight as they commence the next stage of their circuits of the Western Mediterranean.

Chapter 1
The origins of cruising

From the appearance of the first sea-going steamship, Henry Bell's the *Comet*, which began sailing on the River Clyde in 1812, the development firstly of coastal steamer services and, shortly after, of international liner routes, was rapid. Ashore and at sea, steam power enabled transport services to be regularised according to published timetables. Early on, coastal steamships were additionally used to provide short leisure trips for a curious public who soon found that, in clement weather, viewing coastal scenery from offshore while eating, drinking and even dancing could make for a pleasant afternoon outing. So far as government was concerned, steam power enabled military superiority to be projected overseas and so 'deep sea' passenger and mail-carrying liners and warships became mutually supportive in the creation and maintenance of imperial might. Arguably the first international liner operator of steamships was Britain's Peninsular & Oriental Steam Navigation Company (P&O), founded in the 1830s to commence a mail, cargo and passenger service from London to Gibraltar.

By the mid-1840s, Peninsular & Oriental was running a network of mail and cargo routes round the Mediterranean and these provided opportunities for travellers to visit various places of interest along the way by booking aboard a series of connected sailings. P&O's largest ships of the day, the *Great Liverpool* and the *Oriental*, each offered only about 100 passenger berths that were typically otherwise lightly booked. Such trips were a privilege of the wealthy, having sufficient money and time to travel for two months or more, and were rooted in the tradition of the classic 'Grand Tour', the purpose of which was to view the cultural treasures of classical and Renaissance art and architecture in Italy, Greece and elsewhere. Since the early seventeenth century, young aristocratic men had made the Grand Tour for enlightenment, discovery and personal enrichment.

The time needed in each port for handling mails and cargo, provisioning and coaling allowed P&O's passengers a stay of a night or sometimes longer, thus, inland travels could be arranged. In 1844, P&O gave the popular London satirist, novelist and author William Makepeace Thackeray (1811-1863) tickets for a connected series of voyages around the Mediterranean in return for which he wrote a short book telling of his experience as an enticement for others to also make the tour. His *Notes of a Journey From Cornhill to Grand Cairo* was published in 1846.

Thackeray was obviously thrilled to have had an opportunity to make such a trip as he relates in the opening passages of his narrative: 'The Peninsular and Oriental Company had arranged an excursion in the Mediterranean, by which, in the space of a couple of months, as many men and cities were to be seen as Ulysses surveyed and noted in ten years.'[9] He sailed from Southampton on 22nd August 1844 aboard P&O steamer the *Lady Mary Wood*, bound for Vigo, Lisbon and Gibraltar. There, he transferred to the *Tagus* to continue his journey eastwards across the Mediterranean, calling at Valetta, Athens, Smyrna (now Izmir), Constantinople (now Istanbul), Rhodes, the ancient ruins of Telmessus, Beirut and Jaffa, where he left the ship and made his first of two overland excursions to Jerusalem and the Holy Land. He then sailed aboard the *Iberia* from Jaffa to Alexandria, where he made an overland tour to Cairo, the Nile and the Pyramids at Giza. He then sailed back to Southampton aboard the *Oriental*, and was home again in London by Lord Mayor's Day on 9th November.

Writing under the *nom de plume* M.A. Titmarsh, Thackeray reveals his own imperialistic outlook on the people and sights of the Mediterranean. To him, there were numerous 'malodorous and ill-mannered folk eating horrible messes cooked in filthy pots with their bare and dirty hands' and sleeping in unclean old bedding.[10] Yet he described other encounters with enthusiasm and affection. A small caravan, assembled to take his tour party on the overland trip from Jaffa to Jerusalem, was described in some detail – including how the ladies in the group were carried on a litter slung between two black mules fore and aft, with 'mahogany coloured' men walking at either side to balance the litter as it swayed. He was greatly impressed by the ruins of Telmessus, an ancient Greek city now in Turkey, writing that 'you have but to shut your eyes, and think, and recall it, and the delightful vision comes smiling back, to your order! – the divine air – the delicious little pageant, which nature set before you on this lucky day.'[11]

Above: Early cruises were performed by Orient Line's *Chimborazo* (top), Hamburg-Amerika Linie's *Augusta Victoria* (centre) and P&O's *Tagus* (bottom).

P&O's cruise passenger-carrying liner services continued until 1854 when Britain and France declared war against Russia, and ships were urgently needed to carry troops and armaments to the Crimea. It was later resumed in the 1880s at which point, fortuitously for P&O, the *British Medical Journal* recommended sea travel as being therapeutic. P&O's first dedicated cruise ship appeared in 1904 when the 5,010gt the *Rome*, which had been built in 1881, was converted for this purpose, becoming the *Vectis*.

An alternative to P&O's version of the Mediterranean 'Grand Tour' was to head northward to the Atlantic Isles and the fjords of Western Norway. As Europe was swept by the industrial revolution, some of the wealthy and leisured desired to escape from the man-made squalor and pollution of the modern city and to commune with untamed nature. The romantic

P&O's *Vectis* is pictured top left and the North of Scotland Steam Navigation Company's *St Rognvald* (left) and *St Sunniva* (top right); the latter is seen during a cruise to the Norwegian fjords, for which her aft deck has been covered by a canvas awning to keep any rain off sightseeing passengers. Hamburg-Amerika's pioneering purpose-built cruising yacht, *Prinzessin Victoria Luise*, is pictured below. The visual similarity to the largest private and royal yachts of her era, coupled with a white hull, creates a great impression of exclusive, leisured living.

16 | Cruise Ships: A Design History

A series of images showing the *Prinzessin Victoria Luise*'s social hall, resembling a winter garden of the era in a hotel ashore (top left), her smoking saloon (top right), her exterior (centre) and her dining saloon (bottom right). The disposition of the interiors reflected the era's respectable social norms with dining as a major occasion, hence the saloon's splendid design, but smoking as a 'men only' pursuit, requiring a dark space of masculine character.

vision conjured in such tourists' imaginations by the fjord landscape was not, however, shared by many of those who had to eke out a living in such harsh surroundings. Thus, paradoxically, when the first cruise passengers arrived in Norway in the mid-1880s, Norwegian emigration to America was at its height.

The earliest cruises to Norway appear to have been provided by the North of Scotland Steam Navigation Company, the mainstay of whose operations was to provide a regular ferry service between Edinburgh (Leith), Aberdeen and the Orkney and Shetland islands. On 8th June 1886, *The Scotsman* newspaper carried the following advertisement:

'The fast and commodious steamship *St Rognvald* is intended to make a special trip with a limited number of cabin passengers on Thursday, June 24 ex Leith and Aberdeen to Bergen and some of the principal fjords and places of interest on the west coast of Norway.'[12]

Ninety passengers would be carried, paying £10 each. Although relatively expensive by the era's average professional earnings, the cruise was considerably cheaper and therefore more accessible than P&O's Mediterranean circuits.[13] The 984gt *St Rognvald* had been built three years previously by Hall, Russell & Co of Aberdeen and was typical of the coastal passenger, cargo and mail steamers of her era. Such was the popularity of her initial cruise to Norway that more were planned and, very soon, the North of Scotland Steam Navigation Company placed an order for a new steamer primarily for cruising purposes. The *St Sunniva*, delivered from Hall, Russell in 1887, was a little smaller at 864gt but in appearance somewhat resembled a large private yacht. She had a clipper bow with a bowsprit and figurehead and, inboard, she provided only one class of accommodation, with berths for 142 passengers. The dining saloon accommodated the full passenger complement at one sitting and the cuisine was advertised as being equal to that of a first class hotel. In addition, there was a lounge, which had a piano built into the bulkhead as, unlike on today's cruise ships, passengers were expected to entertain themselves. Separate from this were the gentlemen's smoking room and ladies' lounge. Throughout, the vessel was equipped with electric lighting.

The advent of the *St Sunniva* enabled the North of Scotland Steam Navigation Company to offer lengthier cruise itineraries at greater cost to the North Cape and, subsequently, around Britain. During the winter, the vessel was laid up until a charter to the wealthy financier Baron Rothschild was arranged to undertake a private Mediterranean cruise in 1893-1894. Shortly after, the Thomas Cook travel firm also chartered the *St Sunniva* for a cruise to the Eastern Mediterranean.

Soon, the larger 'deep sea' passenger liner companies elbowed into the *St Sunniva*'s summer Norwegian fjords market. By the end of the decade, P&O, Orient Line, Royal Mail Lines, Compagnie Générale Transatlantique, Hamburg-Amerika Linie and Norddeutscher Lloyd were all offering cruises to Norway, often on bigger and better-appointed vessels. For example, in 1889, Orient Line redeployed its London-Melbourne liners the *Chimborazo* and *Garonne* as cruise ships. Measuring around 4,000gt, they far out-classed the little *St Sunniva*. It was on the *Garonne* in 1896 that the famous British social reformer and design entrepreneur, William Morris, following doctor's orders to recuperate from an illness, took a cruise to Norway. Morris was an arch medievalist who had become fascinated by the culture of the Vikings and twenty years previously had even made his own highly imaginative translation of the Sagas.

The first Hamburg-Amerika Linie cruise was by the 7,661gt *Augusta Victoria*, which departed Hamburg in January 1891 on an ambitious 58-day itinerary to the eastern Mediterranean, then through the Suez Canal to ports around the Red Sea and Persian Gulf; 241 passengers were aboard, of whom the majority were Germans. Joining them was Hamburg-Amerika's Chairman, Albert Ballin, whose presence apparently ensured that every effort was expended to make the cruise was an enjoyable experience. Indeed, the company's subsequent annual cruise programmes proved so lucrative that Ballin eventually turned his attention to the commissioning of a purpose-built cruise ship to undertake further voyages. Upon the new vessel's entry into service in 1901, the *Scientific American* reported:

'It is now about ten years ago that the Hamburg-American company made the experiment of sending one of their regular passenger steamers, the *Augusta Victoria*, for a winter trip from Hamburg to the Mediterranean. The venture was looked upon as somewhat in the nature of an experiment, and it was undertaken partly with the object of giving employment to the vessel during the slack season of the trans-Atlantic trade. The tour was such a thorough success that it was determined to make New York the starting point of the next trip, the results of which were such as to justify the company in instituting a regular winter service of this kind. In the earlier years of the venture, the greater proportion of the passengers were European; but of late years Americans have shown such a growing appreciation of these tours that today the bulk of the passengers are taken aboard at New York city.

For some time past the directors of the company have realised that the popularity of these Oriental tours would be greatly increased if a vessel were specially designed and built for the service…'[14]

When Kaiser Wilhelm heard of these plans, he suggested to Ballin that the ideal prototype for such a vessel would be his own very large imperial yacht, the 4,228gt *Hohenzollern*, which had been built in 1893 and more resembled an intermediate-sized passenger liner than it did the typical steam yachts of its era. In 1899, Hamburg-Amerika ordered from Blohm & Voss in Hamburg the similarly-dimensioned 4,409gt cruise ship *Prinzessin Victoria Luise*, taking the name of the Kaiser's daughter, which would have a capacity for 180 passengers. The vessel would have much less powerful engines than the *Hohenzollern* to maintain a genteel 15-knot service speed (whereas the imperial yacht cruised at 21.5 knots). To give greater stability for long 'deep sea' voyages, the *Prinzessin Victoria Luise* was also deeper drafted. Perhaps due to her conventional triple-expansion machinery and unexceptional speed, however, the English-language shipping technical journals gave her scant coverage – whereas the *Scientific American*'s reportage was highly detailed, particularly with regard to the passenger accommodation and facilities. Of course, it was precisely the type of journal likely to be read by potential American passengers, who would have been highly educated and probably with wealth earned through owning industrial premises.

Inboard, the *Prinzessin Victoria Luise*'s prosperous passengers were given the impression that they were cruising aboard one of the European royal yachts. Whereas passenger ships intended for liner service required holds for cargo and

Right: The *Meteor* is seen during a Norwegian fjords cruise.

mail, as the *Scientific American* reported, the *Prinzessin Victoria Luise* was 'entirely given up to the accommodation of passengers and crew. There are no Second- and Third Class accommodations...'[15] At that time, Hamburg-Amerika's trans-Atlantic liners were considered to offer their First Class passengers the ultimate in commercial shipboard luxury – indeed, it was Albert Ballin's intention that the style and service on these vessels should be commensurate with the finest European hotels. The *Prinzessin Victoria Luise* replicated the ornate interior design of their First Class saloons in somewhat miniaturised form. The two main spaces were vertically stacked forward of amidships on three decks with the dining saloon on the lowest passenger deck level. Above was a two-deck-high light shaft with a glazed cupola cutting through the social hall on the Promenade Deck. These saloons both featured ornate baroque and rococo wood carvings, gilding and decorative panels. The *Scientific American* noted that 'a particularly pleasing feature in the [dining] saloon is a series of high-class paintings representing the harbours of Constantinople and Sydney, and various landscapes in Germany and in North America.' The social hall had a barrel-vaulted deck-head, the framing for the cupola being of floridly-patterned cast iron (this was lined internally with panes of cut crystal). The curvaceous lines and mannered details of this ensemble gave the space an air of fashionable 'jugendstil', which was perhaps appropriate to conjure the atmosphere of a contemporary shipboard equivalent of a winter garden. It was 'furnished in red, the walls being enriched with a series of beautiful paintings illustrative of scenes in the Mediterranean and the Orient.' The smoking saloon (for gentlemen only) was 'finished in carved oak and the walls… relieved with numerous majolica paintings, illustrative of various aquatic sports.'[16] The cabin accommodation was similarly elegant, there being only lower berths. The grandest of the rooms was the State Suite, which was included in case Kaiser Wilhelm ever wished to sample the vessel. The *Scientific American* noted that 'the staterooms are loftier and more roomy than those which are found on the trans-Atlantic service.'[17]

In line with growing fashions for fresh air and exercise as means to recuperation and good health – as found concurrently in new spa hotels ashore – the vessel had spacious, uncluttered outside decks and exercise facilities:

'Agreeably to her duties as a yacht, the *Prinzessin Victoria Luise* affords a particularly spacious promenade… and a novel feature… is the provision of deck shelters which are formed by extending aft the walls and roof of two of the deck houses, thus providing an open air shelter, where the passengers can get the sea air without being exposed to wind and spray. Immediately aft of the larger of these shelters is [an outdoor] space intended to afford a smooth dancing floor. A permanent awning framework is provided with a view to entirely enclosing this over with canvas, and thus affording a sheltered ballroom, the orchestra being placed in the permanent shelter, described above. Another novel feature which has been carried out on quite an elaborate scale is the gymnasium… fitted with Dr Zander's system of gymnastic apparatus, of which there are fully a dozen different electrically-operated pieces installed. One of these, which is known as 'the horse', is intended to imitate the movement of a trotting horse… There is also a bicycle, a form of rowing machine and the customary chest weights, dumb-bells and Indian clubs. Most of the apparatus, however, is designed to enable the user to subject himself to a more or less violent mechanical massage, the rubbing and kneading being performed by rapidly reciprocating rubber-tyred wheels.'[18]

The *Prinzessin Victoria Luise* entered service in 1900 and soon became very well regarded by rich German and American passengers. According to the *Scientific American*:

'The yacht's first cruise of 35 days is to the West Indies and Venezuela… Here, it may be mentioned that on account of the great number of landings which are made in the course of a tour, the yacht is provided with two large naphtha launches, each capable of holding 40 passengers. On her return to New York, the vessel will start on a 57 days' cruise to the Mediterranean and the Black Sea, then a three weeks' trip to England, Ireland and Scotland to be followed by two trips to the North Cape and the season will close with a voyage through the Baltic, touching at the important ports, including St Petersburg.'[19]

The *Prinzessin Victoria Luise*'s career was sadly short, however, as in December 1905, while making the first of what had been intended as a series of Caribbean cruises, she ran aground off the coast of Jamaica on an uncharted ridge newly formed by an earthquake. It was not until the following morning that passengers were rescued by German warship the *Bremen*. Having supervised the evacuation, the *Prinzessin Victoria Luise*'s captain retreated to his cabin, where he unlocked his pistol and shot himself dead.[20] Pounding by waves soon ensured that the unfortunate vessel became a total loss. Almost immediately, however, Hamburg-Amerika ordered a replacement cruise yacht from Blohm & Voss. Named the *Meteor*, she was slightly smaller at 3,613gt but with a larger 220-passenger capacity. This vessel was, like her short-lived predecessor, a commercial success but this prosperity continued only until the outbreak of the First World War.

The war brought radical changes to the map and politics of Europe. Germany's feudal monarchy was superseded by a Social-Democratic republic. Notwithstanding the fact that Germany had deposed Kaiser Wilhelm and created its own new constitution, the terms of the Treaty of Versailles was particularly harsh. Germany was forced to demilitarise and to make swingeing reparation payments to the war's victors, money which the now bankrupt nation could ill afford. Largely as a result of the Treaty's arguably unreasonable demands, in the post-war years, Germany struggled to reinvigorate itself, suffering high unemployment, hyper-inflation and, increasingly, sharply divisive political tensions. As Germany had previously been continental Europe's economic 'powerhouse', its now sluggish economy had negative effects for all of its neighbours. Hamburg-Amerika lost much of its fleet in the war and in post-war reparations but the cruise ship, the *Meteor*, which had survived unscathed, was now regarded by the company as an unaffordable luxury and was offered for sale. Her purchaser in 1921 was Det Bergenske Dampskipsselskap, which, as with the North of Scotland Steam Navigation Company, was primarily an operator of passenger, cargo and mail services, linking Western Norway with the UK and the Continent. Det Bergenske wished to commence its own programme of Fjord cruises and the *Meteor* appeared to be the ideal vessel for this purpose.

Shortly, another Western Norwegian steamship company, Det Nordenfjeldske Dampskipsselskap, headquartered in Trondheim, which having lost its existing steamer for fjord cruises, the *Haakon VII*, during the First World War, negotiated to purchase the laid up British Royal Yacht the *Alexandra*. This large yacht had been built by A&J Inglis in Glasgow on the River Clyde for H.M. King Edward and H.M. Queen Alexandra's use. As the latter was Danish, there had been a need for the senior royals to make not infrequent North Sea crossings to Copenhagen. In appearance, the *Alexandra* was rather conservative, being very similar in outline to the previous British Royal Yacht, the *Victoria and Albert*; even the funnels were anachronistic-looking with elliptical tops – but these belied the fact that the vessel was in fact powered by state-of-the-art steam turbines.

The outbreak of the First World War led to the yacht being laid up and she was never reactivated by the British Royal Navy. Det Nordenfjelske had the vessel rebuilt as a commercial ship and she entered service in 1926 as the *Prins Olav*. Although the passenger accommodation was more simply decorated than that of the *Meteor*, perhaps reflecting King Edward's taste for a navy-style design approach, the British royal connection ensured the *Prins Olav*'s success for Det Nordenfjeldske, particularly in attracting moneyed American tourists to Norway. During the winter, Mediterranean itineraries were offered – and these were sold in the USA with return trans-Atlantic passages included. Prices for a 46-day cruise from Marseille began at $1,700 and to occupy the former King's cabin would have cost $5,500.

Above: The 'Royal' stateroom on the *Prins Olav*, which in the vessel's earlier career as a British Royal Yacht, had been occupied by H.M. King Edward and Queen Alexandra. This gave the space a unique kudos, particularly with wealthy American passengers. In the eras since, upmarket cruise ships have attempted to associate their images with royal and aristocratic lineages for the same reason; among the cultural conservatives who comprise a majority of their passengers, royal links are very desirable.

Below: The *Prins Olav*'s external appearance was little-changed from her earlier phase as the *Alexandra*.

20 | Cruise Ships: A Design History

Swedish American Line's *Kungsholm* is shown departing Gothenburg in the mid-1930s; the vessel was successful both as a trans-Atlantic liner and as a cruise ship, a 'dual-role' approach that would become increasingly commonplace in the 1950s and '60s. The vessel's modern romantic interiors reflected late-1920s Swedish high taste in the decorative arts and there was even a large heated indoor swimming pool – a remarkable feature for a liner of her intermediate size.

Det Bergenske Dampskipsselskap, buoyed by the success of the *Meteor*, decided in the mid-1920s to have an even larger cruising yacht purpose-built. By that time, Scandinavian-headquartered shipping companies (and several British ones besides) had largely switched over from steam to diesel propulsion for their new vessels and Det Bergenske was no exception, specifying for the vessel twin 8-cylinder Burmeister & Wain diesels to give a 15-knot cruising speed. Headquartered in Copenhagen, Burmeister & Wain had pioneered diesel navigation for sea-going commercial ships and was one of two major designers of marine diesel engines, the other being Sulzer of Winterthur in land-locked Switzerland. Although the initial costs of diesel engines were greater than for steam reciprocating or turbine plants, operationally a diesel ship was much cheaper, offering far better fuel economy and requiring a smaller crew.[21]

Det Bergenske placed an order for the 5,020gt *Stella Polaris* with the Götaverken shipyard in Gothenburg. The vessel would carry 198 passengers in great comfort. The cabins were located aft of amidships, following the traditional approach for steam yachts. These comprised four suites, each with a separate sitting room and bathroom, twelve double staterooms also with private bathrooms, the remainder being an even mix of single and double cabins, sharing toilets and bathrooms that were located across the corridors along the centre line. The public rooms – consisting of a lounge, writing rooms and dining saloon – were decorated in a national romantic idiom, commonly found at that time in Norway and, indeed, throughout much of northern Europe. The saloons were enriched by Norwegian 'folk art' in the form of bas relief sculptures, tapestries and decorative moulded glass panels.

Delivered in 1927, the *Stella Polaris* created a distinct impression of 'old world' grandeur and exclusivity; with her graceful hull lines, bowsprit, counter stern and tall buff-yellow funnel, she resembled steam yachts of the late Victorian and Edwardian eras more than typical passenger vessels of the latter 1920s. This traditionalism, however, concealed modern innovations; apart from her purring diesel engines, she was fitted throughout with a forced-air ventilation and heating system, meaning that there were neither noisy ceiling fans nor bulky electric heaters to clutter the interiors.

The *Stella Polaris*' cruise itineraries not only included Northern Europe and the Mediterranean but also the West Indies and the Caribbean and, as with the *Meteor* and *Prins Olav*, she was notably popular with American passengers. Although the vessel developed a very loyal following, as with the other cruising 'yachts', hers was an exclusive niche market of the exceptionally affluent and leisured. In wider Western society, however, significant shifts in wealth and status were underway and it was the middle classes experienced some of the largest relative income gains. In addition, during the 1920s, middle income earners benefitted from a substantial fall in the cost of living. More significantly, the overall numbers of 'white collar' workers grew exponentially between the wars, meaning that a larger proportion of the population had more disposable income for spending on leisure pursuits.[22] Ashore, this was reflected in growing expenditure on hotel and

Above: The Norwegian-owned cruise ship *Stella Polaris* retained the yacht-like external appearance layout of her Edwardian era predecessors, but married these with up-to-date comfort-giving technologies, such as forced ventilation and heating.

Below: Part of a general arrangement drawing of the *Stella Polaris*, showing how the disposition of her promenade deck public rooms continued to follow the precedent of Edwardian cruise yachts; relative to the size of the ship, there was also a great deal of uninterrupted outdoor deck space.

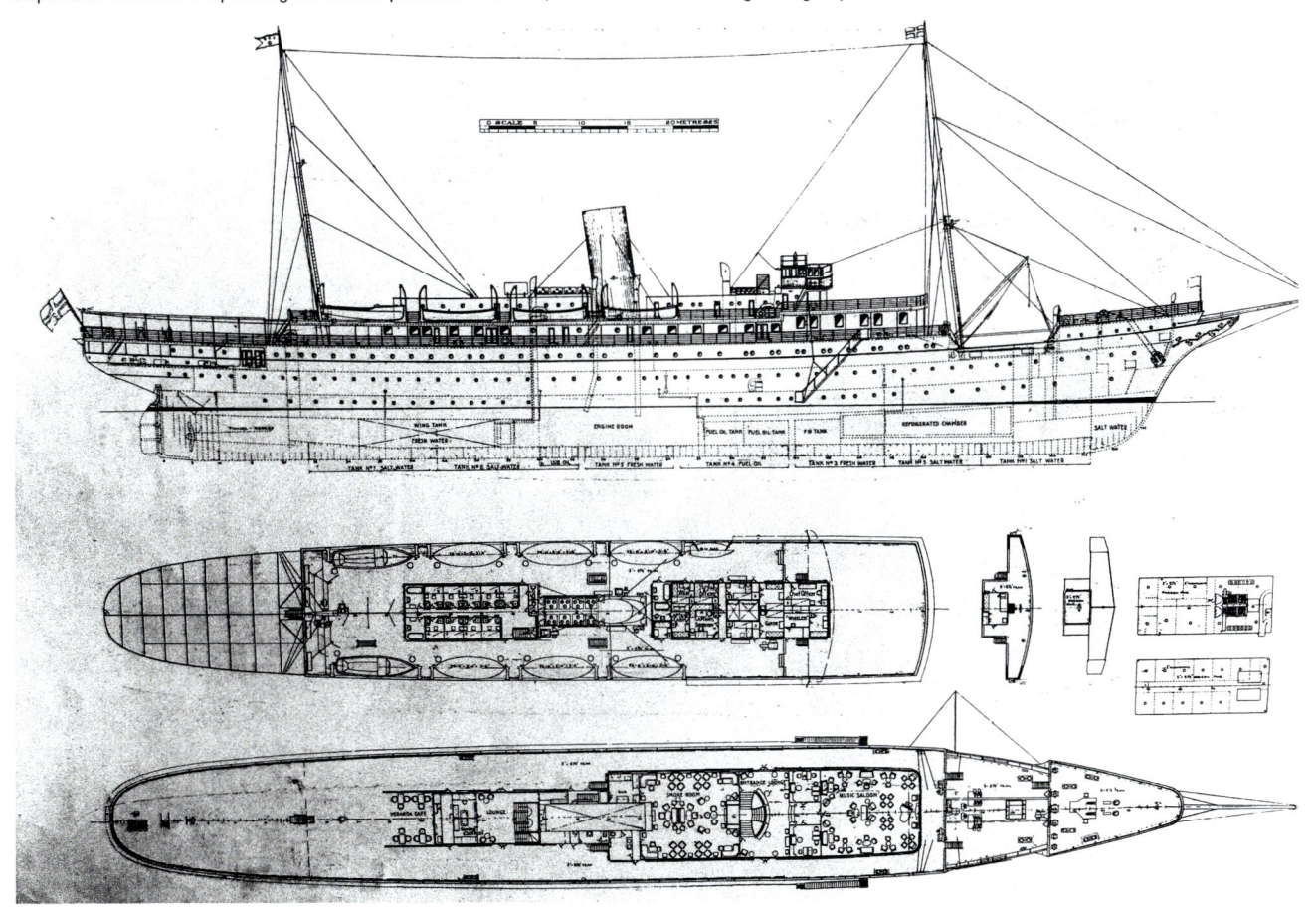

Above: The *Stella Polaris* at anchor during a Norwegian fjords cruise in the 1930s.

restaurant services.[23] The era's bouts of severe economic turbulence and political instability most negatively affected the poorest, whose jobs in heavy industry were precarious as orders for large manufactured items – such as ships – were among the earliest casualties of sharp downturns.

For shipping companies engaged in the liner trades, meanwhile, the 1920s gave rise to major challenges – particularly for the operators engaged in the trans-Atlantic liner trades. Since the First World War, emigration to America had declined to a third of its pre-war level. The United States applied a quota system to reduce numbers further and, besides, in the immediate post-war years, preferential space on ships was given to soldiers returning home. Trans-Atlantic liner companies noted changing travel patterns with an increase in the numbers of tourists from America wishing to book eastbound passages. Often, these travellers had earlier travelled west as migrants. Having made money in their new country, they now wished to go on holiday to Europe to visit their relatives.

Cunard – arguably the leading Atlantic liner company – was in a strong position to cope with this new reality. Its flagship liners, the *Mauretania* and the *Aquitania*, both of which dated from the pre-First World War era had, from the outset, been designed with an all-cabin third class, rather than the dormitories provided for emigrants by other lines. In the latter-1920s, Cunard's rivals built new tonnage, specifically aimed at attracting the tourist market. The French Line's *Ile de France* of 1927 was perhaps the most celebrated of these vessels. Thanks to her sumptuous and modern interiors, which were largely the work of architects and designers who had worked on French exhibits at the 1925 Exposition des Arts Décoratifs et Industriels Modernes in Paris, the liner created a sensation on both sides of the Atlantic. While America was experiencing prohibition, the *Ile de France* had numerous chic cocktail bars at which drink and where conversation flowed freely among the fashionable set. Indeed, the liner even made her way into popular song: 'You're just as hard to land as the *Ile de France*/I haven't got a chance/ this is a fine romance!'[24]

Although smaller and less prominent than the *Ile de France*, the Swedish American Line's 21,250gt trans-Atlantic motor ship *Kungsholm*, built by Blohm & Voss in Hamburg and introduced in 1928, was equally influenced by the Paris Exposition. As American tourists to Scandinavia tended to prefer visiting in summer, the North Atlantic liner trade was largely seasonal from the latter-1920s onward, those brave enough to face the ocean in its winter fury being relatively few. Swedish American Line's parent company, Broström AB of Gothenburg, therefore decided to make the *Kungsholm* a dual-purpose Atlantic liner and cruise ship.

Decoratively, the *Kungsholm* was radically different from previous Scandinavian ships. During the 1920s, Swedish architecture, art and design earned a solid international reputation for craftsmanship and innovation. The liner's interiors were designed by Carl Bergsten, the architect of the highly regarded Swedish Pavilion at the Paris Exposition. The richly coloured modern romantic décor was highly distinctive stylistically, but shared a similar palette of exotic and colourful finishes to that of the *Ile de France*. A particular attraction for cruise passengers was the *Kungsholm*'s large indoor swimming pool – a remarkable feature for a liner of the intermediate size category. The emphasis given to health and fitness anticipated the coming cult of the 'body beautiful' – which would cut across aesthetic and political boundaries in the 1930s.

Chapter 2
Cruising in the wake of the Wall Street Crash

The new liners of the latter-1920s were soon to face the severest of economic challenges. During the period between 1924 and 1929, share values in the United States of America increased five-fold. Playing the stock market had become a popular pastime in the 1920s and many of the speculators were private individuals who had themselves borrowed the money they invested. As the value of shares had grown, an increasing disparity emerged between the value of publicly-quoted businesses' assets and of their shares. On 29th October 1929 there was a major correction and share prices on the New York Stock Exchange collapsed, 17 per cent being wiped off their worth, equating to 14 billion dollars. Their value then continued to fall for a whole month. In the weeks leading up to the crash, the market had been unstable with repeated waves of stock selling, rallying share prices and then renewed purchasing. By Christmas, there was a partial recovery, followed by a second, more severe decline. From 1930 onwards, there was a breakdown in international trade, the negative effects of which were particularly acute in countries whose economies depended on exports. Businesses and individuals consequently defaulted on their loans and this in turn caused banks to collapse, further compounding the problem. Germany suffered renewed hyper-inflation as American banks withdrew their support for its industries. As Germany therefore could no longer afford to make any repayments to France and Britain, their economies suffered a second blow after the initial shock of the crash itself. In September 1931, Britain withdrew from the Gold Standard and the pound fell in value against the dollar by 20 per cent. On 8 July 1932 a new crash occurred from which the Dow Jones Industrial Average of shares did not fully recover for over 20 years.[25] These events led to a widespread and catastrophic loss of confidence in the market which left many destitute and brought about a Great Depression in economies throughout much of the Western World.

Their effects on the shipping industry as a whole were disastrous, especially for less efficient companies that were forced to put their vessels into lay-up and, in the worst cases, to declare bankruptcy. Perhaps inevitably, there was an immediate and severe drop in passenger liner patronage. For the leading trans-Atlantic companies, the least-worse option was to redeploy their least competitive tonnage on short, inexpensive cruises from New York to take the better off among city's depression-struck multitudes out with the twelve-mile coastal limit of prohibition. Once at sea, the liners' bars could be opened so that passengers could obliterate with alcohol their worries about the dire economic situation ashore. Thus, some of the grandest trans-Atlantic liners of the pre-First World War era were sent cruising – including Cunard's the *Berengaria* (the former-German *Imperator*, which had been ceded to Britain as a war reparation ship) and the former-Blue Riband holder the *Mauretania*, which was subsequently repainted with a white hull for cruising purposes.

Throughout this difficult period, there remained a small elite market for luxury cruises, served primarily by the Norwegian *Stella Polaris* and also by Royal Mail Lines, a British liner company known primarily for its services from the UK to South American ports. Since the ending of the First World War, the company had operated its former *Asturias* of 1908 as the cruise ship *Arcadian*. In 1929, it converted the larger 1913-built *Andes*, which originally had carried 1,330 passengers in three classes, into the one-class, 450-passenger cruise ship the *Atlantis*.

Another major British liner company hitherto primarily engaged in the South American trades to offer cruises was the Blue Star Line, the principal business of which was the importation of meat to the UK from Argentinean cattle ranches. In addition to its large fleet of refrigerated cargo vessels, Blue Star also ran combined passenger-cargo liners with exclusively First Class accommodation, one of which, the *Arandora* of 1927, was extensively rebuilt in 1929 as the cruise ship *Arandora Star*. This involved converting cargo holds into decks of passenger cabins and the extension of her superstructure fore and aft to double the passenger capacity to 354.[26] A swimming pool and a gymnasium were also installed during the conversion. The low passenger densities and relatively high fares of the *Atlantis* and *Arandora Star*, however, belonged to a disappearing era of grand luxury. In future, a majority of purpose-built or converted cruise ship tonnage would be aimed at the upper end of the middle market.[27]

The Kraft durch Freude fleet

It was in 1930s Germany that cruises for the mass market were first successfully offered as a 'sweetener' by the National Socialist regime, which came to power in 1933. Quickly, the Nazis established a *Deutsche Arbeitsfront* (German Labour Front) to supersede the existing trade union moment. Independent unions' political agitation could not be tolerated, particularly as most existing unions had unacceptable leftist leanings. In order to make the German Labour Front appear attractive to the working and lower middle classes who were strongly encouraged to become members, a propaganda division was created, entitled *Kraft durch Freude* (Strength through Joy). This was founded by a leading Nazi propagandist, Robert Ley, with the aim of structuring and controlling the free time of German workers. Ley and his henchmen realised that cruises were not only highly aspirational – and hitherto out with the budgets of working people – but also enabled 'captive' shiploads of passengers to be fed propaganda while otherwise having enjoyable experiences of eating, drinking, sunbathing and entertainment. As numerous German liners had been withdrawn or were struggling to continue in service in the face of depression conditions, a further useful side-effect of arranging a cruise programme would be to provide

24 | Cruise Ships: A Design History

Blue Star Line's *Arandora Star* was considered among the finest in the nascent British cruise market of the inter-war era, as images of a cabin, her dining saloon, veranda café and smoking saloon demonstrate. The veranda's Spanish-style décor shows that architectural theming has long been applied to cruise ships, just as it has to holiday hotels and resorts ashore. The vessel is seen (left) at Miami in the 1932, where she was one of the first ever cruise ship visitors and (above) following rebuilding work on the Clyde in 1937, during which her main mast was removed and her superstructure was extended.

Left: Cunard's famous trans-Atlantic liner *Mauretania*, repainted with a white hull for cruising purposes during the first half of the 1930s.

renewed employment for German seafarers. At first, a variety of liners were chartered from the Norddeutscher Lloyd of Bremen.

Kraft durch Freude's offer of inexpensive cruises to the Baltic, Norway and the Mediterranean was a great success – so much so that the organisation drew up an ambitious programme that envisaged the completion of thirty vessels specifically for cruising, with the declared objective of accommodating at least two million German workers each year.[28] In the end, only two such vessels were actually built – the 25,484gt, 1,465-passenger *Wilhelm Gustloff*, which was delivered from Blohm & Voss in 1938, and the slightly larger 27,288gt, 1,774-passenger *Robert Ley*, which was completed the following year by Howaldtswerke A.G. Initially, it had been planned that the first of the pair should be named the *Adolf Hitler*, but instead it was decided to memorialise Gustloff, who was a Swiss Nazi assassinated in 1936.

For cruising, the sizes and capacities of these vessels were unprecedented. In fact, they were nothing less than prototypes for a new kind of cruise ship, the general arrangement of which was adopted in other countries after the Second World War. Being designed for capacity rather than speed (as would have been the case with passenger ships intended for liner service), their hull lines were relatively bluff, thereby maximising the area of deck within. The external profiles of the two ships, while not identical, were compact, simple and clean: a single funnel of elliptical form being placed centrally on a long superstructure distinguished by the absence of ventilators and other cluttering elements.

Mechanically, they also represented very advanced thinking. While the former was powered by four diesels, coupled in pairs via gearboxes to twin propellers, the latter instead used a diesel-electric propulsion solution. Although the idea of using diesel engines to power electrical generators dated back to diesel power's early years, this was the first time that such an approach had been attempted on a large passenger ship. Apart from achieving an admirable compactness of machinery layout, the other major advantage was that the main engines could be used to provide power for shipboard services, thereby avoiding the need also to install auxiliary machinery.

The vessels' overall white livery and use of a 'brand identity' consisting of an emblem of propeller blades containing a Swastika also prefigured the kinds of corporate identity strategies nowadays widely used in passenger shipping – and, indeed, throughout the contemporary hospitality and leisure industries. The advanced structural and technical design was not, however, reflected in the vessels' interiors, which followed the traditionalist directives of the Nazi regime. In order to ingratiate themselves with a majority of the German populous, Nazi-approved design sought to reflect the mainly conservative tastes of 'ordinary people.' In practice, this approach actually closely reflected the less adventurous strains of architecture and design for public and commercial environments throughout the Western World at that time. The Nazis believed that peoples' homes should appear *gemütlich* in German vernacular styles, while the state and civic authorities should employ Roman imperial neo-classicism. Only when up-to-date technologies were involved – for example, cars or aircraft – were modern aesthetics tolerated (incidentally, this approach was simultaneously applied in Stalin's Soviet Russia). With regard to passenger ships' interior design, the methodology also reflected that of a majority of liner operators internationally. Indeed, similar decorative conservatism continues to be preferred for the design of a majority of cruise ship interiors of the present era.

On both the *Wilhelm Gustloff* and the *Robert Ley*, all cabins had portholes and the public rooms were logically-arranged on the Promenade Deck. In addition, there were generous outdoor spaces for sports activities. The standard of crew accommodation matched that for passengers.[29] The *Wilhelm Gustloff*'s interiors were designed by the neo-classical architect Woldemar Brinkmann, who had formerly been an assistant of Paul Ludwig Troost, whose uncluttered approach he sought to emulate. Furniture was simple but solid, while the bulkheads were adorned with murals by German artists of romanticist outlook, featuring

Below: The Royal Mail liner *Atlantis* was another Edwardian-era liner converted for cruising purposes in the era following the Wall Street Crash. Here, we see passengers posing on deck in fancy dress; mimicking the 'exotic' by imitating the appearances and national dresses of peoples from around the world has for long been a cruising tradition which enhances the sense of escapism and cosmopolitanism of shipboard life.

folk costumes and bucolic landscapes.[30] The exception was the Wilhelm Gustloff Halle, in which the panelling was of dark wood with gilded bronze lamps, dominated by a portrait of Adolf Hitler, whose gaze was unavoidable.

In designing the *Robert Ley*, Brinkmann placed greater emphasis on decorative elements. The ship's two main public rooms, the *Theatersaal* and the *Tanzsaal*, differed from those on the *Wilhelm Gustloff* in being two decks high with galleries, one square and the other circular. Both rooms had large dance floors of polished wood and featured decorative reliefs set into the walls. Ornate balustrades, in the form of crossed swastikas, and electric candelabra completed the décor.[31] Hitler's trusted architect Albert Speer chose these two rooms to represent the regime's interior architecture, illustrating them in his 1941 book *Neue Deutsche Baukunst* which, as a celebration of anti-modernist architecture, opened with the Munich buildings of Troost.

So far as KdF passengers were concerned, few of whom would ever previously have gone on a cruise, the *Wilhelm Gustloff* and *Robert Ley* must have seemed unbelievably glamorous. It is easy to imagine that while the wine and beer flowed, hearty German cooking was served up and there was dancing to folk tunes and classical recitals in the lounges, most passengers would have gained an exceedingly favourable impression of National Socialism. The reality ashore of persecution, deportations, enslavement, executions and the orchestrated looting and destruction of Jewish property of Kristalnacht would, most likely, have gone unnoticed by KdF's leisured multitudes. Encouraging the switching off of passengers' critical faculties (beyond commenting on the standard of hospitality received on board) arguably continues to be one of mass market cruising's characteristics even today.

When the Second World War broke out, the *Wilhelm Gustloff* and *Robert Ley* first became hospital ships, then floating military barracks. Towards the end of the war, the *Wilhelm Gustloff* was re-activated to evacuate German refugees ahead of the advancing Red Army and, in this role, she was tragically torpedoed by a Soviet submarine in the southern Baltic in January 1945. It is estimated that 9,400 drowned when the heavily over-loaded vessel sank in what was one of the worst tragedies in the history of passenger shipping.

In the latter-1930s, no other nation could boast cruise ships commensurate with the size and technical modernity of the *Wilhelm Gustloff* and the *Robert Ley*. Sometimes, very grand and modern trans-Atlantic and colonial passenger liners were sent cruising for short periods. Examples were the P&O flagship the *Viceroy of India* (which had been built in 1927) and the magnificent French Line *Normandie*, dating from 1935 and possibly the most magnificent passenger ship ever seen, which in 1939 made a cruise from New York to Rio de Janeiro. Generally, a majority of the inter-war era's dedicated cruise tonnage consisted of converted liners of older vintages and so, in terms of design advancement, out with Germany, cruise ships lagged behind the great leaps forward in naval architecture and interior design that were exemplified by other types of passenger ships, such as liners, Channel packets and ferries. Towards the end of the decade, a small number of liners were built with the possibility of future use as cruise ships. Royal Mail Lines' steam turbine-powered UK-South America vessel the *Andes*, completed in 1939 by Harland & Wolff of Belfast and measuring 25,689gt, boasted a very high quality of accommodation throughout and a dining room in which a majority of passengers could be

Below: The German Kraft durch Freude cruise ship *Wilhelm Gustloff* was the first large example of the genre built for a 'mass market' clientele, but also served as a propaganda vehicle for a very unsavoury political organisation.

Cruising in the wake of the Wall Street Crash | 27

Top: Kraft durch Freude's *Robert Ley*'s bluff hull configuration clearly demonstrates the requirement for internal volume to boost capacity in a vessel offering popularly-priced cruises, thereby long prefiguring the standard approach to 'mass market' cruise ship design from the 1980s onwards.

Below: Interiors of the *Wilhelm Gustloff* show the comfortable but conservative approach to shipboard design favoured in the KdF fleet, which aligned with National Socialist architectural policies ashore. KdF advertising, meanwhile, reflected standard international practice for travel posters and brochures.

28 | Cruise Ships: A Design History

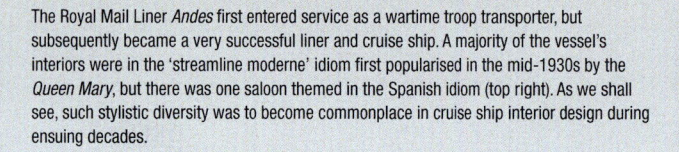

The Royal Mail Liner *Andes* first entered service as a wartime troop transporter, but subsequently became a very successful liner and cruise ship. A majority of the vessel's interiors were in the 'streamline moderne' idiom first popularised in the mid-1930s by the *Queen Mary*, but there was one saloon themed in the Spanish idiom (top right). As we shall see, such stylistic diversity was to become commonplace in cruise ship interior design during ensuing decades.

accommodated at a single sitting.[32] As with Blue Star's the *Arandora Star* in her original liner service configuration as the *Arandora*, there were also extensive refrigerated cargo holds, which were typical features of liners in the trades to Argentina.[33] Upon completion, the *Andes* was used as a troop ship, but – unlike the Kraft durch Freude fleet, the *Viceroy of India* and the *Normandie* – she survived the Second World War largely unscathed. It was not until 1955, however, that she eventually came to be used for regular cruises.

In the mid-1930s, Swedish American Line, which arguably had pioneered modern dual-purpose liner-cum-cruise ships with the *Kungsholm* of 1928, ordered a new flagship to be named the *Stockholm* from the Cantieri Riuniti dell'Adriatico at Monfalcone in Italy, also with the intention of operating a mix of summer trans-Atlantic liner voyages and winter cruises. As with the *Wilhelm Gustloff*, the *Stockholm* would be a motor ship, albeit powered by three Sulzer diesels with a triple-screw propeller arrangement. Indeed, in several fundamental respects, the *Stockholm* was planned as a two-funnelled version of the German vessel. (The *Stockholm*'s forward funnel was, however, a dummy, included merely for aesthetic reasons at the insistence of Swedish American Line's recently-appointed technical director, Eric Christiansson, to balance her silhouette.) She too would boast an all outside cabin layout, in which the cabins were accessed from corridors running along the centre-line, pairs of cabins being inter-locking L-shapes. The exhaust uptakes were routed upward from the engines' aft ends, their casings being located approximately two-thirds aft. This meant that the 'midships section of the passenger accommodation could benefit from open planning, lending a greater feeling of spaciousness and flow from space to space than was typical of passenger ships of her size and era.

The design of the *Stockholm*'s interiors involved co-operation between a number of forward-looking architects and naval architects from both Sweden and Italy. Her principal public rooms were the work of Nils Einar Eriksson, one of the architects previously involved in the ground-breaking 1930 Stockholm Exhibition, which had first brought modern Scandinavian architecture and design to the attention of an international audience. On the *Stockholm* project, he was assisted by another Gothenburg architect, Gustav Alde, and the detailed execution of their work was supervised at Monfalcone by a like-minded Italian, Nino Zoncada, who also contributed the connective spaces and hallways. Thus, a high degree of coherence was achieved. It was intended that up to 1,350 passengers would be carried in three classes when in Atlantic liner service between Gothenburg and New York but, when cruising, the First and Tourist Class accommodations would be amalgamated and the third-class areas closed off entirely, reducing her capacity to a mere 620. Among the special provisions made for cruise operation were an open air swimming pool (most unusual for a Scandinavian trans-Atlantic vessel at that time) and spacious sun decks. All cabins and public rooms to be used in cruise service were completely air conditioned. This, in itself, was noteworthy at a time when many liners designed exclusively for tropical services offered this comfort only in their First Class dining saloons and, perhaps, in one or two other major public rooms.[34]

Most unfortunately, while nearing completion, the *Stockholm* was virtually destroyed by fire and subsequently was partially scrapped, then rebuilt in a slightly enlarged form. The vessel now measured 30,390gt but, when in 1941, she ran trials in the Gulf of Trieste, it was found that she had serious stability problems. Consequently, delivery was postponed until sponsons were fitted on either side of the hull below the waterline. By the time modifications had been made, the Second World War had begun and, as it would have been risky to have attempted a delivery voyage, the *Stockholm* remained in Italy, where she was sold by Swedish American to Italy's Fascist Government only subsequently to be destroyed by Allied aerial bombardment while at anchor in the Adriatic, near to the Italian coast.

Above & left: Swedish American Line's *Stockholm* of 1931 was mechanically similar to the *Wilhelm Gustloff*, but with up-to-date Swedish and Italian interior design. Here, we see a cabin, a hallway and the vessel's aft-located Showboat Restaurant. Her open-plan layout, evident in the centre image, was enabled by splitting the exhaust flues and vertical servicing to run upwards through ducts closer to each beam. Left, we see the nearly-complete liner during trials in the Gulf of Trieste.

Chapter 3

The post-war shift from liner to cruise

The Second World War both decimated Europe's merchant fleets and disabled its economies. Many ships had been sunk by torpedoes, bombardment and sabotage in the interim and so the priority for all shipping nations was to build afresh. As the most prestigious trans-Atlantic express liners were faster than torpedoes, they were not easily targeted and so those lost during the war years were destroyed in port – the defeated Axis Powers' fleets being particularly badly affected.

By 1945, Britain – whose pre-war merchant navy had dominated the world's shipping lanes – was bankrupt and the post-war settlement did not favour it. Necessity won, however, and so its rebuilding programme was mostly a continuation of 1930s practices. Cunard quickly ordered from John Brown & Co of Clydebank a new 34,183gt dual-purpose trans-Atlantic liner and cruise ship, the *Caronia*, for delivery in 1948.[35] As Cunard's American clientele were comparatively wealthy relative to most Britons, the idea was that the vessel would earn dollars for the company and hence also for the British exchequer. As the New York-based liner and cruise ship historian John Maxtone-Graham observed, Cunard's aim was to attract 'a travelling elite from both sides of the Atlantic… shipboard aficionados with a great deal of money, time on their hands, no particular destination in mind, and a penchant for booking with the same friends year after year on a vessel that seemed more a club than a cruise ship.'[36] Externally, the *Caronia* had a single exceptionally large funnel, a tripod mast and a raked bow – features which were subsequently widely emulated in post-war passenger liner naval architecture – and the vessel's hull and superstructure were painted in shades of green to reduce the glare of tropical sunlight. Yet, the fact that the vessel was required to make regular North Atlantic crossings meant that her promenades were enclosed, unlike the open ones found on liners and cruise ships primarily intended for use in tropical climes.

According to the ship design historian Philip Dawson, the *Caronia*'s 'contribution to the history of cruising was that, rather than breaking any new ground in naval architecture, she established a gold standard of top-quality deluxe' service and style.'[37] Dawson observes how the layout of her First Class public rooms on Promenade Deck was very similar to that of the Edwardian-era trans-Atlantic liner the *Aquitania* – and of practically every other significant Cunard passenger ship delivered in the period since. Yet, such a great success was she that Cunard subsequently converted other liners for cruising purposes, adding bigger sun decks with swimming pools and painting them in the same predominantly green livery.

The interior design followed Cunard's somewhat eclectic pre-war Art Deco formula, as demonstrated so successfully by the trans-Atlantic liner the *Queen Mary*, which had entered service twelve years before. The polished hardwood veneer used throughout to line the saloons may have been pre-war in taste and in workmanship – 'instant *Queens* with cruise seasoning', as Maxtone-Graham characterised it.[38] Yet, in an era of continuing austerity in Britain, the sumptuous effects of combining shiny surfaces with rich textures, sumptuous upholstery and carpeting created an aura which would have been considered luxurious – indeed, it is arguable that, even today, these qualities continue to manifest in 'aspirational' passenger ship interior design. The fact that the individual elements barely acknowledged each other seemingly did not matter. Maxtone-Graham reflected that the *Caronia*'s interiors 'cocooned one in comfort and luxury as it took one to nice places; decorative nit-picking was secondary and probably non-existent.'[39] In any case, by the 1950s, the *Caronia* had gained a formidable reputation for her expensively-priced luxury cruises – and a very loyal, though mainly elderly, clientele. The liner and cruise historian Peter C. Kohler wrote evocatively of the *Caronia*'s passengers' lives of leisure:

Right: Cunard's *Caronia*, completed in 1948 and pictured here in New York, successfully combined the roles of trans-Atlantic liner and cruise ship. Her single exceptionally large funnel and tripod mast anticipated 1950s naval architectural fashion, while her green livery reduced glare in tropical light.

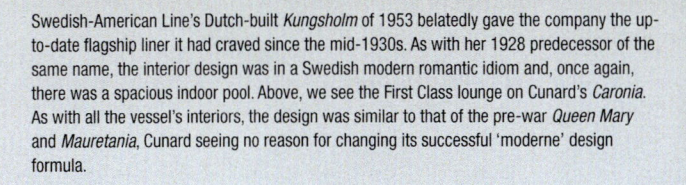

Swedish-American Line's Dutch-built *Kungsholm* of 1953 belatedly gave the company the up-to-date flagship liner it had craved since the mid-1930s. As with her 1928 predecessor of the same name, the interior design was in a Swedish modern romantic idiom and, once again, there was a spacious indoor pool. Above, we see the First Class lounge on Cunard's *Caronia*. As with all the vessel's interiors, the design was similar to that of the pre-war *Queen Mary* and *Mauretania*, Cunard seeing no reason for changing its successful 'moderne' design formula.

Above: Royal Mail Line's *Andes* is seen in 'cruising white' in the early-1960s; the liner's Mediterranean and African itineraries were immensely popular with Britain's 'affluent society' of the late-1950s and throughout the 1960s.

'Among the Palm Beach and Bar Harbor socialites who were the ship's bread and butter, was a real cast of characters. One woman had fresh flowers delivered to her stateroom each of the 80-plus days at sea on a world cruise. Some passengers literally lived on the ship; Clara Macbeth of New York, stayed aboard for over 15 years, and a Texas ranch owner, Mrs Howard Jones, had the same cabin for years, both contributing millions to Cunard's coffers… After a full day ashore in some hot and dusty port, the *Caronia*'s passengers would come home…in one of those immaculate teak-trimmed launches, manned by seamen in starched whites, stepping aboard to that familiar smell of polish and fresh flowers and a drawn bath. The dressing gong was followed by the clatter of anchor chains, and over cocktails in the Raleigh Bar, the gowned and bejewelled *Caronia* set watched another island fade behind the churning wake…'[40]

By the mid-1950s, significant social shifts were underway in Britain as the end of post-war rationing and changes in government policy encouraged would-be entrepreneurs to make money. Growing wealth – at least for some – and the advent of new tonnage encouraged Royal Mail Lines to use its pre-war liner the *Andes* as a cruise ship. For the next fifteen years, the vessel attracted a broad clientele of upwardly-mobile mainly British passengers with voyages to Scandinavia, the Mediterranean and the Caribbean, depending upon the season.

In 1950s America, meanwhile, the *Caronia* was only one of several dual-purpose trans-Atlantic liners and cruise ships sailing regularly from New York. The appearance in 1952 of the first commercial jet passenger airliner, the DeHavilland *Comet 1*, heralded a major threat to the profitability of the passenger liner business and so the ability of new liners also to perform effectively in cruising roles came to be seen as advantageous, especially by private-sector liner operators. By contrast, state-owned companies, such as United States Lines, French Line and Italian Line would continue to build and operate pure express liners well into the 1960s by which time the advantages of jet flight had decimated the trans-Atlantic passenger trade.

Swedish American Line, which had pioneered dual-purpose liner-cum-cruise ships with the *Kungsholm* of 1928, ordered for delivery in 1953 a new 21,141gt, 802-passenger vessel of the same name from the Koninklijke Mij. De Schelde of Flushing. This was built in to a design developed from that of the lost pre-war *Stockholm*, albeit using twin Burmeister & Wain diesels, rather than the earlier vessel's three propeller arrangement. Early renderings suggested that the new *Kungsholm* would have twin slender exhaust stacks towards the stern, but, for Swedish American, this was a step too far and so, as with the *Stockholm*, twin conventional funnels were fitted. Again similarly, the cabins were all accessed off central corridors and their 'inter-locking' L-shaped layouts enabled every one of them to have a porthole.

The *Kungsholm*'s interiors were designed by the Swedish architects Per Lindfors, Rolf Ahberg and Margaretha Engströmer with supervision of the outfitting by the Dutch firm of H.P. Mutters & Zoon. The vessel was highly regarded by liner and cruise passengers, so much so that the company went on to order a broadly similar near-sister, the 23,191gt, 842-passenger *Gripsholm*, which was delivered in 1957 from the Ansaldo shipyard at Genoa in Italy. Her interior design involved the collaboration of same Swedish architects as on the *Kungsholm* with considerable input from the Italian Nino Zoncada, who was a veteran of the pre-war *Stockholm* project and who not only oversaw the fitting out process but also designed all the hallways and stairwells, plus the forward lounge/ballroom. A significant difference from the *Kungsholm* was the partial elimination of the enclosed promenade decks that had been features of trans-Atlantic liners since the latter-nineteenth century. Instead, the air-conditioned public rooms filled the full width of the superstructure, except towards the stern where vestigial promenades remained.

Cruise itineraries for vessels such as these included relatively lengthy sea segments between the ports of call, of which there were relatively few by present-day standards. One reason was that appropriate foreign currency was harder to obtain in the 1950s, whereas aboard ship, everything could be paid for in dollars. Another reason was that the era's cruise passengers actively enjoyed being at sea with its mix of relaxation and shipboard social life. There was relatively little by way of professional entertainment – perhaps only a ship's orchestra for dancing – and anything else by way of quizzes or fancy dress balls was organised by the vessels' hotel staff. Typically, there was a crew-to-passenger ratio of approximately one crew member for every two passengers.

The Holland America Line followed Swedish American's lead in specifying a dual-role approach when planning its new 38,650gt, 1,456-passenger steam turbine-powered trans-Atlantic liner the *Rotterdam*, which was completed in 1959 by the Rotterdamsche Droggdok Mij. The liner's internal layout represented a significant departure from established approaches.[41] On all existing vessels of her type, First Class passengers occupied an exclusive 'island' amidships where there was less sea motion, the remaining accommodations being split fore and aft. On the *Rotterdam*, by contrast, First and Tourist Class spaces were divided horizontally on alternate decks. This meant that each class had a complete run of public rooms from end to end of the superstructure and cabin decks extending fully fore and aft. A key feature of this arrangement was the *Rotterdam*'s

Below: The design of the Italian-built Swedish American liner *Gripsholm* of 1957 was developed from that of the four-year-old *Kungsholm*, albeit with hull lines similar to other recent liner tonnage from her Genoese builder.

unique 'scissors' arrangement of double interleaved stairways. Concealed sliding panels could be closed on each deck lobby to segregate the two sets of stairs during Atlantic crossings. With the panels opened for cruises, all passengers had the complete run of the ship.[42] Unusually for a large trans-Altlantic vessel, there was only a single engine room, containing four boilers, and this arrangement both saved space and labour, enhancing the vessel's economy. As with the Swedish American Line's vessels, the *Rotterdam*'s exhaust uptakes were routed aft of amidships to allow for a greater amount of open space throughout the passenger accommodation. Yet, unlike the conservative Swedes, the Dutch apparently had no qualms about fitting slender exhaust stacks in place of funnels, meaning that there was also a great deal more uncluttered deck space outdoors. Amidships, where a funnel might have been expected to have been located, there was instead an observation lounge with an outdoor viewing platform above; this feature avoided an awkward 'gap' in the silhouette.[43]

The *Rotterdam*'s interior design reflected the contemporary architecture and outlook of its namesake city. By the 1950s, Rotterdam's harbour, at the mouth of the Rhine, was being marketed as 'Europort' and was overlooked by the 'Euromast.' By designing a 'European' ship, Holland America would be able to offer potential passengers the best of everything – from French cuisine served on Delft porcelain to an Italian ice cream parlour, all arranged within an abstract modernist framework. The *Rotterdam*'s interiors may have been outfitted using traditional materials such as hardwoods, leather and Delft ceramics but, in style, they were very up-to-date, being characterised by trapezium shapes, zigzags and patterns of atoms; similar forms to these adorned the new facades of the post-war city of Rotterdam.

The First Class suite of public rooms was on the upper promenade deck and consisted of the circular-shaped Ambassador Club, designed by J.A. van Tienhoven of Amsterdam in the bright red, dark blue and gold colours of a Heinz tomato soup can, the Smoking Room by Carel L. W. Wirtz of Rotterdam – which had a gently undulating ceiling and banquettes with swing backs, allowing passengers to either face in or towards the sea – and the Ritz Carlton ballroom. It was a double-height space with a balcony and a wide, curved staircase. The forward bulkhead was adorned with a mural by Cuno van den Steene in lacquered teak, depicting scenes of the Aegean Sea. The architects Mutero & Zoon designed it and the adjoining Tropic Bar, plus the library.[44]

The Promenade Deck spaces, intended for Tourist Class use in Atlantic service, consisted of a spacious main lounge of asymmetrical layout which extended the full width of the ship. The floor was slightly terraced around a commodious kidney-shaped dance floor, itself set slightly off the centreline. To port, the adjacent Ocean Bar continued the lounge's full-height windows. The forward part of both public decks was occupied by an egg-shaped cinema auditorium, designed by the architect Cornelius Elffers, whose work ashore in the city of Rotterdam included a bank headquarters building along the City's Blaak thoroughfare.[45] The dining rooms for both classes, located lower in the hull forward and aft of the mid-ships main stairs, were of double-height and nearly identical in decoration. The galley was immediately below, connected by escalator.[46] Continuing further downward, passengers reached a commodious indoor swimming pool. For a liner in her size category, the *Rotterdam* had a remarkable variety of types and scales of space, the relationships between which were very well thought through. The vessel was found to make an ideal cruise ship and for the next forty years developed a very loyal following among older, prosperous, mainly American passengers, many of whom returned year after year to enjoy her familiar shipboard atmosphere and the company of the same travelling companions. Indeed, such loyalty to particular vessels was a characteristic of 'classic' cruising but one that gradually was lost as the cruise industry was 'massified.'

In the same year as the *Rotterdam* entered service, there appeared for the first time in New York a full-time cruise ship: Incres Line's the *Victoria*, which had been ingeniously rebuilt in Italy from the ageing UK-South Africa liner the *Dunnottar Castle*, which was a 508-passenger motor ship, dating from 1936. Incres Line was a subsidiary of Home Lines, which had been established in 1946 primarily to serve the post-war migrant trade from Europe to the Americas and Australia. Headquartered in Switzerland and flying the Panamanian flag, the company's founder and 'guiding light' was Greek shipping entrepreneur, Eugen Eugenides. Its capital came largely from the Swedish American Line and the Italian Cosulich shipping company, which was headquartered in Trieste.

Eugenides – whose companies would go on to make major impacts on the New York cruise market – had been born in 1882 and grew up in Constantinople (Istanbul). Having served as an agent to British shipping firms, be began importing timber from Scandinavia, which brought him into contact with Broström AB, the Swedish American Line's parent company. During the Greco-Turkish War of 1919-1922, he relocated to Piraeus, where he continued to represent Broström's interests and to encourage trade links between Greece and Scandinavia in general. During the Second World War, he moved to South Africa and then to Argentina, between which he established new liner services. Home Lines' initial purpose was to

Above: Whereas the *Kungsholm*'s interiors were largely traditional in style, those of the *Gripsholm* merged together Swedish and Italian modernism, indicating Swedish American's acceptance of a significant shift in visual culture during the mid-1950s. Here we see her dining saloon, smoking saloon and veranda lounge.

Holland America Line's *Rotterdam* of 1959 featured aft-located machinery and a splendid array of magnificent public rooms, reflecting the very best in Dutch post-war design. Here, we see the vessel's Ambassador's Club (centre left), Ritz-Carlton ballroom (bottom left) and the interiors of the Odyssey and La Fontaine dining rooms, which featured extensive Delft ceramic wall and ceiling decorations.

carry migrants from Europe to the Americas. Not only did Swedish American Line provide capital but also the initial tonnage, comprising older trans-Atlantic liners, including the former-*Kungsholm* of 1928, which had all survived the war thanks to Sweden's neutral status. Home Lines' shipboard staff and cuisine were, however, Italian.

In 1950, Incres Line had purchased the 1922-built liner the *Rimutaka* (ex-*Mongolia*) from the New Zealand Shipping Company, which was a P&O subsidiary, for use in the Europe-Australia emigrant trade for which she was renamed as the *Europa*. After less than a year, she was rebuilt in Genoa as a cruise ship, the *Nassau*, which as the name suggested was for operation between New York and the Bahamas. In particular, the cargo holds aft of her superstructure were decked over while derricks and other clutter were removed to create large expanses of outdoor space for sunbathing. Although the vessel was aged and had fairly basic amenities, the *Nassau*'s cruises proved successful – so much so that by the latter-1950s, Incres Line was looking for a more suitable replacement. At that time, the only vessel available was the *Dunnottar Castle*.

In 1958, the vessel was sent to the Wilton Fijenoord shipyard at Schiedam, near Rotterdam, for a very extensive reconstruction into the *Victoria*, which was to be a far superior cruise ship to the *Nassau*. The vessel's modified external silhouette and interiors were designed by Gustavo Pulitzer Finali, a prolific and highly-regarded Italian architect of liner interiors from the mid-1920s onward. Born in Trieste in 1887, Pulitzer's initial shipboard project was to work on interiors for the Cosulich Line's trans-Atlantic motor ship the *Saturnia*, completed in 1925. Inboard, she was a highly ornate 'floating palace', to which various architects and decorators contributed – but when Pulitzer was given complete control of a subsequent ship interior project for a Lloyd Triestino Mediterranean service liner to be completed in 1931 and co-incidentally also named the *Victoria*, his approach was notably progressive, eschewing rich ornamentation in favour of smooth surfaces and clean lines. Thereafter, he designed or co-designed numerous famous Italian trans-Atlantic and other passenger liners of the 1930s and 1950s. Between 1939 – when he helped design the Italian Pavilion for the New York World Fair – and 1947, Pulitzer lived in the USA, where he absorbed forward-looking and glamorous American design ideas, which he brought back to Italy.[47]

As we shall see, Incres Line's the *Victoria* was the first of three very significant post-war cruise ships in which Pulitzer had a significant design input. After nearly a year's work, she emerged completely transformed in terms of layout and appearance. The conversion first reduced her to an empty hull with only the shell of the mid-ships superstructure otherwise retained; even her engines were replaced. A new pointed forepeak was added along with forward and aft extensions to the superstructure in place of cargo hatches and cranes. Pulitzer designed a streamlined aluminium alloy forward superstructure, reflecting the most up-to-date constructional and aesthetic trends in passenger ship naval architecture, as well as a conical-shaped funnel casing combined with mast, which were also fabricated from aluminium.[48] The originally open lower promenade deck was plated in and the cabins extended outward, every one being given a private bathroom. Altogether, 214 new cabins, accommodating 368 passengers, were built in the emptied hull and superstructure, as was a new dining saloon in place of the original First Class one (while the one for Tourist Class was replaced by cabins). Ahead of this in the forward hull, a fan-shaped theatre auditorium with tiered seating was installed within the forward cargo hold, making good use of the tapering space. Although most large- and intermediate-sized liners had cinemas, this was possibly the first ever proper theatre complete with a proscenium stage and with dressing rooms on a cruise ship. It was only much later on in the 1980s that such facilities became commonplace. In the superstructure, the public rooms were arranged on a single deck, which already had a lofty deck-head thanks to its airy 'country house' style design for the 1930s Union-Castle service. Towards the stern, overlooking the lido deck through an extensively-glazed, aft-facing bulkhead was a two-deck-high ballroom and nightclub, called the Riviera.[49]

Flying the Liberian flag, the *Victoria* made her maiden cruise from New York in 1959 and, thereafter, continued to cruise for various owners until 2002 – much longer than her initial career as a UK-South Africa liner had been.

Back in the 1950s, many of the migrants travelling from Europe to Argentina to begin new lives were Germans who sailed from Hamburg. Home Lines ran a well-patronised migrant service from there to Buenos Aires. The company's operations in Hamburg were managed by a youthful and energetic Danish-born shipping agent called Axel Bitsch-Christensen, whom Eugen Eugenides had employed in 1952. Following Eugenides' death two years later, his son and successor, Nicolaos Vernicos Eugenides, took over Home Lines. In the early-1960s, he and Bitsch-Christensen decided that the company should build a new predominantly Tourist Class trans-Atlantic liner to operate on a route from Genoa to Montreal but, soon, it became clear that the rapid growth of air travel would mean no long-term future for such a line. A far better alternative would be to take inspiration from the *Victoria*'s success as a cruise ship operating from New York and to build a brand new additional vessel for this increasingly lucrative trade. The outcome was the innovative and immensely popular *Oceanic*.[50]

The *Oceanic* was Italian-designed by the famous naval architect Nicolò Costanzi and built by the Cantieri Riuniti dell'Adriatico shipyard at Trieste, which was home to the Cosulich company whose technical staff could therefore easily supervise the construction, with delivery scheduled for 1965. Born in Trieste in 1893, Costanzi had overseen the design of nearly all of the significant Italian-owned post-war liners and was widely regarded as one of the world's leading experts in passenger ship design. In addition to his prominent role as a naval architect, however, he also found more local fame as an abstract painter and sculptor and his 'artist's eye', coupled with a deep knowledge of hydrodynamic theory, enabled him to devise hull forms that were visually striking and operationally effective in equal measure. As with other recent Costanzi designs, the *Oceanic*'s bow was concave at the waterline but convex above, thereby simultaneously giving a slender entry at the waterline while maximising the deck area above. Amidships, the hull topsides gently sloped outwards towards the waterline to enhance stability and, aft, the sheer of the stern was almost as pronounced as that of the bow. Although spoon-shaped above the waterline, a transom below increased the effectiveness of water flow over the propellers.[51] This design was used by Costanzi on subsequent vessels – and was revived by the British naval architect Stephen Payne in his designing of the stern for the giant 2004 Cunard flagship, the *Queen Mary 2*. Payne has observed

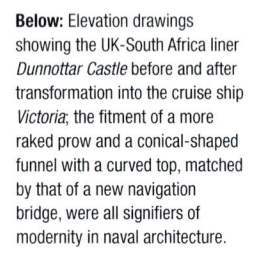

Right & above: Originally P&O's colonial liner *Mongolia*, the Incres Line cruise ship *Nassau* became very popular in the 1950s for voyages from New York to the Caribbean. The elderly vessel's external decks were, however, somewhat cluttered by cranes and hatches, which were relics of her original use.

Below: Elevation drawings showing the UK-South Africa liner *Dunnottar Castle* before and after transformation into the cruise ship *Victoria*; the fitment of a more raked prow and a conical-shaped funnel with a curved top, matched by that of a new navigation bridge, were all signifiers of modernity in naval architecture.

that, in terms of speed and fuel economy, the *Oceanic*'s hull was one of the most effective ever built for a passenger ship.[52]

Furthermore, Costanzi enthusiastically adopted the latest thinking with regard to the specification of machinery and the arrangement of passenger and crew accommodation. The *Oceanic*'s overall layout was to a large extent inspired by that of P&O's recently-introduced 44,807gt UK-Australia liner the *Canberra*, which had entered service in 1961. With an aft-located engine room and lifeboats 'nested' in recesses on either side of her lower superstructure, the topmost decks were able to fill the vessel's entire width with consequently much more space available for passengers to enjoy the outdoor life.[53] The officers' accommodation and bridge formed a separate block above the superstructure's forward end – and this approach was also emulated on the *Oceanic*, which measured 39,200gt – only marginally smaller than *Canberra*.[54] (The idea of nested lifeboats had a much longer history, however, the Rotterdam Lloyd Netherlands-Dutch East Indies liner the *Willem Ruys*, designed in the late-1930s and completed in 1947, having had this feature.)

The *Oceanic*'s very large lido area was protected by glazed screens on either side and from above by a retractable glazed 'magradome' roof, making it usable all year round. The lido itself contained two oval-shaped bathing pools in free-form mosaic surrounds with shallow water in which to relax. The decking was laid in a 'crazy paving' pattern, like the terrace of a contemporary hotel. It was a real 'sun trap' and the prototype for the swimming pool areas of the vast majority of subsequent purpose-built cruise ships.[55]

The interiors were largely the work of the Italian architect Nino Zoncada, who had been involved in designing the pre-war *Stockholm* and numerous other passenger liners since. In addition, contributions were made by other prominent Italian architects with previous experience of shipboard interior design – such as Giò Ponti and Gustavo Pulitzer Finali. The most exclusive cabins, located abaft the bridge, even had their own private verandas. Although unusual, this was not innovative because as far back as the mid-1920s, the Cosulich liners the *Saturnia* and *Vulcania* had similar accommodation.

Although the *Oceanic* had been planned as a two-class liner, the nominally First Class areas were fairly small compared with those of Tourist and, when operating as a single class cruise ship it was nearly impossible to spot where the divisions lay. The principal public rooms were located on the promenade deck and comprised two large ballrooms – the Italian Hall, located forward, and the Aegean Room amidships, with the Skål Bar and Europe Observation Lounge aft (Home Lines'

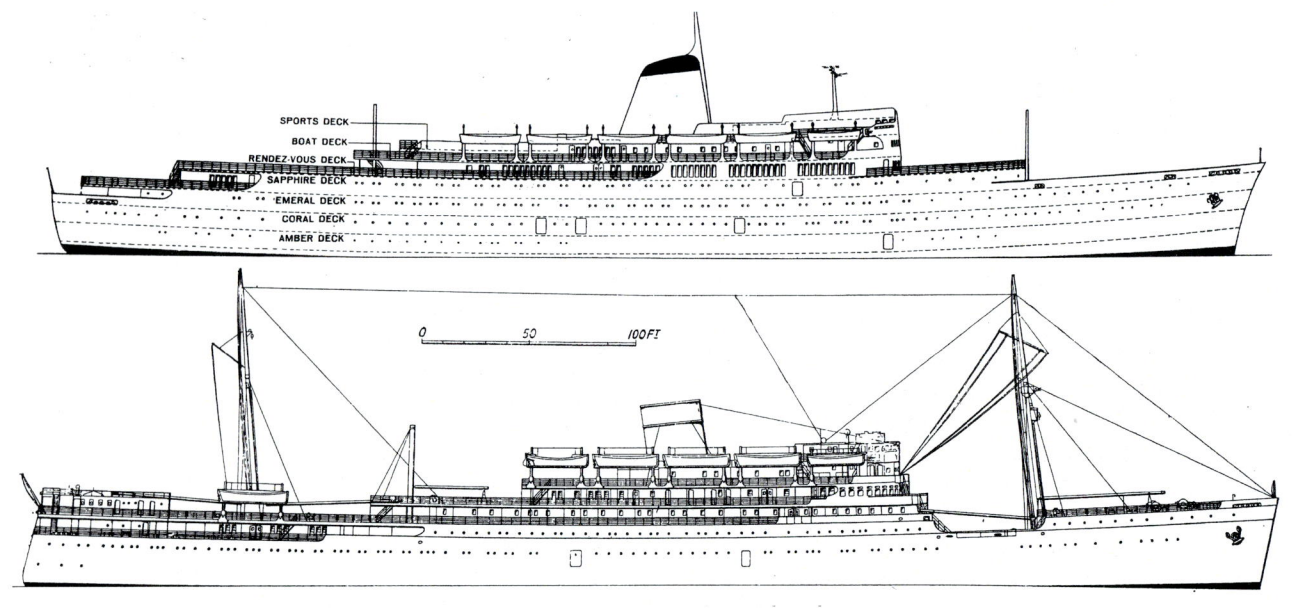

The post-war shift from liner to cruise | 37

The *Victoria* is seen off New York (top), the raking light picking up inequalities in her old hull shell plating, thereby revealing her true vintage. Her interiors, however, were all-new and reflected an up-to-date Italian design approach. The dining saloon, nightclub and cinema-theatre were all double-height spaces, while the forward-facing observation lounge echoed the curving shape of her modernised forward superstructure.

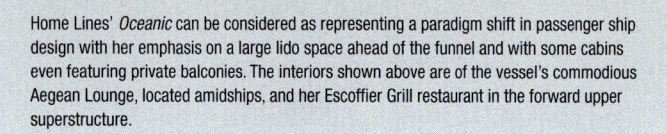

Home Lines' *Oceanic* can be considered as representing a paradigm shift in passenger ship design with her emphasis on a large lido space ahead of the funnel and with some cabins even featuring private balconies. The interiors shown above are of the vessel's commodious Aegean Lounge, located amidships, and her Escoffier Grill restaurant in the forward upper superstructure.

pan-European ownership structure was reflected in these names). The fore and aft spaces were oval-shaped, following the curving and slanted forms of the superstructure and these forms were visually reinforced by cove-lit ceilings, arranged in concentric rings and focusing attention on the dance floors. Bright velour-clad furniture, abstract artworks and festoon blinds completed the effect. Filling full width of the hull two decks below was the main dining saloon, which was one of the largest single-span spaces on any ship, its rectangular ceiling dome, decorated with abstractly-patterned tiles by the ceramicist Emanuele Luzzati, punching through to the deck above. The tables in the middle of the room were circular and arranged in groups of three around lighting standards with three shaded globes on arms to light each group individually. Passengers booked in the most expensive cabins dined in a separate grillroom, named the Escoffier and located in the forward superstructure.[56] Soon, the *Oceanic* developed a very favourable reputation among prosperous New Yorkers, not only for the luxury and modernity of her accommodation but also for the warmth and charm of the Italian officers and crew.

In addition to the *Oceanic*'s successful New York debut in 1965, the port also witnessed the maiden arrival the same year of Norwegian America Line's new dual-purpose trans-Atlantic liner and cruise ship, the *Sagafjord*. As with the *Oceanic*, a very high standard of accommodation was provided throughout, meaning that the relatively small suite of First Class rooms for Atlantic service blended easily with the remainder when the vessel was cruising. Just like the Norwegian America's two earlier post-war passenger liners, the *Oslofjord* of 1949 and the *Bergensfjord* of 1956, the *Sagafjord* was designed by the company's in-house naval architect, Kaare Haug as a twin-screw motor vessel with an all-welded aluminium superstructure, the front of which and funnel casing were elegantly streamlined. In September 1962, a contract for the construction of the ship was signed with the French shipbuilders, Société des Forges et Chantiers de la Méditerranée at La Seyne, for delivery in 1965.[57]

With cruising in mind, the interior design approach was to represent a significant change in direction since the *Oslofjord* and *Bergensfjord* had been completed. In line with the upsurge in Norwegian national sentiment following Norway's liberation from Germany, the interiors of its previous passenger vessels had been in the national romantic style, drawn up by Arnstein Arneberg, who was best known for having designed Oslo City Hall. In contrast, to make the *Sagafjord* more appealing to the wealthy, cosmopolitan clientele whom Norwegian America's directors now hoped to attract, a team of progressive, mainly Scandinavian architects and designers was assembled under the co-ordination of Fritjof S. Platou, whose firm was based in Oslo. The most spacious room was the Tourist Class ballroom, designed by Finn Nilsson. With its high ceiling and a floor area covering 8,000 square feet, a bright colour scheme and subdued lighting, it was spacious, yet instantly welcoming. From this room, glass doors led out onto the lido deck and open-air swimming pool which had an illuminated fountain at night. The two-deck-high Saga Dining Room, amidships in the lower hull, was designed by Platou and his assistant Njål Eide and, in terms of layout, was comparable with that of the *Oceanic*. A splendid staircase led down from the deck above, passengers making a grand entrance through doors in a double height glazed bulkhead.[58] As we shall see, in the 1970s and 80s, both Finn Nilsson and Njål Eide went on to become significant cruise ship interior designers, mainly working on behalf of other Norwegian ship owners. Increasingly, their work came to reflect their perceptions of popular American taste, rather than the rarefied and exclusive Scandinavian modernism of the *Sagafjord*.

Kay Kørbing, who was a Dane, designed the *Sagafjord*'s relatively compact but exquisitely detailed suite of First Class public rooms, which were located at the forward end of her Veranda Deck. The circular Garden Lounge, located towards the bow, was built on split levels around a sunken circular dance floor and ingeniously combined the daytime role of a quiet, airy sitting room with that of an intimate nightclub. This was achieved by means of four vertically slatted matt gold metal screens, which gave the space a cosy and warm-toned inner area and a bright and airy perimeter. The ceiling above the central section featured lighting coves with a colour-change system for use at night when there was lounge dancing. The First Class hallway, immediately behind, was an impressive oval-shaped multi-deck space with a dramatic under-lit open tread staircase plunging downward and appearing to float in front of a gently curving wall, panelled in strips of teak and onyx marble. Moving further aft, the library, writing room and North Cape Bar were on either beam. The latter was well lit through large windows by day, but full-length curtains ensured that it was dark and sociable by night.[59]

The *Sagafjord* was eventually delivered six months behind schedule in the Autumn of 1965, the expense of her construction coupled with rapidly increasing labour costs having brought her builder to the verge of bankruptcy. Yet, she soon was established as one of the finest cruise ships afloat and spent an increasing part of the time in this role. It soon became Norwegian America's policy that its older vessels should maintain the trans-Atlantic liner service while the newest would cruise full-time; this was a complete reversal of its earlier practice and demonstrated changed commercial perceptions of which activity was the more prestigious and lucrative.

Norwegian America's Scandinavian rival, the Swedish American Line, meanwhile, had decided to update its fleet, replacing the 1953-built *Kungsholm* with a new, larger and considerably more sophisticated liner of the same name, measuring 26,678gt. Indeed, a clear design lineage could be traced back to the pre-war *Stockholm*. The new *Kungsholm* would be the naval architect Eric Christiansson's final major project for the company (indeed, he retired while the design was in progress, leaving others to oversee its completion).[60]

Having previously built its major passenger ships in Italy and the Netherlands, this time the order went to the famous Clydebank shipyard of John Brown & Co in Scotland, which, having built a succession of acclaimed liners for Cunard, was now hoping to win an eventual order for that company's planned new Atlantic liner. To maintain continuity of employment for its skilled workers until that order came to fruition, it bid low to win the *Kungsholm* project. As with the *Sagafjord* débacle at La Seyne, this was to prove unwise.[61] When the project was announced, Swedish American's directors had explained to the shipping press that they were instituting what they described as a 'build and sell' policy to ensure a young and technically state-of-the-art fleet, the implication being that a succession of further liners would in future be ordered. As events unfolded, however, the new *Kungsholm* was to be the final passenger ship ever built for the company.[62]

The *Kungsholm* was intended to cruise for 80 per cent of the year with only occasional Atlantic crossings. Senior staff from Swedish American's Passenger Department and Technical Department carried out extensive surveys and made large-scale mock-ups of various aspects of the new liner's design in an attempt to ensure the best possible outcome. As a majority of regular cruise passengers were American, the company's New York office had a great deal of input into the design development process.

The *Kungsholm* had been due for delivery in November 1965 but labour problems during the fitting out stage delayed her by four months, causing Swedish American to invoke penalty clauses. In all, John Brown & Co lost £3 million on what was a £7 million contract.[63]

There was, however, widespread praise for the vessel's graceful external design and for the quality of the craftsmanship of her interiors. For trans-Atlantic service, her capacity was 750 but, when cruising, only 450 were accommodated in the lower berths with a crew of 438 – a remarkably high ratio, indicating the liner's luxury status. The approach to commissioning the vessel's interior design emulated the *Sagafjord*, Swedish American likewise selecting a diverse team of architects and designers to give a sense of variety, albeit sharing a common Swedish modernist aesthetic formula.[64]

Given that Swedish American's North American passengers greatly appreciated anything with a connection to the Swedish Royal Family, the company commissioned Count Sigvard Bernadotte, who was a well-known industrial designer and the second son of H.M. King Gustav VI, to collaborate with the architect Veit Betlike in designing the *Kungsholm*'s main forward lounge on Boat Deck. Beneath this was the liner's cinema-theatre, designed by British architects, Tabb & Haselhurst, who were also employed to oversee the entire interior outfitting at the shipyard. The main lounge, located amidships, was the work of a young Swedish interior designer, Robert Tillberg, who would go on to have an outstanding career in passenger ship interior design. Towards the stern was a further lounge and smoking room for use by Tourist Class when in trans-Atlantic service. The dining saloon was located amidships, four decks below and was by Rolf Ahberg. Folding partitions could be drawn across to split it into two sections for liner service. Out on deck, the *Kungsholm*'s two funnels mitigated against the expanses of recreational space found topsides on the *Rotterdam* and the *Oceanic* and so, instead, a lido area was located between the funnels with over-hanging 'wings' of deck protruding on two levels between the lifeboats. These were surrounded by glazed shelter screens, creating an attractive 'suntrap', even in windy weather. As on the *Sagafjord*, a majority of outdoor deck space was located aft of the superstructure, there being a large fantail area.[65]

On her maiden trans-Atlantic crossing, the *Kungsholm* carried only 304 passengers, a disappointingly small number for a prestigious new liner, but the vessel soon found a niche in cruising from New York, where she joined a whole armada of significant vessels of recent construction. Apart from the dual-purpose *Rotterdam*, *Oceanic* and *Sagafjord*, described above, there were also the pure trans-Atlantic liners the *United States* and *France*, plus the Italian *Leonardo da Vinci*, *Michelangelo* and *Raffaello*. In addition, the American Moore-McCormack Line's the *Brasil* and *Argentina* sailed to South American ports. Within a decade, every one of these loss-making liners would be withdrawn from service as, increasingly, the future of 'deep sea' passenger shipping lay with cruise ships.

In terms of the design aesthetics of passenger ships (and, indeed, of merchant shipping in general), the mid-1960s witnessed the beginnings of a radical change of approach. Since the latter-1930s, progressive naval architecture and shipbuilding practices had increasingly come to favour 'streamformed' superstructure elements. An increasing confidence in the use of aluminium alloy and of welding techniques encouraged double-curvatures in bridge fronts and funnel tops and this approach – which added additional construction expense – arguably reached its apotheosis with the *Sagafjord* and *Kungsholm*, the languid forms of which were acclaimed for their visual harmony and poise. In other words, these relatively large vessels were intended to be 'read' by observers as inheritors of the tradition of yacht-like passenger ship design, perpetuated from cruising's early years in the latter nineteenth century.

A more economical alternative which was to become increasingly commonplace in ensuing decades was to avoid unnecessary curvature wherever possible as every piece of bent steel represented an input of labour. Instead of sheer and camber throughout a hull's length, its decks could be flat with only sheer where it was really needed at the bow. The *Michelangelo* and *Raffaello* reflected this approach, which was accentuated by equally angular superstructure and funnel detailing, creating a quite severe but nonetheless pleasingly coherent overall effect. An early cruise ship design to employ a similar approach was the West German-owned 24,950gt *Hamburg* of 1968.

As with Home Lines' the *Oceanic*, the *Hamburg* project was the brainchild of Axel Bitsch-Christensen, who, back in the mid-1950s, had succeeded in persuading his boss, Nicolaos Veronicos Eugenides, to provide him with an investment of six million deutschmarks to enable the establishment of a new passenger liner company to commence a Hamburg-New York trans-Atlantic service. The Hamburg-Atlantik Linie began operations in 1958 using the 1930-built former-*Empress of Scotland* which was substantially rebuilt as the *Hanseatic*. During the winter, she was also used for cruises from New York and Fort Lauderdale to Caribbean ports and, by the mid-1960s, had become nearly a full-time cruise ship, attracting a loyal clientele of mainly Americans of German origin.

As the *Hanseatic* was ageing, Bitsch-Christensen investigated ways of part-financing a purpose-built replacement, designed primarily for cruising. His solution was to issue shares to former passengers. This was successful but, before a contract could be signed, the *Hanseatic* was badly damaged by a serious fire in the autumn of 1966. Very soon after, an order was placed with the Deutsche Werft in Hamburg and, as a stop-gap, the four-year-old French-built Israeli trans-Atlantic liner the *Shalom* was purchased in 1967 to enable the *Hanseatic*'s cruise programme to be continued. Elegantly-appointed and up-to-date though the *Shalom* was, she had been unsuccessful for her initial owner; it is claimed that this was due to the fact that her cuisine was entirely kosher, thereby excluding many non-Jewish passengers' favourite foods. Under German ownership, she was re-named the *Hanseatic* (II) but was otherwise little-altered. Meanwhile, her new owner re-branded from Hamburg Atlantik Linie to Deutsche Atlantik Linie in anticipation of its new flagship cruise liner the *Hamburg* being delivered in 1968.

As with the *Oceanic* and *Hanseatic*, ex-*Shalom*, the *Hamburg* was a steam turbine vessel, yet in overall concept she

Norwegian America Line's *Sagafjord* was an exclusive cruise ship, the interiors of which were in a Scandinavian modernist idiom and were the work of a number of Norwegian and Danish architects. Here we see her dining saloon by Fritjof Platou and Njål Eide of Oslo, the sitting area of one of her suites and her Garden Lounge by Kay Kørbing of Copenhagen. The vessel's curving lines and harmonious details reflect the commercial and national pride of her owner.

Above and below: Swedish American Line's *Kungsholm* of 1966 was the ultimate iteration of a design trajectory begun in the mid-1930s with the *Stockholm*. The new liner's mid-ships lounge (below) was an early work by the Swedish designer Robert Tillberg and featured a ceramic bas relief by Carl Harry Stålhane, while the dining saloon (bottom) had vitrines containing collections of historic tableware from the East Indies.

was most similar to the recent Scandinavian motor ships the *Sagafjord* and *Kungsholm*. Where the *Hamburg* completely differed was her much more advanced hull form, which featured flat decks, angled upward at the bow. Her convex bow form above the water was reminiscent of the *Oceanic* – as well as several recent West German-built refrigerated cargo ships, the idea being to increase slightly the deck area for more spacious cabins. In addition, the entire vessel was of steel construction, rather than using weight-saving aluminium for the upper decks, funnel and mast, as was the case with so many other recent liners, the *Sagafjord* and *Kungsholm* included. The reason for this was simply to save money as aluminium not only cost more but was also more time-consuming to work.

Rather than the inter-locking L-shaped cabins preferred by Swedish American Line, on *Hamburg*, there were inside and outside rooms accessed off centre-line main corridors; all of the cabins had private bathrooms, however. A maximum of 790 could be accommodated, though the upper limit of berths typically sold was only 652. This was because her cruises were so costly that passengers rightly expected to be accommodated in lower berths, rather than upper bunk beds. In order to achieve undivided cabin decks, the dining and galley facilities were located unusually low down in the hull with the result that, to maintain the necessary watertight compartment subdivisions, they were split into three separate spaces (as opposed to the single grand-scaled equivalents on the *Oceanic*, *Sagafjord* and *Kungsholm*). Four decks above, the *Hamburg*'s public rooms were arranged with a multi-functional ballroom and entertainment space filling the full width of the forward superstructure, aft of which was a series of intimate bars, lounges and club rooms, accessed from a long central hallway and sandwiched between enclosed promenade decks. Towards the stern, there was a theatre. On Boat Deck, above, a large observation lounge with a circular cocktail bar faced forward. Amidships, there was an ingenious deck arrangement, exploiting the fact that the forward and aft saloons had particularly lofty deck heads. It was thus possible to squeeze an extra deck level of intimately-dimensioned spaces in between, one of which was a nightclub, forming a U-shape around the swimming pool tank.

The *Hamburg*'s interiors were designed by a Munich-based architect, Georg Manner, who had previous experience of passenger ship interior design, having worked in the latter-1930s with the Italian Gustavo Pulitzer Finali and, post-war, having been heavily involved in the conversion of the pre-war French liner the *Pasteur* into Norddeutscher Lloyd's trans-Atlantic liner the *Bremen*. Manner's the *Hamburg* interiors were in an international modernist idiom, sober yet glamorous and very typical of West German hotel and hospitality design during the country's post-war 'economic miracle.'

The *Hamburg*'s most distinctive design feature, however, was her funnel. In common with several prominent liners of the 1960s, research was undertaken to find the most effective smoke-dispersal strategy. The recent Italian trans-Atlantic vessels the *Michelangelo* and *Raffaello* had demonstrated the benefits of having large smoke-deflecting fins at their

The post-war shift from liner to cruise | 43

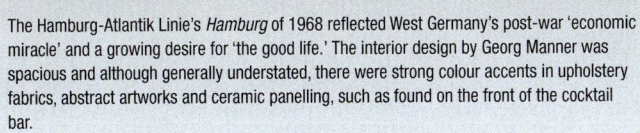

The Hamburg-Atlantik Linie's *Hamburg* of 1968 reflected West Germany's post-war 'economic miracle' and a growing desire for 'the good life.' The interior design by Georg Manner was spacious and although generally understated, there were strong colour accents in upholstery fabrics, abstract artworks and ceramic panelling, such as found on the front of the cocktail bar.

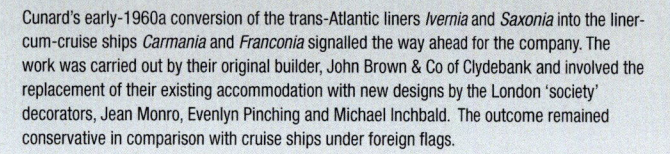

Cunard's early-1960a conversion of the trans-Atlantic liners *Ivernia* and *Saxonia* into the liner-cum-cruise ships *Carmania* and *Franconia* signalled the way ahead for the company. The work was carried out by their original builder, John Brown & Co of Clydebank and involved the replacement of their existing accommodation with new designs by the London 'society' decorators, Jean Monro, Evenlyn Pinching and Michael Inchbald. The outcome remained conservative in comparison with cruise ships under foreign flags.

Left: The aft superstructure of the *Carmania* and *Franconia* was entirely reconfigured with new tiered sun decks and a swimming pool, surrounded by glazed shelter screens. Here, the *Franconia* is seen leaving the Clyde at the end of her transformation, repainted in a *Caronia*-like green livery.

funnels' summits, supported on open lattice structures to enable an airflow to blow beneath, thereby reducing downward suction to the rear. The *Hamburg*'s funnel used a similar approach, but was conical shaped with a 'flying saucer'-shaped smoke deflecting plate held high aloft by the boiler stovepipes, which were splayed outward. This distinctive solution, coupled with the vessel's commodious appointments, led to her being marketed as 'The Space Ship.' (Referencing space travel was one fashionably effective means of out-manoeuvring the jet airline industry.)

So far as clientele was concerned, liners such as the *Oceanic*, *Sagafjord*, *Kungsholm*, *Hanseatic* and *Hamburg* attracted mainly Americans, a majority of whom were from New York itself, or the most prosperous parts of the industrial northeast. There was a strong correlation between many of these passengers' European origins and their preferred cruise ship – Italian-Americans, for instance chose the *Oceanic*, on which they could enjoy cuisine served by waiters from the 'Old Country.' Americans of Scandinavian origin obviously preferred the *Sagafjord* and *Kungsholm*, while those of German background were particularly attracted to the Deutsche Atlantik Linie's two ships. In all instances, these liners developed very loyal clienteles with significant numbers of repeat passengers who enjoyed simple relaxation in spacious, understated environs of high design quality in which social interaction with similarly affluent and like-minded fellow passengers was guaranteed. As the environs of New York's piers fell into post-industrial decline, the luxury cruise ships calling there provided their fortunate passengers with seemingly ideal and protected spaces, safely aloof from the decay surrounding them. When calling briefly at ports in third world countries, the same situation was true.

In post-war Europe, the situation was somewhat different as there simply was not yet the same level of prosperity as in large parts of the USA. Yet, the situation was changing. In Britain, post-war rationing finally ended in 1955 and, thereafter, government policies sought to encourage entrepreneurship, leading to a large nouveau riche emerging to challenge the strictures of the established class hierarchy. A mid-1960s BBC documentary, presented by Alan Whicker, records the atmosphere and changing passenger demographics of Royal Mail Lines' pre-war built the *Andes*, one of several ageing British liners by then finding employment in the expanding cruise market. Whicker explains that in 1960, around 35,000 Britons took cruises, but by 1965, that figure had quadrupled.

A majority of the *Andes*' passengers were older, single women, several of whom bemoaned the democratisation of luxury. 'I came because I expected millionaires,' says one, 'but all I found was a load of Huggets' (a reference to a working class family in a radio sitcom). Another observed what she saw as 'the bad manners and the dirty habits' of some of her fellow passengers, pointing out orange peel littering the deck. 'I take it you're not enjoying your cruise?' asked Whicker, 'Well, I am in a way,' she replied 'but there's very, very mixed fare. In normal life, you wouldn't quite mix with those people.' Of the newly prosperous, one male passenger was the sales director of a textile company who additionally worked four evenings a week as a bookmaker at greyhound racing circuits and was now able to enjoy 'the good life' aboard the *Andes*. Throughout, a running theme was passengers complaining about the behaviour of one unidentified boy who apparently responded to everyone he met with 'shut your cake-hole!'[66]

In the mid-1960s, a cruise on the *Andes* would have cost between £7 and £23 per day, the average price for Whicker's cruise to North Africa being £300, which was a very large sum back then. For Royal Mail Lines, the liner's break-even point was achieved by selling 85% of the berths for their full price; discounting was practically unheard of.[67]

British liner companies initially responded to cruising's potential by modifying their existing tonnage. For example, in 1964 the Pacific Steam Navigation Company – which traditionally operated a UK-West Coast of South America liner service via the Panama Canal – sent its newest liner, the eight-year-old, 20,234gt *Reina Del Mar*, back to her builder, Harland & Wolff in Belfast. There, forward and aft cargo holds were built over with an extended superstructure, containing additional cabins, public rooms and sun deck spaces. These new facilities included what was claimed to be the longest bar at sea, extending around three sides of the extended forward-facing Coral Lounge. The plan was that the *Reina Del Mar* would henceforth be operated by a consortium called 'Travel Savings Ltd', the subscribers to which could pay monthly instalments for future cruises, thereby spreading the cost. Although the vessel's conversion was aesthetically detrimental to her formerly sleek profile, the overall approach set the pattern for numerous subsequent liner-to-cruise ship rebuilds for a wide variety of operators. The *Reina Del Mar* went from being a three-class 766-passenger capacity liner to a one-class, 1,047-passenger cruise ship. Her relatively high revised capacity indicated the addition of many relatively economical four-berth

46 | Cruise Ships: A Design History

Upon completion, the *Queen Elizabeth 2* was considered a major triumph for British contemporary design – a situation reflecting the influence of approaches used by the airline industry. Here, we see (top left to bottom right) the vessel arriving at New York on her maiden voyage, her Double Room ballroom by Jon Bannenberg, her circular entrance foyer, Britannia Restaurant and Columbia Restaurant by Dennis Lennon and a bow-quarter exterior view at Cape Town.

The post-war shift from liner to cruise | 47

A series of images showing the *Queen Elizabeth 2*'s Tourist Class library, her Look-Out observation lounge by Theo Crosby, one of her shops, the Q4 Room nightclub by David Hicks, the Queen's Lounge and the port-side promenade deck. Many of her interiors had a space-age quality, resulting from the extensive use of moulded fibreglass to encase columns and as a ceiling finish. Such a co-ordinated approach was only rarely used on subsequent cruise ships, however, and even *QE2*'s interiors were quickly fragmented by numerous alterations.

The *Vistafjord* represented the end of an era, being arguably the final large passenger ship built to a design primarily developed for 'deep sea' liner service. Her interiors were by the same team of Scandinavians as were responsible for the *Sagafjord*; here we see a lounge space, her restaurant, which – in common with those on *Queen Elizabeth 2* and most subsequent cruise ships – was located in the superstructure, her library and Norse Bar.

cabins, making her cruises – which departed from the UK and South Africa – affordable for a wider demographic than had hitherto been typical of the cruise industry in general.

Britain's Cunard Line, hitherto the dominant force in trans-Atlantic passenger shipping, had been pondering how best to respond to the rapidly-changing trading conditions brought about by the jet age and to equally profound changes in the make-up of sections of its American, British and continental European passenger demographics. By the mid-1960s, Cunard was operating no fewer than four major liners in cruise service for a majority of their time with only occasional trans-Atlantic crossings interspersed. The UK-Canada liners *Ivernia* and *Saxonia*, which had first entered service in 1954 and 1955 respectively, were extensively reconfigured in 1962-63 by their original builder, John Brown & Co, with light and spacious new interiors by the London-based society decorators Michael Inchbald and Jean Monro. Renamed the *Carmania* and *Franconia*, both joined the *Caronia* in making combinations of liner voyages and cruises, mainly for the American market. By the mid-1960s, however, cruising was all three vessels' predominant activity and they were joined in this role by the trans-Atlantic liner the *Mauretania* – and even occasionally by the *Queen Mary* and *Queen Elizabeth*, though they were really unsuitable on account of their great size, lack of proper air conditioning and passenger facilities that were solely intended for three-class liner service.

In the early-1960s, Cunard had planned to commission a new Southampton-New York express liner, a project code-named 'Q3', which would in essence have been a variation of the *France* and the most recent Italian trans-Atlantic vessels, none of which were particularly suited for cruising purposes. Given the rapidly changing passenger travel market, however, it was fortunate that in 1964, Cunard superseded Q3 with a smaller 65,862gt, 1,025-passenger liner-cum-cruise ship, code-named 'Q4'. She was subsequently completed in 1969 by Upper Clyde Shipbuilders as the *Queen Elizabeth 2*.[68] (Upper Clyde Shipbuilders was the former-John Brown & Co shipyard at Clydebank that had been nationalized and amalgamated with other yards as a result of financial difficulties caused by the loss-making *Kungsholm* project).

Shortly after Q4 was announced, Cunard's Chairman, Sir John Brocklebank, resigned due to poor health. His replacement, Sir Basil Smallpeice, was the former Managing Director of British Overseas Airline Corporation (BOAC), where he had played a key role in introducing de Havilland Comet and Vickers-Armstrong VC10 jets. Cunard's operations were familiar to him due to trans-Atlantic cooperation between the two companies, which had formed Cunard-BOAC to offer combined air-and-sea travel packages. Smallpeice's aim – so far as was possible – was to bring Cunard's image and service approach into the jet age.[69] An early move was to discard Cunard's traditional three-class stratification of trans-Atlantic liner travel in favour of a two-class arrangement that could easily be dissolved for cruising.[70]

As a cruise ship, Q4's hull dimensions would be constrained by a need to fit the Panama Canal's locks. Yet, to incorporate the broad range of leisure facilities imagined by Cunard and their designers, the vessel would also need a relatively tall superstructure in comparison with trans-Atlantic liners of the past. Inspired by the example of the recent Orient Line UK-Australia vessel the *Oriana*, the solution was to make very advanced and extensive use of light-weight aluminium alloy.[71] Of course, the upper decks and funnel casings of several recent liners (with the notable exception of the *Hamburg*) had made use of varying amounts of aluminium – but none on the scale proposed for Q4. Her four upper decks were to be entirely constructed of the material with more forming an 'inner core' of the decks below, surrounded by a deep and massively strong U-shape of steel hull and lower superstructure. Rather than the typical propulsive solution for large trans-Atlantic liners of having two engine rooms, which was deemed too costly and inefficient, the Q4's steam turbine plant would be located in a single unit, following the precedent of the *Oceanic*, with only three boilers supplying steam to drive twin-screw propellers.[72]

So far as the layout of the passenger accommodation was concerned, Cunard applied knowledge gained from experience with its existing liner-cum-cruise ships, particularly the *Caronia*, and its technical staff also examined in detail a wide range of recent passenger ships to see what innovative ideas could be learned and incorporated into Q4. Yet, the final solution was surprisingly radical as the design evolved into a floating version of a modern luxury hotel resort in which all of the public rooms, including the restaurants, were located on three of the superstructure decks. Moving upward, these were known as 'Quarter Deck', which was exclusively First Class in trans-Atlantic service, 'Upper Deck' and 'Boat Deck', both of which were for Tourist Class passengers. A very significant innovation for Cunard was that every cabin would be *en suite* – an approach emulating the standards of Q4's New York-based competitors and also pointing ahead to the forthcoming generation of purpose-built, full-time cruise ships. Indeed, the overall layout of the cabin decks was subsequently widely copied in subsequent cruise ship design. Rather than the central axial corridors, these had parallel corridors on either side of the centre line with casings containing vertical services, stair towers and inside cabins between.[73]

To give the vessel an up-to-date image, Cunard retained the industrial design consultant James Gardiner, who had previously been employed by BOAC and had recently developed external styling suggestions for the stillborn Q3, working in close co-operation with its Chief Naval Architect, Dan Wallace.[74] In designing the exterior, not only did Gardiner achieve a notable sense of visual integration but also a subtle suggestion of science fiction fantasy. Rather than the broad barrel-shaped funnels of past Cunard vessels, research by the National Physical Laboratory had shown that a tall, slender stovepipe would be most efficient in carrying exhaust gases high above the ship. A scoop at its base used the airflow over the superstructure to add an extra updraft. The bridge was dramatically sculptural, its windows being recessed in a horizontal slot, thus achieving the illusion of it pulling the remainder of the upper works in its wake. Above, the 'space needle'-like mast – containing a galley flue – complemented the funnel. In place of Cunard's black, red and white livery, a charcoal grey and white scheme was introduced with 'Cunard' emblazoned in red on the forward superstructure, much like the corporate graphics of a jetliner's superstructure. The outside decks were generously proportioned and entirely lacking in any of the clutter of derricks, ventilators or guy wires found on previous Cunard liners – indeed, even the two electric cranes mounted ahead of the superstructure were encased to harmonise with the overall design concept.[75]

A number of prominent interior architects and designers were inherited from the Q3 project – including the London-based Dennis Lennon and the society interior designers Michael Inchbald and David Hicks, plus a young Australian émigré,

Jon Bannenberg. Gardiner recommended to Smallpeice a greater role for Lennon, who was promoted to overall coordinator. Recently, he had designed critically well-received hotel and restaurant interiors for the catering company J. Lyon & Co's Albany chain and a similar approach was adopted for Cunard. In addition, the Council of Industrial Design advised Smallpeice that the interior design team should be augmented by Misha Black, Gaby Schreiber (who, like Gardiner, had been a BOAC designer) and the graphics specialists Crosby, Fletcher, Forbes.[76]

Although launched on schedule, the completion of the *Queen Elizabeth 2* was beset by labour shortages, which delayed the completion of her outfitting, followed by technical problems with her steam turbines, meaning that she was at first rejected by Cunard pending rectification and was therefore unable to enter service until April 1969. Only then could Cunard's great design achievement be widely appreciated.

Of the *Queen Elizabeth 2*'s many diverse public rooms, several were of notably striking design. The circular 'midships embarkation lobby continued the 'space age' theme of the exterior with extensive use of moulded white fibreglass for a central 'trumpet' column and the ceiling, which radiated as a series of concentric rings – indeed, the liner was promoted in Cunard's publicity material as 'the most exciting thing to be launched since Apollo 1' and – just like the *Hamburg* – as 'The Space Ship.'[77] In First Class, the Queen's Room lounge and ballroom, by Michael Inchbald, likewise made extensive and imaginative use of fibreglass for furniture and to encase columns, the futuristic sense of lightness and 'uplift' being heightened by a white lattice ceiling. Its Tourist Class equivalent in trans-Atlantic service was the two-deck-high Double Room by Jon Bannenberg, in which two levels were linked by a dramatic, spiral staircase with red carpeting and smoke-tinted glazed balustrades, which continued around the upper-level. Throughout, shiny brushed aluminium bulkhead and ceiling finishes contrasted with red and orange lounge chairs.

Using similar finishes, Dennis Lennon's Grill Room restaurant was entered by a curved staircase similar to those accessing the Boeing 747 Jetliner's upper deck. The First Class Columbia and Tourist Class Britannia restaurants – also by Lennon – were decorated respectively in shades of brown leather and in the bright colours of the Union Flag. These were served by a single large galley complex, located ahead of the Columbia Restaurant, from which the Britannia and Grill Room on the deck above were also accessed – though at risk of the food occasionally becoming a little tepid *en route*. Soon, such few teething difficulties were resolved, however and, in service, the *Queen Elizabeth 2* proved an immediate and enduring success. In her trans-Atlantic liner role, she appeared to represent the end of an era – but as a cruise ship, she presaged the beginning of a new one.

In the next 34 years, only one more trans-Atlantic liner-derived cruise ship was commissioned. Norwegian America's 24,292gt the *Vistafjord*, built by Swan Hunter on the River Tyne and delivered in 1973, was broadly similar to the company's eight-year-old the *Sagafjord*, albeit with a larger superstructure which contained a *Queen Elizabeth 2*-style dining room with large windows. Whereas the *Sagafjord*'s cruises and her passengers mostly originated from the USA, the *Vistafjord* tended to be based in Europe for much of the year, attracting a clientele of Europeans and Americans. With the *Vistafjord*, the classic passenger liner with a fine-lined, deep drafted hull and a low passenger density reached its apotheosis.

Right: A night-time view of the *Queen Elizabeth 2* at her berth in New York; the liner's sweeping bow and the incidental floodlighting of her superstructure create an ethereal, other-worldly image, but one that is very seductive. In the imagination, the idea of being aboard, surrounded by luxury, enjoying *haute cuisine* and romance is very appealing. Cruise ship design reflects and encourages such desires.

Chapter 4
Small and specialized

In the 1960s, there remained a niche market for small and exclusive cruise ships of similar tonnage and dimensions to those that had carried the wealthy plutocrats of the Edwardian 'gilded age' on grand voyages. Towards the end of the decade, the advent of wide-bodied jet aircraft brought a realization among some cruise entrepreneurs that specialist tonnage could be stationed remotely in 'exotic' locations with entire ship-loads of passengers being brought from Europe or the USA on a single jet flight.

The new era of the large cruising 'yacht' coincided with the latter years of operation of the finest such vessel from the twentieth century's first half – the *Stella Polaris* of 1927. Having come through the Second World War largely unscathed, the vessel had been refitted, then returned to cruise service, initially for her original Norwegian owner and, from 1951 onward for the Swedish Clipper Line, owned by a Gothenburg-based ship owner, Einar Hansen. By the latter 1960s, the *Stella Polaris* proved increasingly problematic to keep certified due to more stringent fire safety regulations having been introduced. The vessel was therefore withdrawn in 1969, by which time a number of new cruise ships of commensurate size had entered service.

The first of these was commissioned by an entrepreneurial West German ship owner, the Lübeck Linie, which, as its name suggested, was based in Lübeck. Established in 1924, it had traditionally operated small cargo vessels in the Baltic trades. In the post-war era, it augmented its operations by acquiring a number of older coastal passenger ships for use on tax-free shopping day excursions between Denmark, Sweden and West Germany. (Such trips were highly popular as they enabled Scandinavians and West Germans to buy cheaper drinks and tobacco than were available ashore.)

In 1965, the Lübeck Linie rather bravely decided to enter the nascent West German cruise market by commissioning a purpose-built 5,933gt, 276-passenger cruise ship, named the *Regina Maris* from the local Flender Werke shipyard. Underpinning this order was a belief that, as West Germany's 'economic miracle' was underway, there would, once again, be enough passengers to re-kindle a German cruising tradition of summers trips in northern Europe and winter voyages to warmer climes.[78]

Although the *Regina Maris* was a relatively small twin-screw motor ship, she was never intended to be particularly 'exclusive' or 'luxurious' in the way that the German cruising yachts of the early twentieth century had been. Indeed, in terms of layout and propulsion, she was actually rather similar to typical passenger ships and car ferries that had entered service on Baltic and Scandinavian overnight routes in the previous decade. Her passenger accommodation consisted of forward-facing lounges on Main Deck and Boat Deck with the restaurant aft on Main Deck and the galley to starboard amidships. Aft on Boat Deck was a small and cosy saloon bar. Cabins occupied the two main hull decks, there being almost equal numbers of insides and outsides, accessed from two axial corridors along each deck. Though all cabins were *en suite*, they were compactly dimensioned while the interior design was similar to that of West German ferries of the same generation, being unfussy and with a preponderance of dark woodwork.[79] This was unsurprising as the construction of the *Regina Maris* followed directly after that of TT-Linie's Travemünde-Trelleborg ferry the *Peter Pan*.

At first, the *Regina Maris* was apparently successful, but subsequently the West German cruise market grew increasingly crowded with superior vessels, which offered better economies of scale and so she was chartered out for operation in Canadian waters instead, returning briefly to West Germany in the early-1980s. Subsequently, she became a private yacht, owned by the Greek shipping, banking and petro-chemicals tycoon, John Latsis.

Shortly after the advent of the *Regina Maris*, another, somewhat larger, purpose-built was completed in Italy. The 12,219gt, 452-passenger *Italia* had been ordered from the Cantieri Navale Felszegi at Muggia, near Trieste, by a group of Italian business entrepreneurs who correctly believed that fly-cruising represented the best hope for the cruise industry's future development. Indeed, the vessel was specifically dimensioned to carry the same load as that of an up-to-date wide-bodied jet aircraft of the era. The *Italia* was designed by Nicolò Costanzi, who had recently drawn up the highly-acclaimed *Oceanic*, the overall layout of which was been a great influence, particularly with regard to the nesting of the lifeboats, enabling a consequently unencumbered lido deck above. Interior design, meanwhile, was by Gustavo Pulitzer Finali, the project being the swansong for both of these talented and experienced men, each of whom died shortly after.

With the inputs of such figures, the *Italia* should have been a great success from the outset. Unfortunately, both the owner and the yard went bankrupt during construction and so the unfinished hull was taken over by the major creditor – the Banca Nazionale del Lavoro, which completed her through a subsidiary company in 1967, then chartered her out to other cruise operators.[80] The *Italia*'s wedge-shaped funnel and very large public room windows made her very distinctive, if somewhat quirky, though her economic diesel propulsion helped her succeed and to find useful niches in developing new cruise markets on the U.S. West Coast, Latin America and, subsequently, in the Far East and elsewhere.

By contrast, the 2,841gt *Lindblad Explorer*, completed two years after the *Italia*, was arguably the world's first

Below: The Italian-built and -owned cruise ship *Italia* was, in terms of layout, a much smaller iteration of the *Oceanic*, but was intended to carry a jet-load of passengers on fly-cruises. Rather than airline competition being considered as the enemy, as had been the case in the past, for cruise ship operators, it was now a useful ally.

purpose-built expedition cruise ship and was designed by the Copenhagen-based consulting naval architects Knud E. Hansen A/S.[81] The idea for building such a vessel originated with a Swedish explorer and entrepreneur, Lars-Eric Lindblad, who had emigrated to Conneticut in 1951. There, he developed a successful adventure travel business, Lindblad Travel. The *Lindblad Explorer* was built by Nystads Varv AB in Finland, where all shipbuilders had a good working knowledge of ice-strengthened hull design and construction. Although only built to ice class 1C (a rather low ice class level), the vessel was nonetheless capable of sailing among Antarctic ice floes, carrying only 118 adventurous passengers. The segregation of her hull into watertight compartments extended above bulkhead deck level and into her superstructure, all compartments having direct vertical access to Main Deck. Fuel tanks were arranged along the centre line within cofferdams well inboard of her sides and machinery spaces were contained between additional longitudinal watertight bulkheads. Externally, the vessel's tomato red hull echoed the high-visibility approach typically used on Antarctic research vessels.

Although she had a number of hair-raising scrapes, among the most serious being a grounding at La Plaza Point in the Antarctic in 1972, which necessitated a full evacuation, she was deemed a success and she opened up a new frontier in the cruise business. From 1992, she operated as the Liberian-registered *Explorer* until November 2007 when she struck submerged ice in the South Atlantic. Fortunately, her passengers and crew were evacuated before she heeled over and sank.

Above & Below: The West German cruise ship *Regina Maris* (top and bottom) and the pioneer purpose-built adventure cruise ship *Linblad Explorer* (below) represent early attempts by cruise operators to target niche markets.

Chapter 5
The Caribbean mass market

At present, over seven million cruise passengers take Caribbean cruises each year, a majority on vessels with capacities for between 3,000 and 6,000 guests. The growth of the mass market Caribbean cruise industry since the mid-1960s is among the more remarkable leisure phenomena of the past half century.

If 'Luxury Liner Row' in Manhattan is where one went to see the newest, most exclusive and expensive cruise ships and hybrid liner-cum-cruise vessels, it was in the port of Miami that inexpensive, informal 'mass market' cruising was first established in a North American context. During the 1950s, a number of very large hotel resorts were established along South Miami Beach, using essentially Taylorist principles to accommodate, feed and entertain thousands of holidaymakers in modern, air-conditioned comfort. Standardisation and 'economy of scale' were the keys to the business models of the Sans Souci, Eden Roc, Fontainebleu and other flamboyant new hotels, most of which were designed by the Miami-based architect, Morris Lapidus. Not only were these developments impressive in scale, but they were also flamboyantly decorated with highly imaginative – some would have said 'vulgar' – mixes of baroque, rococo and modernist 'space age' imagery and design features. In particular, Lapidus was a master at designing grand multi-level hallways with 'feature' staircases, Lucite chandeliers and ornamental fountains. Another of his talents was in designing outdoor pools and sun terraces with bars, cafés and bandstands, all arranged in informal patterns and accessorised with tropical vegetation and colourful parasols. Indeed, Lapidus' hotel resorts were eventually to influence greatly the interior and exterior design of forthcoming generations of purpose-built, mass-market cruise ships.

Back in the 1950s, however, Miami's passenger shipping scene was regarded as a trivial backwater in comparison to that of New York, or even Fort Lauderdale, immediately to the north, where a majority of vessels berthed *en route* to the Caribbean.

Miami's history as a cruise port dated back to the spring of 1913, when a 3,786gt coastal passenger ship named the *Evangeline* commenced a series of 11-night Caribbean cruises. Her owner was the Jacksonville-based Peninsular & Occidental Steamship Company, known as P&O but entirely unconnected with the famous British liner operator also using these initials. Instead, the company was a joint venture of the Plant Line and a Florida railroad owner called Henry Flagler who had built the railway linking Miami and Key West. The *Evangeline* had been completed in 1912 by the London & Glasgow Shipbuilding Company of Govan a Canadian owner, based in Nova Scotia. Her cruises from Miami were suspended after the 1914 season due to the First World War. From January 1927 onward, Miami once again had a regular cruise ship in the form of the Canadian-owned *New Northland*, owned by the Clarke Steamship Company of Quebec, which during the winter months ran weekly Caribbean circuits, returning to Canada each spring for coastal service there. In an era before the widespread shipboard application of air conditioning, in Caribbean waters, the atmosphere on board would have been uncomfortably hot and humid during the remainder of the year. The effects of the Great Depression caused a suspension of cruises from 1931 until 1935, when the *New Northland* returned, additionally operating short and therefore inexpensive cruises from Miami to Nassau in the Bahamas. In 1936, Eastern Steamship Lines had placed its nine-year-old, 5,002gt *Evangeline* in winter cruise service from Miami and, soon after, the Clarke Steamship Company had added a second, much bigger and more modern vessel, the three-funnelled 6,893gt *North Star*, which dated from 1930. The outbreak of the Second World War, however, caused the suspension of cruise operations from Miami. (The first foreign-flagged cruise ship to visit Miami, incidentally, was Blue Star Line's the *Arandora Star* in February 1932 and again in January 1935.)

In 1948, a Miami-based business entrepreneur by name of Frank Leslie Fraser established the Eastern Shipping Corporation to operate regular cruises from Miami, initially chartering the former *New Northland*, which had recently been purchased by the Dominican Republic's main shipping line Flota Mercante Dominicana and renamed as the *Nuevo Dominicano*. Its initial plan had been to operate her in liner service from New York to New York, Puerto Plata and Ciudad Trujillo (now Santo Domingo) – but this initiative soon proved a failure. Fraser's main business was the importation of bananas from Jamaica on cargo coasters but he was also involved in other related activities, including serving as Flota Mercante Dominicana's General Administrator. Under Eastern Shipping Corporation's management, the *Nuevo Dominicano*'s typical nine-night Caribbean itineraries were interspersed with short two night Miami-Nassau-Miami 'party cruises', which proved highly successful – though with space for only 177 passengers, there was little profit margin and so, after three years, the charter ceased and, shortly thereafter, the vessel sank.

In 1954, Eastern Shipping Corporation purchased from Eastern Steamship Lines its coastal liner the *Yarmouth*, which was the *Evangeline*'s sister ship, for cruises from Miami to Jamaica, Nassau and Havana. Soon, she was renamed as the *Queen of Nassau* and, having 500 berths, she proved a good profit-earner. Doubtless very satisfied with her performance, some months later, Fraser bought the *Evangeline* as well. For these cruises, the typical clientele consisted of holidaymakers who had booked a week or longer in one of the new Miami resort hotels but who soon found their days lounging by the pool in tropical heat tediously monotonous. Taking a short cruise to the Bahamas enabled them to enjoy refreshing sea air and a change of scene. Yet, on board, these 1920s-vintage steamers were decidedly old-fashioned, their strictly symmetrical saloons with Corinthian pilasters and coffered ceilings reflecting the very formal approaches to shipboard decoration in the twentieth century's first decades. This was in complete contrast to the designs of Miami's latest hotel-resorts, in which large numbers of their passengers would have been staying prior to embarkation. At least the retro-fitting of air conditioning kept their interiors satisfactorily cool and comfortable while broad external promenades provided

The Miami-based Eastern Steamship Lines cruise ships *Evangeline* and *Bahama Star* are seen top left and top right. Subsequently, the former passed to Yarmouth Cruise Lines, becoming the *Yarmouth Castle*, pictured in Nassau (centre left). Her dining room (centre right) clearly shows her origin as an American coastal liner of the 1920s. After a disastrous fire in 1965, ageing vessels of this type were replaced by up-to-date chartered European ferry tonnage, the Israeli-owned *Bilu* (above left) and *Nili* (right and below) thereafter being used by various Miami cruise entrepreneurs. The latter was marketed as the 'Jamaica Queen.'

shade from the sun and tropical downpours.

In 1959, Fraser acquired the *Bahama Star*, which had been built in 1931 as the American coastal liner *Borinquen*, and, in the following year, he also took over the four-year-old West German-owned cruise ship the *Ariadne* (which had originally been a Swedish-owned North Sea passenger steamer). Eastern Shipping Corporation's vessels flew the Panamanian flag and their crews came mainly from the Dominican Republic and elsewhere in the Caribbean area. In other words, their combination of 'flag of convenience' registry and low-wage 'third world' staffing set an early precedent for the mass-market cruise industry's subsequent development. By contrast, passenger ships operating in United States coastal service had to be American-built, registered and crewed and, since the mid-1930s, all new examples were required to comply with very tough fire safety regulations.

By the early 1960s, Frank Leslie Fraser's health was failing and so, in 1961, he sold the Eastern Shipping Corporation to a new owner, William R. Lovett of Jacksonville, Florida, a 71-year-old businessman who, like Fraser, had been a banana importer before going on to found the Winn-Dixie supermarket chain. Fraser died only a few months after the sale, aged only 57. Lovett sold the ageing *Yarmouth* in 1963 to another Miami company, Yarmouth Cruise Lines, and soon after, also disposed of the *Evangeline*, which became the *Yarmouth Castle*, both vessels operating on short cruises to Nassau and Freeport in the Bahamas, marketed as 'The Fun Ships.'

In 1964, one observant and experienced cruise passenger, Denny Bond Beattie wrote a trenchant critique of the *Yarmouth Castle* to his travel agent:

> 'For an overnight sail the majority of the cabins would be adequate. For the most part they are tiny, furnished with fixed lower and upper berths (circa 1927) one washbasin, one wall phone and four coat-hooks… At the foot of one stairway in the passenger accommodation was a large pile of trash. The aroma indicated that it had been there for some time. Other working areas and offices showed this same care in housekeeping. The crew are a mixed bag… [who] appeared to have been scrounged from the waterfront and service and discipline were of dubious quality. Those I did see did not appear to be familiar with the ship… Within an hour after embarkation had begun, passengers were lined up at the Purser's Office. Some had been given keys to the wrong cabins; some found that the locks would not work; and not a few had found other passengers already settled in 'their cabins.' Many were just plain disappointed with the quality of their accommodations. 'Come back at six o'clock and maybe I could do something for you' seemed to be the solution to each problem.'[82]

In November 1965, the *Yarmouth Castle* suffered a very serious fire, caused by an electrical malfunction, as a result of which 87 lives were lost. Her Captain was among the first to leave by lifeboat, though he later claimed that he had been going ashore to solicit help. At a subsequent inquiry, it was found that neither the fire alarms nor the sprinklers were in working condition, the fire doors did not shut and there was insufficient water pressure to use the fire hoses; even some of the wooden lifeboats burned before they could be launched. American marine safety officials, who had little jurisdiction to ensure the same fire safety standards on 'flag of convenience' vessels as on American-flagged ones, now began toughening their inspection regimes to marginalise such ageing and run-down tonnage, the original construction of which had involved the extensive use of easily combustible woodwork.

In 1966 two further serious fires occurred on cruise ships trading from American ports – one at sea aboard the Norwegian-owned *Viking Princess* (originally French South American liner the *Laviosier* of 1950) and the other at Fort Lauderdale on the German *Hanseatic*, which dated from 1930 and was previously the British trans-Atlantic liner the *Empress of Scotland*). In the same year, new international SOLAS (Safety Of Life At Sea) regulations were introduced with the specific aim of bringing non-American passenger ships' resilience in the event of fire into line with the standards expected for U.S.-flagged tonnage.

To modernise the Miami cruise fleet, operators looked to Europe, where large and very well-appointed overnight car ferries were being introduced in significant numbers. As with the Caribbean cruise industry, European ferry services were to a large extent seasonal. The ferries there carried summer holidaymakers but often would run nearly empty during the winter months. Ferry hull forms soon proved themselves ideal bases for cruise ships as, being relatively regularly-shaped, shallow-drafted and flat-bottomed, they enabled relatively high capacity, manoeuvrability and economy. An Israeli company called Somerfin Lines was planning to introduce a summer service from Naples to Piraeus, Limassol and Haifa. Its 6,445gt the *Bilu* was delivered in 1964 from Cockerill's shipyard in Hoboken, Belgium. Designed to offer economical transportation and marketed as a 'boatel', the *Bilu* could carry 524 passengers, berthed in 172 cabins, many of which shared bathroom facilities, 120 cars and up to three buses, all loaded and discharged via her stern. To spare construction costs, none of the cabins had portholes, making them uniformly claustrophobic.

In December 1964, the *Bilu* transferred to Miami where she began a season of three- and four-day cruises to Freeport and Nassau in the Bahamas and to Montego Bay in Jamaica, marketed by Somerfin Lines' American subsidiary, Swiss Cruise Lines Ltd, which had offices in New York and Miami. After her inaugural Caribbean cruise season, she returned to the Mediterranean in March 1965. Somerfin's second ferry, the 7,851-ton *Nili*, while similar in overall layout to the *Bilu*, was a somewhat more substantial vessel. Constructed by the Fairfield Shipbuilding & Engineering Company of Govan,

Above: Inboard, the *Nili* featured rubber-tiled floors and a lot of Formica panelling – hardly luxurious, but certainly fire-retardant. The vessel enjoyed brief success in making winter trips from Miami to the Bahamas, but her arrest when her Israeli owner went bankrupt led to more suitable tonnage being found instead.

56 | Cruise Ships: A Design History

The Norwegian ferry *Sunward* was intended for an 'upmarket' service from Southampton across the Bay of Biscay to northern Spain, her interior design by the Danish Mogens Hammer reflecting typical approaches on large ferries in Scandinavia. The vessel's maiden call in Southampton coincided with a prolonged seafarers' strike, during which much of the British merchant fleet was in enforced lay-up. Behind her in the bottom image are the cruise ship *Reina Del Mar* and the trans-Atlantic liner *Queen Mary*. The *Sunward*'s sleek external design and comfortable, modern appointments subsequently fitted in very well in the Caribbean cruise market.

Glasgow and delivered to her owner in 1965, she could carry 544 passengers, all berthed, and 120 cars. Although fully air-conditioned and of modern construction, the *Bilu* nor the *Nili* were high-density ships with ferry-like 'wipe-clean' interiors and, to save building costs, none of the cabins had portholes as 'insides' were considered perfectly acceptable for overnight ferry services.[83]

During the 1965-66 winter season, the *Nili* was chartered to Pan American Cruise Lines, a new operator founded by Frank Leslie Fraser's son, Leslie, but it cancelled the contract for the following winter, perhaps having discovered that the vessel's Israeli owner was in a parlous financial state and teetering on the verge of bankruptcy. Instead, during the 1966-67 season, the *Nili* was to be chartered to yet another upstart Miami cruise entrepreneur, Ted Arison. He was to become arguably the most famous name in the history of mass market cruising. Born in Tel Aviv in Palestine in 1924 and educated at the American University in Beirut, he had served as a soldier in the British Army and, subsequently, as an officer in the Israeli Defence Force during the War of Independence. He then worked for a shipping agency in Israel but, sensing greater potential business opportunities in the USA, he left for New York in 1954, where he founded an airfreight forwarding business and became El Al's U.S. agent. Tired by hard work, he decided to take early retirement and relocated to Miami. Finding himself unable to relax and do nothing, there he founded the Arison Shipping Company, which initially ran cargo vessels.

For Arison, an advantage of the *Nili* was that, while cruise passengers occupied the superstructure, the vehicle deck could still be used to carry freight between Miami, Nassau in the Bahamas and Montego Bay in Jamaica. Marketed as the 'Jamaica Queen', the *Nili* was beginning to attract cruise passengers in appreciable numbers when, suddenly, her owner, Somerfin, went bankrupt and she was arrested by creditors. None of this was Arison's fault and he was consequently left with plenty of willing passengers, but no ships on which to carry them.

In Europe, meanwhile, a Norwegian shipping entrepreneur, Knut Kloster – who was a youthful and dynamic director of the Lauritz Kloster Rederi of Oslo, founded in 1906 – had recently inaugurated Sunward Car Ferries to bring British holidaymakers from Southampton to Vigo, Lisbon and Gibraltar (from which the Costa del Sol could be accessed).[84] The company's brand new vessel was the 8,666gt *Sunward*, built by the Bergens Mekaniske Verksteder to a design by a prolific Copenhagen-based naval architecture firm by name of Knud E. Hansen A/S. Since establishment in 1937, it had specialised in ferry design and, in recent years, had produced plans for a large number of such vessels, mainly for Scandinavian routes. The majority of these vessels were devised by one of the firm's employees, Tage Wandborg, who, having become a leading expert in ferry design, subsequently also became a very significant designer of the forthcoming generation of purpose-built mass market cruise ships.[85]

Unfortunately for Kloster, growing diplomatic tension with Spain over Gibraltar's status, coupled with a major strike by British seafarers which paralysed the port of Southampton, and British Government restrictions on currency for foreign travel led to there being insufficient passengers to enable Sunward Car Ferries to be viable. This situation led Kloster to cut his losses by withdrawing the *Sunward* and laying her up in Oslo, pending a charterer or buyer. When Ted Arison discovered that the vessel was available he contacted Kloster and persuaded him to place her in service out of Miami, using his company as sales and marketing agents in exchange for 22% of revenue. She was marketed under the 'Norwegian Caribbean Line' brand (often abbreviated as NCL). Carrying both passengers and freight loaded by forklift from Miami to Nassau in the Bahamas, Montego Bay in Jamaica and Port au Prince in Haiti, the *Sunward* was an immediate success and the company went from strength to strength.

NCL's emphasis on Norwegian-ness was an important selling point. In American ports, Norwegian-owned merchant ships of all types were widely regarded as being scrupulously clean, and well-run with high safety standards. Just as Norwegian trans-Atlantic liner companies had drawn on romantic 'Viking heritage' and links with North America dating back to Leif Erikson's explorations at the end of the 10th century, so NCL emphasised on similar themes. Yet, unlike the Norwegian trans-Atlantic liners, which heavily emphasised national colours and used Norwegian modern romantic art and furnishings, the *Sunward*'s design identity was more international and corporate, albeit with a strong Scandinavian flavour. Her name primarily suggested warmth and escapism, rather than anything Norwegian, and her livery of white with blue stripes and gold 'compass' motifs was similarly culturally non-specific.[86]

The *Sunward*'s passenger accommodation was relatively commodious and of a high quality for what was essentially an overnight ferry. Her public rooms were at Boat Deck level and amidships on Bridge Deck, above which there was a 'skybar.' This and the main lounge, two decks beneath, gave fine views over the bow. The dining room was located aft and, in between, there was an arcade on the starboard side, off which a small grillroom was accessed, while the galley space was adjacent on the port side. Cabins filled an entire deck above her car deck, and also most of Main Deck, where there was also a reception lobby. The interior design was the work of the Danish architect, Mogens Hammer, and was typically Scandinavian with dark wood veneer wall panelling, modernist Danish furniture and lighting; the cosy atmosphere engendered being more appropriate for European service than in the tropics.[87]

The *Sunward*'s inauguration fortuitously coincided with the ready availability of flights to Miami by jetliner. Hitherto, most long-established operators of passenger ships in liner service had considered airlines to be a dangerous enemy, but NCL and the other fledgling Miami-based cruise operators instead saw an opportunity to bring in passengers quickly and efficiently from all over North America and beyond. From being something of a backwater, Miami suddenly became easily accessible and an obvious choice as a departure point for Caribbean cruises. Therefore, Knut Kloster

Below: The *Starward*, a combined trailer-ferry and cruise ship, was purpose-built for Norwegian Caribbean Line's operations from Miami to the Bahamas and Jamaica. The vessel's design represented a development from that of the *Sunward*, there being two outdoor pools, the one ahead of the funnel being partially sheltered by a solarium, which was known as the 'Tropicana Garden.'

Above: A deck scene on the *Starward* (top), looking into the triple-level 'Tropicana Garden' space; this enabled sheltered relaxation and spectatorship around an outdoor pool. The image below shows a dock-side scene of the vessel at Miami, showing her vehicle deck access door open with a lorry trailer being pulled ashore by a tractor.

and Ted Arison decided that more ships would be needed to cope with market expansion. Meanwhile, the Port of Miami began the construction of a large new cruise terminal on Dodge Island, where there was plenty of parking space and also considerable room for future expansion.

Knut Kloster asked Tage Wandborg to plan two more substantial 12,940gt combined ferry and cruise vessels specially tailored for the Caribbean trade from Miami and geared to the tastes of American passengers. Built by AG Weser Seebeckwerft in Bremerhaven, each represented a further development of the *Sunward*'s design. The construction process was somewhat unusual as the ships were built in two halves which were joined together in dry-dock. First to be finished was the *Starward*, assembled in only twelve months and delivered in November 1968.[88]

The *Starward* could carry 540 passengers, all berthed in *en suite* cabins, and 220 cars, loaded through the stern which had a special lifting visor covering the ramp to continue the lines of the hull so that while at sea, she looked more a passenger liner than the passenger and trailer ferry she actually was. Certainly, the *Starward* had a most distinctive appearance, emphasised by her all-white colour scheme with blue accents and streamlined funnels, located towards her stern. Ahead of the funnels, there was a sheltered lido area with a three-storey glazed sun lounge above the bridge. Known as the Tropicana Garden, it was a remarkable shipboard environment, partially enclosed on three sides by glazing and with two aft-facing balconies accessed by a spiral staircase. Altogether, Tage Wandborg had created for NCL a very compelling and up-to-date tropical cruise design identity.[89]

The *Starward* was constructed and outfitted in accordance with American 'Method 1' fire protection standards. These specified the use of non-combustible materials throughout the passenger and crew accommodation. In Scandinavia, it was more common to use the British approach, 'Method 2', in which non-fire-retardant finishes could be utilised in conjunction with a sprinkler system.[90] Thus, the *Starward* was rather different in atmosphere from the earlier *Sunward*. The new ship used a lot of laminate, aluminium and glass fibre for wall and ceiling finishes as well as for furniture, giving a light and fresh ambience more like that of a modern hotel than any previous Scandinavian-owned passenger vessel. Once again, Mogens Hammer was responsible for the interior design and, by using bright colours and a variety of finishes and textures, he adapted well to the Method 1 approach. Indeed, the *Starward*'s interior ambience proved ideal for Caribbean service and the project's successful outcome led Hammer to become the first specialist designer of cruise ship interiors.[91]

The *Starward*'s Scandinavian ferry origins showed, however, in her rather cramped cabins, in which lower berths could be converted into settees for daytime use, a solution reputedly inspired by the layout of staterooms on South Africa's famous 'Blue Train.' To save time and money, the builder developed an innovative prefabrication technique to assemble the shower and toilet cubicles as complete units, prefacing the widespread use of modular construction for ship interiors during the ensuing decade.[92] The car and freight deck ran down the middle of the hull with two levels of outside cabins on each side and more cabins on Main Deck above. Below the vehicle deck, two very compact 16-cylinder 8,690 bhp MAN V-diesels, chosen for their high power output and relatively low height, provided a 21-knot speed. Apart from powerful air conditioning, able to cope with the most extreme tropical humidity, there were heated swimming pools, Jacuzzis, sophisticated cold stores for food and well-equipped galleys able to supply fresh meals nearly 24 hours a day. All the public rooms were on a single deck with the main lounges forward and amidships and the dining saloon located aft. This was an early instance of the mass market cruise industry's eventual favoured division of shipboard service provision with entertainment facilities forward-located and catering aft.[93]

One sharp-eyed visitor to the *Starward* in May 1969 was the cruise aficionado Denny Bond Beattie, who provided his travel agent with a detailed written report:

> 'The Venus Lounge, forward on Galaxy Deck, is the largest room aboard *Starward*, and is the centre of the ship's social life. Aft of the dance floor is a large, irregularly shaped, three-sided bar. Hot colours predominate, red, orange and copper. The bar stools are covered in 'genuine' fake zebra skin. The Atlantic Deck is the site of *Starward*'s business centre, and I do mean 'business.' There is a long centreline corridor flanked by a large shop, barber's shop, beauty salon, pinball and slot machine casino, and a large studio devoted to nothing but photos taken by the ship's photographer. Officers and operating crew of the *Starward* are Norwegian. The hotel staff, however, appear to be a mixture of Jamaican and Bahamian. There were a number of attractive young Scandinavian ladies stationed strategically about the passenger accommodation to answer questions and provide directions. *Starward* was spotless everywhere I went, above and below decks.'[94]

Beattie's report gives an insight into the *Starward*'s colourful interior design and, more intriguingly, the way in which the ship had been planned with the purpose of generating significant onboard revenues. The presence of a shopping arcade amidships on the Main Deck was a feature repeated on nearly all new mass market cruise ships built thereafter. Indeed, it was arguably the point of origination for the large, multi-deck indoor malls found on many of the latest 'mega' cruise ships of the present era.[95]

For Norwegian Caribbean Line, the *Starward* was a notable success and the subsequent delivery of her near-sister, the *Skyward*, brought Kloster's investment in the Miami cruise business to over $100 million. When she arrived there in December 1969, she received a tumultuous welcome and was feted by the Miami Chamber of Commerce. Whereas the *Starward* had a trailer deck, the *Skyward* was arguably the first pure purpose-built cruise ship for the Caribbean with berths for 750 passengers. Later, in the mid-1970s, the *Starward* was stripped of her vehicle-carrying capacity and the space was used for additional cabins and for a cinema/theatre called 'The Four Vikings.' These were installed gradually while she remained in service using prefabricated components.[96] The advent of the *Skyward* enabled NCL to introduce week-long itineraries, as well as the short half-week cruises offered by the *Sunward* and *Starward*, fitting in with their freight shipments to the Bahamas and Jamaica.

From a design historical viewpoint, one notable – though seldom seen – interior space on the *Skyward* was the captain's day room, which was decorated to resemble how its equivalent on an eighteenth century warship would have appeared. There was ornate panelling, a beamed ceiling, brass fittings and, on one inner partition wall, a series of back-lit leaded glass windows, behind which was a painted seascape diorama. At the touch of a button, the captain could bring this scene to life with moving waves, leaping fish and changing lighting effects. Its purpose was to provide a point of conversation in the event of passengers being invited to visit; presumably few Norwegian master mariners were confident about 'small talk' in English – especially with non-seafarers – and so a distraction which guests might find 'cute' and 'amusing' would hopefully avoid stilted conversations with awkward silences.[97] The design was arguably the starting point of themed interiors for modern cruise ships – an approach to interior design that, as we shall see, is perpetuated in the present.

A further key vessel to have entered service almost concurrently with the *Starward* in 1968 was the 10,448gt *Freeport*, an overnight cruise ferry jointly owned by US Freight of New York and the Bahamas Development Corporation, who jointly marketed their service as Freeport Cruise Line. She operated daily from Miami, bringing tourists and freight from Miami to Freeport on Grand Bahama Island, as well as American holidaymakers to Miami who made 20-hour return 'mini-cruise' trips. Also designed by Tage Wandborg and his colleagues at Knud E. Hansen A/S, the *Freeport* was built by Orenstein & Koppel in Lübeck and was broadly similar to the *Starward* in overall dimensions and layout.[98]

A further ferry-type cruise vessel to appear in Miami late in 1968 was the 10,328gt, 540-passenger *Bohème*, owned by a West German subsidiary of the Swedish shipping company, Olof Wallenius.[99] The vessel was the last of a quartet of near-sisters ordered by various owners from the Wärtsilä shipyard at Turku in Finland. The first of the four, named the *Finnhansa* and the *Finnpartner* were for Finland-West Germany service and the second pair were for North Sea operation between Bremerhaven and Harwich.[100] Once the first of these, named the *Prins Hamlet* and belonging to the Swedish company Lion Ferry, was delivered in 1966, it turned out that the market on the route was only big enough to support a single vessel.

Fortuitously, at the same time, a Florida hotelier, Sanford Chobol, went into partnership with a former manager of Yarmouth Cruise Line, Edwin Stephan, to establish a new company named Commodore Cruise Line. Chobol had previously attempted to run Caribbean cruises in 1962 using a chartered Brazilian liner, the *Princess Leopoldina*, but for his second attempt to operate cruises from Miami, he realised that a vessel similar to NCL's the *Sunward*, would be preferable. While the *Bohème* (which originally was to have been named the *Prins Albert*) was in the early stages of construction, Wallenius was approached by Chobol and Stephan, who negotiated an agreement to provide marketing and ticket sales; this was similar to the initial relationship between Arison Shipping Company and Klosters Rederi. The *Bohème*'s layout was modified with most of her vehicle deck space replaced by cabin accommodation.[101] Commodore Cruise Line promoted her with considerable success as 'The Happy Ship.'

While participating in the establishment of Commodore, the ambitious Stephen was hatching plans for a further, much more ambitious Caribbean cruise operation. To find partner ship owners, in 1967, he contacted the ship brokerage arm of the Norwegian shipping company Fearnley & Eger, who suggested that it would be worth inviting the cargo liner operator I.M. Skaugen to form a joint venture. When it turned out that a minimum of two new cruise ships would be needed to ensure profitability, a further Norwegian ship owner, Anders Wilhelmsen, who operated oil tankers and fishing trawlers, agreed to become involved. Later, it was decided that a third vessel would be required and so Skaugen suggested that Gotaas-Larsen, which was likewise primarily a tanker operator, should become an additional member of the consortium. Their cruise line would be known as Royal Caribbean.[102]

Development of a design for the three planned vessels was coordinated by Martin Hallen, the chief naval architect of I.M. Skaugen, who worked in close co-operation with Knud E. Hansen A/S in Copenhagen. Meanwhile, potential builders were also contacted with the Finnish company Wärtsilä particularly enthusiastic about building more cruise ships following the success of the *Bohéme*.[103] Wärtsilä was therefore asked to attend a meeting in Copenhagen with representatives of Knud E. Hansen A/S and of the Norwegian ship owners. Alas, Wärtsilä's team failed to see eye-to-eye with those from Knud E. Hansen A/S, each side refusing to acknowledge any superior attributes in the other's initial design proposals. Indeed, an unseemly brawl was only narrowly averted by Anders Wilhelmsen's shipbroker, who quickly suggested that the combatants should all go for dinner and drinks in the Tivoli amusement park.[104]

Wärtsilä tendered successfully to build all three members of the new Royal Caribbean fleet at their Helsinki shipyard. The final design emerged as a hybrid of elements proposed by Wärtsilä's drawing office with others put forward by Knud E. Hansen A/S and other still by Martin Hallen, plus various architecture and interior design consultants. Measuring 18,346gt and accommodating 714 passengers each, they were to be named the *Song of Norway*, *Nordic Prince* and *Sun Viking*, choices clearly reflecting their owners' national identity. Despite being nearly twice the size of NCL's the *Starward* and *Skyward*, their passenger numbers were about the same, indicating bigger average cabin sizes and a lower accommodation

Above: The *Skyward* was Norwegian Caribbean Line's third vessel from Miami, but the company's first 'pure' cruise ship; although of almost identical external appearance to the *Starward*, where the latter had a trailer deck, there were instead additional cabins.

Below: The Swedish Wallenius-owned, but Commodore Cruise Line-operated, *Bohème* was likewise essentially a ferry with additional cabins where there would otherwise have been a vehicle deck. Here, she is seen at Miami in the late-1960s.

density overall. Indeed, so far as passenger demographic and pricing were concerned, Royal Caribbean sought to position itself slightly upmarket of NCL – though still as an essentially 'mass market' cruise line with an emphasis on onboard revenue generation.

In terms of propulsion, the vessels represented a major step forward by having four compact Wärtsilä-Sulzer diesel engines of a recently-developed design, coupled in pairs to each propeller shaft, rather than only two large examples. Apart from the engine room occupying less space, a four-engine solution gave a greater ability to vary speed depending on the length of voyage from one port to the next and to provide better redundancy, enabling one or more to be shut down for maintenance whilst at sea. Together, they enabled a 20.5-knot service speed to be easily maintained.[105] In future, similar four-engine solutions would become more-or-less a standard specification throughout the cruise industry.

In an age before port security was anything like as rigorous as today, passenger ships were much more easily seen by their passengers and passers-by, who could in most locations walk along the quays. Thus, Royal Caribbean felt a strong need for an up-to-date, yet distinctive exterior design identity to make its vessels immediately recognisable and easy to differentiate from those of NCL and other operators. Apart from their silhouettes, these vessels deployed a strong but simple corporate identity, the centrepiece of which was a logo comprising of a stylised anchor with a crown immediately above. Just as the 1930s Kraft durch Freude cruise ships used a propeller and swastika symbol, Royal Caribbean's logo communicated two clear elements – a nautical tradition and being treated like royalty – and could be applied equally to ships' funnel casings and to brochures, business cards, souvenirs and many other brand-associated items. Within shipping, this approach was a departure from the usual combination of funnel livery and house flag as means of communicating identity.[106]

The initiator of their strikingly distinctive and innovative exterior styling was a youthful Finnish industrial designer, Heikki Sorvali, who was employed by Wärtsilä Turku shipyard to produce conceptual designs for futuristic passenger ship exteriors. Sorvali's initial sketches and models contained many of the essential elements of the rather futuristic-looking overall silhouette eventually realised.[107] As the vessels were not expected regularly to meet high waves, it was decided that a very pronounced 'clipper'-shaped bow profile would be attractive to passengers, perhaps reminding them of the romance of the days of sail. Near the summit of the funnel casing, a protruding cocktail lounge was proposed (this idea was reputedly suggested by Edwin Stephan, however).[108] Sorvali's design proposal was worked on further by the Norwegian modernist architect Geir Grung who had previously styled the superstructure of Wilhelmsen's Japanese-built oil tanker the *Wilstar*, which had entered service in 1967. For the cruise ships, Grung added glazed shelter screens around the lido decks and restyled the cocktail bar on the funnel, making it resemble a circular concrete observation room he had previously designed for visitors to a hyro-electric power station in Røldal in Norway. Thereafter, it became known as the 'Viking Crown Lounge.'[109]

In terms of internal planning, the vessels had a similar circulation pattern to the *Skyward*, with two aisles along the length of the public room decks reflected in the cabin deck corridors and transverse lobbies containing the stairwells and lift shafts in between. On the cabin decks, the inside cabins were built in blocks across the hull between these main end-to-end corridors. Again like the *Skyward*, their interiors were designed in compliance with American 'Method 1' fire prevention standards.[110]

Wärtsilä developed an innovative assembly system for internal non-load-bearing walls, using special composite sound-insulated and fire-proof panels with laminate surfaces, which slotted between enamelled steel vertical framing strips. That way, cabins and corridors could be built much more quickly and cheaply than if traditional joinery methods had been used. Another important development was the large-scale usage of vacuum-flush toilets. As these used a tenth of the quantity of water than gravity systems and consequently generated considerably smaller amounts of sewage, it became much easier to have private facilities in every cabin. Indeed, bathrooms were pre-fabricated as complete units, built in a temporary fabrication hall adjacent to the shipyard.[111]

Lounges and restaurants were hotel-like and unashamedly designed to appeal to Middle America. Interior finishes made much use of laminates, plastics, glass fibre mouldings and enamelled aluminium. The majority of the interior design was by Mogens Hammer while some public rooms were by the Finnish interior designer Vuokko Laakso.[112] Typically of the early-1970s, the colour palettes were bright and the spaces were accented by wide ranges of specially-commissioned artworks to add visual richness. Public rooms were named and themed after well-known Broadway musicals (the 'Can Can Show Lounge', the 'King and I Restaurant' and so on) and the cabin corridors named after the main streets of Oslo.

Topsides, there were large expanses of sun-deck with spacious lido areas extending over the sides aft of the funnel and between it and the mast. Some of these areas were planked in varnished pine, following

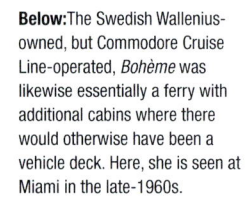

Norwegian tradition, while others had cost- and weight-saving Astroturf, which was considered pleasant to walk upon with bare feet, but which unfortunately also served as an effective propagator of pungent-smelling mould in the warm and humid Caribbean climate.[113]

The *Song of Norway* was delivered in October 1970, the *Nordic Prince* following in July 1971. The third example of the class, named the *Sun Viking* was completed in November 1972 to a modified design with 882 berths. Externally, she was distinguished from her otherwise identical sisters by her bow plating which was carried up an extra deck, thus giving a more imposing forward profile. American passengers responded well to the informal atmosphere on the three vessels, enjoying their discos and casinos, steel bands playing Calypso music on deck and waiters balancing trays of exotic cocktails on their heads. Royal Caribbean chartered wide-bodied jet aircraft – including Boeing 747s – to bring passengers to Miami. In particular, it focused on affluent California as a major market for fly-cruise packages to the Caribbean. Soon, increasing numbers of Europeans were also attracted by the company's fly-cruise offers. Clearly, a highly successful formula had been created.

Knut Kloster and Ted Arison's Norwegian Caribbean Line was also proving highly lucrative – so much so that it was decided to order a further two examples of the *Skyward*-type ferry-derived cruise ship. When Kloster let slip to the naval architect, Tage Wandborg, that this was his plan and that contracts had already been negotiated with a shipyard in Italy, the Cantieri Navali e Riuniti of Riva Trigoso, Wandborg told him that this was a mistake. Rather than repeating the existing design, given the opportunity, he could produce a far better solution, optimising the vessels for cruise passengers, rather than still retaining remnants of earlier vessel's ferry origins. Kloster agreed and, by that time, the only solution was for Wandborg to be sent directly to the shipyard to carry out a hasty re-design there.[114]

What emerged was a slightly longer 16,607gt cruise ship design with the superstructure re-arranged in the manner of the *Oceanic* and the *Italia*, described above, both of which had been the work of Wandborg's naval architecture hero, Nicolò Costanzi. As on these vessels, the lifeboats were to be 'nested' on each side of the lower superstructure, enabling a full-width lido area between the bridge deck and funnels. On either side, a tapering line of glass screens would provide shelter from cross-winds. Another positive effect of this layout was that it was possible to gain extra height for the dining room, which was located between the lifeboats at main deck level, and for the mid-ships lounge, directly above. The latter had a sunken floor in the centre with raised wings above the lifeboat recesses on either side, ensuring that most passengers had a reasonable view of the stage and dance floor.[115]

At Riva Trigoso, ships were usually launched in a nearly completed state but, because the yard was busy, the first of the new NCL cruise ships, named the *Southward*, took to the water somewhat earlier and was completed at a wharf in Genoa. She entered service in December 1971 but work on the *Seaward* was abandoned when industrial unrest at the shipyard increased her price by more than 50 per cent. By the time the Italian Government intervened by nationalising the yard, Knut Kloster had decided to cancel the contract because the original agreement had not been honoured. Instead, the unfinished hull was bought by the British liner company P&O, which was winding down its extensive network of passenger liner services to concentrate instead on cruising. As with NCL and Royal Caribbean, it had ambitions to break into the lucrative North American market. Yet, none of its ageing liner fleet would have met American cruise standards of comfort and modernity and so the plan had been to design from scratch and have built new vessels. Because the Caribbean was judged a crowded market, these would operate from San Francisco and Los Angeles on the U.S. west coast. When the incomplete *Seaward* became available, it seemed too good an opportunity for P&O to miss and so the vessel was completed in 1972 according to modified specifications as the *Spirit of London*. The *Southward*, meanwhile, had successfully entered service for NCL from Miami, giving the company a four-ship fleet. The oldest of these, the six-year-old *Sunward*, was really too small and too much of a ferry to compare favourably with the *Starward*, *Skyward* and *Southward* and so cancelling the *Seaward* contract had been a mistake on Kloster's part. Even if the vessel had cost more than Kloster had initially agreed, as P&O soon found out when operating her as *Spirit of London*, her earnings would soon have offset this extra sum.[116]

While the *Southward* and the abortive *Seaward* projects were under construction in 1972, Knut Kloster was developing plans for a cruise ship of around 20,000gt – twice as big as NCL's existing new buildings – which would have had a conventional bow, aft of which the hull would divided into a catamaran design. One advantage was a gain in stability while another was that the vessel could be unusually wide, enabling enough space for facilities more akin to those of a beach resort hotel or shopping mall. On the other hand, a catamaran hulled vessel would be significantly more expensive to build than a conventional single-hulled design. The project, which was code-named 'Elysian,' never progressed beyond the planning stages because suddenly and quite unexpectedly, NCL was plunged into a managerial crisis with damaging economic consequences for the company.[117]

Knut Kloster discovered that his business partner Ted Arison had been withholding and re-investing a pool of earnings from advance sales of cruises, rather than passing the money promptly to NCL. Arison allegedly kept the interest earned from these undisclosed investments for himself and, consequently, Kloster felt cheated and aggrieved. He therefore refused to have any further business dealings either with Arison personally or with the Arison Shipping Company. As it had been responsible for generating all

Above: The *Freeport* operated daily from Miami on short cruises to Grand Bahama Island, carrying mini-cruise passengers, some private cars and a good deal of freight.

Below: When planning the Royal Caribbean cruise business, its Norwegian owners sought to create an identity distinct from that of the existing NCL operation at Miami. An exaggerated clipper-shaped prow and a funnel casing incorporating an elevated cocktail lounge formed important parts of its vessels' unique, futuristic silhouettes. Here, we see the *Nordic Prince* shortly after her entry into service in the early-1970s.

of NCL's business, the sudden split led to a dramatic fall in ticket sales and revenue. This led to a brief financial crisis at NCL which Kloster resolved by selling the *Sunward*, reducing the fleet to only three vessels.

Meanwhile, the company had to build up a new sales organisation from scratch. Because the cruise industry was quite small, it was impossible to poach experienced sales executives from rivals and so the new NCL sales and marketing staff were mostly recruited from the airlines. This influx of air industry executives encouraged idea of selling fly-cruises with plane tickets included, rather than would-be passengers buying their cruises and planning their travel to Miami separately.[118] As a result, it became easier for the cruise lines to reach out to a wider market in terms of age and geographical spread. A new marketing employee brought in from Eastern Airlines, Bruce Nierenberg, suggested that NCL should introduce a western Caribbean itinerary to include Cancun in Mexico, Grand Cayman and Ocho Rios in Jamaica (located on the opposite side of the island to Montego Bay). None of these destinations were yet served by any of the cruise lines – whose focus was on eastern Caribbean routeing – and, due to their lack of suitable berthing facilities, it was necessary at first to anchor offshore, transferring passengers by tender. NCL's western Caribbean cruise initiative was to prove immensely popular and helped the company's return to profitability. It also kick-started the rapid development of the tourist industry in the destinations now visited.[119]

Ted Arison, meanwhile, had plans to begin a new cruise company to take on and beat Kloster's NCL. With the assistance of business associates Meshulam Zonis, who had been Arison's partner in chartering the *Nili*, Meshulam Riklis – who was a financier and owner of American International Travel Services (AITS) – and a shipbroker, Ellie Schalit (who, like Arison, was a veteran of the Israeli War of Independence), Arison sought out a suitable vessel. At first, Schalit directed Arison to Cunard regarding the possibility of taking over one or both of its recently laid up cruise ships: the *Carmania* and *Franconia*. Its Chairman, Victor Matthews, refused to sell them to Arison, presumably out of concern that these might be used to under-cut members of the company's current fleet in the Caribbean. In London, meanwhile, a small naval architecture firm called Technical Marine Planning had produced a conversion plan to transform the redundant Canadian Pacific trans-Atlantic liner the *Empress of Canada* into a cruise ship for Home Lines to partner its successful the *Oceanic* – but this scheme had failed to come to fruition. One of Technical Marine Planning's three partners, Jacob Viktor, had previously been employed by Somerfin Lines, who had owned the *Nili*. Through Meshulam Zonis, Viktor

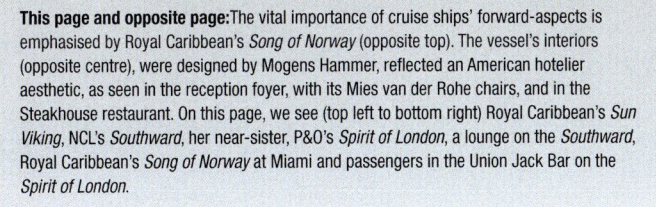

The Caribbean mass market | 63

This page and opposite page: The vital importance of cruise ships' forward-aspects is emphasised by Royal Caribbean's *Song of Norway* (opposite top). The vessel's interiors (opposite centre), were designed by Mogens Hammer, reflected an American hotelier aesthetic, as seen in the reception foyer, with its Mies van der Rohe chairs, and in the Steakhouse restaurant. On this page, we see (top left to bottom right) Royal Caribbean's *Sun Viking*, NCL's *Southward*, her near-sister, P&O's *Spirit of London*, a lounge on the *Southward*, Royal Caribbean's *Song of Norway* at Miami and passengers in the Union Jack Bar on the *Spirit of London*.

Above: The Canadian Pacific trans-Atlantic liner *Empress of Canada*, showing CP Ships' 'Multimark' design identity, which formed the basis of the Carnival Cruise Lines livery when they acquired the ship.

Below: Carnival Cruise Line's *Mardi Gras* (ex-*Empress of Canada*) is seen at Miami in the mid-1980s, the 'Multimark' having been altered into a crescent moon-shape and the colours having changed to an all-American red, white and blue.

suggested that Arison ought to consider the *Empress of Canada* for his new cruise ship. The vessel was only a decade old, measured 27,284gt and accommodated 1,048 passengers, more than any existing Miami-based cruise ship. With Schalit as broker, the vessel was purchased by Riklis for 6.5 million dollars and placed under Arison's management. As there was hardly any money for conversion work, after not much more than a cursory repaint which even retained Canadian Pacific's 'multi-mark' funnel logo, the vessel was sent to Miami, where she entered cruise service in January 1972 as the *Mardi Gras*.[120] She was the first member of Carnival Cruise Lines, which is nowadays the world's biggest cruise ship operator.[121]

The *Mardi Gras*' inaugural cruise for travel agents was beset by difficulties. NCL booked all of the cruise berths at the Port of Miami's Dodge Island terminal to prevent Carnival getting access and so it was necessary to use a freight berth instead with minimal waiting areas to protect Carnival's guests from the heat and humidity.[122] On leaving Miami, the liner ran aground on a mud bank, causing NCL's crews and passengers great hilarity (on the *Starward*, the bar tenders are alleged to have served up a new cocktail called 'Mardi Gras on the Rocks'). Later on, when it was necessary to pay a fuel bill, Ted Arison is alleged to have emptied the slot machines in the casinos to raise enough cash.[123]

Carnival was developed with such haste that just about its entire identity was 'borrowed' from elsewhere. The company livery was essentially that of Canadian Pacific; when the latter complained of violation, Carnival changed the 'multi-mark' into a crescent moon shape (the logo still used today). Even the company's marketing strapline 'The Fun Ships' had previously been used by Yarmouth Cruise Line to promote the *Yarmouth* and the ill-fated *Yarmouth Castle*. Yet, the company's apparently patriotic red, white and blue colours appeared appropriately festive, while appealing to a petit bourgeois sense of American nationhood. Paradoxically in that context, the *Mardi Gras* was registered in Panama and was crewed by Italian officers with crew from Honduras and elsewhere in the Caribbean and Central America (by contrast, both the NCL and Royal Caribbean fleets flew the Norwegian flag with its associated higher costs). Although during the *Mardi Gras*' first cruises, passengers experienced a slightly dowdy formerly-British trans-Atlantic liner, over time, the vessel was superficially refitted whilst remaining in service with a large casino, discotheque and other 'fun ship' elements. Thus, Carnival's now well-known strategy of providing inexpensive, informal entertainment-filled cruises, somewhat akin to Las Vegas afloat, only emerged gradually as the 1970s progressed. In the same period, Royal Caribbean developed a slightly more 'upmarket' reputation with NCL occupying the territory between.

Rivals from the outset, NCL, Royal Caribbean and Carnival all became major players in shaping the future of the mass market cruise industry. Indeed, today, all three have become the main global industry giants.

Had circumstances been slightly different, there might have been a fourth major Caribbean cruise operator. In the late-1960s, a Texan entrepreneur called Steedman Hinckley, who was chairman of Overseas National Airways, with a charter airline he had founded in 1950 in New York, began planning a new fleet of sail-assisted cruise ships to be based at San Juan in Puerto Rico, to which passengers would be flown by his airline for embarkation. Such an integrated fly-cruise

The Caribbean mass market | 65

The exterior of the *Cunard Ambassador* was styled by the *QE2* industrial designer, James Gardiner, with a 'drooping' bow profile and a forward-slanting funnel (top and bottom right). The vessel's economic design and interiors resembling American mid-market hotels came as a shock to Cunard traditionalists, who preferred the company's grand liners of the past. In the bottom left image, we see early morning arrivals at Miami, with NCL's *Southward* and *Skyward* nearest the camera and Carnival's *Mardi Gras* in the background.

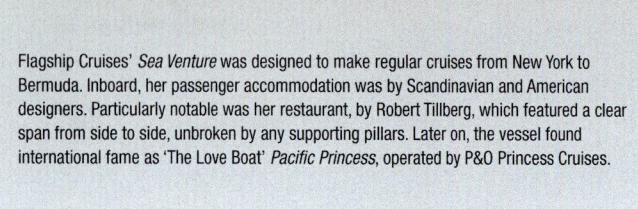

Flagship Cruises' *Sea Venture* was designed to make regular cruises from New York to Bermuda. Inboard, her passenger accommodation was by Scandinavian and American designers. Particularly notable was her restaurant, by Robert Tillberg, which featured a clear span from side to side, unbroken by any supporting pillars. Later on, the vessel found international fame as 'The Love Boat' *Pacific Princess*, operated by P&O Princess Cruises.

offer with both airline and cruise line under the same overall management was certainly ahead of its time, as was the idea of building clipper-like three-mast cruise ships, providing all modern conveniences while romantically evoking the maritime past. A suitable design was drawn up to designs by Knud E. Hansen A/S and orders for two examples placed with shipyards in Rotterdam in the Netherlands – J.P. Smit & Son and the Rotterdam Drydock Company. The steel was delivered and cutting commenced to form the hull sections, but before work could proceed further, the owner had a change of heart. Construction stopped abruptly when it was decided instead to build two bigger, but more conventional vessels without sails, somewhat resembling NCL's the *Skyward* in terms of design concept and dimensions. This brought about the unusual situation of the shipyard invoking penalty clauses in the contract for delays against Overseas National Airways.[124]

As Hinckley had recently crossed the Atlantic on Cunard's newly-delivered the *Queen Elizabeth 2*, the appearance of which had impressed him greatly, he invited its industrial designer, James Gardner, to style his two vessels, giving them similarly 'futuristic' bridge and funnel detailing – and an exaggerated prow that appeared to 'droop' slightly.[125] While construction was underway, however, Overseas National Airways got into financial difficulties and, via the broker Ellie Schalit, a majority interest in both vessels was sold to Cunard. The intention was to form a joint venture, benefitting from Cunard's expertise in passenger ship operation.[126] When shortly after the airline withdrew, Cunard bought the vessels outright, the first entering service in October 1971 as the *Cunard Adventurer* with the second, named the *Cunard Ambassador*, following a year later.

Following Overseas National Airways' intention, Cunard employed the vessels mainly for Caribbean fly-cruises, much as Hinckley had intended. In summer, Cunard additionally stationed the *Cunard Adventurer* on the U.S. West Coast for cruises to Alaska, while the *Cunard Ambassador* operated from New York to Bermuda – which was also a popular cruise destination, albeit without any ports *en route*. Unfortunately, the vessels' essentially light-weight construction, small cabins without much closet space and synthetic interior finishes and furnishings appalled the company's traditionally-minded clientele, so different were they from the old fashioned solidity of the converted liners they superseded. Indeed, the contrast between the heavy construction and lustrous woodwork of the *Caronia* of 1948 and the melamine and fibreglass of these new vessels served to show not only how much the design of cruise ships had progressed in less than a quarter-century but also the extent to which the perceived market for cruises had popularised. Rather than floating clubs for the exceptionally wealthy, in terms of style, these new Cunarders were more akin to the Holiday Inn motels beloved of aspiring Middle America.

A further American-based cruise line project was proposed jointly by the Norwegian ship owners Øivind Lorentzen, Bergenske Dampskibsselskab and Fearnley & Eger, the latter of which had helped to bring about the establishment of Royal Caribbean and was keen to become more deeply involved in the potentially lucrative Caribbean cruise business. As Bergenske's directors preferred plan was to operate cruises from the U.S. Western seaboard, they lost interest early on, leaving Øivind Lorentzen and Fearnley & Eger jointly to form Flagship Cruises in 1968 – though even they disagreed as to where the two new cruise ships they planned to build should be located. Øivind Lorentzen, whose liner shipping activities were based in New York, was much more keen on a service from there to Bermuda for most of the year than he was on year-round the Caribbean cruises Fearnley & Eger would have preferred, and it was his position that came to prevail. After all, Home Lines' the *Oceanic* had appeared to demonstrate that with a modern and appropriately equipped vessel, year-round cruises from New York could indeed be viable. During the worst winter months, it was planned to station just one vessel briefly in the Caribbean with the other cruising from the U.S. West Coast to the Mexican Riviera.[127]

The New York-Bermuda trade had traditionally been the territory of the British liner operator Furness Withy, which had won the USA-Bermuda mail contract from the British Government in 1919. In 1933, the company's Furness Bermuda Line subsidiary introduced the first of a pair of luxuriously-appointed three-funnelled liners, the *Queen of Bermuda*, followed soon after by the *Monarch of Bermuda*. With a 40-hour passage from New York and four days in Hamilton, during which the vessels served as floating hotels, it was possible for a week-long holiday to be enjoyed. Although primarily a liner service, the ambience was cruise-like. Both survived the Second World War, though the *Monarch of Bermuda* was so badly damaged by fire while being re-converted for civilian service that Furness Bermuda Line replaced her with a smaller liner, the *Ocean Monarch*, which appeared in 1951. Only fifteen years later, though, the service was abandoned as the Royal Mail was sent by air instead. During the summer months, warm weather was guaranteed, but in winter the North Atlantic could be very rough indeed, meaning that experiencing seasickness was a high possibility.

Øivind Lorentzen's technical department took responsibility for the design of Flagship Cruises' two vessels, with assistance from Knud E. Hansen A/S. To be named the *Sea Venture* and *Island Venture*, each would measure 19,903gt and their builder was the Rheinstahl Nordseewerke shipyard at Emden in West Germany. In order to fit the quay in Hamilton harbour, their length was constricted to only 168.76 metres (compared with the 238.44 metres of the *Oceanic*, which was more typical of the length of passenger ship using New York). An unfortunate result of the new sisters' relative shortness was that they would be unable to ride more than one Atlantic wave and trough at a time, giving rise to a pronounced pitching motion in anything more than relatively moderate seas.[128]

Another consequence of the vessels' dual North Atlantic and tropical spheres of operation was that they not only required extensive lido areas for sunbathing, but also sheltered semi-enclosed space for use in inclement Atlantic weather conditions. The ingenious solution was to place a retractable glazed roof over the lido so that it could be fully enclosed in poor weather; this was no doubt inspired by the success of a similar feature on the *Oceanic*. Forward of the lido, there was an observation lounge and cocktail bar above the bridge. All the other entertainment spaces were arranged in open plan on a single deck, connected by a side arcade with large picture windows, while the dining room was three decks lower in the hull, perhaps another concession to the possibility of encountering Atlantic storms. To give a clear span without the need for columns to support the weight of the decks above, the longitudinal cabin corridors running above were constructed as box girders, while deep lateral beams crossed the entire width of the ship.[129]

Throughout, the interior design was a successful combination of up-to-date Scandinavian design and West German craftsmanship. The saloon deck had a lofty ceiling height with lounges fore and aft, seating arcades on either side with a slightly tiered show lounge amidships between the forward and aft stair and lift lobbies. An American interior designer, Mildred Masters, designed the forward lounge, which was circular and with seating focused on a white marble dance floor. The aft lounge, meanwhile, was by a Norwegian designer, Finn Nilsson; this was a double-height space with a fully glazed bulkhead looking out on the lido area, the two levels being linked by a spiral staircase. The space was decorated by the Swedish designer, Robert Tillberg, who emphasised the structural framing with lighting troughs which were reflected by curved ceiling recesses between. The most impressive space, though, was the double-height purser's square. Its centrepiece was a wrap-around white marble panel, weighing seven tons, adorned by an abstract metal artwork made by students of the Oslo College of Art. Unfortunately, such weighty fixtures and fittings made the ship top heavy and the situation was only solved by removing some of the teak covering from the topmost external decks and by fitting lead bars into the bottom of the hull. After these changes, the vessels performed well from an operational viewpoint.[130]

The *Sea Venture*, which was wholly owned by Øivind Lorentzen, was completed in 1971 and introduced as planned between New York and Bermuda. Fearnley & Eger, who owned the second, to be named the *Island Venture*, meanwhile had developed such grave misgivings about Flagship Cruises' focus on Bermuda, rather than the Caribbean was misguided that they arranged to charter her instead to P&O, which wished to boost its U.S. West Coast cruise operations. Rather than developing its own purpose-built cruise fleet, in 1972, P&O purchased an up-and-coming American cruise line, Princess Cruises, headquartered in Los Angeles.[131] Founded by Stanley McDonald, it had begun operations only in 1965, initially chartering Yarmouth Cruise Line's remaining vessel, the *Yarmouth* to offer trips on the Western Seaboard of North America to ports in Canada, Alaska and Mexico. Shortly, she was replaced by a Canadian Pacific-owned coastal steamer, the *Princess Patricia*, which was of post-war construction and designed for service in these waters. After the *Princess Patricia*, the fleet comprised two chartered Italian-owned liners – the *Carla C.* of Costa Line, which was marketed as *Princess Carla*, and the *Italia*, which was sub-chartered from Costa. The former had been rebuilt in Italy in the latter 1960s from the 1952-vintage French transatlantic liner the *Flandre* the latter had been purpose-built for cruising in 1967 (as described above). Under P&O's management, Princess Cruises was successfully developed during the 1970s and it too became a prominent and popular cruise brand in America.[132]

P&O re-named the *Island Venture* as *Island Princess* and, subsequently, in 1975, acquired the *Sea Venture* as well, which was renamed the *Pacific Princess*. The sisters gained a formidable reputation and usually sailed filled to capacity with delighted passengers. Almost simultaneously, the *Spirit of London* was re-branded as a Princess ship and renamed the *Sun Princess*.

Caribbean, Mexican Riviera and Alaska cruise operations all had the advantage of being repetitive, meaning that shore-based catering and hotel supply operations, baggage handling and passenger check-in, interfaces with port agencies and the running of shore excursion programmes could soon be made to run like clockwork. Long-term contracts with suppliers, port authorities and agents also spared costs – all in line with Fordist and Taylorist business efficiency theories.

The cruise ships purpose-built for NCL, Royal Caribbean, Cunard and Flagship Cruises were unprecedentedly efficiently planned from technical and operational perspectives. Diesel propulsion used between half and one-third of the fuel burned by typical steam turbine passenger vessels. Relatively shallow-drafted, flat-bottomed hulls with modern hydrodynamic design, built using welding rather than riveting to spare the weight of lapped plates also aided fuel economy while increasing manoeuvrability. Controllable-pitch main propellers, twin rudders and lateral-thrust propellers allowed speed and direction to be precisely regulated and this spared the use of tug boats. Inboard, careful attention to the layout of hidden servicing in terms of goods elevators and crew stairs enabled baggage and supplies to be efficiently loaded and moved to where they were needed while garbage was simultaneously offloaded. As a result, the new cruise ships could turn around in under twelve hours by arriving early and sailing again with new passengers later the same afternoon (whereas, traditionally, passenger liners had needed several days to unload, load and re-store). Powerful air conditioning, vacuum-flush toilets and sophisticated bar and galley equipment enhanced comfort to a level comparable with the most up-to-date hotels ashore and allowed 24-hour food and drink services to be provided.

Up-to-date and technically sophisticated though these vessels undoubtedly were, owing to their compact cabins, mid-range hotel-style interiors, relative lack of quiet, empty space, and popular entertainment they were regarded with disdain by a majority of the more traditionally-minded cruise passengers. They would make known their preference for paying a premium to enjoy the grandeur, commodiousness and greater exclusivity of the *Rotterdam*, *Sagafjord* or *Kungsholm*. Rather than bronzing themselves on sun loungers, packed together on astroturf, they preferred to recline on teak steamer chairs in the cool shade of the promenade deck – or so they wished it to appear. (Evidence suggests that regular cruise passengers in America – such as Denny Bond Beattie, quoted above – enjoyed sampling a wide diversity of ships, if only to criticise the cheaper ones afterwards). The new mass-market vessels may even have been unkindly referred to by some as 'cookie cutter' ships (a reference to their comparatively thin hull plating relative to that of 'true' ocean liners built primarily for trans-Atlantic service), but they represented the future, attracting wider demographics of passengers and, most importantly, generating greater profits for their owners than any passenger ships had ever done before. As subsequent events proved, their welded hulls were actually immensely resilient and most enjoyed lengthier careers with various owners than previous generations of passenger liner – indeed, a few examples remain in service even today. Unsurprisingly, as cruising was popularised, a great deal of social snobbery began to attach itself to the industry, relating to perceptions of their being a hierarchy of types of passenger and what they appeared to be able to afford by way of cruise holidays. Unsurprisingly, the more expensive and therefore elite cruise lines were only too happy to promote such beliefs through the types of language and imagery in their brochures.

Chapter 6
New cruise ships for world-wide itineraries

Traditionally, it was the well-established 'deep sea' liner companies who operated a majority of lengthy cruises to far-flung destinations and who offered annual round-the-world voyages using vessels under-employed in the liner trades during the stormy winter months. By the end of the 1960s, however, the liner companies needed to face up to a revolution in their industry. The advent of wide-bodied jet aircraft, principally Boeing's 747 'Jumbo Jet', was threatening shortly to kill off what remained of passenger liner services while, in the cargo trades, the 'container revolution' promised great efficiency savings but also necessitated very significant capital investment as container ships cost much more to build than general cargo liners. At the same time, wage inflation and so-called 'flag discrimination' (whereby third world governments unfairly delayed or taxed foreign-flag vessels) made traditional liner operations even less profitable (this was one reason why Norwegian cargo shipping companies had formed Royal Caribbean as their radical alternative business strategy).

Germany's major trans-Atlantic liner companies, Hamburg-Amerika Linie and Norddeutscher Lloyd, which had long co-operated, decided in 1968 to pool their cargo services in order to enable the development of a fleet of container ships. Two years later, the companies merged completely to form Hapag-Lloyd with Nordduetscher Lloyd's cruise ship, the *Europa* (originally Swedish American's *Kungsholm* of 1953) henceforth being run by the new company.

Holland-America Line, by contrast, decided to sell off its freight services to Swedish American's parent company, Broström AB, and to concentrate instead on developing its cruise business. The *Rotterdam*'s success as a cruise ship had shown the potential of long, luxury cruises focused on attracting a predominantly American clientele and the company had both extensive lists of repeat passengers and a well-developed agency network. In 1970, Holland America Cruises was established, taking over the *Rotterdam*, plus another, slightly smaller former-trans-Atlantic liner, the 24,294gt *Statendam*, which dated from 1957 and which had been used for cruises since the mid-1960s. A new livery of dark blue hull and orange funnel with a blue and white 'waves' logo was introduced. Next, in 1971, Holland America's cruise expansion began when the Alaskan cruise and tour company Westours was purchased. Next, two redundant American-built and -owned liners, the *Argentina* and *Brasil*, were bought from Moore-McCormack Lines, for whom they had been delivered in 1958 from Ingalls Shipbuilding of Pascagoula for service from New York to South American ports. The pair were renovated in West Germany becoming the cruise ships *Veendam* and *Volendam*.[133] Typically of American-built liners, their construction was immensely strong and their accommodation for 671 passengers each was spacious and very comfortable – yet they were also rather fuel-hungry. Holland America used them mostly for cruises from American ports and they continued to be seen regularly in New York. In addition, a much smaller new 8,566gt, 374-passenger cruise ship, to be named the *Prinsendam*, was ordered from the De Merwede van Vliet shipyard at Hardinxveld in the Netherlands to offer winter itineraries in Indonesian waters and cruises to Alaska in summer to develop the recently-purchased Westours business. In terms of overall design, layout and propulsion, the *Prinsendam* was radically different from any of Holland America's existing fleet, being much smaller in size and propelled by diesels, rather than a fuel-hungry steam turbine plant.[134]

An ambitious new entrant into the world-wide cruise market in the early-1970s was the Royal Viking Line, owned by yet another consortium of Norwegian shipping companies. The idea for a new upmarket cruise line to offer lengthy voyages to far-flung destinations originated with the long established Bergenske Dampskibsselskab, which much earlier on had operated the cruise yachts *Meteor* and *Stella Polaris*, both described above. In more recent time, from the mid-1960s onward, the company had run winter cruises from the UK to Madeira and the Canary Islands on its 1931-vintage North Sea passenger ship the *Venus*, which operated as a ferry between Bergen and Newcastle for the remainder of the year. In addition, the company's 1955-built *Meteor* – which was a near-sister of the small passenger vessels it also operated on the Norwegian west coast 'Hurtigrute' passenger, cargo and mail service – ran cruises, mainly in Norwegian waters. The *Venus* was however retired in 1968 due to being unable to meet new safety regulations. Consequently, Bergenske's directors felt a strong urge to build a new vessel so as to remain in the cruise business. In 1966, the company had been poised to order a new cruise ship from Swan, Hunter & Wigham Richardson in the UK, but this never materialized as BDS began to investigate alternative options for the future.[135] In 1968, BDS considered forming of a new American-based cruise subsidiary, working jointly with two other Norwegian ship owners, Øivind Lorentzen and Fearnley & Eger (who went on to establish Flagship Cruises without Bergenske's involvement, as described above). It appears that what Bergenske's directors really wanted was to order an additional similar vessel to the one proposed by these potential partners on their own account, either as well as or instead of sharing ownership with other partners.

Although Bergenske's directors had examined a number of recently liners for inspiration, for any company wishing to build modern high-quality passenger ships for world-wide cruising, Cunard's the *Queen Elizabeth 2* was an obvious precedent to follow. Indeed, both in their interior layout and in their external appearance, the directors were keen that the up-to-date style of the new Cunarder should be closely emulated.

In 1969, Bergenske signed a contract with Wärtsilä's Helsinki shipyard for a 21,847gt cruise ship with delivery planned for 1972. The intention was that she would be named the *Stella Polaris*. Once an order was placed, Bergenske was

The exterior of Royal Viking Line's *Royal Viking Sea* shows some similarities to the *Queen Elizabeth 2* – particularly in the design of her funnel casing. The Royal Viking fleet's interiors were, like those of Royal Caribbean's recent Finnish-built cruise ships, assembled from pre-fabricated components, thereby saving time and money. While the spaces were akin to those of contemporary hotels, there was a greater sense of spaciousness, reflecting the relatively high prices Royal Viking charged.

approached by two other Norwegian shipping companies, Det Nordenfjeldske Dampskipsselskap and A.F. Klaveness & Co. as they too wished to explore the possibility of ordering similar vessels and perhaps operating them jointly with Bergenske. Both Bergenske and Nordenfjeldske had long co-operated in the Hurtigrute service, but Klaveness was new to the passenger market. In the Autumn of 1970, the three partners founded the Royal Viking Line with a head office for operations was in Oslo and a sales department was in San Francisco, headed by Warren Titus, whose enthusiastic promotional work ensured the company's early success. Each would contribute one ship, built by Wärtsilä in Helsinki using the design recently developed by Bergenske in conjunction with the shipyard's drawing office.[136] A succession of renderings was published showing how the completed vessels were intended to look, the influence of the *Queen Elizabeth 2* becoming increasingly apparent as the project developed. Indeed, the funnel design was very obviously copied from the Cunard flagship. The Royal Viking Line corporate identity sought to emphasise Norwegian 'heritage', the funnel logo featuring a stylised Viking horn while the company livery used the Norwegian national colours. Even the stewardesses wore a simplified version of the national dress.

As with the Royal Caribbean ships concurrently under construction in Helsinki, the machinery space and funnel on new Royal Viking Line vessels were located aft, thereby opening up an expanse of recreational space on the topmost deck. Another similarity was their long, rakish bow profile, flaring up from otherwise straight hull lines. While this may have looked impressive, in worldwide cruise service, it proved impractical, especially as, in rough weather, head-on seas very easily damaged the forepeak.

As Royal Viking Line aimed upmarket, the internal use of space needed to be more generous than on the similarly-dimensioned Royal Caribbean vessels. Yet, even with an extra deck of superstructure, only 536 passengers were carried. With the exception of the cinema theatre, amidships on the lower decks, and an observation lounge atop the bridge, nearly all public rooms were on the main and boat decks and these were both commodious and with lofty deck heights. The restaurant was amidships and could accommodate all of the passengers at a leisurely single sitting. Just as on the *Queen Elizabeth 2*, the galley filled the forward part of the superstructure. The main lounge and ballroom was towards the stern and there was a further lounge and cocktail bar aft on Boat Deck above.

A majority of the interior design work was carried out by the Norwegian architects Finn Nilsson F.S. Platou, working in conjunction with the Finnish Claes Olof Lindquist. As the Royal Viking fleet was designed for long cruises, cabins were large and many had their own sitting areas. The external deck spaces were equally generous and there was a wide wrap-around promenade at boat deck level with more spaces round and in front of the funnel and a tier of sun-decks aft.

The first of the three new cruise ships, the *Royal Viking Star*, was delivered to Det Bergenske Dampskibsselskab in June 1972. The remaining two vessels arrived in 1973, the *Royal Viking Sky* being introduced in July by Nordenfjeldske and the *Royal Viking Sea* entering service in December under A.F.Klaveness ownership. For the next decade, the three liners developed an excellent reputation and a very loyal clientele – but Royal Viking Line's owners found that providing world-wide itineraries was considerably more expensive than the Caribbean cruise companies' repetitive weekly circuits from Miami. At each new port, special arrangements needed to be made long in advance and this meant employing large numbers of office workers to plan itineraries and to correspond with port agents around the world. Thus, Royal Viking Line was ultimately less profitable than its owners had hoped. For the Norwegian-owned mass market Caribbean cruise operators, by contrast, there were great operational and economic advantages in repeating exactly the same cruise itinerary, week after week after week.

Above: Holland America Line's transformation from a trans-Atlantic liner company into an international cruise operator with a focus upon the American market was completed in the early-1970s when a new midnight blue and orange colour scheme was introduced, seen here applied to the company's flagship, the *Rotterdam*.

Below: The *Prinsendam* (below) was a new, small Holland America cruise ship for Alaskan and Indonesian itineraries. The fleet was further augmented by two sisters acquired from American owners, one of which was the *Veendam* (bottom).

Chapter 7

Under Mediterranean flags

In the post-war era, small numbers of surviving 'deep sea' liners, belonging to the major northern European liner companies offered occasional Mediterranean cruises, it was not until the mid-1950s that cruising in the region began to develop. With an end to post-war rationing within sight, in 1954, a British travel agency named Swan's Tours recommended 'grand tours' by sea of archaeological sites, initially chartering a small two-year-old Greek-owned passenger vessel, the *Miaoulis* of Nomikos Lines, for this purpose. The *Miaoulis* had been built for ferry service from Piraeus to islands in the Aegean. After five seasons, a substantially larger Turkish-owned liner, the *Ankara* – which had been built in the USA in 1927 as the *Iroquois* for the Clyde Line's coastal service and which was very similar to the Miami-based *Evangeline* and *Yarmouth* – was chartered instead. When not cruising for Swan's, the vessel operated in liner service between Istanbul and Marseille, via Piraeus and Naples.

During the Second World War, the Greek and Italian merchant fleets had been decimated, the former mostly by the Axis powers and the latter by Allied actions, coupled with German sabotage to prevent vessels from falling into Allied hands. Under the terms of the American-orchestrated Marshall Plan, which sought to revitalise the defeated nations' economies and to rebuild their infrastructure, Greece and Italy gained access to numerous American war-built merchant ships, some of which were ingeniously converted from cargo to passenger use for the carriage of emigrants who wished to begin new lives in South America or Australia. Indeed, some entrepreneurial Greek and Italian ship owners sought to purchase any potentially suitable vessels that were available, then to extensively convert them for the migrant trades. Little-known names such as Angelo Costa of the Armatori Costa S.p.A. and the Compagnia Genovese di Armamento (in which Costa owned a shareholding), both of Genoa, Alexandre Vlasov, the Russian émigré owner of Sitmar, the operations of which were likewise initially based in Genoa, Achille Lauro of Naples, the brothers Aldo and Guido Grimaldi, also of Naples, and John D. Chandris of Piraeus (though originally from the island of Chios) all purchased motley collections of second-hand tonnage. While some of these vessels re-entered service with hardly any changes, others were extensively rebuilt. Examples of the latter approach were Cogedar's 15,465gt *Flavia*, which was converted in 1961 in Genoa from Cunard's 14-year-old passenger cargo liner, the *Media*, and Lauro's 23,629gt the *Achille Lauro* and 24,377gt *Angelina Lauro*, which were reconfigured in the mid-1960s from the Dutch colonial liners the *Willem Ruys* and *Oranje*. In all three instances, new, fully air conditioned passenger accommodation was installed, designed in a manner similar to contemporary Italian trans-Atlantic liners, and the vessels' external appearances were modernised with new funnels featuring smoke-deflector fins at their summits and superstructure additions. When post-war migration declined and airlines took over the Europe-Australia and Europe-South America routes, nearly every one of these companies turned to cruising instead (the only exception being Cogedar, who sold the *Flavia* to Costa for cruises from Fort Lauderdale in Florida).[137]

Alexandre Vlasov's Sitmar company had first been established in 1937 as an operator of cargo vessels in the tramp trades. A decade later, its tramping operations were augmented by a successful migrant-carrying liner service from Genoa to Sydney, the tickets for which were subsidised by the Australian government under its 'Assisted Passage' scheme.[138] In 1968, Sitmar purchased two Cunard UK-Canada liners, the *Carinthia* and *Sylvania*, which were near sisters of the *Saxonia/Carmania* and *Ivernia/Franconia*, initially with the intention of using them on its migrant service but, due to a downturn in trade, they remained in lay-up in Southampton until Sitmar decided instead to enter the North American cruise market – which was a very different and much more demanding sphere of operations from anything it had tried before.[139]

In 1970, the former *Carinthia* and *Sylvania* – which had already been renamed in Sitmar style as the *Fairsea* and *Fairland* – were very extensively rebuilt at the San Marco shipyard in Trieste as 16,627gt cruise ships, accommodating 884 passengers (before entering service, the *Fairland* became the *Fairwind*, however). A new, more extensive upper superstructure was added to each with a single saloon deck containing a series of relatively intimate lounges, bars, nightclubs, a library and a casino. Clean-lined, modern Italian design by Umberto Nordio – who had previously worked on various Italian-owned trans-Atlantic liners – entirely replaced the previous rather fusty 1950s neo-Regency decoration from the Cunard era. Many new cabins were installed and the better existing ones refurbished. The promenade deck windows, which had provided useful protection in North Atlantic liner service – were removed to allow tropical air to flow through. Externally, the most striking change was the fitment of new funnel casings and wheelhouses of up-to-date, slightly streamlined design. Aft, a series of tiered sun decks was developed with swimming pools and Jacuzzis. The conversions were very comprehensive and, upon completion, the vessels looked so convincing in their new guises that, to an untrained eye, it would have been hard to tell that they had ever been anything other than very successful cruise ships.[140]

The Greeks – enjoying beautiful island scenery and with the protection of strong cabotage legislation preventing non-Greek shipping companies from running cruises stopping at more than one Greek port in succession – developed a highly successful cruise industry, based in Piraeus. This

Below: The Turkish *Ankara* was among the earliest Mediterranean passenger ships to be used for cruises in the post-war era. The vessel was very similar to the former-American coastal liners concurrently being used as cruise ships from Miami.

Under Mediterranean flags | 73

The Flotta Lauro flagship, *Achille Lauro* (top), was converted from the Dutch *Willem Ruys*; although intended for liner service, the vessel's advanced design with nested lifeboats made her ideal for cruising. The Italian Sitmar company rebuilt former-Cunard liners as the cruise ships *Fairsea* (pictured centre left) and *Fairwind*. Greek owners Potamianos of Epirotiki Line and Kioskoglou of Sun Line radically converted redundant 1950s-vintage Dutch and French liner tonnage, Holland America's *Ryndam* (centre right) becoming Epirotiki's *Atlas* and Messageries Maritimes' *Cambodge* (bottom left) being transformed into Sun Line's *Stella Solaris* (bottom right).

Above: Royal Cruise Line's *Golden Odyssey* represented a Greek attempt to emulate Royal Caribbean's winning formula in a Mediterranean context, offering fly-cruises to predominantly American passengers. The vessel's Scandinavian naval architecture was coupled with contemporary Greek interior design in what should have been a winning formula. Due to rising travel costs in the wake of the Oil Crisis however, she was instead often based in North American waters, where she developed a very loyal following.

Below: A table setting in the *Golden Odyssey*'s restaurant, showing a pastel-coloured op-art mural by the Greek artist and interior designer, Michael Katzourakis.

blossomed during the 1960s and continued to grow during the 1970s and 80s. Due to Greece being a military dictatorship from 1967 until 1974, it was hard for Greek cruise entrepreneurs to raise sufficient capital to construct new vessels and so the Greek cruise lines became particularly adept at carrying out radical conversions of second-hand liner and ferry tonnage. Alongside Nomikos and Chandris, another leading Greek cruise line to develop in using this technique was Epirotiki, owned by the Potamianos family, whose origins as ship owners could be traced back to the mid-nineteenth century.[141] The company's first cruise ship was the approximately 3,000gt, 150-passenger motor ship the *Semiramis*, bought second-hand in 1953 from the Elder Dempster Lines, for whom she had been built in 1935 as the *Calabar* for West African coastal service. Following conversion, the *Semiramis* made her first Aegean cruise in 1954 and is generally credited as being the first Greek-flagged passenger ship to be used exclusively for cruising. Subsequently, Epirotiki bought Danish, Norwegian and Canadian coastal passenger steamers, followed by a couple of motor ships built since the war for Irish Sea overnight services.[142]

In 1972, Epirotiki bought from Holland America Line its out-of-work Tourist Class-only steam turbine trans-Atlantic liner the *Ryndam*, which was one of two sisters built by Wilton Fijenoord in 1951 to provide an 'economy' trans-Atlantic service. Having been laid up, the vessel was taken to Greece, where she was rebuilt into the cruise ship *Atlas*. Epirotiki's reconstruction of the accommodation decks was less thorough-going than Sun Line's the *Stella Solaris* rebuild had been. Rather than complete demolition and replacement of the existing cabins, some of the originals were combined to create more space and to allow for the installation of private bathrooms, while other, slightly larger ones had shower and WC units installed in a corner. The result was a rather complicated layout, but one that provided quite adequate accommodation for Epirotiki's price level and market segment. The most remarkable change was external.

In converting ageing tonnage for cruising purposes, Greek ship owners' overwhelmingly desired to disguise the fact that, in other circumstances, the same vessels might well instead have gone for scrapping. The most effective way of achieving this was to modernise the external silhouette – sometimes quite radically – and the *Ryndam*-to-*Atlas* conversion was a paradigmatic example of this approach.

To achieve Epirotiki's desired effect, the *Ryndam*'s rather mundane silhouette was augmented with a great deal of additional steelwork, added mostly to the funnel casing, as well as additions to the forward superstructure. The forms of these new elements were very bold – either angular or sweepingly curvaceous – and appeared to reflect the type of brutalist concrete architecture being used concurrently ashore in Greece for numerous buildings (the main liner terminal in Piraeus being a very good example of this genre).

From the late-1960s and early-1970s, Greek shipping entrepreneurs bought nearly the entire passenger fleet of the French colonial liner operator Messageries Maritimes, whose vessels linked Marseille with ports in French Indo-China. Five of the company's diesel passenger-cargo liners, built in the early-1950s and measuring approximately 11,000gt, were bought by Efthymiades for Mediterranean ferry services but most of these were subsequently re-sold, and then fairly superficially converted by a variety of Greek owners for cruising purposes. Epirotiki, for example, bought the former *Jean Laborde*, converting her as the *Oceanos*, while the *Tahitien* became Med Sun Line's the *Atalante* and the *Ferdinand de Lesseps* became the Greek-Cypriot-owned *La Perla*.[143] In all instances, the vessels were immediately recognisable from their original French incarnations, albeit with variable amounts of additional superstructure augmenting their original mid-ships-located accommodations. One example of a broadly similar, if somewhat larger, class of three steam turbine-powered Messageries Maritimes liners of the same era built for France-Japan service also went to a Greek owner – but her transformation into a cruise ship was altogether more thorough.

The 13,217gt, 595-passenger *Cambodge* had been completed in 1953 by the Chantiers de France in Dunkerque to link Marseille and Yokohama. In 1970, she too was sold to a Greek ship owner, Haralambos Kioscoglou, who had begun his career as an employee of Home Lines under Eugen Eugenides and who left in 1959 to found his own cruise company, which he named simply Sun Line. His initial fleet consisted of a couple of small vessels – a converted naval frigate and a German-built day excursion vessel which he used successfully on Greek island itineraries; the *Cambodge* was of a different magnitude relative to these.

Temporarily renamed the *Stella V*, the liner was taken to Perama, a shipyard area adjacent to Piraeus, for a thorough rebuild. As with Icres Line's conversion of the *Dunnottar Castle* to *Victoria*, described above, this first involved completely gutting the entire vessel, returning her to a steel shell. The superstructure was extended forward and aft over the cargo holds, effectively trebling its length. In the hull and lower superstructure, new cabins were built, again following much the same layout approach as on the *Victoria* (those in the mid-ships superstructure extended into what had previously been open promenade decks, but were now plated in). In all, 700 berths were provided with 514 being lower berths. All of the public rooms, however, were located in the superstructure, the majority on a single saloon deck which was very similar in terms of layout to the *Queen Elizabeth 2* and to the three Royal Viking sisters, which were at that time under construction in Helsinki and for which deck plans were available. The galley was forward-located with the dining saloon amidships with the main lounge aft. Kioscoglou employed the Italian architect Nino Zoncada, with whose work he was familiar from Home Lines' the *Oceanic*, to design the interiors in his typically understated and elegant manner.[144]

The conversion took almost three years to complete and the vessel was finally ready to enter Sun Line's service as the *Stella Solaris* for the 1973 Mediterranean summer cruise season. During winter months, she was re-located to the Caribbean and soon gained an enviable reputation with both European and American cruise aficionados.

Shortly after, similar conversions were undertaken on two British cargo motor ships, the *Port Sydney* and the *Port Melbourne*. Dating from 1955, the former had been built by Swan, Hunter & Wigham Richardson in Newcastle and the latter by Harland & Wolff in Belfast for Port Line's UK-New Zealand liner service. By the early 1970s, the introduction of new container ships had caused them to be prematurely retired. Vessels such as these offered excellent conversion opportunities; as they had been designed to carry large weights of cargo, extra superstructure was unlikely to cause serious stability problems and their twin-screw diesel propulsion was not only fairly economical but also offered enough redundancy for safe operation with passengers. Furthermore, they could be purchased for not much more than scrap value.

Their purchaser was the Greek shipping magnate, John C. Karras. At first, Karras planned to have them rebuilt as side-loading Adriatic car ferries, to be named the *Akrotiri Express* and *Therisos Express*. With this in mind he contacted Knud E. Hansen A/S to act as the project naval architects. Karras then changed his mind and requested instead that they be transformed into cruise ships with accommodation for a little over 500 passengers.[145]

Each rebuild took two years to complete at a shipyard at Chalkis, near to Rafina. The centre part of the existing superstructure was kept up to Promenade Deck level and extensive new accommodation was added around this. As with the *Stella Solaris*, most of the public rooms were on one deck with the galley forward, serving a large dining saloon amidships, and a multi-purpose main lounge towards the stern. Aft, there was an expansive lido area, protected from headwinds by shelter screens, and there were even six cabins with private balconies amidships. Renamed as the *Daphne* and the *Danae*, the two ships came to be regarded as amongst the finest in the Greek cruising fleet. The contrast between the futuristic styling of the upper decks and the riveted hull with lapped plating certainly made the ships very distinctive.[146]

The *Daphne* was completed in 1975 with the *Danae* following in 1977. The two were used on cruises of the Mediterranean, the Caribbean and even occasional voyages to the Far East and around the world, beginning and ending in Marseilles. Karras' experience of running the ships was disappointing, however. Much like Royal Viking Line, he found that offering diverse world-wide itineraries created larger than expected administrative overheads.

Among the very few purpose-built cruise ships delivered to Greek owners in the 1970s was the 6,757gt *Golden Odyssey*, completed in 1974 by Helsingør Skibsværft for Royal Cruise Line, owned by the Greek shipping tycoon Pericles Panagopoulos. He was a nephew of Eugen Eugenides, proprietor of Home Lines, for whom he was first employed as a teenager. Subsequently, in the mid-1960s, he joined Sun Lines, the eventual owner of the Stella Solaris, before establishing his own Royal Cruise Line in the early-1970s.[147]

Designed by Knud E. Hansen A/S, the *Golden Odyssey* was designed to carry a single wide-bodied jet-load of passengers, Panagopoulos' business concept being to extend the American 'fly-cruise' concept from the Caribbean to the Mediterranean. In particular, his plan was to bring plane-loads of American passengers to Athens Airport for Aegean cruises, providing a commensurate level of quality to Royal Caribbean (hence, the 'Royal…' name adopted by his company).[148] As with NCL and Royal Caribbean, he needed an American business partner to sell his cruises in the United States and he was fortunate in finding a very energetic and effective one in the travel entrepreneur Richard Revnes, who personally fronted the venture in brochures and advertising, thereby making Royal Cruise Line seem more American and Greek to passengers who might otherwise have been put off by anything too 'foreign' or 'exotic.'

In terms of layout, the *Golden Odyssey* was effectively a very heavily compressed version of Royal Caribbean's the *Song of Norway* and her sisters. Her exterior was styled by Knud E. Hansen A/S' Tage Wandborg, who produced a silhouette slightly reminiscent of a large motor yacht with a pronounced bow flare and a fin attached to the rear of the funnel casing. The interior design was carried out jointly by Wandborg and a Greek contemporary artist, Michael Katzourakis, who designed abstract bulkhead murals for the vessel's hallways and public rooms (subsequently, he became a well-known cruise ship interior designer, producing in addition similar interiors for Karras' the *Danae* and *Daphne* conversions).[149] In terms of scale, the vessel was ideal for Aegean cruising as she could enter relatively small harbours. Unfortunately for Panagopoulos, political instability in the eastern Mediterranean made Americans less willing to travel there. The solution was to redeploy the vessel from the North American west coast ports of San Francisco and Vancouver for much of the year, where she became very popular.

Above: Part of the *Golden Odyssey*'s nightclub with another Katzourakis mural behind the bar and Eero Saarinen 'Tulip' chairs and tables in the foreground; the light colours were intended to create a distinctly 'Mediterranean' ambience, albeit offset by futuristic-looking furnishings of American origin.

Chapter 8
The Oil Crisis and after

In the Middle East, Arab nations in the Organization of Petroleum Exporting Countries (OPEC) decided to retaliate against the United States and its allies to punish them for supporting Israel in the Yom Kippur War. In the autumn of 1973 they slashed oil production by between 5 and 10 per cent per month, hoping that resulting political pressure would force Israel to withdraw from the areas it had occupied. Since the Second World War, oil prices had remained more or less stable at around ten dollars a barrel but during the latter part of 1973 they quadrupled, precipitating a global downturn and an end to the steady growth experienced in the Western World since the Second World War. Shipping companies, which were amongst the heaviest commercial oil users, were particularly badly affected and shipbuilders too suddenly found themselves with empty order books.

The so-called 'Oil Crisis' had a profound effect on the cruise industry's subsequent development. Many projects for new ships were postponed, or cancelled altogether. A large number of old steam turbine-powered passenger liners, latterly in use as cruise ships, were withdrawn and sold for scrapping. P&O – Britain's biggest cruise operator – withdrew all but three members of its Southampton-based fleet, sending them to Taiwan for breaking. Even the *Canberra* was threatened with premature withdrawal in 1974 after an ill-judged programme of cruises out of New York the previous summer; the former-liner's many cabins sharing public bathrooms had demonstrated how unsuitable she was for a non-British clientele. Another major British cruise operator, Shaw Savill, withdrew from the sector altogether when its directors decided henceforth to concentrate only on the cargo liner sector. As a result, its 12-year-old the *Northern Star* and recently-upgraded *Ocean Monarch* (ex-*Empress of England*) were sold for scrap in 1975 as no willing buyers could be found.

By the mid-1970s, the effects of the hike in fuel costs caused by the Oil Crisis had led to soaring inflation, making the employment of European hotel staffs prohibitively expensive. One solution was to swap traditional European flags for those of Panama, Liberia or the Bahamas, enabling the employment of low-cost third world crews – a policy already practiced by Carnival Cruise Lines, for example. Some ship owners who refused to follow this approach decided instead to withdraw from the sector altogether, an example being the Swedish American Line, owned by Broström AB of Gothenburg, which withdrew and sold its highly-regarded the *Gripsholm* and *Kungsholm* in 1975. The former assumed the Greek flag while the latter was bought by Øivind Lorentzen's Flagship Cruises and was re-registered in Liberia.

One of the very few cruise operators to take delivery of new vessels in the second half of the 1970s was Cunard. In 1974, the two-year-old *Cunard Adventurer* had been badly damaged by fire during a positioning voyage, leaving a gap in the fleet. Through the shipbroker Ellie Schalit – who had previously arranged the company's purchase of the *Cunard Adventurer* and *Cunard Ambassador* – Cunard acquired the only two realised examples of what had been intended as a class of eight identical 17,496gt, 947-passenger cruise ships.

They too were initiated by Overseas National Airways which, having resolved its financial difficulties, apparently wished to make a second attempt at entering the cruise industry. This time, it intended to do so in partnership with the well-known film and entertainment conglomerate MGM, which would have owned the remaining six vessels, none of which were built. Had they been so, the eight-strong fleet would have been positioned in the Caribbean, the Mediterranean, the Indian Ocean and the South Pacific, capitalising on what was expected to be a boom in long distance air-sea cruising. Unusually, the hull and superstructure steelwork and the machinery installation for each vessel were to be built at the Burmeister & Wain shipyard in Copenhagen, using designs supplied by Knud E. Hansen A/S. They would then be towed to Italy for completion by the Industrie Navali Merchaniche Affine shipyard at La Spezia.[150]

The vessels' hulls were sixteen metres longer than those of the *Cunard Adventurer* and *Cunard Ambassador* and this gave them superior sea-keeping qualities. The design was unusual as the topsides tapered outwards towards the waterline – thereby increasing stability – and the stern was a curving transom design, more like that of a container ship. Cheaper to construct than a traditional tapering stern, this increased the aft deck area and also lent additional rigidity. While tumblehome was rarely used for cruise ship hulls, transom sterns were widely used. As with the Royal Caribbean and Royal Viking vessels, four medium-speed diesels, geared to twin shafts, were installed, albeit ones of Burmeister & Wain's own design. These enabled a relatively fast cruising speed of 21.5 knots to be maintained with advantages in terms of operational flexibility.

The first of the pair, named the *Cunard Countess*, was delivered in the summer of 1976 but the second was delayed by a shipyard fire in April 1976, and was not introduced until March 1977. For sea trials, she was named the *Cunard Conquest*, this being changed to the *Cunard Princess* before entry into service. By this point, Cunard's senior management was evidently so pessimistic about the

Below: The *Cunard Princess* was, according to Cunard, likely to have been the last ever new cruise ship as the Oil Crisis caused great pessimism about the industry's future. Here, the sleek vessel is seen leaving New York at the beginning of what turned out to be a long and successful career.

future of the cruise business that its Chairman, Victor Matthews, declared in a speech made at the naming ceremony in New York that she would be 'the last cruise ship.'[151] Matthews, a self-made businessman from London's East End whose earlier career had been in property development, also had strong views about Cunard's identity, which since the advent of the *Queen Elizabeth 2*, had attempted to emulate airline aesthetics, rather than the traditions of the passenger liner trade. Given Cunard's heritage, Matthews perhaps saw this as a missed opportunity and so, prior to entering service, the *Cunard Princess* and *Cunard Countess*' white funnel casings were repainted in Cunard's traditional red and black livery, complete with black hoops (which on the old liners had held the funnel casings together, but were redundant on modern tonnage with welded funnel casings). Whether he realised or not, Matthews' instinct was very much in line with the emerging approaches of the 'heritage' industry and with what would subsequently become known as 'retro design.' Only much later on would similar 'retro' stylings significantly impact upon cruise ship design more generally, however, as in the mid-1970s nearly all operators continued to prefer up-to-date aesthetics for their vessels.

From the outset, the *Cunard Countess* served almost without interruption in the Caribbean, sailing on weekly circuits from San Juan. The *Cunard Princess* also operated in the Caribbean, as well as the Mexican Riviera and to Alaska during the summer.

At this point, Cunard sold the *Cunard Adventurer* to Norwegian Caribbean Line which, after an economically troubled period was now resurgent and wishing to re-enter the short 3-4 day cruise market from Miami to the Bahamas (which it had exited when it sold the *Sunward* three years previously). The *Cunard Adventurer* was rebuilt to a design by Knud E. Hansen A/S better to match the external and interior style of NCL's three other vessels with slanted twin exhaust stacks in place of the original single funnel, re-entering service from Miami as NCL's *Sunward II*.[152] The extent of this work on a vessel of such recent construction demonstrates the extent to which the outward image of Caribbean cruise ships was important to their owners in the 1970s. (The fire-damaged *Cunard Ambassador*, meanwhile, had been abandoned to her insurer and the wreck was sold to a Danish owner for conversion as a livestock carrier.)

In the latter-1970s, the *Sunward II*'s only rival in the Miami-Bahamas trade was Eastern Steamship Lines' the *Emerald Seas*, a converted World War 2-built troop transporter which, due to having had concrete ballast incorrectly installed to counterweight her enlarged superstructure, sailed with a permanent list. Since 1968, Eastern Steamship Lines had been owned by the Norwegian company Gotaas-Larsen, which was, of course, also a part-owner of NCL's great rival, Royal Caribbean. In comparison with the *Emerald Seas*, the *Sunward II* was superior in terms of comfort, aesthetic and technological modernity.[153]

While Cunard's directorate were unduly pessimistic about the future of cruising, the highly successful Royal Caribbean was seeking cost-effective means of providing additional capacity in order to cope with sharply increasing demand. When in 1977 the Royal Viking Line partner Nordenfjeldske Dampskibsselskab decided to withdraw from cruising and to sell the *Royal Viking Sky* on the open market, Royal Caribbean considered purchasing the vessel to expand its own fleet. Before an offer could be made, however, Royal Viking's other partners intervened, jointly acquiring her so as to retain a three-strong fleet in the hope that better times lay ahead. (The difference between Royal Caribbean's profitability and Royal Viking's struggles to break even reflected the fact that the type of luxury world-wide cruising in which it specialised involved far greater operational overheads than the Caribbean operators' repetitive weekly itineraries from Miami.)

Royal Caribbean's alternative strategy, therefore, was to have two of its three-strong existing fleet lengthened amidships; this was in any case a more cost-effective solution as having two bigger ships would improve economies of scale in all areas of operation, whereas buying an extra vessel would have entailed additional purchase and operational costs. Thus, in 1978, the *Song of Norway* and *Nordic Prince* were sent back to their builder in Helsinki for this work to be carried out and when they returned to service, their capacities had risen from 724 to 1,196 with a gross tonnage of 22,945. A welcome side effect was that the longer hulls were less likely to experience extreme pitching motion during rough weather.[154]

Carnival Cruise Lines, meanwhile, had introduced two further second-hand cruise ships, converted from redundant liners. The 32,326gt *Carnivale*, introduced in 1975, had originally been Canadian Pacific's trans-Atlantic liner the *Empress of Britain* of 1956, a former fleet mate of Carnival's existing the *Mardi Gras*. More recently, the Greek Line had used her as a cruise ship, the *Queen Anna Maria*, but had withdrawn her due to bankruptcy in the wake of the Oil Crisis. Usefully, her superstructure had been extended fully aft by Greek Line, providing an additional large lounge space which, with

Above: In the Caribbean, it was possible to sail slowly, meaning that even fuel-hungry, steam turbine-powered former-liners could be made profitable. Carnival Cruise Line therefore acquired the UK-South Africa vessel *S.A. Vaal*, which is seen leaving Southampton under her new name of *Festivale*, bound for Japan and rebuilding (top). A show lounge and many new cabins were added in a greatly enlarged superstructure, as the centre image shows. Out with the Caribbean, only the Soviet Union was bullish about the future of passenger shipping and, among many other purchases in the 1970s, the Soviets bought a new Danish-designed and -owned cruise ship, the *Copenhagen* (above), which was renamed the *Odessa*.

Above: The Soviet cruise fleet's flagship was the formerly-West German-flagged *Hamburg*, which became the *Maxim Gorkiy* in 1974, albeit for chartering henceforth mainly to West German tour operators.

Below: The *Gruziya* was one of a fleet of five Finnish-built cruise ferries, intended for Black Sea routes. As the Soviets had too few cars, but a strong desire to earn hard currency, most instead became cruise ships in the Western market.

further modification, could be made suitable for cabaret shows. With two ships, Carnival was at last was satisfactorily profitable and so, in 1978, a third, much larger vessel was acquired, the *S.A. Vaal*, a Southampton-Cape Town passenger and mail liner, dating from 1960 and originally the *Transvaal Castle*. A large, modern one-class ship, she offered considerable potential for conversion into the type of popular floating entertainment resort Carnival henceforth wished to provide. Renamed the *Festivale*, the vessel was sent to Japan for a rebuilding masterminded by Technical Marine Planning of London, who were henceforth to be Carnival's preferred naval architects. Large new superstructure additions were fitted forward and aft, the former containing cabins and a large tiered cabaret lounge, enabling table service of drinks and snacks during staged performances. In form and style, it followed closely the layout of the 'Copa rooms' found in Las Vegas resort hotels. Arguably, it was the first of its kind ever on a cruise ship (although quite what constitutes a 'Copa room' or 'show lounge' is open to debate).

Throughout, new interiors were designed by a youthful Miami-based interior architect, Joe Farcus, who was an assistant of the well-known Florida and New York hotel designer, Morris Lapidus (best known for the Fontainebleu and Eden Roc hotels at South Miami Beach). Although existing Miami-based cruise ships, such as those of Royal Caribbean, utilised themed interior decoration similar to these hotels, Farcus' work sought to be much more brash and flamboyant to generate the intended 'festive' atmosphere. Clashing, garish colours and kitsch references, such as plastic palm fronds or beer barrels for tables, were juxtaposed with bold graphics and colour-change lighting. This 'scenography' proved highly effective and the *Festivale* – which now measured 38,175gt and accommodated 1,432 (twice as many as before) – re-entered service in the autumn of 1978, transformed from a somewhat conservatively-decorated liner into a particularly glittery Caribbean party cruiser. She was an early and influential example of a wilfully post-modern design approach used in a shipboard setting. The emphasis on live shipboard entertainment also pointed the way ahead for the mass market cruise industry.

Under the Soviet flag

While there was still money to be made in North American waters if a cruise operator had the right business concept, the mid-1970s was a rather fallow period for cruising's development in the wider world. Profit margins were slim and operating costs, high. Only the Communist Bloc, consisting of the Soviet Union and its satellites, appeared exempt from the economic downturn affecting the wider world. Quite remarkably, in light of the anti-bourgeois character of Communist ideology, during this period, the Soviets assembled the world's biggest cruising fleet. The Soviet Union was energy-rich and its economy was structured around five-year plans, thereby avoiding the booms and major corrections that characterised western economies (and, to Communists, seemed illogical). Yet, as the Soviets needed to earn hard currency to pay for imported goods, running cruise ships seemed a sensible source of this revenue. Besides, in practice, Soviet Communism was imitative and usually tried to emulate western ideas – whether skyscrapers, pop music or cruises.

The core of the Soviet passenger fleet, operated by the Black Sea Steamship Company, was the so-called 'Writer class' of trans-Atlantic liners built in East Germany in the mid-1960s for service from Odessa and Leningrad to Canada. These were augmented by various classes of smaller liner for shorter Baltic, Mediterranean and Far East routes. By the early-1970s, several of these vessels had been given over to cruising. Soon, they were augmented by second-hand acquisitions fom western owners, such as Cunard's the *Carmania* and *Franconia* (which became the *Leonid Sobinov* and *Fedor Shalyapin* in 1973) and the very modern and superbly-appointed Deutsche-Atlantik Linie vessel the *Hamburg*, which in 1974 became the Soviet flagship, the *Maxim Gorkiy* following the bankruptcy of its previous owner.

The Black Sea Steamship Company's liners were used as cruise ships in markets where passengers were less fussy about comfort than in the USA. Few of their cabins had private toilets and their communal spaces were rather spartanly appointed. On the plus side, they were generally clean and well-run and, what they lacked in terms of hotel-like comfort and facilities, they made up for with very cheap bar prices. In Australia, the cruise industry developed to a large extent thanks to the presence of Soviet vessels. There, very strict city licensing regulations ensured that all pubs closed at 6pm and so the phenomenon of the 'six o'clock swill' emerged, whereby drinkers would line up glasses of beer and down one after another before this deadline. On a Soviet cruise ship, by contrast, the bars remained open for most of the day and night and so short trips from Sydney on these vessels were essentially 'booze cruises.' Better appointed vessels, such as the two former-Cunarders, were chartered to European travel agencies, who sold the berths. In London, CTC Cruises was established especially to market cruises on Soviet passenger ships for the British market. The *Maxim Gorkiy*, meanwhile, was chartered to West German travel agencies, continuing to attract a similar clientele as when she was the *Hamburg*, albeit with far lower operational costs due to her Soviet ownership and crew.

In 1974, the Black Sea Steamship Company took delivery of its first brand new, purpose-built cruise ship. The 13,750gt *Odessa* had been designed in the late-1960s by Knud E. Hansen A/S for a Danish owner, K/S Nordline A/S. It consisted of 850 investors who, encouraged by a tax-break, had intended to use the vessel mainly for Baltic cruises from Copenhagen. The *Copenhagen* Early publicity material suggested she would be named the *Prins Henrik af Danmark* in honour of the Danish Prince Consort, but this was subsequently changed to the *Copenhagen*.[155]

In 1970 Nordline placed an order with the long-established British shipyard of Vickers in Barrow-in-Furness. Before she could be finished, however, her owners got into a dispute with the yard over escalating costs, leading to the contract being cancelled. After some time elapsed, the partially completed vessel was towed to Wallsend on the River Tyne where she was fitted out by Swan, Hunter & Wigham Richardson, which had recently completed the Norwegian-America liner the *Vistafjord* and was doubtless anxious to find similar work to keep its skilled employees occupied. Having been fully finished, the *Copenhagen* returned to Barrow, where she was laid up. Upon being taken over by the Black Sea Steamship Company, she was sent to the USA, where she cruised from New York, New Orleans, Vancouver and, subsequently, from Mediterranean and Baltic ports.

By the early-1970s, the Soviets were concerned that much of their domestic passenger fleet operating Black Sea coastal services was antiquated and therefore potentially dangerous. Since the ending of the Second World War, new tonnage built overseas, consisting mainly of freight ships, had been purchased through the so called 'Comecon' system, whereby the Soviet Union paid the governments of countries supplying it with manufactured goods of all kinds with an equivalent value in oil and gas. The most regular foreign shipbuilding nation providing ships for the Soviets was Finland and, as well as building the usual mix of cargo vessels, fish factory ships, tankers and icebreakers, the Wärtsilä shipyards – as we have seen – also had great expertise in passenger ship construction. The Black Sea Steamship Company therefore commissioned no less than five substantial cruise ferries from Wärtsilä's Turku yard for delivery in 1975.[156]

Their primary purpose was to modernise Black Sea passenger routes, but they could also be useful as troop and military supply transporters in the event of a war breaking out. Above all, they could be more lucratively deployed in the western cruise market. As car ownership in the USSR was very low, there was actually no need for car ferries in the Black Sea and so it was as cruise ships that they were mostly deployed.[157]

The vessels measured around 16,400 tons, could be quickly constructed and outfitted with deliveries taking place at five-monthly intervals. All were given the names of Soviet republics – the *Belorussiya*, the *Gruziya* and the *Azerbaizhan* being completed in 1975 with the *Kazakhstan* and the *Kareliya* following in 1976. Each could carry 1,009 passengers, 504 of whom were berthed, and 256 cars. Twin Wärtsilä-built Pielstick diesels ensured a 21-knot service speed.

The design was most clearly influenced by Wärtsilä's recent Royal Caribbean and Royal Viking Line cruise ships – although the Soviet cruise ferries had straighter lines and bluffer bow profiles. Their exterior aesthetics displayed a distinctly Soviet 'space age' quality particularly evident in the design of their funnels. As with Norwegian Caribbean Lines' the *Starward*, outside cabins filled the broad casings on each side of the vehicle deck, which was provided with bow, stern and side doors. Above, there was a deck given over almost entirely to cabins with the main Saloon Deck above that. This had a similar arrangement to Royal Caribbean's cruise ships with lounges forward and aft and a large dining room amidships. The vessels were strongly-built, economical and popular, and all five were employed at the 'budget' end of the cruise industry. Their arrival effectively doubled the number of Soviet passenger ships suitable for cruising in the western market and the Black Sea Steamship Company soon entered negotiations with Wärtsilä for a further series that would have been bigger and better still, but these plans apparently met with opposition at a higher level of Soviet bureaucracy and so failed to come to fruition.

In the United States of America, meanwhile, the showing in 1976 on the ABC Television network of a made-for-TV movie entitled 'The Love Boat' was such a popular hit that it spawned a weekly television soap opera of the same name. This was filmed aboard cruise ships operated by the P&O subsidiary Princess Cruises. The resulting extensive positive publicity for cruising in general, and for the Princess fleet in particular, was enormous. The series, which reached tens of millions of Americans, promoted a fashionable, youthful and glamorous image – cruising was now perceived as fun and available to everyone, not just older and richer holidaymakers. Within five years, 'The Love Boat' was being cited as one of the prime factors influencing the growth of the cruise industry in North America.

Above: Cunard's *Carmania* and *Franconia* also joined the Soviet cruise fleet in the 1970s, becoming the *Leonid Sobinov* and *Fedor Shalyapin*. The former is seen here at Southampton shortly after swapping the Red Ensign for the hammer and sickle.

Chapter 9

West Germany's new cruise fleet

The recovery of West Germany from the ruination of the Second World War to become Europe's dominant economic and industrial power was considered miraculous by many observers. Between 1970 and 1980 the economy grew by nearly a third with GDP rising from 200 billion dollars to 290 billion and with statistically full employment. Against this background of growth and prosperity, West German investors were persuaded to finance the first examples of a new generation of cruise ships.

The first of these was the 7,813gt, 330-passenger *Berlin*, which was built by Howaldtswerke Deutsche Werft's Kiel shipyard and delivered in 1980 to Peter Deilmann, a ship owner based at Neustadt in Holstein whose shipping business had begun in the latter-1960s operating cargo coasters in the Baltic trades. Later on, in the early-1970s, he ran tax-free shopping day-trips from West German Baltic ports to the Danish island of Bornholm. The *Berlin* was ordered as a result of Deilmann having secured a 5-year charter deal to the West German tour operator Neckermann, which specialised in cruises and had for several years chartered the Soviet *Maxim Gorkiy*, amongst other vessels.[158]

The *Berlin*'s internal planning and interior design was heavily inspired by emerging practices in the Baltic ferry industry, with which both Deilmann and Howaldtswerke would have been very familiar. In the late-1970s, the world's most advanced and prestigious ferry was the *Finnjet*, a very large and fast gas turbine-powered vessel, operating between Helsinki and Travemünde. Although the vessel's jet propulsion system remained unique, her deck layout would be widely emulated during ensuing years on new ferries and cruise ships, not least in the *Berlin*. The *Finnjet* was designed with all cabins forward-located, forming a 'hotel block' in the quieter front half of her superstructure and with public rooms astern. Soon, another large Baltic ferry, the *Viking Sally*, built in West Germany by Meyer Werft at Papenburg and delivered in 1980, was given a similar layout. Inboard, the Berlin was public rooms and cabins used similar dark imitation wood laminate finishes and muted fabric tones to recent German-owned Baltic ferries; this discreetly understated approach was an aesthetic very different from the showy finishes found on typical American-based cruise ships and, to an extent, it may have reflected the undemonstrative taste of a generation of West Germans for whom memories of the Second World War and of post-war austerity remained.

Hapag-Lloyd, the inheritor of Germany's great trans-Atlantic liner shipping and cruising traditions had, since the mid-1960s, operated the former Swedish American liner the *Kungsholm*, which dated from 1953, as its cruise ship the *Europa*. By the latter-1970s, this fine vessel, which had a 50% repeat clientele, was in need of replacement if a high quality of operation was to be reliably maintained. Hapag-Lloyd's starting points for generating a suitable design came from two sources – the ferry *Finnjet*, for its vertically-segregated layout, and Hapag-Lloyd's most recent twin-screw container ships for their overall hull forms, which were considered a well-proven basis for a cruise ship intended for world-wide itineraries. In comparison with *Finnjet*, however, the new *Europa* would have a lower passenger density with 316 large cabins for all 600 passengers (who would be served by a crew of 300, the 1:2 ratio being indicative of the intended elite clientele). The cabins filled the forward two-thirds of five hull and superstructure decks. To give the public rooms, aft, a greater sense of spaciousness, each had a higher deck head than the cabin areas. The lowest passenger deck, on which the dining room was located, was entirely flat with a progressive split-level appearing progressively, through the upper hull and superstructure, cleverly modulated by the 'mid-ship stairs. Situated among the crew accommodation in the lower hull was a theatre auditorium and, further down, a health spa with indoor pool. The galley was beneath the dining room and, above it was the large Europa Lounge with slightly terraced seating. A smaller bar and sitting areas were aft on Boat Deck, above again. In addition, an observation lounge was placed above the bridge, this being similar to those found on Royal Viking

Below: The *Berlin* used a 'cabins forward, public rooms aft' layout, much like a majority of the newer Scandinavian and West German ferries of the early-1980s. Her interiors were likewise reminiscent of those of ferries operating on southern Baltic routes, as this image of the dining saloon demonstrates.

Line's vessels. Between this and the funnel was an outdoor swimming pool with a retractable glazed roof. The layout was ingenious, being logical in planning, yet providing a broad range of facilities on a variety of scales and with diverse atmospheres.

Measuring 33,618gt, the new *Europa* would be the biggest vessel to date intended only for cruising. Initially, it was planned that steel sections would be built by a coalition of three shipyards in the Bremen area – Bremer Vulkan of Vegesack, A.G. Weser and the Hapag-Lloyd yard in Bremerhaven. In the end, however, Bremer Vulkan built the entire ship, sustaining a loss of 100 million Deutschmarks on the 180 million contract. This notwithstanding, the *Europa* was considered a prestigious 'showcase' for West German shipbuilding and technical expertise and, in an era when orders were few and far between, very welcome employment was generated. (Shortly after withdrawing from the *Europa* project, A.G. Weser won orders for two large North Sea car ferries, the *Olau Hollandia* and *Olau Britannia*, the overall layout of which was similar).

To spare expense while improving the quality and precision of finish, the cabins were all prefabricated by an external contractor, Horst Warneke Metalbau, to a series of standard modular sizes based on a 3.5x7.45-metre module. (Although the *Finnjet* had been designed for the use of this technique, in the end, her cabins were built *in situ* instead.) Warneke had made the manufacture of ships' cabins a niche activity since the early-1970s, when his company had supplied complete interiors, including cabins, in kit form for Swedish-owned ferries being built in Yugoslavia (the *Visby* and *Gotland* of 1972-73).[159]

Unlike the Finnish-built cruise ships of Royal Caribbean and Royal Viking Line, all of which had four medium-speed diesels, the Europa had instead twin slow-speed, direct-drive engines, a robust and reliable solution similar to those selected for Hapag-Lloyd's container ships. The vessel was, however, state-of-the-art in terms of its re-use of waste energy to generate electricity, to purify and to heat water. Generators mounted on the ends of the crankshafts generated auxiliary power under normal operating conditions (with back-up from dedicated auxiliary units). Meanwhile, heat from exhaust gases was used to boil water, the funnel casing containing boiler cylinders, condenser units and associated pipework for this purpose. These installations reflected the growing reputation of West German mechanical engineers for devising innovative yet effective design solutions and so the *Europa* was arguable a relatively 'green' ship long before environmental consciousness became widely fashionable.

Drawings and models suggested that, in external appearance, the *Europa* would closely emulate the *Finnjet* with twin funnels and a plated-in forecastle – but in the end, a more harmonious solution was achieved with a single funnel, surrounded by a streamlined cowl, and a more elegant treatment of the bow profile and forward superstructure.

Inboard, the vessel's interiors, designed by the architects Joachim Buchwald and Wilfred Köhnemann used neutral pastel shades, following a similarly understated approach to those of the *Berlin*. Although all spaces were only one deck high, throughout, a sense of spaciousness was achieved through the generous dimensioning of corridors and aisles and the avoidance of clutter. Furthermore, fixtures, fittings and surface finishes were of a very high quality. In essence, the vessel was a safe, orderly piece of the best of what West Germany could offer by way of design, technology and hospitality, taking its privileged to exotic places, safe in the knowledge that, if the 'exotic' became too intimidating, they could retreat to the calm environment on board where everything worked exactly as it should – just like Lufthansa Business Class or a Mercedes-Benz limousine.

The Hamburg-based Hafen-Dampfschiffahrt A.G., founded in 1888 and known as 'Hadag' was an operator of harbour excursion boats and River Elbe ferries in Hamburg, owned by the Hamburg Municipality. In 1979, it entered into a partnership with the travel company TUI and with the tobacco company Reemtsma to build a new cruise ship for Baltic

Above: The Hapag-Lloyd cruise ship *Europa* was considered among the finest anywhere in the 1980s; intended for world-wide operation, her lido deck was enclosed by an *Oceanic*-style 'magradome' retractable roof.

Above: The *Astor*, pictured here departing New York, was painted externally in the colours and graphic style of Astor cigarettes. The vessel's interiors were, however, rather understated and conservative in style. Her dining room, for example, was actually quite similar in terms of furnishings and design details to that of the 1930s KdF cruise ship *Wilhelm Gustloff*.

and Mediterranean itineraries. Reemtsma had been frustrated by the West German government's recent banning of the advertising of tobacco products on television and so its management decided that a cruise ship could act as a floating advertisement for cigarettes that would be impossible to censor. While Hadag's management suggested the name 'Hammonia', Reemtsma insisted on the *Astor*, which was one of its cigarette brands. Indeed, the vessel would be painted in the same colours as an Astor packet, with the name on the hull in the same font and even the funnel would be designed to resemble an open cigarette packet with the exhaust stovepipes protruding like four smouldering cigarettes. As cruising was obviously considered an aspirational activity, this plan was ingenious in theory at least. Successfully building and operating a cruise ship, however, required far greater expertise than any of the three partners actually possessed.

The *Astor*, which would measure 18,853gt and have a capacity of 633 passengers, was ordered from Howaldtswerke Deutsche Werft's Hamburg shipyard with delivery scheduled for the summer of 1981. Inboard, a horizontal layout was selected, similar to that of the Royal Viking Line fleet, with a majority of public rooms on a single deck with cabins above and below. Decoratively, again, the approach was similar to the *Berlin* and *Europa*, the interiors being rather neutral in tone. As it was expected that the *Astor* would only ever cruise sedately, her propulsion, consisting of four six-cylinder MAN diesels, was selected to give a typical speed of no more than 18 knots, acceptable for Baltic cruises with short distances between ports, but too little when attempting more complex itineraries further afield. The vessel's completion was delayed by a fire, the damage from which took several months to rectify and so it was not until winter that her maiden cruise took place in the Mediterranean.

As a one-ship operation, unfortunately, the *Astor*'s operational overheads outstripped her earnings potential and, as her owners had no loyal passenger base as yet, she sailed just over half-full.

Inspired by the success of 'The Love Boat' on American television; the West German ZDF channel decided to make its own version, entitled 'Das Traumschiff.' The first series was filmed aboard Norwegian America Cruises' the *Vistafjord*, which was a popular ship with West German passengers. For the second series, ZDF was offered free accommodation as an inducement to film aboard the *Astor* – but even although the series attracted high TV ratings, these did not translate into enough bookings of cruises; unlike some of their American counterparts, the types of West Germans who watched TV soap operas were apparently insufficiently wealthy as yet to consider actually taking a cruise. The *Astor* was, therefore, chartered overseas in 1983 and sold shortly after. 'Das Traumschiff' was subsequently filmed on Deilmann's the *Berlin*. The *Astor*'s initial failure reflected a flawed business model as, unlike Deilmann with his Neckermann charter agreement, or Hapag-Lloyd with their large clientele of loyal repeat passengers, the *Astor*'s owners had no way of guaranteeing patronage and thereby securing the necessary profit margin for such a high-cost one-ship operation under the West German flag.

The *Astor*'s purchaser was the South African Marine Corporation (Safmarine) which planned to use her to re-introduce a liner service between Cape Town and South Africa. After only a short time, the Astor was found to be working at her absolute limit in terms of speed, fuel and fresh water capacity (she had been designed for a relatively sedate 18-knot service speed to carry out itineraries with regular port calls to enable re-fuelling). Apart from this fundamental difficulty, Safmarine was apparently pleased with the *Astor* – so much so, in fact, that the solution was to order a new vessel of the same name, built to only slightly modified plans with a hull 12 metres longer than the existing vessel, more powerful engines and greater fuel and water capacities.

This time, the order went to Howaldtswerke Deutsche Werft's Kiel shipyard with delivery expected in 1987. The 'new' *Astor* would measure 20,606gt with a capacity of 650 passengers. While she was under construction, the introduction of anti-apartheid sanctions against the South African Government meant that it would be impossible for her to be used as intended. Safmarine therefore set up a company in Mauritius to own the vessel 'offshore', thereby escaping the restriction and she was run as a cruise ship, initially for a British operator. In the long run, both the first and second *Astor*s were to prove very successful.

Chapter 10

The 1980s cruise ship generation in North America

The election in 1979 of a new Republican President of the United States, Ronald Reagan, brought a profound change to American economic thinking. Reagan and his advisers believed in low taxes and small government, finding their hero in Milton Friedman, Professor of Economics at Harvard Business School. He believed in small government and in regulating growth only through the adjustment of interest rates. Friedman, in turn, admired the Austrian-American economist Friedrich Hayek, whose interest in what he termed 'creative destruction' made it seem acceptable for established industries and activities to decline and wither without government intervention to save them. The spread of market deregulation was paralleled by economic and social decline in some traditionally industrial areas – not least in America's historically prosperous north-eastern states. Simultaneously, however, there was a significant expansion of the 'white collar' professions who were to enjoy more leisure time and greater disposable income than any previous large social group. They desired to flaunt their new-found wealth in luxury hotels, restaurants, cocktail bars, shopping malls and holiday resorts but, on a cruise ship, these type of experiences could all be enjoyed in a single floating entity.

Hitherto, cruising had mainly been the preserve of wealthy, older people – but during the 1980s its popularity would spread to the middle-aged and even to those with young families and teenagers. Bigger ships would enable the necessary economies of scale while providing enough internal and external space for ever wider ranges of revenue-generating entertainments. As the decade progressed, mass market cruise lines' profit models changed from achieving over 90% of revenue from ticket sales to generating between 30% and 40% on board.

The France-to-Norway conversion

By the latter-1970s, NCL's fleet was fully booked for months ahead and the company therefore had no option but to turn away trade. While this may have seemed an enviable position from a business viewpoint, it was bad for the company's reputation to disappoint would-be passengers who were hoping to enjoy a cruise holiday. NCL's senior management reasoned that, one way or another, it would be necessary to add an additional, significantly larger vessel to its fleet. Any such vessel would, however, not necessarily be able to tie up alongside at many of the existing Caribbean port facilities.

NCL's unrealised 'Elysian' semi-catamaran project of the 1970s would have made a virtue of anchoring offshore, delivering passengers to most island ports by tender. In addition, NCL's success with western Caribbean itineraries had proven that the constricted dimensions of most Caribbean islands need not limit the size of vessels and, moreover, were a cruise ship sufficiently large, it could become the major attraction – effectively, a mobile artificial island. Kloster's thinking was very advanced but it proved impossible to convince enough potential financiers to back his project. The next best option was to choose one of the several large out-of-work trans-Atlantic liners for a radical conversion.

NCL's technical staff paid visits to the American Blue Riband-winning liner the *United States*, which at that time was in fully intact condition, but rejected her as too expensive either to acquire or rebuild (any work would have needed to be undertaken in an American shipyard). The Italian *Michelangelo* was inspected, but she and her sister, *Raffaello*, had a complex three class layout with too few cabins having private facilities. Following these disappointments, in 1979 an inspection was made of the magnificent French Line flagship the *France*. Withdrawn from service in 1974, the vessel had been acquired from the French Government in 1977 by a Saudi Arabian businessman Akram Ojjeh (it is said as compensation for a failed arms deal). Plans had been announced by his company for her conversion into a floating hotel and resort to be moored at a jetty off at Daytona Beach in Florida – but, as these had met with opposition, she was effectively for sale once more. Knut Kloster and his Finance Director Bjørnar Hermansen apparently immediately realised the vessel's potential for they agreed to purchase her. The total cost of the acquisition was 65 million dollars.[160]

Constructed by the Chantiers de l'Atlantique at St. Nazaire with the help of a massive government subsidy and introduced in 1961 on the Le Havre-New York route, the *France* had been President Charles de Gaulle's *grand projet* – a spectacular and very chic showcase of all that was best in French technology, design and decoration. A quadruple-screw, steam turbine-powered vessel, she measured 1,035 feet in length – the longest liner in the world. Viewed externally, she had been designed to impress with a

Below: The trans-Atlantic liner *France* as she appeared before conversion for cruising purposes; the vessel's layout emphasised indoor activity, meaning that a great deal of additional outdoor deck space needed to be added for Caribbean cruises.

Above: The newly-converted *Norway* is seen at night in Southampton, where she called during her delivery voyage to Miami; two large ship-to-shore tenders have been mounted on her bow for use at Caribbean islands where she was too big to berth alongside.

Below: The *Norway*'s Leeward dining room was converted from the *France*'s Tourist Class (Rive Gauche) facility. Throughout, the interior designer Angela Donghia overlaid the original designs with glamorous new elements, in this instance adding a spiral staircase with glazed balustrades and a chandelier composed of stainless steel rods.

dramatic, tapering whaleback bow and two massive funnels, topped with giant wings to throw smoke away from her sides. Having agreed to buy the vessel, Knut Kloster contacted his regular naval architecture collaborator, Tage Wandborg of Knud E. Hansen A/S, who had previously been responsible for the designs for all of NCL's existing vessels. Wandborg was given three weeks by Kloster to produce an outline conversion plan. To do so, he set up a design office on board, from where a team from Knud E. Hansen A/S would work for the next fourteen months. Their proposal would involve 'opening up' the largely enclosed superstructure to the sun by adding new decks and pools and all segregations between First and Tourist Class would be removed. By converting the enclosed promenade decks into 'main streets', not only would passenger circulation be improved but also new retail opportunities could be created, generating additional onboard revenue. Meanwhile, her passenger capacity would be increased through the installation of additional cabins. Furthermore, the vessel would be made more fuel economic through the elimination of half her boiler capacity by closing the forward of her two engine rooms with the removal of the outer pair of her four propeller shafts. As a trans-Atlantic liner, it was necessary to maintain speeds of around 28 knots, but as a cruise ship, only half that speed would be acceptable. As the *France* was deep-drafted and required the assistance of tugs when manoeuvring in port, the solution was installing three lateral thrusters in the bow plus two in the stern, enabling her to turn within her own length in the port of Miami without any help from tugs. To bring passengers ashore at the various Caribbean islands, Wandborg's ingenious proposal was to store two landing craft, each for 450 persons, on the foredeck.[161]

The *France* was towed to the Hapag-Lloyd shipyard in Bremerhaven which estimated the cost of the conversion at 42 million dollars. As events unfolded, however, this sum would grow by a third. One reason was that when converting an existing vessel, many unexpected difficulties can arise, causing delays and increasing costs. Another is that Knut Kloster became increasingly excited by the prospect of operating the world's biggest cruise ship under the Norwegian flag and, having begun the *Norway* project as a purely commercial proposition, it gradually transformed into the creation of a Norwegian 'national flagship.' As the project progressed, Tage Wandborg suggested new ideas to Knut Kloster, some of which – such as rebuilding the funnels with flat smoke-deflecting plates – were rejected while a great many others were enthusiastically endorsed.[162]

Knut Kloster appointed the well-known New York-based interior designer Angelo Donghia to work alongside Knud E. Hansen A/S's naval architects to make the ship's interiors more appealing to American passengers going on tropical cruises. He transformed the former First Class promenades into lively 'shopping streets' named Champs Elysses and Fifth Avenue, with some themed décor to engender something of the atmosphere of Paris and New York. Accessed from these, the imposing double-height former First Class *fumoir* (smoking saloon) was transformed into an elegant nightclub and cocktail lounge called the Club Internationale. Smaller spaces, such as the Salon Debussy, were converted to shops and the First Class ballroom, amidships, became Chequers' Cabaret. Of the former Second Class spaces, the smoking saloon became a large casino and the ballroom became the North Cape Lounge. A small grillroom was located aft of these, overlooking the stern. The indoor Second Class swimming pool became a flashy discotheque called 'A Club Called Dazzles' with an under-lit plate glass dance floor where the water had been. The dining saloons, amidships on the lower decks, had been among the most impressive spaces on board the *France* and the First Class Chambord was left largely unaltered, while its Second Class counterpart was one of Donghia's most successful redecorations. A new spiral staircase in brushed aluminium was introduced to connect its two levels and a chandelier, consisting of closely grouped aluminium tubes of different lengths, was installed above the void. Not only did this work glamorise the space and make it appear almost the equal of its former First Class counterpart, but also Donghia's design was entirely in keeping with the original décor.

Externally, what had been a courtyard with surrounding cabins on the bridge deck between the funnels was converted to an amidships swimming pool while aft, three vast tiered sun-decks, the lowest and largest of which had another larger pool, were added. This involved a great deal of new steelwork as the decks were cantilevered over the sides of the ship's fine-lined stern.[163]

As some of the former-Second Class cabins did not have private facilities and, as the existing plumbing was a gravity system, it was decided to entirely replace this with an up-to-date Evac vacuum installation in all cabins.[164] Altogether, the ship's capacity rose from 2,044 as the *France* to 2,400 as the *Norway*. The 1,100-strong French Line staff was replaced by an international (i.e. low-wage, non-unionised) crew of 800. As with the remainder of the NCL fleet, the officers were Norwegian, but no less than 32 other nationalities represented among the engine room, deck and hotel staff. All of these changes were to make the once unprofitable *France* a moderately acceptable dollar-earner for NCL.[165]

The *Norway*'s arrival in Miami in June 1980 marked the beginning of a new epoch for the cruise industry. Because her mainly American passengers were used to constant entertainment whilst on vacation and, sailing from Florida ports, they would have been familiar with such theme parks as Disneyland at Orlando, NCL placed great emphasis on hiring well-known entertainers to perform on board. Whereas the earlier NCL ships were relatively small and thus offered only a limited choice of entertainment and activities, the sheer size of the *Norway* opened up a world of new possibilities. She was a floating resort with a theatre big enough to stage Broadway musicals and she had a vast range of sports facilities. Earlier cruise ships had shuffleboard and tennis courts, but she had basketball and volleyball courts too, as well as a golf driving range. The entertainment staff organised as many as five or six different activities for the passengers to choose between at any one time; this was unprecedented in the history of cruising. For instance, there were make-up demonstrations, foreign language classes, ballroom dancing lessons, exercise classes, cocktail hours, chess tournaments and trivia quizzes.[166]

At the suggestion of Bruce Nierenberg, NCL purchased an uninhabited small island in the Bahamas for 3.5 million dollars for the exclusive use of its passengers, which extended the leisure possibilities of cruising even further. There, the *Norway*'s guests could participate in scuba diving, barbecues, sports tournaments or simply relax in a hammock tied between palm trees. Across expanses of white sand beach and turquoise water, the great ship made an impressive sight as she rode at anchor. According to Nierenberg, passengers' feed-back indicated that the 'private island day' was their favourite part of the cruises.[167] (The image of a great European-owned passenger ship aloof in the middle distance, surrounded by palm fronds and tropical foliage, had been commonplace in colonial shipping companies' advertising imagery since the latter nineteenth century.)

In the end, the total cost of the *Norway*'s purchase and conversion was 130 million dollars. NCL pointed out that this was only half the price of a somewhat smaller newly-built cruise ship. Nonetheless, the payment of this sum emptied the company's cash reserves and meant that it was in no position to afford further cruise ships in the ensuing five years – an era when the wider mass market cruise industry grew substantially.[168]

While the *Norway* conversion had been under way, Knut Kloster had initiated a project for a giant purpose-built Caribbean cruise ship, code-named 'G-6' and measuring over 250,000gt. At first he worked with a youthful Norwegian designer, Petter Yran, who had been trained as an architect but had been inspired to draw speculative designs for futuristic cruise ship concepts in the early-1970s. Later in the decade, Yran was briefly employed by Knud E. Hansen A/S, where the initial project development for G-6 was carried out.[169] When the *Norway* entered service, Yran's senior colleague, Tage Wandborg took over

Above: A stern-quarter view of the *Norway*, showing the over-hanging sun decks added above her slender aft-body.

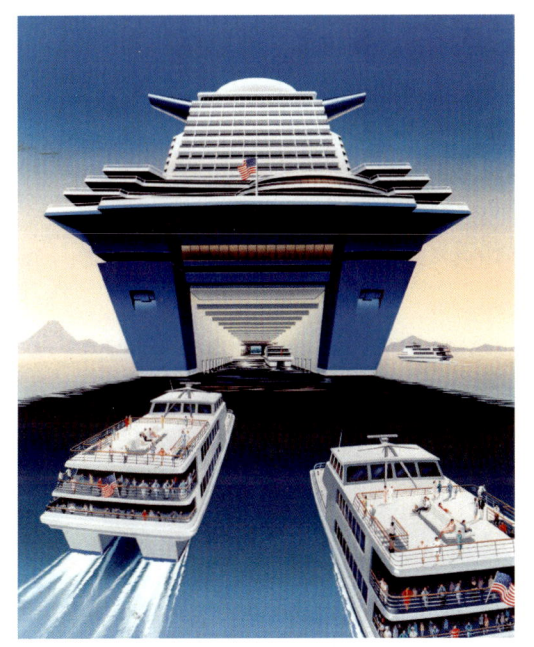

Left & below: Two renderings of Tage Wandborg's 'Phoenix World City' giant cruise ship concept for NCL; various iterations of the design for a vessel with several accommodation towers were produced, but it proved impossible to raise sufficient capital to take the project forward. At the stern, there would have been a docking bay for ship-to-shore tenders.

Right: Carnival Cruise Line's *Tropicale* was the first purpose-built 'Fun Ship' for the Caribbean market. Although of up-to-date appearance and with straight hull lines, the vessel's layout was heavily influenced by that of the converted liner, *Mardi Gras*. The winged funnel design was to become a Carnival trade-mark.

and henceforth the project became known as 'Phoenix World City' – but, as Kloster's ambition was far ahead of what financiers believed that the cruise market could withstand in terms of capacity, he struggled to raise enough money to bring this vision to fruition. Instead, other cruise operators began ordering more and bigger vessels, the sizes and capacities of which increased on a gradual basis.[170]

Although Knut Kloster was immensely proud of the *Norway* and was convinced that significantly bigger vessels would eventually be needed to cope with growth, he also began to worry that bringing large numbers of prosperous American cruise passengers to Caribbean islands was a new form of colonialism. Typifying the thinking of many progressive Scandinavians of his generation, he began to wonder how passengers might be encouraged to engage more constructively with the local cultures to learn about them at a deeper level and perhaps to go home with a more complex and nuanced view of what they had experienced. One of Kloster's suggestions was that local representatives might be invited aboard to have lunch with groups of passengers to discuss Afro-Caribbean culture and local concerns. Apparently, Kloster was horrified to discover colleagues in his Miami office referring to this idea disparagingly as 'inviting a nigger for lunch cruises.' Nothing further was attempted, therefore, and Kloster apparently began to lose interest in NCL's day-to-day operations, concentrating instead on the technical development of the 'Phoenix World City' with his like-minded friend, Tage Wandborg.[171]

Without his strong and visionary leadership of NCL, as the 1980s progressed, the company began to lose ground to its rivals, Carnival and Royal Caribbean.

Carnival's first new buildings

By the early 1980s, Carnival Cruise Line was in a position to build anew, and Ted Arison commissioned an outline design from the company's usual naval architects, Technical Marine Planning on London. In terms of overall layout, this was remarkably similar to the company's first cruise ship, the former-trans-Atlantic liner *Mardi Gras* and, initially, Carnival even suggested using steam turbine propulsion, rather than diesels, as their engineering staff were most familiar with this fuel-hungry system (unlike diesels, steam boilers cannot quickly be switched off and on and so turbine-powered vessels continue to guzzle fuel while in port). Soon, however, the benefits of diesels over steam were realised to be overwhelming – but the situation reveals the extent to which the new vessel was conceptualised from the company's existing knowledge base. To build her, Arison approached the best known builder of modern cruise ships, Wärtsilä in Finland, with a view to ordering possibly more than one example. At that time, Wärtsilä's order book was full and, besides, as Arison was a first-time buyer of new tonnage, the Finns perhaps were less than fully confident about the seriousness of his intention to follow through with an actual order.[172]

Below: With a younger clientele expected than was typical of other recent cruise ships, the *Tropicale*'s facilities included a state-of-the-art discotheque with an illuminated dance floor.

Meanwhile, at a Danish shipyard, Aalborg Værft – which had no previous experience of building cruise ships but which was a successful builder of large ferries – there was a high expectation of winning an order for two such vessels for the Swedish Sessanlinjen's service across the Kattegat. Although Aalborg Værft designed the new Sessan ships, at the last moment, the Swedish Government granted a subsidy to the Arendal Shipyard in Gothenburg, meaning that they secured the building contract instead, leaving Aalborg Værft with a gap in its order book. At this point, Ted Arison contacted the yard. Needless to say, its management were relieved and delighted by this unexpected, but welcome, change in fortune. Time was tight, however, as the *Tropicale* was expected to enter service during the 1981 winter Caribbean cruise season.[173]

Although Aalborg had a large and able drawing office, the 22,919gt *Tropicale* would be the biggest and most complex passenger ship yet built there and so both Technical Marine Planning and Knud E. Hansen A/S were employed in to carry out large portions of the vessel's detailed design. Unusually, the deal struck between Carnival and Aalborg Værft stipulated that she should be owned by a Liberian subsidiary established by the yard, AVL Maritime of Monrovia, then leased to Carnival for ten years. The fact that Aalborg Værft agreed to this unusual requirement demonstrates their desperation to win the order – and also Carnival's apparent inability to finance the vessel's purchase cost through capital plus a mortgage.

The *Tropicale*'s underwater hull design was similar to the recent Aalborg-built North Sea ferry the *Dana Anglia*, having a pronounced bulbous bow to alleviate the rather bluff entry and a transom stern configuration. Between, the hull lines were straight with the superstructure extending well forward and aft. The yard's location was actually

The 1980s cruise ship generation in North America | 87

The *Holiday*, Carnival's second new-building, further developed the 'Fun Ship' concept. Inboard, the Blue Lagoon Lounge (centre left) had an 'under sea' theme, using moulded fibreglass for ceiling, column and furniture finishes, while an indoor promenade, linking the various public rooms, featured a burger bar and café in a restored Bedford bus (centre right). At the time of completion, the *Holiday* was among the world's biggest cruise ships, though deadweight problems discovered during her initial sea trials necessitated the installation of fins to add buoyancy at her stern (bottom left). The subsequent Swedish-built *Jubilee* (lower centre) and her sister, the *Celebration*, avoided these difficulties, however.

rather constricted, meaning that the vessel's hull and superstructure required to be constructed in two sections, which were fitted together in a floating dock. Propulsion was by twin Sulzer diesels with a mechanically straight-forward direct drive arrangement.

Two decks of public rooms filled the upper superstructure, their arrangement mostly following a similar pattern to those on the old *Mardi Gras*. Even the dining room was located low down in the hull amidships in trans-Atlantic liner style. The five lowest passenger decks were otherwise given over entirely to cabins, accommodating 1,422. These were unusually large given the relatively inexpensive cost of Carnival cruises (in comparison with the prices charged by NCL and Royal Caribbean, whose vessels had far more compact standard cabins). The main reason was that Carnival believed that, as a large part of their broad passenger demographic was younger than was typical of the wider cruise industry; larger hotel-like cabins would provide couples with more romantic possibilities while extra upper berths could enable whole families to be accommodated. The forward part of the two public room decks was filled by a large show lounge, inspired in part by the one installed on the *Festivale* and also by a design produced by Aalborg Værft for the Sessanlinjen ferries (with similar tiered fenestration). Decoratively, the *Tropicale*'s interiors, designed by Joe Farcus, also followed the *Festivale*'s successful precedent, being very much in the style of recent Las Vegas resort hotels. Farcus additionally designed the vessel's distinctive winged funnel, which thereafter became a Carnival trademark (though the design exhibited considerable similarities each of the *Norway*'s two stacks).

Even the *Tropicale*'s machinery installation was unremarkable and the layout of her public rooms was rather conservative, at least the layout and equipment of her hidden service infrastructure was progressive. In Miami, the vessel would have eight-hour turnarounds – slow by ferry standards but very fast relative to passenger liners of commensurate size built as recently as the mid-1960s. On a cruise – unlike a ferry trip – a very large amount of passenger luggage needed moving from cabin corridors to the lower decks and ashore for collection with the same procedure then happening in reverse during the embarkation of the next cruise's passengers, fresh catering and hotel supplies. Once again, Aalborg Værft's recent ferry design work for the *Dana Anglia* and for the Sessan ferries informed the overall approach to the arrangement of the vertical and horizontal flows of catering, retail and hotel supplies.[174] On the ferries, fresh supplies were pre-loaded in containers then embarked via the vehicle deck, where they were moved by elevator to the galley and other storage areas. On the cruise ships, by contrast, passenger baggage and supplies were loaded through side hatches aligning with the quay. Within the hull, an unobstructed area of steel deck was an equivalent of a ferry's vehicle deck, enabling marshalling and dispatch to the appropriate store, or by elevator to whichever deck.

So satisfied was Carnival with the *Tropicale*'s performance that, immediately after her delivery, they began work with Technical Marine Planning, Knud E. Hansen A/S and Aalborg Værft and on a further, considerably larger version, otherwise mostly following the successful formula established by the *Tropicale*.[175] The 46.052gt *Holiday* was delivered in 1985, the biggest vessel ever built by Aalborg Værft and, once again, constructed in two sections that were subsequently co-joined. In terms of layout, the *Holiday* differed from the *Tropicale* primarily in having a wide arcade to starboard on her main saloon deck to link her wider range of public rooms and in having two restaurants located amidships and aft in the upper superstructure with the galley located between. These had large windows and slightly raised centre sections, enabling many diners to enjoy sea views. The arrangement followed the approach first used on NCL's *Starward* in the late-1960s and, with the main entertainment lounge being towards the bow, it represented the next stage in the development of what was to become the most commonplace layout solution for large, mass-market cruise vessels. In terms of the range of facilities on offer, the Holiday was intended to please a very diverse clientele in terms of age and background. Their designer, Joe Farcus, specified a vintage Bedford bus, containing a diner, as a focal point in the arcade, while one of the lounges attempted an 'under sea' theme and the library was panelled in wood veneer with buttoned leather chairs. Such varied post-modern theming negated any sense of visual harmony or continuity – and was stimulating, rather than soothing as was most 'conventional' cruise ship décor at that time. Out on deck, the *Holiday* had large expanses of teak planking for sunbathing (Carnival tended to specify more resilient finishes than Royal Caribbean as midnight disco pool parties needed surfaces on which passengers could dance). The 'mid-ships pool, tiled in black, red and yellow stripes, had a slide, making it especially popular with older children and teenagers – two groups never specifically catered to by any cruise line (although some liners in the trans-Atlantic and UK-Australia trades had had teenage rooms).

Alas, the *Holiday*'s sea trials were problematic and she quickly took on a severe list, causing some loose fittings to roll overboard. The problem was that, much as with the *Sea Venture* and *Island Venture* just over a decade previously, her interior fit-out included too many overly heavy items, including real brick walls in the pizzeria and marble floor slabs in the internal promenade. Aalborg Værft's supervisory staff, who should have vetoed their installation, apparently lost control over how many extra tons were being built into her upper superstructure. The only solution was to retrofit sponson fins to her stern in order to provide additional buoyancy – a costly modification that also meant that she could not quite attain her contractual maximum speed.[176] The outcome was that what should have been a profitable contract for Aalborg turned into a loss-maker. Carnival, however, had already ordered two near-sisters, this time from Kockum's of Malmö in Sweden as Aalborg now lacked the resources to build any further cruise ships. Having followed the *Holiday* project's progress, Kockum's naval architects decided to lengthen the design amidships by three metres and to use a thicker grade of steel for the underwater hull plating, both measures improving stability. The *Jubilee* and *Celebration* entered service in 1987-88 and, operating regularly from Miami, all three proved very successful. Indeed, thanks to their economic propulsion and high on board revenue earning potential, it is believed that they paid for themselves in just three years.[177]

Royal Caribbean's response

Carnival's upmarket competitor, Royal Caribbean, meanwhile, further expanded its own capacity to take account of ongoing market growth. While construction work on the *Tropicale* was underway, the company had begun planning its own new cruise ship, likewise specifically optimised for the seven-day market from Miami and therefore providing an interesting comparison with Carnival's fairly conservative approach to vessel layout. Early on, it was decided that the vessel's passenger capacity should be double that of the existing *Song of Norway* in un-lengthened condition. As with Royal Caribbean's previous new buildings, the 37,584gt vessel, to be named the *Song of America*, was ordered from Wärtsilä's Helsinki shipyard in Finland.

In comparison with her older fleet mates, the *Song of America* had proportionately many more cabins but only a little extra crew accommodation. Flying the Norwegian flag (whereas the *Tropicale* was Panamanian-registered and therefore with cheaper deck and hotel crews), it was necessary for Royal Caribbean to spare expense through cost-effective manning. This and speedy turnarounds at Miami would be achieved in part through very careful attention to the arrangement of service spaces to enable the most efficient use of labour. A similar strategy was thoroughly applied to the design of catering supply infrastructure, hotel services, baggage handling, refuse disposal and bunkering. In addition, the greatest possible use was made of standardised and reliable machinery and materials. Indeed, the vessel was designed around her cabin areas and service flows, for which a significant precedent was provided by the very large Wärtsilä-built Baltic ferry the *Finnjet*, which had been completed in 1977. Shortly after, the yard had inaugurated a vast shed, covering the building dock and enabling entire vessels to be constructed with complete protection from the treacherous Nordic winter climate. Although the shed was intended primarily to allow the building of large ice-breakers, it proved particularly advantageous for building cruise ships, which had relatively delicate external finishes and deck furnishings, the installation of which was better carried out amid temperate conditions. The investment in the building dock and shed were measures which greatly helped to ensure Wärtsilä's future success in the cruise sector.[178]

The *Song of America*'s hull was 4.4 metres wider than those of Royal Caribbean's existing fleet, thereby enabling a *Finnjet*-style high-density cabin layout with inner blocks and corridors across the beam to be achieved. Furthermore, the *Finnjet*'s 'cabins forward, public rooms aft' layout was copied in the *Song of America*'s superstructure plan. Ingeniously, a four-deck-high hotel block, filling the front third of the superstructure was married to only three decks of public rooms which consequently had higher deck-heads; this solution was similar to Hapag-Lloyd's the *Europa* – though being aimed at the luxury market, the latter's passenger accommodation was of much lower density overall. The junction was between the two blocks made at the point where the forward staircase was located, each cabin deck being accessed from one of the half-landings. With a further three cabin decks in the upper hull stretching all the way to the stern, the *Song of America*'s lower berth capacity was 1,575 (as against 724 on the *Song of Norway*).

The *Finnjet*'s very short two-hour turnarounds showed how the rationalisation of work-flows could result in substantial savings of time and manpower.[179] As with the *Finnjet*, the *Song of America*'s layout was structured around two vertical service cores for the vertical movement of luggage, catering supplies, hotel stores and garbage, connected by a wide linking fore-to-aft passage on Deck 2, where supplies were embarked and waste removed through side hatches. As superstructure cabins were located towards the bow, the forward service core dealt mainly with hotel supplies and the laundry was located at its base.

So far as propulsion was concerned, Wärtsilä's favoured arrangement of four medium-speed Sulzer engines was perpetuated, albeit using four-stroke, rather than two-stroke units to give better variable-speed control to optimise fuel economy during overnight legs of variable length between ports. The auxiliary engines burned the same heavy fuel as the main ones which greatly simplified bunkering operations.

Where the *Song of America*'s design approach differed greatly from Wärtsilä-built ferries of the era in terms of aesthetics, the fore-square silhouettes of the *Finnjet*, *Viking Song* and *Viking Saga*, *Silvia Regina* and *Finlandia* showed clear icebreaker parentage; a great deal of effort was expended to make the *Song of America* appear elegant and futuristic. As with the earlier *Song of Norway*-class, the Norwegian architect Geir Grung was employed to 'style' the vessel's exterior, while her interiors were by the Danish interior designer Mogens Hammer, who worked in concert with two experienced Norwegian specialists, Njål Eide and Finn Nilsson.[180]

Grung's interventions to re-shape the funnel, the glass screens around the lido deck and the forward superstructure were highly effective both functionally and aesthetically.[181] His design for the Viking Crown Lounge entirely surrounded the funnel casing, its forward and aft-ward projections being echoed in the shapes of the overhanging glass-enclosed lido area, tiered after decks and bridge wings. At the superstructure's forward end, Grung added observation decks, the angular, slanting forms of which were further emphasised by a wide blue band around the upper hull which widened aft of the cabin block to surround two decks of public room windows, making the vessel appear longer and lower than she actually was. The angles of this band matched the other design elements, creating a striking, yet harmonious overall effect. Consequently, the *Song of America* appeared to be big, impressive and thoroughly up-to-date.[182]

In thinking through the economic arguments for building the *Song of America*, Royal Caribbean's and Wärtsilä's managements realised that she would most likely attain a peak of profitability when approximately twenty years old and thus fully written down as an asset. Thus, her passenger facilities would need to anticipate as best possible market conditions in the early-2000s. The Scandinavian interior designers employed by Royal Caribbean decided to use the latest American hotel-resorts as their favoured design precedent.[183] With a view to the future, they attempted to avoid selecting anything that would date obviously and quickly with the result that the *Song of America*'s public rooms, while undoubtedly spacious and well-finished, were nonetheless for the most part rather blandly pastel-shaded. In line with the emerging design taste of the period, a great deal of smoke-tinted glass, polished metal railings and indirect lighting were employed throughout. The greater ceiling height of the public rooms – achieved by having each deck's height equivalent to one-and-a-half cabin decks – enabled bold ceiling treatments to be used, particularly by Njål Eide in the aft-located Oklahoma Lounge and the Guys and Dolls nightclub, which was amidships. Finn Nilsson's entrance lobby and dining rooms were less memorable in this regard.

Upon entering service in November 1982, the *Song of America* fully lived up to Royal Caribbean's expectations. Though

90 | Cruise Ships: A Design History

The exterior treatment of Royal Caribbean's *Song of America* was notably successful, her extruded forward superstructure decks, white and blue paintwork and futuristic funnel design cleverly disguising what could otherwise have appeared as a harshly rectilinear composition. Inboard, the vessel featured a wide variety of sleek public rooms, the Viking Crown Lounge in her funnel (centre left) and her 'Can Can' show lounge (centre right) being notable spaces. Topsides, her extensive lido area was carpeted in Astroturf (bottom right).

considerably smaller than her nearest rival, Norwegian Caribbean Line's converted steam turbine ocean liner the *Norway*, she was – as expected – much more economical to operate. Within only a short time, Royal Caribbean was planning cruise ships based on the Song of America's design formula, but even bigger than Norway. What Royal Caribbean and Wärtsilä failed to predict, however, was the speed with which cruise ship standard cabin sizes and layouts would transform from high-density overnight ferry-derived spaces of minimal dimensions (intended also to force occupants to spend as much of their time in public space, spending money) to much bigger hotel-like staterooms, many with private balconies. In this regard, the *Song of America* eventually fell short of American market expectations and so in 1999 she was sold to the British package holiday provider Airtours to become an entry-level vessel, rather than the upper mid-market one she was originally intended to be.

New cruise ships for other operators

Of the half-dozen significant new cruise ships of the early-1980s for the American market, the *Song of America* was the most advanced in terms of layout, propulsion and external design aesthetics. The others, by contrast, all demonstrated similarly retrogressive design characteristics to Carnival's *Tropicale*. This was unsurprising as operators looked to mix design characteristics that were known to have worked well on their existing converted liner tonnage with up-to-date construction techniques and some new features, suitable for the coming era. Diverse examples of this approach were Home Lines' 35,123gt, 1278-passenger the *Atlantic* of 1982, Holland America Cruises' 33,930gt, 1214-passenger the *Nieuw Amsterdam* and *Noordam* of 1983-1984, and Sitmar's 46,087gt, 1,600-passenger the *Fairsky* of 1984. All four were ordered from shipyards in France, thereby benefitting from the state's support of shipbuilding. The *Atlantic* and *Fairsky* were constructed at La Seyne on the Mediterranean coast, respectively by Constructions Navales et Industrielles de la Méditerrannée (CNIM) and by Chantiers du Nord et de la Méditerranée, while the two Holland America vessels came from Chantiers de l'Atlantique at St Nazaire. A famous builder of some of France's greatest passenger liners, this yard now sought to become a leading cruise ship builder.

The *Atlantic*'s design was developed in-house by Home Lines' technical staff, working in consort with her builder, and very obviously developed from that of the company's existing vessels, the highly successful *Oceanic*, dating from the mid-1960s and her smaller, second-hand fleet mate, the *Doric* (which had originally been the Israeli trans-Atlantic liner the *Shalom*). A further influence was the new generation of Scandinavian cruise ferries – which were being built concurrently according to so-called 'large block principle' design where the superstructure was both considerably taller and more extensive than on any previous passenger ships, the idea being to maximise the internal deck area (and therefore profit potential). The *Atlantic* turned out as a curious – and not entirely successful – hybrid of these influences. The hull form was very similar to that of the *Oceanic* and, most unusually for a cruise ship of her era, retained her spoon-shaped stern in favour of the more common transom variety. In terms of internal layout, the *Doric*'s design was the major influence.

So far as overall dimensions were concerned, however, the *Atlantic* was actually much more similar to Carnival's the *Tropicale*, being relatively short and tall with straight lines and a stubby bow, more resembling a ferry than a traditional liner. As the vessel was intended for year-round cruising from New York, the lifeboat deck was enclosed to form a promenade – much like on the *Oceanic*. Amidships between the promenades, the *Atlantic* had an *Oceanic*-style lido area with a 'magradome' retractable roof. Alas, due to an infelicitous combination of the lifeboats being atop the superstructure, rather than being 'nested' lower down, coupled with the topsides' greater height, the *Atlantic*'s mid-ships section appeared as a featureless, slab-sided box. Worse still, her combination of slender lines, thin shell plating and a high superstructure raised her centre of gravity, meaning that she had a tendency to pitch and corkscrew even in relatively slight seas. (Many subsequent cruise ships overcame the problem by adopting fuller hull forms to increase their displacement, thereby lowering the centre of gravity with a positive impact on overall stability.)

Inboard, the *Atlantic* was the work of five different interior design consultancies. The Italian Studio DeJorio – which subsequently came to specialise in cruise ships – drew up the Atlantic Lounge and the dining room (as on the *Oceanic*, this was located down in the hull), Ennio Cantu designed the main entrance, Observation Lounge and bar and domed pool area and Studio Bertolotii drew up the cabins and shopping arcade. The Swiss-based Groupe 3 produced the Hamilton Bar and Bermuda Lounge, disco, cinema, the aft outside pool area and the lido bar. These spaces reflected the era's tendency towards bright colours and shiny metal finishes, there being also an extensive usage of Murano glass fixtures. A combination of too many talents being involved and the relative crudity of the prefabricated wall and ceiling finishes available at that time meant that the *Atlantic*'s interiors very obviously lacked the *Oceanic*'s level of craftsmanship and coordination. Overall, the vessel appears to have divided opinion between those passengers who appreciated her newness, relatively large cabins and up-to-date comforts and those who considered her as significantly retrograde in terms of space and style when compared with her older fleet mate.[184] Although twin-engine diesel propulsion and a relatively efficient layout made the *Atlantic* much cheaper to operate, her ungainly appearance and reputation for poor sea-keeping also failed to win many admirers. She did, however, represent an interesting early attempt at designing a new generation of cruise ship for the 1980s. By the end of the decade, she had been sold out of the fleet for further use in the relatively calm seas between Florida and the Bahamas, where she appears to have found much

Below: By contrast, the exterior of Home Lines' *Atlantic* was slab-sided and with few positive distinguishing features. The vessel also suffered from having too high a centre of gravity, meaning that her sea-keeping was not very good.

greater acceptance.[185]

The *Nieuw Amsterdam* and *Noordam*, by contrast, proved immediate and enduring successes for Holland America Cruises. With regard to the size, style and scope of passenger facilities, these vessels' overall design approach was in large part influenced by the company's 1959-built *Rotterdam*, which continued to be regarded as the company's flagship liner, and also partly from lessons learned at a smaller scale on the *Prinsendam* of 1973 (which most unfortunately had been destroyed by fire in 1980 while cruising in Alaska, though all 520 passengers and crew were rescued).[186] A third significant design influence came from the shipbuilder Chantiers de l'Atlantique, which had gained knowledge of efficient construction techniques through their building of large oil tankers; during the 1970s, these had become the yard's speciality. In this period, very substantial investments had been made in new infrastructure with fabrication shops erected in which large tanker hull sections could be built. The *Nieuw Amsterdam* and *Noordam*'s hull design, therefore, was developed to enable construction from a series of large pre-fabricated sections, each weighing up to 680 tons. To cut building costs further, curved plates were avoided wherever possible and so the transom stern configuration was formed as a series of flat planes. At the bow, a knuckle-joint added rigidity, but its presence allegedly caused some consternation in Holland America's marketing department, which would have preferred uninterrupted expanses of smooth plating for aesthetic reasons. At least in profile the bow had an exaggerated 'clipper' shape and, for publicity photographs, the knuckle could always be air-brushed out.[187]

Apart from the fact that the vessels' public rooms filled the full length of the superstructure on Main Deck, the overall layout had many similarities to that of Hapag-Lloyd's recent the *Europa*, the catering facilities and service provision being aft-located with a majority of cabins in the forward hull and superstructure sections. Also similar was the observation lounge above the bridge – yet there was no mid-ships lido, nearly all of the sun deck space being located towards the stern. This latter approach was similar to most of the existing Holland America cruise fleet. From the *Rotterdam* came the idea of having a double-level lounge-cum-ballroom, the lower part of which filled Main Deck amidships with the balcony level on Boat Deck, above. The new vessels had none of the *Rotterdam*'s sweeping curves, however, as these would have been too costly to replicate, even in the public rooms. Instead, many of the spaces (and, indeed, the aft end of vessels' fantails, were distinguished by the repeated use of 45-degree angles, giving rise to hexagon- and trapezium-shaped spaces. Throughout the interiors, the muted colour palette also was reminiscent of the *Europa*; neutral brown and grey tones were chosen by the interior designers De Vlaming, Fennis, Dingemans of Utrecht to act as a backdrop for collections of Dutch colonial antiquities which were displayed in vitrines strategically placed throughout the passenger accommodation.[188] On the *Nieuw Amsterdam*, these items told the story of the Dutch West India Company, while on the *Noordam*, they related to early Dutch settlement of North America. This approach won acclaim from regular passengers and from the shipping industry press as it appealed greatly to travellers who considered themselves as more educated and discriminating than those of other cruise operators. Through being surrounded by 'exhibitions' of museum-quality antiques, they apparently felt flattered and gratified that their feelings of higher status had been acknowledged and catered to.

Although the internal finishes of bulkheads and ceilings were mostly identical to those used on less 'exclusive' ship types of the same era, such as European overnight ferries and the more mass market cruise ships, Holland America sought to engender a sense of grandeur by paying closer attention to memorable details – for example, by serving food on Rosenthal china, rather than the generic robust-looking flatware typical of the 'mainstream' hospitality trade, thereby linking one esteemed Dutch brand with another. Such precise attention to the material culture of the shipboard experience arguably has a major impact in forming and re-enforcing passengers' perceptions of a cruise's level of quality. It also involved an increasing emphasis on the fetishisation of minor differences, rather than on architectural qualities of spatial arrangement and level of finish. As the economic and safety cases for outfitting even supposedly 'luxurious' vessels with generic regulatory-approved materials were overwhelming, however, increasingly the upper end of the cruise market would henceforth emulate Holland America's approach.

Sitmar's the *Fairsky* may have been among the largest and most capacious of the early-1980s generation of cruise ships – but she was also arguably the most conservative in terms of design, being essentially an updating of the company's existing mid-1950s vintage the *Fairsea* and *Fairwind*, albeit with straight hull lines, a transom stern and a short, pointed bow, similar to that of Home Lines' the *Atlantic*. Fortunately, lessons were learned from the *Atlantic*'s stability problems

Above: Sitmar's *Fairsky* combined traditional and relatively fuel-hungry steam turbine propulsion with passenger accommodation that fused together recent Italian approaches to ship interiors and an up-to-date Californian hotel aesthetic. Here, we see one of the vessel's dining rooms (centre) and her piano lounge (above).

and so the *Fairsky*'s massing was more similar to that of the *Nieuw Amsterdam* and *Noordam*, with wide Boat Deck promenades directly above Main Deck. Whereas Carnival initially considered, then rejected, the possibility of steam propulsion for the *Tropicale*, Sitmar actually installed a turbine plant so that the crews of all three of their vessels were interchangeable. Inboard, the *Fairsky* shared the older Sitmar cruise ships' overall layout with numerous relatively small public rooms, outfitted to designs by a variety of architects and interior designers. They were Dennis Lennon, famous for having in the past co-ordinated the *QE2* interiors, Giacomo Mortola of Genoa and Claes Olof Lindqvist of Helsinki. Barbara Dorn of San Francisco was selected to produce designs for the cabins and suites, the idea being that these should have particular appeal to Sitmar's predominant American passenger demographic.[189] The outcome of involving such varied talents was a considerable variety of atmosphere from one space to the next, albeit within a vaguely modernist design framework. The overall effect was, however, much calmer and better coordinated than on the *Atlantic* – indeed, if anything, the *Fairsky* was criticised for being too hard-edged by cruise critics and passengers who had become used to the softly upholstered and carpeted hotel-like expanses of Royal Caribbean. Instead, the *Fairsky*'s décor more closely resembled that of an ocean liner of the 1950s-60s period than it did any other contemporary cruise ship.[190]

Nonetheless, Sitmar found the *Fairsky* to be highly popular, with cruise after cruise fully booked. Unfortunately, later on, her boilers and turbines proved her undoing due to their greater fuel and maintenance costs. Consequently, her career was rather short in comparison with the other cruise ships of her generation (after four years in lay-up, she was scrapped in 2013).

While most of the new cruise ships built in the early 1980s were broadly successful, albeit with aspects that could have benefitted from greater design development, only one was an outright failure. In the late-1970s, the Danish ferry and liner operator DFDS (Det Forenede Dampskibs-Selskab) was persuaded by New York Port Authority executives and American cruise entrepreneurs – led by Bruce Neirenberg (previously of Norwegian Caribbean Lines) – to introduce a coastal cruise-ferry service between New York and Florida, the idea being to transport American holidaymakers and their cars in cruise-style comfort.[191] DFDS established a new subsidiary named Scandinavian World Cruises and commissioned the building of a very large and well-appointed vessel, the design of which was derived from recent Scandinavian overnight ferry tonnage. To an even greater degree than Home Lines' the *Atlantic*, such vessels were designed using what ferry naval architects referred to as a 'large block principle' to maximise the amount of regularly-shaped vehicle deck space and superstructure, thereby ensuring the maximum payload – indeed, the superstructure extended fully aft above the stern mooring deck.[192]

Built by the Dubigeon Normandie shipyard at Nantes in France, the 26,747gt, 1,606-passenger the *Scandinavia* was well-appointed internally, having a 'cabins forward, public rooms aft' layout; this was similar to other contemporary ferries and the West German cruise ships the *Berlin* and *Europa*. Her upper superstructure layout, however, resembled that of Home Lines' the *Oceanic* with a lido area extending above recessed lifeboats and enclosed by a magradome. The *Scandinavia*'s undoing was her excessively bluff hull configuration, which would not have mattered on a Baltic ferry route but which proved hopelessly inadequate for the stormy waters of Cape Hatteras, across which she traversed on every voyage. Another problem was that DFDS had failed to realise that the Jones Act of 1920, which had been intended to encourage the development of the US merchant marine and shipbuilding capacity by protecting domestic trade from competition from foreign vessels, would prevent a direct New York-Miami service by this French-built, Bahamian registered vessel. Instead, the route would need to terminate at Freeport in the Bahamas with feeder services by different ferries from there to Florida ports.

The *Scandinavia* entered service in the autumn of 1982 and, over the next year lost so much money that her operation nearly bankrupted DFDS. Too few Americans were persuaded to cruise from New York via the Bahamas to Florida when a cheap jet flight would take them there in a couple of hours. In addition, stormy winter weather stove in the bow plating and caused other structural damage. After just over a year of delayed sailings and poor loadings, DFDS withdrew the *Scandinavia* and she was brought back to Europe for ferry service between Copenhagen and Oslo. Because the vessel's hotel services had been designed to provide a cruise-style service, this was not very successful there either because she needed many more crew than was typical of an overnight ferry. Subsequently, she returned to the USA where, for subsequent owners, she found success cruising to Alaska as Sundance Cruises' the *Stardancer* and, later still, in the Mediterranean as the budget cruise ship the *Island Escape*. Her initial difficulties showed the dangers for cruise entrepreneurs of a poorly thought through concept coupled with an unsuitable ship design.

Above: Holland America's *Nieuw Amsterdam* had a low boat deck, much like the *Fairsky*, but her very spacious interiors were rather muted in colouration, relying on vitrines containing displays of antiquities for their effects. Above, we see her dining room in which the quality of the tableware and cuisine were emphasised.

Below: The Danish-owned cruise ferry *Scandinavia* had a bluff hull form similar to those of recent overnight Baltic ferries. Unsurprisingly, the design proved unsuitable for year-round operation through the rough seas off New York.

P&O Princess Cruises' *Royal Princess* was arguably the outstanding cruise ship of her generation. Her combination of nested lifeboats and cabins with balconies on the decks above was widely emulated in numerous subsequent designs. The vessel's pastel-shaded 'Californian modern' interiors were highly reflective of the ideal to which most cruise operators attracting American passengers at that time aspired.

Chapter 11
The Wärtsilä concept ships and their derivations

The greater hull-width of the early-1980s generation of cruise ships meant that the centres of public room decks inevitably felt more isolated from the sea than those of their late-1960s/early-1970s precursors. This, however, gave greater opportunities to increase shipboard revenues by surrounding passengers with shops, cocktail bars and casinos. As the Finnish naval architect Kai Levander – who ran the Project Department at Wärtsilä's Helsinki shipyard – observed in a 1982 paper delivered to fellow passenger shipping professionals in Athens: persuading each passenger to spend an extra $5 every day on board would increase a cruise ship's profitability more than saving ten per cent in bunker costs.[193] Most unusually for a naval architect, Levander's expertise in ferry and cruise ship design development and engineering was paralleled by a sociological interest, which enabled him to analyse cruise market trends in great detail and to produce sound economic arguments to underpin his design ideas.

In order to stimulate demand for new cruise ship and ferry orders during the fallow years of the latter-1970s Levander had overseen the development of a wide variety of futuristic 'concept ships.' He had realised that radical new thinking would be needed to meet the greater expectations of the 'baby boom' generation who would form the bulk of ferry and cruise passengers from the latter-1980s until the new millennium. Being used to shopping mall environments and regular overseas holidays, they would expect a higher degree of physical comfort and broader ranges of facilities and entertainments than the generation whose formative experiences were during the deprivations of the war years and post-war rationing. In addition to addressing changes in the 'mainstream' cruise market, there would also be opportunities for smaller, specialised cruise ships to target particular niches.[194]

Levander was inspired in large part by documentation he had read pertaining to a Massachusetts Institute of Technology course in Creative Engineering which emphasised four vital research areas for engineers designing for consumer markets. These were:

- Increase of function: how can a product be made to do more things?
- Increase in performance level: how can a product be given a longer life-span and also be made safer, more reliable and easier to repair?
- Lowering of costs: how can excess parts be eliminated and cheaper materials be introduced, while reducing the need for manual labour, or using full automation?
- Increase in saleability: how can we improve a product's appearance, or package it more attractively and sell it more effectively?

Levander's design team at Wärtsilä's Project Department in Helsinki consisted of Pirjo Harsia, Ilkka Penttinen, Birger Trygge and Jan Kingo. Together, they devised five different concepts for future passenger ship types. One was an 'All Outside Cabin' (AOC) cruise liner, adaptable for capacities of between 500 and 1,500 passengers. Another was 'Ferry 85', a large jumbo ferry type with a huge superstructure filled with cabins and retail space, overhanging the hull at the bow. A third was a broad, twin-hulled cruise ship, referred to as a 'Small Water plane Area Twin Hull' (or 'SWATH') vessel, the wide decks enabling new and more expressive architectural possibilities. The fourth was a 'Yacht Cruiser' for around 120 passengers with a shallow draft to enable visits to 'exotic' destinations off the beaten tracks of other bigger cruise ships. The fifth was a variation on the Yacht Cruiser concept known as a 'Wind-cruiser'; this would use hybrid diesel and sail propulsion to conjure up a romantic image while also saving fuel.[195]

Levander's team apparently did not originate all of these ideas in-house; the Finnish industrial designer and former Wärtsilä employee Heikki Sorvali claims to have first devised the SWATH catamaran cruise ship idea.[196] Furthermore, several notable passenger ships of the inter-war era – such as the French trans-Atlantic liner the *L'Atlantique* of 1931, the German Kraft durch Freude cruise ship the *Robert Ley* and the Swedish American Line trans-Atlantic liner and cruise ship the *Stockholm*, both of which were completed in 1939, had solely outside cabins 40 years before Wärtsilä's naval architects supposedly 'invented' the concept. Be that as it may, Levander's approach proved effective as a means of engaging with and even of 'wowing' potential Wärtsilä customers who were disinterested in the origins of the ideas being presented, though keenly engaged by what appeared to be money-spinning opportunities.

Of these five design concepts, the 'All Outside Cabin' solution was one of the more immediately marketable for the simple reason that a cabin with a window could be sold for around 25 per cent more than an inside room.[197] Whereas existing cruise ships typically had cabins in their hulls with public rooms above, Wärtsilä's concept inverted this, enabling the full with of the hull to be used for revenue-generating public rooms, with a narrower cabin block forming the superstructure above with lifeboats stowed outboard. This would contain cabins of uniformly rectilinear shape and in a limited range of standard sizes. Inboard were parallel cabin corridors on either side of a service core running the length of the vessel's centre-line, containing vertical circulation, storage and servicing – including the air conditioning plant. The idea of a cabin block growing out of a bigger hull was not new either, it having first been proposed by the Danish naval architect Tage Wandborg of Knud E. Hansen A/S for 'Project Phoenix' which was a concept design for a vast 250,000gt vessel featuring four 'skyscrapers' containing hotel-like staterooms, initially devised for Norwegian Caribbean Line in the early-1980s but never built due to a lack of funding.

Cruise Ships: A Design History

Above: The Japanese-owned and -built *Crystal Harmony* (top), which was aimed largely at a wealthy American clientele, copied features of the *Royal Princess*' layout. Later on, Crystal Cruises ordered from Finland the *Crystal Symphony* (right), pictured at Cape Town, as a fleet mate. Another new Japanese-owned cruise ship of the era was the *Nippon Maru*, which was aimed at the Japanese market.

One potential client for Wärtsilä's 'All Outside Cabin' cruise ship was the British shipping and property conglomerate P&O's American-headquartered subsidiary, Princess Cruises. Its existing three-strong fleet, comprising the *Pacific Princess*, *Island Princess* and *Sun Princess*, was already highly regarded and very profitable and so a new cruise liner, more than twice their size, would be a lucrative investment. So intrigued were P&O's directors by Levander's economic arguments in favour of an AOC design that a contract was signed for a 1,200-passenger, approximately 45,000gt vessel to be named the *Royal Princess* with delivery scheduled for October 1984. Wärtsilä agreed not to reveal any details of the project – indeed, renderings of a much more conventional 'decoy' design were released to the press, revealing none of the new ship's special features.[198]

P&O's in-house naval architecture subsidiary, Three Quays, worked closely with Wärtsilä on the *Royal Princess*' design. P&O also employed Knud E. Hansen A/S to assist with this work. Her provisions handling arrangements were derived from the *Song of America*'s successful precedent. To style the exterior, P&O hired the Norwegian cruise ship specialist Njål Eide, who replicated the *Song of America*'s forward-projecting observation decks; on the *Royal Princess* these successfully disguised the fact that the cabin decks would otherwise have appeared as a severely rectilinear block.[199] The external detailing referenced emergent 'high tech' trends in public and commercial architecture ashore. The prominent placement of lifesaving equipment possibly reflected the fitting of services on the exteriors of Renzo Piano and Richard Rodgers' Centre Georges Pompidou in Paris and on Rodgers' forthcoming Lloyd's building in London. The use of steel slats to form the funnel casing with an extruded steel tube forming its summit further developed this language.

To achieve an 'All Outside Cabin' solution, even with a narrowed superstructure, the cabins would inevitably be thin and deep. Upon closer analysis and after discussions about what American cruise passengers would tolerate, P&O decided that Wärtsilä's 2.45-metre-wide spacing was too little to allow comfortable free movement and so a more commodious 2.52-metre standard was finally agreed. As the uppermost two cabin decks were to have balconies projecting over the lifeboats, the greater width would enable space for a sliding door to be accessed between two single beds.[200] A great deal of intensive design work was carried out to optimise the cabin and public room arrangements while tank tests in Copenhagen and Trondheim helped to refine the hull lines for maximum efficiency at the vessel's required 18-knot service speed (her maximum was 22 knots). Although four medium-speed Sulzer diesel engines were installed, under normal operational conditions, only two of these would be in operation, giving excellent fuel economy.

A lightweight construction with shallow frames economised on weight in the *Royal Princess*'s superstructure, the lowered stowage positions of the lifeboats also helping in this regard. To save additional weight, Wärtsilä chose lightweight, fireproof panels for cabin partitions.[201] As the public rooms were to be in the hull's upper deck, immediately below the strength deck, the need for large window openings threatened to bring about structural problems as only every fourth frame was uninterrupted. The solution was to use steel plating of high-ductility in the critical areas of the upper hull and lower superstructure for added resilience and flexibility.[202]

Njål Eide was also involved in co-ordinating the interior design, although the schemes for the cabins and public rooms were largely devised by the Los Angeles-based firm of Hirsch-Bender, who had no prior shipboard experience but who could authentically create the style of a Californian hotel resort; this would appeal to the American passengers P&O hoped to attract in large numbers. As with the *Song of America*, the *Royal Princess*'s interiors used mainly pastel shades, offset with tinted glass and shiny metallic details. Her circular three-deck-high lobby was notably impressive; P&O had in fact wanted it to fill the entire height of the superstructure, but were thwarted by the United States Coastguard's stringent fire-containment regulations. The main public room deck featured a one-deck-high show lounge towards the bow – subsequently a standard location for such a feature on cruise ships – with a nightclub at the stern and a casino, boutiques, card room, photo gallery and cinema between. The main restaurant was amidships on the deck below, supplied from a large galley immediately adjacent. Atop the superstructure was an extensive lido area with a buffet restaurant nearby. Around the base of the funnel was a cocktail lounge, reminiscent of the elevated 'Viking Crown' lounges on Royal Caribbean vessels, albeit much bigger as it filled the whole width of the ship, slightly overhanging the superstructure on either beam.[203]

P&O had great hopes for the *Royal Princess* and from the outset she more than lived up to them. HRH Princess Diana named the vessel in Southampton in November 1984. Thanks to the glamorous young royal, who was becoming a global media superstar, the naming ceremony attracted worldwide attention. The maiden voyage was trans-Atlantic to the Panama Canal and this sold out in only three hours. P&O had options to build two further vessels based on the *Royal Princess*' design but, due to the need to fight off a hostile take-over attempt by another British conglomerate, Trafalgar House Plc, which at that time owned Cunard, the opportunity further to expand the Princess Cruises fleet was wasted.

In February 1984, *The Times* newspaper provided an insight was given into the economics underpinning the design and operation of the *Royal Princess*:

> '…Though P&O cruising had been consistently profitable, the profits were never big enough it seemed until 1982 to justify the massive cost of a big new cruise ship like the *Royal Princess*. Capital costs alone, at more than £100 million, require earnings of about £60,000 a day to service; and operating costs – pay for 600 staff, fuel, repairs, maintenance, insurance, food and drink, port charges, etc – come to substantially more. What this adds up to is a charge of around £200 a day per passenger to make a viable proposition… Some 20 million people in the US can afford to pay those kind of prices for a holiday, of whom some four million are ready and willing to do so on a Princess cruise… provided *Royal Princess* offers what the Americans want…'[204]

The *Royal Princess* was arguably the most innovative and influential cruise ship of her era. Indeed, elements of her design were subsequently perpetuated in several other vessels built by Wärtsilä and its successors and elsewhere in the world. The most faithful copy was the 48,621gt *Crystal Harmony* of 1989, designed by Knud E. Hansen A/S and built by Mitsubishi Heavy Industries in Nagasaki, Japan for Crystal Cruises, a newly established upmarket cruise subsidiary of the

Above: The Japanese *Asuka* (top) was, like the *Nippon Maru*, aimed at the Japanese cruise market. As with the Crystal Harmony, her design showed considerable similarities to the *Royal Princess*. The Saudi and Iraqi royal and presidential yachts *Abdul Aziz* and *Al Mansur* (centre) provided design precedents for the 'Yacht Cruiser' concept, of which the *Sea Goddess I* (bottom) and *Sea Goddess II* were the first examples.

famous and long-established Japanese shipping company, Nippon Yusen Kaisha (NYK). Although Japanese-owned, Crystal was aimed mainly at the upper end of the American cruise market and so the Swedish-based cruise ship interiors specialist Tillberg Design was used to provide a post-modern design aesthetic of marble slabs, Tiffany glass and neo-classical pilasters suitable for this clientele. Indeed, the only overtly Japanese influence to be found was a small sushi restaurant.

Alas, the *Crystal Harmony* was to prove controversial as, during the design development for the *Royal Princess*, Wärtsilä had patented in the USA certain construction details relating to the 'All Outside Cabin' layout. Neither Knud E. Hansen A/S nor NYK were aware of this, but Wärtsilä's lawyers informed them that if the *Crystal Harmony* berthed in a US port, NYK might be sued for infringement. As Knud E. Hansen A/S had been heavily involved in the *Royal Princess*' realisation and as there was a tradition in naval architecture of sharing good ideas, this came as a nasty surprise, particularly for the Japanese ship owner, who may have feared a loss of face. For its next new building, the broadly similar though slightly larger 51,044gt *Crystal Symphony*, delivered in 1995, Crystal Cruises ordered from the former-Wärtsilä, by then renamed Kværner Masa Yards, and this solution removed any threat of legal action to the satisfaction of all concerned.[205]

Prosperous Japan itself had a growing cruise market and an ageing, yet wealthy clientele keen on exploring the wider world from the safety and comfort of a comfortable 'piece of Japan' at sea. Thus, Nippon Yusen Kaisha ordered from Mitsubishi a broadly similar, though smaller cruise ship, the 28,717gt, 584-passenger *Asuka*, for delivery in 1991 to serve this market. Inboard were cabins with tatami mats, communal 'onsen' baths and other uniquely Japanese design features. The *Asuka* was just one of several new cruise ships for the Japanese market to appear around this point; others were Japan Cruise Line's 21,884gt 606-passenger the *Orient Venus*, delivered in 1990 by Ishikawajima-Harima Heavy Industries of Tokyo, and Mitsui O.S.K. Line's 23,340gt, 603-passenger the *Fuji Maru* and 22,472gt, 607-passenger the *Nippon Maru*, completed in 1989 and 1990 respectively by Mitsubishi Heavy Industries' Kobe shipyard. Each of these vessels was based to an extent on Japanese ferry design precedents developed by the same shipyard drawing offices.

Back in 1980s Finland, in addition to Wärtsilä's 'All Outside Cabin' concept coming to fruition with the building of the *Royal Princess*, so too did its 'Yacht Cruiser' proposal. As we have seen above, the first ever purpose-designed cruise ship, Hamburg-Amerika's the *Prinzessin Victoria Luise* of 1890, was in essence a very large steam yacht for the pleasure of a very wealthy and exclusive fare-paying clientele. During boom periods in the western world, further conceptually similar vessels were constructed in the years before the outbreak of the First World War and again in the latter-1920s. The 1980s – with its great growth in the financial services sector – appeared to be giving rise to a new wave of *nouveau riche*, enough of whom would enjoy experiences akin to those first offered by Hamburg-Amerika to make viable a new generation of 'Yacht Cruiser.'

Design inspiration came from a number of royal and state yachts built in Denmark and Finland in the early-1980s for the ruling families of the oil rich Gulf states of Iraq and Saudi Arabia. The Helsingør shipyard in Denmark built the 2,200gt *Qidissiyat Al Saddam* for use by the Iraqi president, Saddam Hussein, to cruise on the Euphrates.[206] Subsequently, the same yard delivered the *Abdul Aziz* to the Saudi royal family. Next, a second, much larger Iraqi yacht, the *Al Mansur*, was built by the Wärtsilä shipyard in Turku for ocean-going use and with a capacity of no fewer than 300 passengers.[207]

In his 1982 presentation in Athens on 'Increased Productivity for Passenger Ships', Kai Levander explained the logic underpinning Wärtsilä's 'Yacht Cruiser' concept:

> 'The cruise market today shows a very evident gap and demand for high-class cruise vessels for 50 to 200 passengers. Some people find the existing bigger cruise liners too crowded or the ports visited uninteresting and spoiled by excessive touristic exploitation. On the other hand, the yachts that can be chartered and taken to unspoiled islands do not offer the comfort, service and safety that many passengers wish to have. Today, there is great interest in both sailing and motor cruise liners to fill this gap between the big and the small… The profitability depends on the economy of scale. For a small vessel, this means that it has to be special or attractive in some distinctive way to justify the higher ticket prices… A small ship must offer the 'consumer' something he or she wants and cannot get on a bigger ship.'[208]

This sales pitch greatly interested a former Norwegian Caribbean Line executive, Helge Naarstad, who, like Levander, believed there was a market niche for cruise ships offering greater exclusivity than those of existing upmarket operators, such as Cunard or Royal Viking Line. In particular, Naarstad wished to target affluent people who were not attracted by

Above: Inboard, the Sea Goddesses were designed by Yran & Storbraaten of Oslo, who produced pastel-shaded, hotel-like designs for the cabins and public rooms.

these operators' rather conservative shipboard atmospheres, which were mainly attractive to experienced repeat passengers.[209] Naarstad therefore founded a new ship-owning company, Kommanditselskabet A/S Norske Cruise, which ordered a pair of 4,253gt, 121-passenger 'Yacht Cruisers' from Wärtsilä in May 1982. Finance was raised from 500 private individuals, each shareholder being promised a 20% discount on all cruises. The contract price for the ships was circa 34 million US dollars a-piece.

Design work was carried out jointly by Wärtsilä's own staff and Knud E. Hansen A/S with considerable input coming from an up-and-coming Norwegian architect, Petter Yran, a former KEH employee who had earlier on worked on NCL's unrealised 'Phoenix World City' project.[210] The design that emerged showed considerable similarities both to the Iraqi presidential yachts, for which Knud E. Hansen A/S had produced drawings, and the *Abdul Aziz*. From the *Al-Mansur* the idea of placing the lifeboats aft of amidships was perpetuated, thereby enabling the superstructure's forward two-thirds to be given over entirely to 61 commodious outside staterooms – including an owner's suite and two single cabins. The *Al-Mansur* also provided a precedent for the vessels' propulsion by four Wärtsilä-Vasa vee-diesels, geared to twin shafts.

Naarstad's operation was marketed as Sea Goddess Cruises and the two ships were named the *Sea Goddess I* and *Sea Goddess II*. The 'Sea Goddesses' would visit small islands and 'hidden' bays, where their more active passengers could enjoy scuba-diving, snorkelling and surfing. Leisurely dining on *haute cuisine* would be another attraction, the restaurant – which was located aft of amidships – being sufficiently commodious to seat all passengers at once (although an open-seating approach was actually employed to give an enhanced sense of individual freedom of choice). Unlike existing small expedition cruise ships, such as the *Linblad Explorer*, described above, on which the focus was on adventure travel, the 'Sea Goddesses' would emphasise a relaxed and luxurious lifestyle involving fine dining, casino gaming and other 'glamorous' leisure pursuits. Petter Yran designed interiors using marble slabs, tinted glass and pastel colours to achieve the desired 'exclusive' effect. His stateroom interior design for the vessels won considerable praise for its well-thought-out details, including timber inlays and shallow arches in the ceiling to suggest a separation between the sleeping and sitting areas. At a time when typical cruise fares were in the $150-250 range per person per day, the $500 rate charged by Sea Goddess Cruises placed the vessels at the apogee of the industry.

Initially, the *Sea Goddess* twins were to have been built at Wärtsilä's Helsinki yard. However, after the pair was ordered, the Helsinki yard received a lucrative contract to build a pair of car-passenger ferries and as a result the decision was made to subcontract the steel fabrication and assembly of the hull and superstructure for the *Sea Goddess I* to the Hollming shipyard in Rauma with only outfitting taking place in Helsinki.

The *Sea Goddess I* and *Sea Goddess II* entered service in 1984 and 1985 but their high capital cost coupled with expenses of marketing and day-to-day operation caused their owner to experience disappointing financial results. In 1985, the hijackings in the Mediterranean of the Italian cruise ship, the *Achille Lauro,* and a Trans World Airlines jet caused a sudden collapse of American tourism in Southern Europe, meaning that Sea Goddess Cruise Line's summer Mediterranean-based cruises ran nearly empty. Consequently, the company had such severe difficulties in staying afloat that Wärtsilä threatened to re-possess the vessels for non-payment of purchase instalments. This piqued the interest of other, better capitalised luxury-sector cruise lines, principally Cunard and Royal Viking Line, both of whom sought to acquire the Sea Goddesses. Cunard successfully negotiated a deal whereby the Midland Bank would acquire Sea Goddess Cruise Line's debt with the vessels being chartered to Cunard thereafter. During the ensuing decade, under Cunard's management, they proved quite lucrative. Indeed, in the longer term, they inspired a whole genre of similar cruise ships for further specially-established operators, principally Seabourn Cruises and Renaissance Cruises – both of which were likewise founded by Norwegians.[211]

Seabourn was the brainchild the business entrepreneur Atle Brynestad, whose plan was to build at least three enlarged 'yacht cruisers.' The 9,975gt, 212-passenger *Seabourn Pride* and *Seabourn Spirit*, which were also styled by Yran, but built by Schichau Seebeckwerft of Bremerhaven, were delivered in 1988-89.[212] One unique feature was an underwater lounge located in the lower hull, the idea being that passengers would gaze through turquoise water filled with tropical fish. In practice, alas, for much of the time only murk could be seen and as the sensation of being below the surface

Above: The subsequent 'Seabourn' sisters, such as the *Seabourn Pride* (top) were enlarged versions of the 'Yacht Cruiser' type, again involving Yran & Storbraaten as stylists. The sail-assisted *Wind Surf* (centre) was a French-built interpretation of another cruise concept originating with Wärtsilä (centre). The *Renaissance One* (above) was one of four Italian-built 'economy' versions of the 'Yacht Cruiser' concept.

Above: The *Delphin Clipper*, built by Rauma-Repola, was a variation on the 'Yacht Cruiser' concept, intended for short cruises across the Baltic Sea.

caused many to feel claustrophobic, the spaces were withdrawn from public use. Seabourn's third vessel, which should have entered service in 1990, was delayed due to a lack of capital and consequently was sold in incomplete condition to Royal Viking Line for whom she entered service in 1992 as the *Royal Viking Queen*.

Almost concurrently with the founding of Seabourn, Renaissance Cruises was established by the Oslo-based shipping company Fearnley & Eger and it placed orders with the Cantieri Navali Ferrari of La Spezia in Italy for four 4,077gt, 100-passenger Yacht Cruisers – the *Renaissance One*, *Renaissance Two*, *Renaissance Three* and *Renaissance Four* – completed in 1988-89. Subsidised construction coupled with a much simpler value-engineered design made them relatively inexpensive compared with the Sea Goddess and Seabourn examples. In addition, Renaissance's concept was to cut operational costs by keeping each vessel on the same itinerary and, while retaining the size and overall ambience of the original Yacht Cruiser concept, to make further savings by not adopting the 'all inclusive' approach favoured by other operators at the cruise industry's upper echelon.

Both Seabourn and Renaissance were, like Sea Goddess before them, unlucky in commencing operations during a downturn in demand – on this occasion brought about by a short but deep recession. Each of the companies was quickly sold to a new owner who helped them to re-capitalise – but their difficulties demonstrated the challenge of making money out of small vessels with their consequently tighter margins. Cunard, owning the Sea Goddesses, at least had the benefit of a long list of loyal repeat passengers who cruised on their other vessels and who could be encouraged also to try yacht cruising.

Perhaps inspired by the Sea Goddesses, another Finnish shipbuilder, Rauma-Repola, whose yard was adjacent to that of Hollming in Rauma, produced a Yacht Cruiser design of its own. Initially, this was intended for a Dutch company, Clipper Cruises, which wished a small cruise ship for European summer and Caribbean winter itineraries but, when an order failed to materialise, the project was offered instead to a Finnish upstart, Delfin Cruises. It planned to use the 5,709gt, 300-passenger vessel, named the *Delfin Clipper*, for 24-hour Baltic cruises to provide upmarket competition for the large ferries dominating the Finnish sea travel market to Sweden. In terms of layout, style and passenger density, however, the design nonetheless had more in common with recent ferries than with the spacious and exclusive Sea Gooddesses, Renaissance or Seabourn Yacht Cruisers. As Rauma-Repola had little work at the time, the Finnish state provided a modest subsidy. During construction, a Singapore-based company offered to buy the *Delfin Clipper* and so Delfin Cruises commissioned a second, slightly larger near-sister, the 7,560gt, 330-passenger *Delfin Caravelle*, as a replacement. Unfortunately, the plan to sell the *Delfin Clipper* fell through, leaving Delfin Cruises with insufficient funds to pay for both vessels; this situation caused the company to declare bankruptcy in December 1990 and, thereafter, the two Yacht Cruisers were chartered out by their builder before being sold.[213]

Subsequently, Rauma-Repola built a further Yacht Cruiser that was larger again, the 8,378gt, 184-passenger *Society Adventurer*. She was ordered by a German company, Discoverer Reederei of Bremen, and had a much lower passenger density than the two 'Delfins', the intention being to attract a wealthy clientele for 'adventure' cruises to remote destinations, including the Antarctic. However, like Delfin Cruises before it, Discoverer Reederei failed to secure the funds needed to take delivery as planned in 1991. Eventually, after two years, another German expedition cruise operator, Hanseatic Tours, stepped in to charter the vessel, which was renamed the *Hanseatic* and thereafter operated very successfully on world-wide itineraries.

As well as the 'All Outside Ship' and 'Yacht Cruiser' concepts, the Wärtsilä Project Department's design for a sail-assisted cruise ship also came to fruition, albeit built in France instead of Finland thanks to a government subsidy and consequently at a more favourable price. In late 1984, a new company called Windstar Sail Cruises placed an order with the Société Nouvelle des Ateliers et Chantiers du Havre for two such vessels – the *Wind Star* and *Wind Song* – paying Wärtsilä a licensing fee to use its design.[214] The sail-assisted concept was a favourite of Kai Levander – who was himself a keen yachtsman – so much so that he had a private yacht modified to demonstrate it at the scale of a very large model.[215]

Windstar Cruises belonged to the same company as ran the Circle Line excursions around Manhattan Island in New York, the head of which was a Finn from the Åland Islands, Karl Gösta Andern. He appointed the former President of Compagnie Générale Transatlantique to lead Windstar and he, in turn, chose a French architect, Marc Held from Paris, to carry out the interior design. Both Frenchmen had a great sense of high style and so, under their guidance, the sail-assisted cruise ship concept developed into a luxury vessel type with facilities akin to the Sea Goddesses, rather than the more elemental design of 'adventure' cruise ship originally imagined by Levander.[216]

The *Wind Star* and *Wind Song* were 134 metres long and equipped with four masts with triangular jib sails with a total area of just under 2,000 square metres, set and furled directly from the bridge. Like a yacht, the hull had a shallow draft and a keel to keep it from swinging away from the wind. Under sail, 12 knots could be maintained and, additionally, a diesel-electric engine was installed, driving twin propellers to enable the same speed when there was no wind. Unlike the vertical subdivision of accommodation on the Sea Goddesses, the *Wind Star* and *Wind Song* had cabins on the lower decks with public rooms above. Marc Held's interior design of the 75 staterooms (accommodating up to 150 passengers) used contemporary luxury yacht and cabin cruiser design as points of reference, using polished hardwood veneers and brass details. Similar detailing was also used in the communal spaces.[217]

The same French builder subsequently constructed a further pair of larger sail-assisted cruise ships –the 14,745gt, 453-passenger *Club Med 1* and *Club Med 2*, which entered service in 1989 and 1992 respectively. Their operator was

Above: The *Hanseatic*, another Rauma-Repola output, had a troubled start, but eventually found success as an 'adventure' cruise ship, serving the German market.

Club Med, a package holiday firm, whose beach resorts were popular with a youthful demographic, seeking a fun and informal atmosphere which the vessels' interior design sought to replicate. The 'barefoot' atmosphere, emphasising sunbathing and buffet dining without the formal trappings of traditional 'upmarket' cruise culture, was therefore closer to Kai Levander's original intention for the sail-assisted cruise concept than what was achieved on the Windstar vessels. For example, although each cabin had a private shower room, toilet cubicles were shared between adjacent rooms to save space and cut costs.[218] The proportion of public rooms was greater, however, with the nightclub-discotheque being an important space.

Just one example of Wärtsilä's Small Water plane Area Twin Hull (or 'SWATH') concept was also eventually constructed and in this instance too, the contract went elsewhere. Following Rauma-Repola's construction of the *Delfin Clipper*, *Delfin Caravelle* and *Society Advenurer*, the yard was keen to secure further cruise ship projects and so it became a partner in a new Finnish-headquartered cruise company, Diamond Cruise Oy. Headquartered in Helsinki, its other main shareholders were various Finnish finance houses and shipping companies. Minority shareholders were international – the American-headquartered Radisson Corporation, and the Japanese Mitsui OSK Lines, Nippon Life and Nippon Total Finance. Initially, Diamond Cruise had an option to build two SWATH vessels though, in the end, only one was contracted. As Radisson would market its operation, the name *Radisson Diamond* was selected.

With a 131.2 metre length and a remarkable 31.96 metre breadth, the 18,400gt vessel was more like a floating hotel resort than a conventional cruise ship. Not only did the broad, twin-hulled layout provide enough space for large staterooms accommodating 354 passengers, wide public rooms and internal atria, but it also guaranteed a high degree of stability. Power came from four Wärtsilä diesels, one eight-cylinder and one six-cylinder unit being located in each hull, giving a speed of 14 knots.

Inboard, the centrepiece was a six-deck-high central atrium, forward and aft of which were a two-deck-high main lounge and dining saloon. The front of the lounge had a double-height window arrangement, overlooking the sea (and reminiscent of similar features on several Finnish-built Baltic overnight ferries of the 1980s). The external sun decks, atop the superstructure, made effective use of the possibilities presented by the vessel's width with a series of pools and lido areas with a variety of ambiences. An intriguing feature was the inclusion of a fold-out water sports platform, stowed behind a shell access door at the stern.[219]

Launching a large catamaran such as the *Radisson Diamond* on a traditional slipway intended for conventional monohulled ships was no easy matter and, when entering the water in June 1991, one of the two bulbous bows was bashed, necessitating a dry docking to replace the crushed steelwork.[220]

Upon entering service, the *Radisson Diamond* initially generated a great deal of curiosity. The shipping industry is, however, usually averse to expensive innovations that are not strictly necessary for generating profit and, as the need to construct two narrow catamaran hulls added significantly to the vessel's cost, she was not viewed as worth emulating by other cruise operators. Furthermore, she was slow and her great width led sceptics to dismiss her as unwieldy (even although she was in fact highly manoeuvrable).[221] Above all, her unusual appearance lacked the impression of length and the all-important soaring clipper-type bow profile which gave 'normal' cruise ships a romantic impression in the minds of the public. Having unique operational characteristics and requirements necessitated crew familiarisation and so it was less easy to transfer navigating officers from one vessel to another. In the end, the *Radisson Diamond* remained one-of-a-kind and her career as a cruise ship lasted only until 2005, when she was sold to a Macau-based gaming company for conversion as a floating casino, operating from Hong Kong. Her great width and guaranteed stability made her ideal for conversion into a series of gaming rooms.

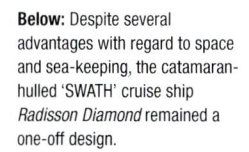

Below: Despite several advantages with regard to space and sea-keeping, the catamaran-hulled 'SWATH' cruise ship *Radisson Diamond* remained a one-off design.

Chapter 12
Expansion and consolidation

While several new cruise lines serving wealthier clienteles were formed in the 1980s, several of the bigger, more established operators, were more concerned by a need for consolidation to cut overheads and thereby achieve better economies of scale. Trafalgar House's attempted take-over of P&O in 1984 might have brought together two significant cruise fleets under a single corporate management. Although, perhaps fortunately, this particular plan was thwarted, the ensuing years nonetheless witnessed the beginnings of a process leading to the creation of a handful of giant international corporations that would eventually come to dominate the cruise industry. Back then, though, several analysts believed that the future giants would be Carnival, P&O, Cunard, Royal Caribbean and Norwegian Caribbean.

In Norway, the first moves involved the take-over by Knut Kloster's Norwegian Caribbean Line of Royal Viking Line through the purchase of the shareholdings of Det Bergenske Dampskibsselskab and A.F. Klaveness & Co. Torstein Hagen, Royal Viking's CEO, however, would much have preferred for the company to have become independent and had arranged and announced a management buyout, financed by the American venture capital firm J.H. Whitney & Co. With hindsight, NCL's purchase of Royal Viking was strategically a poor move, wasting capital that might otherwise have gained much more lucrative returns through building a new generation of bigger Caribbean cruise ships. The three Royal Viking vessels, dating from the early-1970s, were of a design that would shortly be considered obsolescent at the more exclusive and costly end of the cruise market, a sector in which NCL had no previous expertise in any case. Between 1981 and 1983, the trio had been lengthened amidships by 28 metres at the Seebeckwerft shipyard in Bremerhaven, West Germany. Following the acquisition of Royal Viking Line, a new parent company, Kloster Cruise International, was created to manage both fleets. At the same time, the meaning of the NCL initials was subtly changed to 'Norwegian Cruise Line', indicating an intention to expand operations beyond its traditional Caribbean territory.

Kloster Cruise International ordered for each of its operating subsidiaries a single new vessel from the Wärtsilä shipyard in Turku, Finland. Both Norwegian Cruise Line's 42,285gt, 1,504-passenger the *Seaward* and Royal Viking Line's 37,842gt, 768-passenger the *Royal Viking Sun* were delivered in 1988 and each in her own way was an interpretation and amalgamation of design elements of the *Royal Princess* and *Song of America*. Although the two were fairly similar in terms of size, the *Royal Viking Sun*'s much smaller capacity reflected her 'upmarket' characteristic of spaciousness.

In terms of scale, the *Seaward*'s closest comparators in the Caribbean market were the *Song of America* and Carnival Cruise Lines' successful the *Holiday*, *Jubilee* and *Celebration*. Another design precedent was the large Viking Line Helsinki-Stockholm overnight ferry the *Mariella*, which Wärtsilä had completed in 1985. (Furthermore, both vessels' interiors were by the same Swedish designer, Robert Tillberg, who specified a very high proportion of common fixtures and fittings for their outfitting.) For a vessel intended to carry out mainly repetitive week-long cruises from Miami, a ferry precedent was perhaps appropriate in giving the necessary high-density cabin layout.[222]

The *Seaward*'s hull shape was similar to that of the *Song of America*, albeit with a transom stern in place of Royal Caribbean's favoured spoon-shaped variety. The aft half of the uppermost deck and of the lowest superstructure deck were given over to public rooms, connected by a *Royal Princess*-style atrium with a circular void at its centre. The arrangement of the cabin decks was a close derivation of the *Royal Princess* precedent, albeit with smaller cabins, meaning that there was space along the centreline for inside rooms. As the *Seaward* lacked any cabin balconies and as there were no forward-facing observation decks, externally, the visual effect was much more severe, however. One positive virtue of the higher cabin density was that space was freed up for substantially bigger stair hallways connecting the various superstructure decks and these spaces were entirely encased in large panels of tinted glass, creating within a very attractive impression of spaciousness.[223] As with the *Song of America* and *Royal Princess*, the *Seaward* had an overhanging lido deck between her mast and funnel, but this was a single rectilinear expanse, lacking the architectural and spatial variety of the earlier vessels. Indeed, overall, the *Seaward*'s exterior gave a strong impression of having been designed according to a very strict budget which meant that the finer detailing found in previous Wärtsilä-built cruise ships was value-engineered away. The silhouette was, however, given a sense of cohesion by Petter Yran of Yran & Storbraaten, who designed the funnel and mast, as well as adding an exaggerated bow profile and tidying up details such as deck overhangs and fenestration. From a distance, the overall effect appeared as a greatly enlarged version of his earlier 'Sea Goddess' Yacht Cruiser designs.[224]

While the *Seaward* was aimed at NCL's mid-market segment, the *Royal Viking Sun* was intended as a luxury vessel, capable of competing on equal terms with, for example, Hapag-Lloyd's the *Europa* and the Cunard-operated *Sagafjord*, *Vistafjord*, *Sea Goddess I* and *Sea Goddess II*. Since Royal Viking Line had begun operations in the early-1970s, new standards had emerged in this rarefied sector. It was primarily the *Royal Princess*' cabins with private balconies that had created a new benchmark for shipboard luxury and so, for Royal Viking Line, the best solution would be to build a-new to emulate this appealing and commercially apposite design feature.

The *Royal Viking Sun*'s hull layout was derived from that of the original Royal Viking vessels, being planned with a significant number of uniformly-sized external cabins. Although – at a glance – her superstructure very closely resembled that of the *Royal Princess*, in terms of layout, it was actually very different. Where the *Royal Princess* had three decks of outside cabins without balconies, the *Royal Viking Sun* had two decks of public rooms. Appropriately, these were smaller, more varied and intimate than on mid-market vessels, such as the *Seaward* and *Song of America*.[225] Externally and inboard, *Royal Viking Sun* was styled by Njål Eide, whose input lent the vessel a considerable sense of unity. Although the use of lighter colours, mirrors and etched glass, coupled with a greater sense of spaciousness, supposedly indicated higher status, in reality, most of the fixtures and fittings were generic and could be found equally on the latest Finnish-built car ferries, the cabin corridors and stairwells of which were practically identical.[226]

Sovereign of the Seas

In contrast to Kloster's dubious decision to expand by acquiring Royal Viking Line – a cruise operator whose only commonality with NCL's existing operations was its Norwegian ownership – Royal Caribbean astutely chose instead to concentrate resources on growing its core Caribbean operations from Miami. Acknowledging that the new generation of potential cruise guests in the USA was immersed in what might be termed 'mall culture', one way of increasing choice and generating increased shipboard revenue was to include many more retail opportunities when planning a cruise ship. To fit in more shops and bars as well as a very big Las Vegas-style casino, much more internal volume would be needed – and this implied building on a far greater scale than hitherto. Already, the example of NCL's the *Norway* had proven that a vessel of nearly 70,000gt could be a success in the Caribbean cruise trade. While the *Norway*'s rebuilding from the trans-Atlantic liner the *France* involved many compromises, with a brand new purpose-built vessel, it would be possible to optimise the scale of every shipboard facility, placing each next to the most appropriate neighbouring attractions (this is known to cruise ship designers as 'adjacency'). For example, surrounding a casino with bars might encourage drinking before gaming, putting guests in a mood to spend more on the slots and at the tables.

Shortly after the *Song of America* was delivered, Royal Caribbean began working with the Wärtsilä Helsinki shipyard's Project Department on a 73,529gt, 2524-passenger cruise ship for operation from Miami. To establish the project's parameters, a design committee was established, consisting of the Gotaas-Larsen Group's co-managing director and Chief Financial Officer, Richard Fain, I.M. Skaugen's Chief Naval Architect, Martin Hallen, Royal Caribbean's Technical Superintendent, Olav Eftedal, and Wärtsilä's Project Manager and Chief Naval Architect, Kai Levander, as well as representatives of the three Norwegian-headquartered owning companies. This group was split into three sub-committees, researching financing, the growth potential of the North American cruise market, and the development of the new vessel's technical design in light of the first two considerations.[227]

In terms of overall layout, the design solution essentially called for a doubling of the size of the *Song of America* prototype, the new dimensions being 268.3 metres in length by 32.2 metres in width (whereas the *Song of America* was only 214.5 x 28.4 metres). Thus, a significant part of the growth was accounted for by a much wider beam as the length was constricted by the existing quays to be used by the vessel during her regular circuits of the Caribbean. Within such a large hull volume, issues of circulation – not only of passengers and crew, but also of food, drink, hotel supplies, air conditioning, fresh water and sewage – needed careful design development.[228]

As before, a four-engine propulsion solution was specified, similar to the approach favoured on previous Wärtsilä cruise ship and ferry designs. Hull tank tests were carried out in Norway and, after so much work, Wärtsilä's management was confident of winning the order to build the vessel. They were to be sorely disappointed, however.

By the mid-1980s, various European shipbuilding nations were realising that the growth of the cruise industry offered the best option of securing their industries' futures. Cruise ships were, of course, particularly high-value vessels, the construction of which involved a great deal of skilled labour and inputs from many subsidiary suppliers. In France, the Government was particularly keen for the major shipbuilders to increase their involvement in the cruise sector. The Chantiers de l'Atlantique shipyard at St Nazaire – which occupied a commodious site and had a proud history of building some of the most famous trans-Atlantic liners of the mid-twentieth century, including the fabled *Normandie* of 1935 and the *France* of 1960 (later the *Norway*) – was ideal for building a vessel of the size desired by Royal Caribbean.

Above: Norwegian Cruise Line's Caribbean cruise ship *Seaward* was, in some respects, an 'economy' version of the *Royal Princess*, missing the latter's aesthetic refinements. Inboard, she was designed by Robert Tillberg, who made extensive use of pastel-shaded fabrics, white marble slabs, mirrors and illuminated glass typical of 1980s hospitality design.

104 | Cruise Ships: A Design History

The *Royal Viking Sun* updated the successful formula of the original Royal Viking sisters, incorporating elements of the *Royal Princess*' upper decks' layout, including cabins with balconies. Inboard, her interiors, designed by Njål Eide, were in the pastel-shaded idiom found in so many passenger ships and hotels of her era.

Expansion and consolidation | 105

Left: Upon delivery in 1988, Royal Caribbean's *Sovereign of the Seas* was the biggest passenger ship in the world. The all-white vessel's upper decks made extensive use of tinted glass. The design was, in many respects, a development of the successful *Song of America*.

Below: A sumptuously upholstered, pastel-coloured lounge on the *Sovereign of the Seas* and the vessel's two-deck high Windjammer Buffet, with its festive tented ceiling, typified the interior design approach throughout the vessel.

In 1985 Chantiers de l'Atlantique won the tender to build the vessel with a bid of only 180 million US dollars – a mere 30 million dollars more than P&O had paid Wärtsilä shortly before for the considerably smaller *Royal Princess*. For Royal Caribbean, the French quotation was a most attractive bargain and so the giant cruise ship, though largely designed in Finland, was constructed at St Nazaire.[229] Appropriately enough, the name chosen was the *Sovereign of the Seas*.

Exterior styling was carried out by Geir Grung A/S working in consort with a younger Oslo-based architect, Per Høydahl, whose preference was for an all-white exterior with highly curved and streamlined forward and aft aspects, a distinct change from Grung's rather more angular treatment of the *Song of America*.[230]

For the *Sovereign of the Seas* to function effectively when carrying almost twice as many passengers as *Song of America*, it was necessary not only to double the scale of the earlier vessel's facilities but also to re-think entirely some aspects of layout and design to enhance passenger and service flows and orientation. As with the *Song of America*, the arrangement selected had a majority of cabins located towards the bow with public rooms placed aft of amidships. On so large a ship, it was felt desirable to include an impressive central space to act as a focal point, a kind-of internal 'civic plaza.' The model for this type of space was found in recent American hotel architecture.

In the latter-1970s and early-1980s, an Atlanta-based hotel architect and property developer, John Portman, had designed a series of very large hotels in American cities with giant internal atria to provide a visual link between their many floors and a 'wow factor' to impress arriving guests. On *Sovereign of the Seas*, the addition of an extra fire zone allowed for a four-deck-high atrium, a volume of space unprecedented in a shipboard context. Designed by Njål Eide, it featured sweeping curved staircases and projecting pulpit balconies with plate glass balustrades, polished brass trimmings, mirrored ceiling panels and, at the lowest level, there was a white grand piano – just like in the foyer of one of Portman's hotels. Arranged off the atrium's various levels were shops, cafés and other attractions, such as the shore excursion office and ship's photographer's studio. Eide's glitzy design also featured the first ever usage of glass-walled elevators in a ship and these proved a big attraction, enabling passengers to experience movement and spectatorship in combination.[231]

So far as dining was concerned, as it was felt that a single restaurant seating over 1,200 passengers at each serving would be too large and anonymous to function well, the solution was to have two instead, one above the other and each accommodating 650 per sitting. These were accessed from the aft ends of the atrium's two lowest levels and supplied with food and beverages from two galleys, stacked vertically on the decks below. One of these was for the 'mass production' of main menu items, while the other was for the preparation of more specialised dishes, as well

Above: One of *Sovereign of the Seas*' two restaurants and her three-deck-high atrium, which featured glass-enclosed elevators, sweeping stairways and polished brass details.

as providing food for the crew. The main entertainment facilities, including a two-deck-high show lounge similar to the ones on Carnival's recent the *Holiday*, *Jubilee* and *Celebration*, were located all the way aft where vibration from the propellers would be drowned out by loud music and dancing.

Adjacent to the very large lido area atop the superstructure was the Windjammer Café – a two-deck-high space for informal buffet dining, designed by Robert Tillberg, in which food was displayed on a series of serveries with a 'free-flow' circulation arrangement to ease and speed up access. Throughout, the interior design emphasised shiny surfaces and bright pink, turquoise and blue shades, suggestive of the Caribbean. The overall effect was fresh and festive, yet the extensive use of soft furnishings and carpet helped to create a luxurious, hotel-like atmosphere.[232]

Upon entry into service, the *Sovereign of the Seas* attracted world-wide attention. The vessel was regarded as a great achievement and, encouraged by solid bookings for every cruise, Royal Caribbean quickly ordered two sister ships from the same French builder; these were the *Monarch of the Seas* and the *Majesty of the Seas*, completed in 1991 and 1992 respectively and also sailing from Miami. Constructing vessels of such a scale and technical complexity demanded vast influxes of capital, leading Royal Caribbean to issue many new shares and thereby beginning the dilution of its Norwegian ownership.

Almost simultaneously, in 1987, the company's Miami rival, Carnival Cruise Line was restructured through the creation of Carnival Corporation, which was floated on the New York Stock Exchange. It too was now in a position to commence an unprecedentedly ambitious new building programme, as well as mounting a series of successful take-overs, extending its market-reach into other cruise sectors. This was a highly significant and successful move in the cruise industry's gradual process of consolidation.

Carnival Corporation's initial take-over target was Royal Caribbean – a company whose potential for synergies with Carnival's own Caribbean operations appeared highly attractive, at least from the viewpoint of maximising shareholder value. Royal Caribbean's Norwegian owners sought new investors elsewhere, however, and so Carnival was rebuffed, forcing it to look instead to other potential take-over targets. Next, Carnival turned its attention to Holland America Cruises, an upmarket cruise operator quite unlike Carnival itself. Whereas Carnival was strong in the Caribbean mass market, Holland America dominated Alaskan cruising, which was both lucrative and based upon repetitive itineraries from Seattle or Vancouver with consequent benefits in terms of operational efficiency. In 1988, Holland America had bought Home Lines, giving its brand a stronger presence in New York, and had also taken over Windstar Cruises, a niche operator of smallish, sail-assisted cruise ships in the Caribbean and Mediterranean. When Carnival succeeded in acquiring Holland America in 1989, it gained the Windstar fleet as well. Holland America proved an astute purchase as its core market of wealthier, older, mainly American passengers was growing as the population aged overall. Sensibly, Carnival allowed Holland America considerable autonomy to continue serving these discerning passengers in the manner to which they were accustomed.

Prior to Home Lines' absorption by Holland America, in 1986, it had taken delivery of a new 42,092gt, 1,132 passenger cruise ship, the *Homeric*, from the West German Jos. L. Meyer shipyard at Papenburg. Located 41 kilometres up the River Ems, the family-owned yard, which had been founded in 1795, was a novice at building cruise ships, though in recent years it had produced many ferries for Scandinavian owners plus a series of coastal passenger and cargo ships for the Indonesian Government.[233] Soon, however, Meyer Werft would come to specialise in cruise ship construction, making major investments in state-of-the-art shipyard infrastructure to enhance speed and quality of construction.

The *Homeric* was built as a replacement for the 21-year-old *Oceanic* and was in many respects a great improvement over the company's recent *Atlantic*, which was not only considered visually unsuccessful but also suffered stability problems. The *Homeric*'s more fulsome aft hull form with a transom stern helped avoid the latter shortcoming. In addition, her boat deck was at a lower level and her forward superstructure featured streamlined observation decks, similar to those on the *Song of America* and *Royal Princess*. Her internal arrangement was, however, broadly similar to that of the *Atlantic*. Initially, Home Lines intended that the *Homeric* should be significantly longer than the final design as-built. It was the winning of a concession from the Bermudan Government to call at Hamilton on a regular basis that necessitated her length to be limited so as to fit the quay (nonetheless, a double-bulkhead was included amidships to allow any subsequent lengthening to be more easily achieved). When Holland America took over, the vessel was renamed the *Westerdam*, while

Left: The *Monarch of the Seas*, one of two sister ships to the *Sovereign of the Seas*, is seen berthed at Vancouver.

the *Atlantic* was sold. Shortly after, the *Westerdam* was returned to Meyer Werft for lengthening to the original intended length.[234]

Meyer Werft's Chairman (or 'Managing Partner', as he prefers to be known), Bernard Meyer, saw the building of cruise ships as representing the yard's best hope for the future. Such vessels incorporated a great deal of specialised technologies and workmanship. Yet, not only was the Papenburg shipyard far inland, but vessels such as the *Homeric* were launched sideways, a hair-raising and somewhat risky process. To become a serious contender in the cruise ship construction market, it would therefore be necessary to invest in a new building dock, enclosed by a vast shed, similar to the one at Wärtsilä's shipyard in Helsinki.[235]

With local political support, this project was successfully achieved in time for the construction of Meyer Werft's next cruise ship project, the 34,242gt, 1,104-passenger *Crown Odyssey*, which was ordered by Pericles Panagopoulos' Royal Cruise Line for delivery in 1988.[236] Designed by Knud E. Hansen A/S, she had some similarities to the *Royal Princess* in terms of layout and styling. The project development process was lengthy, with numerous iterations and modifications until Panagopoulos and his Technical Manager, Costis Stamboulelis, were sure that their ideal ship design had been realised.[237] Inboard, AMK Design, founded by the Greek artist and interior designer Michael Katzourakis, produced particularly glittering and ostentatious public rooms, aimed at appealing to European and American passengers whose idea of style was influenced by watching the TV soap opera *Dynasty*. The *Crown Odyssey* was a magnificent summation of *nouveau riche* 1980s visual culture – all faceted mirrors and plate glass, polished brass, back-lit Tiffany panelling and pastel-shaded fabrics. (From the outset, the *Crown Odyssey* too was designed to be extended amidships – but it was only after sale to a subsequent owner that this work was carried out.[238])

Soon, another well-established Greek cruise ship operator, Chandris, decided to follow Panagopoulos' lead in ordering from Meyer Werft. Hitherto, Chandris had sweated any remaining value it could extract from a handful of elderly converted ocean liners, several of which were of pre-Second World War vintage, on inexpensive party cruises, mainly from New York and Florida ports. To modernise this fleet, in the mid-1980s, the company's patriarch, John Chandris, considered making second-hand purchases of more up-to-date vessels, such as Home Line's the *Oceanic* or the Danish DFDS-owned New York-Bahamas cruise ferry the *Scandinavia*. An invitation from Howaldtswerke Deutsche Werft in Kiel in West Germany to visit the newly-completed cruise ship, the *Astor*, so impressed Chandris and his colleagues that they left pondering whether to order a substantially larger cruise ship there, based on the *Astor*'s overall layout and standard of finish. Subsequent negotiations with HDW led to the possibility of a joint project with Meyer Werft at Papenburg whereby the steelwork would be built in Kiel with outfitting at Papenburg. Meyer's investment in new indoor construction facilities with the efficiency gains they entailed caused Chandris to switch focus to their yard entirely instead of HDW.[239] By this point, Chandris had made a decision to move his cruise operation substantially upmarket, capitalising on wealthy baby-boomers retiring and wishing to see the world in style. The solution was to create a new cruise brand to avoid confusion with Chandris' existing 'cheap and cheerful' image. Reflecting popular aspirations towards glamorous worlds of fame and fortune, this was named Celebrity Cruises.

As well as being hard-nosed ship owners, John Chandris and his wife, Tina, were well-known art collectors and apparently also possessed a sense of commercial pride common among well-established shipping families. Chandris therefore determined that Celebrity's new passenger ships, to be named the *Horizon* and the *Zenith*, should be aesthetically striking and outfitted to a very high standard. Measuring 46,811gt and accommodating 1,752 passengers, they were completed in 1990 and 1992 respectively.[240]

Below: The dining room on Home Line's *Homeric* had an octagonal faceted domed ceiling. The repetitive use of prefabricated components was now typical of such cruise ship interiors, just as it also was in commercial hospitality architecture and interior design ashore.

Above: The *Homeric* is seen passing through the Dover Strait *en route* from her West German builder to New York; the treatment of her forward superstructure follows the same approach as on *Song of America* and *Royal Princess*, thereby avoiding the monolithic appearance of Home Lines' earlier *Atlantic*.

Below: Royal Cruise Line's *Crown Odyssey*, Meyer Werft's next cruise ship new building, featured nested lifeboats and other characteristics previously seen on the Finnish-built *Royal Princess* and *Seaward*.

To style the exterior silhouettes, Chandris employed the London-based yacht designer Jon Bannenberg, whose career in ship design had begun in the early-1960s when he had worked on interiors for various British liners, including the *Queen Elizabeth 2*. Since that time, Bannenberg had come to specialise in devising aggressive, sports car-like styling for the very large motor yachts beloved of international business tycoons. He applied much the same approach to the Celebrity projects, using a combination of accents resembling car spoilers and broad bands of dark blue paint to create an illusion of greater length and sleekness when the vessels were viewed side-on. From other angles, their sharp corners, flat front and rear aspects and rectilinear funnels were in striking contrast with the softer curves found in all other cruise ships of the era. Their transom stern configurations were unique and were more reflective of recent motor yacht design tactics than they were of contemporary passenger ship naval architecture.

Inboard, the *Horizon* and *Zenith* had much in common with the *Crown Odyssey* in terms of layout, and, again, the interior design was by Michael Katzourakis' AMK Design, which on this occasion produced a rather subdued solution. The liner and cruise ship historian William Miller evocatively detailed the *Horizon*'s interiors upon the vessel's entry into service, finding her to be a:

'…A decorative dreamboat: spacious, soothing on the eye, elegant in tone. Missing, rather thankfully, was that over-mirrored, over-chromed, over-lighted (and sometimes over-neoned) look… The overall feel was actually of a much bigger ship. The America's Cup Lounge, for example, was one of my favourites: large windows overlooking the bow section, an elegantly relaxing feel and a stunning colour combination of navy blue and white. The Plaza Bar was highlighted by beige leatherette and white marble… The Main Lobby, done in terra cotta, had the neo-classical look of some modern-day skyscraper, perhaps a brand new Park Avenue building. Elsewhere, there were touches of the 1930s Art Deco age…'[241]

The interior spaces were all adorned with artworks by a who's who of contemporary practitioners from the Chandris collection. Seemingly, the only aspect of 1980s high style that was missing was Tom Cruise shaking the drinks in the Plaza Bar.

While the *Horizon* and *Zenith* were under construction in Papenburg, Celebrity Cruises was inaugurated using an existing Chandris cruise ship, the 1963-vintage *Galileo*, which had originally been the Italian Lloyd Triestino liner the *Galileo Galilei*. For Celebrity, she was substantially rebuilt by Lloyd Werft in Bremerhaven, emerging with new interiors as a modernised external profile as the *Meridian*. With its two new vessels delivered in 1991 and 1992, Celebrity Cruises' three-ship fleet became a major success, winning critical plaudits from American and European travel critics alike. Chandris therefore began planning for additional new tonnage.

Simultaneously with Chandris' mid-1980s decision to commission new buildings, Boris Vlasov, the owner of Sitmar Cruises, came to the same realisation. Vlasov was delighted by the very positive reception given to the *Fairsky* and so decided to replace the company's 1950s-vintage converted ex-Cunard transatlantic liners the *Fairsea* and *Fairwind* with substantially bigger vessels. Sitmar considered Chantiers de l'Atlantique as the most likely builder, following its successes with the *Nieuw Amsterdam* and *Noordam* and winning the tender to build Royal Caribbean's *Sovereign of the Seas*. As Vlasov remained keen to avoid the noise and vibration that could result from diesel propulsion, yet realised that steam turbines were increasingly expensive to fuel and maintain, while steam-trained engine room crew were a declining commodity, he selected instead a diesel-electric system. Long before he was a ship owner, Vlasov had trained as an electrical engineer and so he had a good working knowledge of how shipboard diesel-electric plants functioned. Rather than the engines being coupled to the propeller shafts, as was the case with conventional diesel installations, they could be entirely separate as they merely generated power for much smaller electric motors which provided the drive. By eliminating the need for precise alignment with long shafts through the lower hull, it was possible to dissociate the engines from the vessel's structure, thereby minimising the transfer of noise and vibration. Other advantages of diesel-electric propulsion were the potentials for redundancy and operational flexibility made possible by using the minimum number of engines necessary to maintain schedule. On a cruise ship, perhaps visiting as many as seven destinations in a week, all various distances from each other, yet typically with

Expansion and consolidation | 109

departures and arrivals at the same times of day, the ability to vary service speed from only a few knots to as much as 22 was highly desirable from both operational and economic perspectives.[242]

Concurrently with the Sitmar's planning for its new fleet, Cunard was preparing to re-engine its mechanically-unreliable flagship liner the *Queen Elizabeth 2* from steam turbine to diesel-electric plant, using nine MAN-B&W medium-speed diesels to power a generator.[243] Meanwhile, Carnival was also planning diesel-electric propulsion for its forthcoming *Fantasy*-class cruise ships (described below). Sitmar's favoured solution was a combination of four MAN-B&W 8-cyliner diesels, powering Alsthom generators.

Following criticism of the very lengthy lifeboat drops from the upper superstructures of vessels such as Home Lines' the *Atlantic*, which some knowledgeable commentators considered too high for assured safe evacuation, Sitmar decided to a return to the solution of 'nested' lifeboats utilised on some ocean liners of the past, such as the *Willem Ruys*, *Canberra* and *Oceanic*, and also seen in modified form on recent cruise ships, for example the *Royal Princess*, *Crystal Harmony*, *Seaward* and *Crown Odyssey* (though in all of these instances, narrowed superstructures were primarily to enable a high proportion of exterior cabins). Although 'nested' lifeboats occupied valuable space on the decks nearest the 'heart' of the passenger circulation (and therefore some of the most commercially lucrative shipboard space) the lower positioning greatly improved slab-sided cruise ships' external appearances by breaking up the rectilinear bulk of their hull topsides and superstructures. This notwithstanding, the design arrived at for Sitmar's 63,524gt, 1,621-passenger new building appeared bulky, the overall effect perhaps indicating an engineers' solution, rather than one in which precedence had been given to aesthetic considerations.[244]

Shortly after, Sitmar entered negotiations with the Italian state-owned Fincantieri shipbuilding group to build two further large cruise ships. Just as the French government had actively encouraged Chantiers de l'Atlantique's entry into the cruise sector, so the Italian Prime Minister, Bettino Craxi, was keenly enthusiastic for Italy to follow suit. Indeed, in 1986, Craxi commissioned the well-known Italian architect, Renzo Piano, to design a concept for a futuristic Italian cruise ship for Fincantieri to build – if a willing customer could be found. Piano – who knew about ships from having grown up close to the port of Genoa, but who had never previously been given such a commission, decided that his concept should look like a dolphin with a whale-back bow to resemble its beak, a heavily slanted forward superstructure, and a dome enclosing the forward portion of the uppermost deck, sleekly shaped like a dolphin's cranium. This design formed the basis of two 69,845gt, 1,900-passenger cruise ships Sitmar subsequently ordered from Fincantieri, which otherwise followed the mechanical and layout solutions developed for its French new building. At about the same time, Fincantieri also commenced negotiations with Costa Cruises for two new buildings for its fleet (described below).[245]

Fincantieri therefore set up two in-house naval architecture teams, one to handle the Sitmar projects, which were to be built at its Monfalcone shipyard and the other to deal with the Costa vessels, to be constructed at its yard in Venice. The Sitmar project group was led by the naval architect Gianfranco Bertaglia while the Costa one was under the leadership of Bertaglia's colleague, Fulvio Cernobori.

While the three Sitmar projects were under construction, in October 1987, Boris Vlasov died. His sudden demise led to a restructuring of Sitmar Cruises, whereby a majority shareholding was acquired by the Monaco-based Italian businessman, Manfredi Lefebvre d'Ovidio, whose existing interests ranged across shipping-related activities and the travel trade. Following this change of ownership, an early decision was made to radically update Sitmar's rather staid visual culture. Instead of buff funnels with the letter 'V' mounted on either side, a new identity was devised, involving an ornate 'S', resembling a swan, with cursive strokes beneath, supposedly looking like waves and a red and blue colour scheme. Not only would this symbol appear on the funnel and on printed matter, as was conventional for shipping companies' visual identities, but it would also be emblazoned on the hull, the 'waves' disappearing below the waterline. Its shape and 'signature' curves were supposed to signify elegance and sophistication – though quite how these qualities would have communicated when rendered at a scale of several decks height is unclear. Subsequently, however, other cruise lines began to deploy similarly bold hull graphics as corporate brands gradually began to usurp the more traditional emphasis on well-proportioned hull, superstructure and funnel arrangements. Sitmar unveiled the new design on a model of the first of its new fleet, which was to be named the *Sitmar Fair Majesty*.[246]

Before any of Sitmar's new vessels could enter service, however, later in 1988, Manfredi Lefebvre d'Ovidio sold the company to P&O which since the great success of *Royal Princess* had wanted to expand its Princess Cruises operations in the USA. P&O's initial plan of building sister ships had been scuppered by the need to fend off a hostile take-over attempt by Trafalgar House. The recently-appointed Chairman, Jeffrey Sterling, whose business acumen had succeeded in maintaining P&O's independence, was now determined to expand in the cruise sector and the fastest way to achieve

Above: The *Crown Odyssey*'s interiors were glitzy, using a great deal of polished metal and expanses of softly-toned fabric, as demonstrated by her nightclub and cocktail bar.

Chandris Celebrity Cruises' *Horizon* (pictured) and her sister, *Zenith*, had very distinctive exteriors by Jon Bannenberg, making ingenious use of bands of dark blue paint to create an illusion of greater height towards the bow. Inboard, there was an emphasis on spatial manipulation, rather than ornate decoration, as the central hallway (centre left) and theatre (centre right) demonstrate. Below, we see the container ship *Axel Johnson*, a sister of the vessel rebuilt into Costa Cruises *Costa Allegra* (above right). The right-hand image shows Celebrity Cruises' *Meridian*, the operation's pioneering ship, converted from the 1960s-vintage former-liner *Galileo*.

Expansion and consolidation | 111

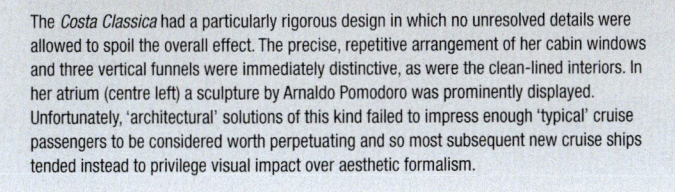

The *Costa Classica* had a particularly rigorous design in which no unresolved details were allowed to spoil the overall effect. The precise, repetitive arrangement of her cabin windows and three vertical funnels were immediately distinctive, as were the clean-lined interiors. In her atrium (centre left) a sculpture by Arnaldo Pomodoro was prominently displayed. Unfortunately, 'architectural' solutions of this kind failed to impress enough 'typical' cruise passengers to be considered worth perpetuating and so most subsequent new cruise ships tended instead to privilege visual impact over aesthetic formalism.

Above: Following acquisition by P&O, the vessel intended to be the *Sitmar Fair Majesty* was completed instead as Princess Cruises' *Star Princess*. Consequently, Sitmar's new visual identity, which had been previewed in promotional models and artist's renderings, was never actually applied on the ship. Painted in Princess Cruises' all-white livery, her bulky silhouette became all too obvious.

Below: The dolphin-shaped *Regal Princess*, the silhouette of which was designed by Renzo Piano, was arguably a more successful design solution with a clearer hierarchy of forms and details. Nonetheless, Piano was allegedly very disappointed that some elements of his styling were omitted for practical reasons by the vessel's builder.

this aim was by taking over an existing cruise line with a similar market positioning as Princess Cruises.[247] P&O paid just £125 million for Sitmar and although its fleet consisted of four rather traditional steam turbine-powered vessels of which only the *Fairsky* was of recent construction, the great attractions were firstly, its strong position in the North American market and, secondly, the three new cruise ships under construction. Upon completion, they would add 5,200 berths to Princess Cruises' capacity. When Sitmar ordered them, shipyard prices were considerably lower than when P&O took over and so the acquisition represented a remarkable bargain, consisting as it did of a total of seven ships plus infrastructure and personnel for not much more than the cost of a single new cruise ship at 1988 prices.

P&O renamed the incomplete *Sitmar Fair Majesty* as the *Star Princess* and the other two vessels in earlier stages of construction at Fincantieri's Monfalcone shipyard near Trieste were named the *Crown Princess* and *Regal Princess*. Inboard, all three were of similar layout with three-deck-high atria amidships, restaurants and galleys aft, entertainment spaces forward and observation lounges above the bridge. The interior design was by the Californian Welton Becket Associates, whose previous work included hotel interiors for Hyatt and Disney. Their approach used pastel shades and shiny finishes, rather similar to Hirsch-Bender's the *Royal Princess* décor, the alchemy of which Sitmar had evidently wished to emulate. Renzo Piano's 'dolphin' silhouette design for the two Italian-built vessels, however, proved too heavy and costly to realise in its entirety and so some of the plating that would have been needed to enclose the sides of the aft decks was excised from the final design drawings. This led to Piano withdrawing from the project in disgust though, in fairness to Fincantieri and P&O, the completed ships were in their important aesthetic elements largely faithful to his original proposal.

The delivery of Sitmar's new buildings to Princess meant that briefly in 1991, P&O was the world's largest cruise ship operator, although the rapid expansion of Carnival and Royal Caribbean soon eclipsed it.[248] Built in France and Italy with interiors designed by Americans, flying the Italian flag and with international crews, the three new Princess ships reflected how internationalised cruising was becoming.

At around the same time as John Chandris and Boris Vlasov took the plunge in commissioning new vessels, the Italian family-owned Armatori Costa of Genoa, which was the parent company of Costa Cruises, also decided that radical action would be needed if it were to remain competitive in the cruise sector. Like Chandris, Costa had hitherto mainly operated older, second-hand liners, the most recent addition to its fleet being the *Costa Riviera*, ex-*Guglielmo Marconi*, a sister of the *Galileo/Meridian*, which had been heavily rebuilt in 1987 for US-based cruising.

Costa's typical passenger demographic was a mix of Italians, Europeans and Americans with custom also coming from the wealthy of the Latin world; in the past when a liner operator, Costa had served Brasil and Argentina, where loyalty remained. Traditionally, the company's post-war liners and early cruise ships were decoratively understated, the emphasis being on stylish Italian modernism, accented with works by leading Italian artists. The *Costa Riviera* was consciously different however, seeking to appeal to a fun-seeking clientele with a more consciously Americanised image of Italy, created by the Italian interior designers Studio DeJorio. Costa's marketing slogan was 'Cruising Italian Style.' The issue was whether in future that would mean the Italy of designer goods and high culture, or the Italy represented in Las Vegas casinos and Mamma Leone's restaurants. Costa's directors in Genoa apparently very much favoured the former approach, while recognising the profitability of the latter, particularly in the American market.

As with Chandris, Costa decided to make such money as was available for investment in fleet modernisation stretch as far as possible by commissioning two entirely new cruise ships and also radically converting two existing vessels. The sources for these latter projects were, remarkably enough, a pair of late-1960s-vintage container ships. Built in Finland for a Swedish owner as the *Axel Johnson* and *Annie Johnson*, they were diesel-powered, twin-screw vessels, making them potentially suitable for future use as passenger ships. Indeed, they were at first purchased by a Greek cruise entrepreneur, Captain Antonis Lelakis, for conversion. To benefit from an Italian Government subsidy to boost employment in the shipbuilding industry, Lelakis had the *Axel Johnson* towed to the Mariotti shipyard in Genoa with the intention of converting her into a cruise ship to be named the *Regent Sun*, but the project was never carried out. Instead, the vessel was sold to an Italian businessman, Bruno Quirconi, who thereafter sold her to Costa, for whom she was transformed into the *Costa Marina*.

The existing superstructure and upper hull were scrapped and an entirely new construction was built upon what remained. Costa entrusted the architectural design of this to Guido Canali from Parma, whose elegant modern buildings ashore had won widespread praise for their spaciousness, slender structural elements and use of natural light. For the Costa project, Canali produced a solution with similar characteristics, his approach being utterly distinct from any established passenger ship design traditions. On the main passenger deck, unusually lofty deck heads and expanses of floor-to-ceiling windows were used. At the stern, the Restaurant Cristallo was terraced with an entirely glazed aft-facing bulkhead. On the topmost deck, the Galaxy Nightclub had a glazed dome with stretched canvas sunscreens, resembling the sails of yachts. Amidships, there was a four-deck-high atrium, also with a glazed deck head. Within, marble and mosaic finishes were used in combination with contemporary Italian-designed furnishings and artworks, the overall effect being rather hard-edged and minimalist; this 'proper architecture' was in complete contrast with the soft furnishings and pastel shades otherwise typifying the era's passenger ship décor. In hot Mediterranean and Caribbean climes, however, the coolness and sense of light and shade worked well, though were perhaps less appealing in Baltic or Alaskan waters. The *Costa Marina*'s severely rectilinear superstructure was capped by a series of six slim vertical tubes for funnels, tightly grouped together.[249]

The *Costa Marina*'s conversion lasted nearly two years but, once the work was completed, the vessel was barely recognisable as her former self; only when viewed from astern did her hull aft body reveal her origin as a container ship. Following trials in the Gulf of Genoa, she joined Costa's cruise fleet in July 1990. She measured 25,441gt and accommodated 1,025 passengers.

Meanwhile, Costa also purchased the *Annie Johnson*, which, in the interim, had been sold by Antonis Lelakis to Mediterranean Shipping Company (MSC), an Italian container ship – and nowadays also a cruise and ferry – operator, owned by Gianluigi Aponte. He had put the vessel back in container service, named the *Alexandra*, but sold her to Costa in August 1990. At the Mariotti shipyard, she was given a similar reconstruction to the *Costa Marina*, but with two key differences; during the conversion, her hull was lengthened amidships by 13.44 metres to provide more cabins, public rooms and deck space and, at the same time, her original engines were replaced with two new ones. Following this work, she measured 28,430gt and had berths for 1,066 passengers. In November 1992, she was named the *Costa Allegra* in Genoa, thereafter setting sail for Miami in Florida and an inaugural winter programme of Caribbean cruises.

The *Costa Marina* and *Costa Allegra*'s vertical funnels subsequently became a key part of Costa Cruises' brand identity. Indeed, when the *Costa Allegra* entered service, she was the first Costa ship painted in an updated livery, utilising a refined Roman font for name graphics and with neither stripes on the hull nor inverted commas around the letter C on her funnel.

While Mariotti in Genoa were undertaking the *Costa Marina* and *Costa Allegra* rebuilds, Costa concluded negotiations with Fincantieri to build two new cruise ships – the 53,700-ton, 1,766-passenger *Costa Classica* and *Costa Romantica* – at their Monfalcone shipyard. Following in the wake of Fincantieri's success with the orders from Sitmar, winning two further contracts for cruise ships for an Italian owner must have been very gratifying.

The initial contract to build the *Costa Classica* was signed in July 1987 and, thereafter, nearly three years of intense design development work followed before her keel was laid in May 1990. In the interim, Fincantieri carried out extensive design work under the leadership of the naval architect Fulvio Cernobori. An outstanding younger member of his design group was Maurizio Cergol, who developed particular expertise in cruise ship design, ranging from concept development to exterior styling. When Cergol had graduated from Trieste University in 1982, he was awarded its Costanzi Prize, which commemorated its most famous naval architecture graduate, Nicolò Costanzi, and was issued to the student whose work best emulated his design talent. Over the ensuing three decades, Cergol would help shape over fifty increasingly large and complex cruise ships built at Fincantieri's yards. Indeed, he came to be widely regarded as among the most outstanding figures in contemporary cruise ship naval architecture.[250] On the *Costa Classica* and *Costa Romantica*, however, his role was subservient to the architects chosen by Costa to design the profile and interiors. They were the critically acclaimed Milanese architecture studio of Gregotti Associati, led by Pierluigi Cerri and Ivana Porfiri. Externally and within, the vessels were designed with a high level of precision echoing the best of Italy's historic and modernist design traditions.

In terms of layout, the *Costa Classica* and *Costa Romantica* had a clear horizontal split between the cabin and public room decks but, unlike the *Crown Princess* and *Regal Princess* projects, the lifeboats were not nested. Externally, the cabin decks were signified by rows of large circular 'porthole'-type windows. While reflecting nautical tradition, they were also practical as they avoided corners where stresses could gather. Above the cabin decks, a theatre auditorium, modelled on a typical Italian Renaissance layout, was located towards the bow. Amidships was a five-deck atrium, around the topmost deck of which the main bars and seating areas were located; formally and functionally, this took the role of a piazza in an Italian town or city centre. Indeed, the distinctly Italian approach to the 'urban planning' of the *Costa Classica* and *Costa Romantica* interiors emphasised social life and the need to see and be seen. The same approach was applied to the lido decks, which were terraced inwards, the better to encourage people-watching. Towards the stern, the main restaurant, casino and lido buffet were vertically stacked. As on the *Costa Marina* and *Costa Allegra*, the deck heads were lofty throughout the public circulation areas. Atop each vessel's the superstructure was a circular 'pod', clad in tinted floor-to-ceiling glazing, which contained a night club. Aft of amidships, a triangular formation of three oval-shaped vertical funnels completed what were crisp, striking and distinctive silhouettes.[251]

As their names suggested, the *Costa Classica* was decorated to reflect Italy's classical traditions, whereas the *Costa Romantica* emphasised the romantic side of Italian culture. Outstanding features of the interiors were their substantial art installations which, in the tradition of previous generations of Italian ocean liners, were fully integrated with the overall designs of the spaces in which they were located. The *Costa Classica*'s atrium featured a spherical bronze sculpture by Arnaldo Pomodoro. Elsewhere on board, the sculptor Sergio Benvenuti produced a series of plaques of The Nine Muses, displayed around the interior promenades. In the theatre, Emilio Tadini illustrated the story of Pinocchio in mosaic panels, while the suites featured abstract tapestries by Renata Bonfanti. On the *Costa Romantica*, the atrium has a sculpture in steel and carbon fibre by the Japanese artist Susumu Shingu, who also produced a striking kinetic sculpture in titanium and steel installed over the swimming pool called 'Message of the Wind.' In the Restaurant Botticelli, Alberto Andreis produced a series of paintings inspired by Italian romantic gardens of the eighteenth century and, in the casino, directly above, Roberto Sambonet designed large abstract mosaics, whose soft grey, green and brown tones were suggestive of coastal scenes.[252]

Above: The spectacular atrium of Carnival Cruise Line's *Fantasy* featured a great deal of multi-coloured neon lighting, making the space an ideal centrepiece for a vessel providing 'party' cruises.

Below: A broadside view of Carnival Cruise Line's *Fascination*, showing how, in appearance, the design was essentially a greatly enlarged version of the earlier *Holiday/Jubilee/Celebration* series.

The *Costa Classica* was christened in Venice in Saint Mark's Basin on 7th December 1991. After an inaugural cruise from Genoa, she sailed trans-Atlantic to Miami to begin her first season in the Caribbean. Nearly two years thereafter, the *Costa Romantica* was also named in Venice, after which she too headed to Miami.

The design of the *Crown Odyssey*, *Horizon*, *Zenith*, *Costa Classica* and *Costa Romantica* reflected the refined taste and commercial pride of family-owned European shipping companies who felt strongly that, as well as earning money, they were in positions of cultural authority to lead taste as well as reflect it. Keenly aware of the great traditions of passenger ship design over the course of the twentieth century, Chandris and Costa were anxious to perpetuate these for a new generation. This culture-led approach was, however, soon largely to vanish, usurped by one led instead by corporate big capital. In the second half of the 1980s, this was best exemplified by the rapid and seemingly exponential growth of Carnival.

The Fantasy-class

Having successfully added the *Holiday*, *Jubilee* and *Celebration* to its fleet, toward the end of the decade, Carnival used money raised on the New York Stock exchange to place orders for a larger number of substantially bigger cruise ships of a size commensurate with Royal Caribbean's the *Sovereign of the Seas*. Indeed, planning work for the initial members of the so-called Fantasy-class first began in 1985 at the London office of Technical Marine Planning.

The project was for a 70,367gt vessel, capable of accommodating 2,634 passengers within a shell measuring 260.6 metres in length by 31.5 metres in beam. Both dimensions were somewhat less than those of the *Sovereign of the Seas*, but were compensated with a more ferry-like massing of the superstructure, which extended further forward and aft than on the Royal Caribbean vessel. In many other respects, however, the Fantasy-class was similar to the *Holiday*, *Jubilee* and *Celebration*, featuring a hull and lower superstructure entirely comprised of highly standardised outside and inside cabins, above which were two decks of public rooms. Filling the forward superstructure on these decks was a very large show lounge with tiered seating at both stalls and balcony level. Due to the overall size of the Fantasy-class, it was felt necessary to add a six-deck-high atrium forward of amidships, uniting all of the decks in the superstructure and acting as a focal point for passenger orientation. This had a cupola, enabling daylight to filter down to the uppermost cabin deck, where the guest services desk was located. As on the *Sovereign of the Seas*, pulpit balconies and glass elevators were prominent features of the space.

The layout of the Fantasy-class reflected an emerging orthodoxy of cruise ship planning which was to entertain passengers towards the bow, where show lounges and nightclubs typically would be located, to feed them towards the stern and to part them from their money in the spaces in between by arranging bars, shops and casinos off long galleries and around the perimeters of multi-deck atria. A consequence of the doubling the capacity of the biggest since the early-1980s generation of cruise ships was that there would be many more passers-by to partake of the shipboard spending opportunities.

As with the Sitmar/P&O Princess new buildings the *Star Princess*, *Crown Princess* and *Regal Princess*, Technical Marine Planning came to the conclusion that the best way to power the Fantasy-class would be a diesel-electric solution. This possibility first arose because one of TMP's naval architects, John Hopkins, had joined the company from Cable & Wireless, whose cable-laying vessels had diesel electric plant to enable very precise speed control when laying telephone cables on the ocean floor. Hopkins was an enthusiastic advocate of diesel-electric systems and so was placed in charge of the machinery design on the Fantasy-class.[253] The power plant selected consisted of four 12-cylinder Sulzer vee-diesels plus three 8-cylinner Sulzer in-line diesels, powering six ABB-Strömberg generators. These were connected to two ABB-Strömberg motors, each driving a propeller. One of Carnival's requirements was for the vessels to be capable to berthing and un-berthing without the aid of any tugs, even against very strong winds and so the installation of three bow thrust propellers plus three stern thrusters was specified.[254]

The tender to build the Fantasy-class was won by the Wärtsilä shipyard in Helsinki. Back in the late-1970s, Carnival had first approached the yard as a possible builder of the *Tropicale* but as it proved impossible to come to terms with regard to financing and expected delivery date, the vessel was instead built in Aalborg. Wärtsilä, of course, had its own

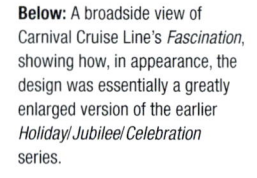

Expansion and consolidation | 115

A bow-quarter view of the *Fantasy* (top), the ornately-decorated Duke's Bar and the Music Café on the *Elation* (centre left and right) and a stern-quarter image of the same vessel.

substantial in-house naval architecture and technical capabilities with considerable accumulated experience in design innovation. As an alternative to Technical Marine Planning's favoured propulsion solution, Wärtsilä's Project Department proposed an innovative so-called 'podded propulsion' solution, using Azipod units. This was being developed jointly by Wärtsilä, Strömberg and Merenkulkuhallitus (the Finnish Maritime Administration).[255]

Azipods consist of stream formed steel casings housing the drive motors with propellers mounted at the forward end, located outboard of the aft hull. Their ability to rotate through 360 degrees gives ships superb manoeuvrability as powerful thrust can be exerted in any direction. Azipods were primarily developed for use on icebreakers to loosen and break up sheet ice – but a much more ambitious and lucrative intention was to supersede shafted propulsion on vessels of all types, including cruise ships. This emerging technology was, however, considered by Carnival's technical staff to be insufficiently developed and therefore potentially of doubtful resilience and so Technical Marine Planning's more conventional shafted solution was decided upon – at least for initial six members of what eventually became a series of eight vessels; these were the *Fantasy*, *Ecstasy*, *Sensation*, *Fascination*, *Imagination* and *Inspiration*.[256] The final two examples of the class – the *Elation* and the *Paradise*, both of which were delivered in 1998 – were indeed fitted with Azipods, manufactured by ABB. Reputedly, Carnival negotiated a very low price to offset the risk of these vessels being test-beds for an 'unproven' technology, at least so far as cruise ship design was concerned. Indeed, the *Elation* was the first ever large merchant ship with Azipods but, since then, the use of podded propulsion has become commonplace in large passenger ships.[257]

Initially, it had been intended that the Fantasy-class would be used on seven-night Caribbean itineraries, but between design and delivery of the first example, there was a change of plan. Instead, it was decided that the *Fantasy* would be used on short 3- and 4-night cruises from Miami to The Bahamas, involving a call in Freeport on Grand Bahama Island, a port with a very difficult access. Shallow water in the channel required the maintenance of significant forward momentum with a quick stop thereafter due to the channel's abrupt end, facing a quay wall. Manoeuvring such a large a vessel in these conditions was thought difficult as several actions would require simultaneous precise co-ordination by the navigating officer. The solution was to install Kamewa joysticks on the bridge control consoles, a new Swedish invention which enabled the main propellers, rudders and thrusters to be optimally controlled by a single action, computer software co-ordinating the various elements to achieve the desired movement by the most effective means. The *Fantasy* was the first cruise ship to be equipped with Kamewa joysticks, which subsequently also have become standard features on vessels of all types.[258]

For Carnival's passengers, these technological innovations were of little significance. What would make a cruise memorable would be spectacular interior design, abundant food and constant entertainment such as would also be found in the latest hotel-resorts in Reno, Atlantic City or Las Vegas. On the Fantasy-class, Carnival's flamboyant Miami-based interior architect Joe Farcus had the opportunity to apply his decorative imagination on an unprecedented scale, using great lengths of coloured neon, dazzling colours, lurid patterns, shiny finishes and outlandish themes. His atrium designs for the vessels were particularly noteworthy, having many kilometres of scintillating neon tubing around the balcony fronts of the various levels. The restaurants were arranged forward and aft of a central galley. There was even a stage with a raised catwalk for song and dance performances between courses by the entertainment staff, maitre d'hotel and waiters. Ensuring fast and accurate food and beverage service in such a large space required careful attention to service design and to the flows between the galleys, serving stations and each table.

Very important revenue-earning aspects of the Fantasy-class were their shops and the casino, all of which were located adjacent to the atrium. The latter formed part of a wider complex of entertainment spaces, also encompassing bars and discotheques that flowed into each other. Within, the décor was designed to break up each space's perimeter, creating an infinite vista of spending opportunities, enriched with effects lighting and the cacophonous sounds of slots, chips being cleared from gaming tables and music of various kinds. Higher up, next to the main outdoor pool was a very large lido buffet and also a stage for outdoor performances. Aesthetically, the Fantasy-class interior design formula was unprecedented in a shipboard context while, economically, the vessels were ruthlessly efficient in generating on board revenue.

The *Fantasy* was scheduled for delivery in August 1989 with the *Ecstasy* and *Sensation* intended to follow at yearly intervals thereafter. Just when the finishing touches were being put on the *Fantasy*, however, disaster struck the Wärtsilä shipbuilding group. In 1987, Wärtsilä's yards in Helsinki and Turku had been merged with those of another Finnish shipbuilder, Valmet, the combined group being known henceforth as Wärtsilä Marine. As the *Fantasy* order had been won with a low bid of 205 million dollars, meaning a loss would be made, and as the costing for her sisters also turned out to be insufficient, the outcome was a very severe financial shortfall. Wärtsilä Marine was consequently declared bankrupt and a major restructuring was put into effect. In the end, a new company was established called Masa Yards, led by the former Wärtsilä Helsinki shipyard Managing Director, Martin Saarikangas, who had in the past been critical of the managerial strategy that had led to this situation.[259] One of the investors was Carnival, which, along with other ship owners with vessels under construction, had a keen interest in seeing them completed and delivered as quickly as possible. The *Fantasy* cost an extra 20 million dollars to complete and entered service from Miami in January 1990, the *Ecstasy* following in April 1991.[260] The remaining sisters – the *Sensation*, *Imagination*, *Fascination*, *Inspiration*, *Elation* and *Paradise* – followed at yearly intervals, the last being completed in 1998. These vessels not only enabled Carnival to offer almost daily departures from Miami, but to begin cruising from New York and Los Angeles as well. The *Paradise* was noteworthy as the first entirely non-smoking cruise ship – but this 'healthy' experiment was eventually abandoned because the on board revenues generated were lower than for the remainder of the Carnival fleet. Perhaps unsurprisingly, the biggest gamblers were often also heavy smokers.'

While the new eight-strong fleet was being delivered, Carnival sought out innovative ways of reaching new audiences who might never have considered going to a travel agent to book a cruise. One successful strategy which, at the time, raised eyebrows within the wider cruise industry was to sell cruises through the Walmart supermarket chain. This ran contrary to cruising's lingering traditions of social elitism – but it certainly helped to fill the ships with fun-seeking passengers. A combination of short cruises, informality and high passenger densities made the experience more similar to the concurrent development of cruise ferries in the Baltic Sea, which were also built by Wärtsilä and its successor, Masa Yards. In US and Caribbean waters, however, where temperatures were tropical, there was a far greater emphasis on outdoor activity. Also, the ferries had all-Scandinavian unionised crews, whereas the cruise ships were staffed by third world labour, subsisting to a large extent on passengers' tips.

Competing with the *Fantasy* in the 3- and 4-day market out of Miami was Royal Caribbean's 48,563gt, 805-passenger the *Nordic Empress*, built by Chantiers de l'Atlantique at St Nazaire and likewise delivered in 1990. The vessel had originally been intended for operation by Admiral Cruises, a company recently created by the Royal Caribbean owning partner, Gotaas-Larsen, and formerly known as Eastern Steamship Lines. Gotaas-Larsen had intended to modernise Admiral's motley fleet of mainly rather elderly vessels with a state-of-the-art new cruise ship for short itineraries from Miami in which new design ideas would be showcased. The project was code-named 'Future Seas.'[261] In many respects, the overall layout with nested lifeboats was similar to that of the *Seaward* but, both externally and within, the Norwegian architects Per Høydahl and Njål Eide were given considerable leeway to create the most up-to-date looking cruise ship they could imagine. Their greatest innovation was the unprecedented extent to which the shell of the superstructure was enclosed by expanses of tinted glazing in place of steel. For example, both sides of the atrium were almost entirely glazed with a cupola in the deck head and the aft-facing, double-height dining room had a glazed aft bulkhead, enabling panoramic views of the ship's wake. These features were complemented by Høydahl's 'futuristic' styling of the superstructure with blunt angular forms, accentuated by blue stripes.[262]

Though stylistically and spatially fairly adventurous, the *Nordic Empress* was mechanically conservative in comparison with the Fantasy-class, having twin Wärtsilä diesels with a direct-drive arrangement. So far as the propulsion of large cruise ships in general was concerned, however, diesel-electric solutions soon became commonplace with a great many subsequent vessels benefitting from the system's inherent flexibility.

Between design and delivery, Gotaas-Larsen decided to abandon Admiral Cruises as a separate brand and to incorporate the *Nordic Empress* into the Royal Caribbean fleet instead, giving the latter a foothold in the 3- and 4-day cruise market, which otherwise was dominated by Carnival.

Miami's initial major cruise operator, Norwegian Caribbean, meanwhile, had conceded market share to Royal Caribbean and Carnival. Partly, the extra cost of the *France*-to-*Norway* conversion was responsible for its loss of momentum. Also, the purchase of Royal Viking Line and the creation of Kloster Cruise International led to a loss of focus. In addition, Knut Kloster was less enthusiastic about

Opposite: The *Nordic Empress* had a futuristic external appearance, utilising large expanses of glazing. The vessel's interiors were characterised by their spaciousness and lightness, as shown by her double-level dining room, which faced aft (centre), and the atrium (bottom).

Below: Norwegian Cruise Line's *Windward* at sea, shortly after delivery.

Right: The *Dreamward*'s tiered, aft-facing dining room enabled passengers to enjoy wide views across the space and through the windows beyond. Such a complex arrangement was, however, less satisfactory for the waiters due to the various changes of level.

'big capital' and the loss of control an increased shareholding entailed, meaning that there was less financial largesse available to build a-new on a large scale. Several projects were designed for NCL, ranging from different iterations of the Phoenix World City concept to more conventional vessels in the 40-50,000gt range – but orders failed to materialise and so the company's original 1970s fleet was still in front-line service in the early 1990s. In comparison with the *Sovereign of the Seas* or *Fantasy*, these ships were decidedly unimpressive and clearly had little future in the Miami market.

In these circumstances, NCL elected to commission from Chantiers de l'Atlantique a pair of 39,172gt, 1,260-passenger cruise ships, named the *Dreamward* and *Windward*, for which Yran & Storbraaten had considerable influence on the exterior design, internal arrangements and décor.[263] In terms of size and capacity, they were more in the class of the *Song of America* and *Seaward* than the newest Royal Caribbean and Carnival giants. Apart from their nested lifeboats, a notable feature of their passenger accommodation was a tiered, aft-facing restaurant in which the tables were arranged around a series of terraces, meaning that each group of diners enjoyed a better view astern than would have been the case in a more typical flat-floored space. The corollary was, of course, that the waiters needed to carry plates of food up and down occasional short flights of stairs. When the completed vessels were undergoing trials in 1992 and 1993, a major challenge for NCL was finding enough money to pay the final instalments owed to their builder but, after some delicate negotiations with financiers, sufficient funds were scraped together, thereby enabling delivery to take place as intended.

Smaller iterations of the same essential concept as the *Nordic Empress*, *Dreamward* and *Windward* were the 19,089gt, 820-passenger *Crown Jewel* and *Crown Dynasty*. These were delivered in 1992 and 1993 to Crown Cruise Line – a new company set up by a Florida-based Norwegian ship owner, Oddmund Grundstad, whose earlier involvement in the cruise business had provided one-day cruises for casino gaming aboard converted ferries of European origin. Crown Cruise Line's initial vessel, the *Crown Del Mar* was also rebuilt from a ferry by the Union Naval de Levante shipyard at Valencia in Spain, thereafter providing two- and five-day trips from Palm Beach. Subsequently, Grundstad placed an order for a purpose-built cruise ship from the same yard, the 15,343gt, 559-passenger *Crown Monarch*.[264]

This was followed by orders for the *Crown Jewel* and *Crown Dynasty* – which were considerably more sophisticated in terms of layout and facilities. Their nomenclature reflected an increasingly common approach of marrying a corporate brand associated with royalty to a 'surname' evoking luxurious imagery; the reference to 'Dynasty' additionally referenced the popularity of the eponymous TV soap opera, starring Joan Collins. The planning of the vessels' passenger accommodation was ingeniously efficient in terms of space utilisation, the cabins being arranged with a similar density to those of recent Scandinavian ferries. Yet, the design solution also incorporated in reduced form the type of hotel-like

Right: The *Crown Jewel* was a smaller derivative of the typical Caribbean cruise ships of the early-1990s.

marble-clad atrium with extensive glazing found on much larger mass-market cruise ships, such as the *Seaward* and *Nordic Empress*. This was achieved by means of an asymmetrical layout with the principal vertical circulation located on the port side. Service facilities were located to starboard – an unusual solution for a Caribbean cruise ship, but one typically found on many ferries.

Between ordering and taking delivery, there was a sharp economic downturn in Europe and the USA, with the effect that Grundstad's business plan was no longer sustainable and so, before either the *Crown Jewel* or *Crown Dynasty* entered service, he decided to sell the Crown Cruise Line fleet to one of the longer-established of the smaller Caribbean cruise operators, Commodore Cruise Line. Since introducing the *Bohème* in the 1960s, Commodore had remained at most a two-ship operation which, in more recent time had been acquired by the Swedish-Finnish shipping conglomerate Effjohn, the main interest of which was operating large ferries in the Baltic Sea under the Silja Line brand. After running the *Crown Monarch* and *Crown Jewel* for just a year with poor results, Commodore decided to charter the Crown Cruise Line fleet *en bloc* to Cunard instead.[265]

When the cruise industry's phase of consolidation began in the mid-1980s, the latter company had been widely tipped to become a leading giant but the parsimony of its owner, Trafalgar House, had meant that little substantive investment was subsequently made while other cruise operators – such as Carnival and Royal Caribbean – grew greatly. Indeed, Cunard appeared to lack a coherent development strategy and instead made opportunistic decisions to charter vessels that had little in common when opportunities arose. By the early-1990s, its fleet consisted of the large and fast trans-Atlantic liner the *Queen Elizabeth 2*, the luxurious though traditional mid-sized cruise ships the *Sagafjord* and *Vistafjord*, the small Yacht Cruisers *Sea Goddess I* and *Sea Goddess II* and the mass-market tropical cruise ships the *Cunard Countess* and *Cunard Princess*. The Crown fleet was intended to augment the latter vessels and, incidentally, the third of Crown's new buildings, the *Crown Dynasty*, was delivered in 1993 already painted in Cunard colours. Furthermore, all three vessels' names were given 'Cunard' prefixes. Cunard shifted Crown's Caribbean operations from Palm Beach to Fort Lauderdale and moved the *Cunard Crown Monarch* to Australia and the *Cunard Crown Dynasty* to Alaska, leaving only the *Cunard Crown Jewel* in the Caribbean – but its involvement in the vessels' operation was very brief. After only a couple of years, their owner, Effjohn, divested itself first of the *Crown Jewel* and then of the *Crown Dynasty*, then when Cunard withdrew cooperation, the *Crown Monarch* was chartered as a casino ship in the Far East.[266] None of these vessels was sufficiently capacious to turn enough of a profit in a mass market sector increasingly dominated by cruise ships of at least double their size and capacity. Clearly, the future of mass-market cruising lay with big capital and even bigger vessels.

In 1996, Cunard's parent company, Trafalgar House, was taken over by the Norwegian Kværner Group, which wanted only Trafalgar's engineering subsidiaries but had no interest in running cruise ships. Two years later, Kværner sold Cunard to Carnival Corporation, giving the rapidly-expanding Miami company control of arguably the most famous name in passenger shipping. What Carnival Corporation actually acquired, though, was a much neglected company, the great potential of which was largely unrealised and, as we shall see, Carnival subsequently invested generously to replace Cunard's existing disparate fleet with new tonnage, suitable for the twenty-first century.

Above: The *Crown Dynasty* in the livery of Cunard, to whom she was briefly chartered. The cursive hull lettering was perhaps suggestive of the handwriting Alexis Carrington (the character played by Joan Collins in the 'Dynasty' soap opera) might have produced using a fountain pen. While it was doubtless supposed to appear sophisticated, instead it arguably looked rather tacky.

Chapter 13

The mid-1990s generation

By the 1990s, the 'baby boom' generation had reached the pinnacles of their professional careers. Their children having mostly having grown up and left home, there was time to enjoy 'the good life.' This situation brought about a further expansion of the cruise industry with an unprecedented number of orders placed for larger vessels which, despite the superficial differences of branding and interior design, actually had a remarkable amount in common. Certainly, the 1990s generation was considerably more homogenised in terms of size, layout and propulsion than those of the 1980s. During this period, exponential economic growth in South-East Asia led to the construction of the first purpose-built cruise ships for operation from Hong Kong and Singapore. Just as architecture and design ashore in these former colonies echoed European and American influences with variations to accommodate aspects of local climate and culture, as we shall see, so too did the exteriors and interiors of the new Asian-based cruise ships.

As nearly all other large mass-market cruise ships were expected to operate during the year in different cruise regions, mainly proximal to the North American continent, it was important for flexibility that they should all be able to fit through the Panama Canal's locks. That way, Caribbean winter seasons and Alaskan summer seasons could be operated with the canal transit itself as a popular cruise itinerary between. 'Panamax' dimensions, requiring a hull width no greater than 32.31 metres, restricted the amount of buoyancy available and thus constrained the heights to which vessels' superstructures could be built. The maximum length dimension allowed by the canal's locks – 294.13 metres – was unproblematic as typical 1990s cruise ships measured in the 220-270 metre range. In any case, making their hulls any longer would have prevented them from calling at many of the most popular cruise ports.

In the 1990s, Royal Caribbean's President, Richard Fain, suggested on several occasions that the maximum possible passenger capacity of a cruise ship would be no more than 2,500; anything bigger would cause disembarkation to take too long. (As we shall see, Fain's position subsequently changed). Typical capacities were, however, mostly in the 1,200-2,400 range with Royal Caribbean's contributions being at the upper end. It is therefore also arguable that the generation of mass market cruise ship built in the 1990s was the last for which the ports of call, rather than the vessels' on board facilities, were the most important aspect of the overall cruise 'experience.'

A further important change impacting upon the layout and appearance of the 1990s cruise ships was the near universal adaptation of 'nested' lifeboats in recesses at Main Deck level. Indeed, SOLAS (Safety of Life At Sea) Chapter III Regulation 13.1.2, introduced in 1996, reads:

> 'Each survival craft shall be stowed as near to the water surface as is safe and practicable, in such a position that the survival craft in the embarkation position is not less than 2 metres (about 6 feet) above the waterline with the ship in the fully loaded condition under unfavourable conditions of up to 10 degrees and listed up to 20 degrees either way.'[267]

Nearly a decade before this regulation was made statutory, however, cruise ship naval architects had begun to anticipate the changes it would necessitate and so, from the late-1980s onward, new vessels incorporating nested lifeboats began to enter service, early examples being the Sitmar/P&O Princess-owned *Star Princess*, *Crown Princess* and *Regal Princess*, described above. The change had a profound effect on the disposition of external deck space; hitherto, outdoor recreational areas on cruise ships had tended to be multiple and varying in shape, size and atmosphere, ranging from a wrap-around promenade beneath the lifeboats – a classic shipboard space – to a spacious fantail at the stern with tiered decks rising above and smaller spaces atop the superstructure. Now that the lifeboat mustering areas were dissociated from the upper decks, the prime focus of outdoor space was increasingly on the topmost decks where communal public sunbathing around the pool became the main possibility; quiet corners were mostly eradicated. Inboard, the tendency to place the theatre or show lounge in the forward superstructure meant that lounges with views over the bow also largely vanished, the theory being that the sight of waves approaching might cause some more sensitive passengers to feel nauseous. (On cruise ships operating itineraries in scenically attractive cruise regions, such as the Norwegian fjords or Alaska, the exclusion of comfortable spaces in which to look ahead as dramatic vistas unfolded was particularly unfortunate.)

Another potential site for a panorama lounge would have been above the bridge but, here, many cruise operators began instead to place increasingly sophisticated gymnasia and spa facilities, reflecting a profound change in leisure culture away from smoking and drinking and towards physical fitness and 'detoxing' (of course, such facilities were lucrative from the point of view of shipboard revenue generation). Perhaps by pedalling furiously on an exercise bike or running on a treadmill overlooking the bow, it was possible to create the illusion that one was actually making the ship move forward? These trends were of course most apparent on cruise ships for the mass market, seeking to attract less experienced cruisers whose idea of shipboard life was less fixed by their previous experiences, or cruising's established traditions, such as pre-dinner drinks requiring certain types of lounge space. Thus, while the new mass market ships increasingly took their design cues from leisure design ashore, those aiming at more upmarket and conservative segments merely added new facilities without displacing those which their existing passengers had come to expect. Indeed, a key emergent difference between mass-market cruise ships and upmarket ones was that, on the former, the most attractive areas were increasingly given over to revenue-generating activities to fend off boredom, whereas on the latter, the same spaces were more likely to be reserved for social display.

As the major Miami-based cruise operators took delivery of new tonnage for the core Caribbean market, they used the smaller, existing vessels to expand into new markets, such as the Mediterranean and the Baltic, albeit continuing to

Left: Holland America's *Maasdam*, one of a series of three Italian-designed and -built cruise ships added to the fleet following Carnival Corporation's take-over. The repetitive forms of the forward superstructure and funnel, combined with orderly fenestration, reflected Fincantieri's growing cruise ship design expertise.

attract a predominantly American clientele. In order to ensure that these passengers enjoyed the precise tastes and textures of foods they were used to, it was felt necessary to supply meat and other victuals by air from the USA. Thus, a passenger ordering a steak on a Royal Caribbean or NCL ship in the Mediterranean would find that it tasted just like the ones they ate back home. The global supply of cruise ships from stores hubs on American soil would become a vital hidden phenomenon of the cruise industry as it globalised in the 1990s.

The new Holland America fleet

Following Carnival Corporation's take-over of Holland America, planning commenced for a pair of new upmarket large cruise ships, measuring approximately 60,000gt and developed from the designs of the existing *Nieuw Amsterdam* and *Noordam*. Negotiations to build these took place with the Bremer Vulkan shipyard at Vegesack, near Bremen in West Germany, but before any deal was concluded, Holland America had a major rethink. This was precipitated by meetings with Fincantieri, whose management were keen to build for the company instead and who could call on substantial government subsidies to win over potential customers. Finding Fincantieri's estimated price to be more appealing than that quoted by Bremer Vulkan, Holland America decided to proceed with the Italian builder instead.[268]

Thereafter, Fincantieri's naval architects, led by Fulvio Cernobori and assisted by Maurizio Cergol, produced their own design, measuring 55,451gt and accommodating 1,266 passengers, using a hull form derived from that of the *Costa Classica* and *Costa Romantica*. Carnival Corporation's naval architects, Technical Marine Planning, meanwhile focused on providing technical specifications for the projects.[269]

Maurizio Cergol's design of the exterior was notably successful, Holland America's simple but dignified combination of a midnight blue hull and white superstructure being accentuated by a slanted forward superstructure, a neat window arrangement and a funnel composed of a series of 'wedge' shapes, raked to match and accented with horizontal ribs. With Alaskan and Baltic cruising in mind, the vessels' external pool areas had retractable 'Magradome' roofs.

A major difference from cruise ships for operation under the Carnival Cruise Line brand was that, as passengers would pay a greater proportion of the cost of the cruise up-front, there would be rather less emphasis on revenue-generating

Left: The *Amsterdam* was the second of a pair of similar cruise ships intended for world-wide itineraries, the external design of which referenced elements of the company's old 1959 flagship, the *Rotterdam*.

Above: The *Volendam* (top) was one of two Fincantieri-built Holland America cruise ships representing a third variation of the company's recent design formula. At the upper end of the cruise market, with perhaps a more critically-engaged clientele, a diversity of design details for individual ships was thought desirable within a recognisably homogeneous overall framework. Holland America's emphasis of Dutch heritage and the traditional nomenclature of its fleet also related to this rationale. The *Rotterdam* (above) is seen in an aerial view, showing the open magradome over her 'mid-ships lido area and also an extension retro-fitted to the aft end of her superstructure, containing additional cabins.

throughout the interior space. Thus, instead of resembling malls or casinos, there would instead be numerous smaller lounges of different types and styles in which to sit and relax. In developing the design strategy, Holland America – which retained considerable autonomy from the Carnival Corporation parent – based the formula on what had been found to work aboard the *Nieuw Amsterdam* and *Noordam*. As with these vessels, the Dutch interior designers De Vlaming, Fennis, Dingemans was retained to design the internal spaces with Carnival's Joe Farcus providing input only for the main entertainment facilities. The outcome was a variation of the increasingly commonplace 'dining aft, entertainment forward and atrium amidships' framework, the spaces between being decorated in dark, saturated colours and enriched with collections of paintings and antiques, including several special commissions depicting historic Holland America vessels by the marine artist, Stephen Card.

The first of the new vessels, named the *Statendam*, should have entered service in 1992, but was beset with technical difficulties, necessitating the replacement of a damaged engine, the removal of which proved complex and time-consuming. There followed an electrical fire in the engine room and rectifying the damage caused further delays, meaning that delivery was the best part of a year late. This meant that Fincantieri had to pay compensation, meaning that the final cost was a bargain.[270] Fortunately, her sisters, the *Maasdam* and *Ryndam*, were completed to schedule in 1994 and 1996 respectively. Soon, their Alaskan and world-wide cruise itineraries developed a loyal following with the result that Holland America soon gave thought to building more of them.

Sharply increasing oil prices from the mid-1990s onward brought into focus the need to replace the 1959-vintage Holland America flagship, the *Rotterdam*, a vessel considered by many as one of the finest ever cruise ships. Although she remained in superb condition considering her advancing years, her steam turbines guzzled fuel in a manner that was becoming unacceptable to the accountants.

The *Rotterdam*'s high reputation and a loyal following among discerning passengers meant that it would be necessary to develop a design for her replacement and namesake with great care. Technical Marine Planning and Fincantieri, therefore, were given the task of jointly producing a suitable concept. In TMP, a rising talent was the naval architect Stephen Payne, who was an enthusiast for ocean liners, the *Rotterdam* being among his favourite vessels. Payne was therefore given a prominent role in coordinating the project, which was known as 'Fastdam.' This title reflected the need for a high 25-knot speed, enabling long trans-oceanic sections of world cruises to be covered relatively quickly. Fincantieri's solution to the hull design problem was a finer bow profile than on the *Statendam* and her sisters, compensated by a wider mid-body to provide additional buoyancy and with tumblehome in the hull topsides, meaning that they sloped outward towards the waterline. (This had been a feature of numerous fast Italian ocean liners of the 1930s-1960s period.) In the engine room, a fifth Sulzer diesel was installed for extra power generation when full-speed was called for; the total available output was 37,500 kW (as opposed to 34,560 kW on the four-engined Statendam-class.[271]

A major design challenge was the avoidance of vibration or cavitation (pressure pulses against the hull and rudders caused by the propellers). Fincantieri and the Swedish propeller designer KaMeWa produced several rival solutions that were tested in a cavitation tunnel until the best combination of hull aft-body, screws and rudder was arrived at (which was by KaMeWa).[272]

The new *Rotterdam*, measuring 59,652gt and accommodating 1,620-passengers, would be built at Fincantieri's Venice shipyard with delivery scheduled for 1997. Apart from hull form and engine power output, in many other respects the vessel was an enlarged and enhanced version of the Statendam-class. Externally and within, however, the homage was paid to her illustrious predecessor, Payne insisting on athwartships twin funnels, a false sheer-line for the hull paintwork and interiors repeating many of the same design motifs and colour schemes as on the 'old' *Rotterdam*.[273] This retrogressive approach, combining new technology with 'historic' visual references was applied to a number of new cruise ships of the mid-1990s, aiming to attract older and more conservative passengers. Indeed, during the subsequent period, the cruise industry's desire to evoke 'ocean liner heritage' would only increase.

A near-sister ship, named the *Amsterdam*, followed in 2000 and, on this vessel, Holland America and Fincantieri decided to emulate the successful precedent of Carnival's recent the *Elation* and *Paradise* in using podded propulsion, rather than propeller shafts.[274] In the interim, Holland America took delivery of two slightly larger vessels, the 60,906gt, 1,824-

passenger *Volendam* and *Zaandam* entered service; all of these were products of Fincantieri's Venice yard. Within this new armada of seven ships, each measuring over 50,000gt, Holland America moved rapidly from being a small but admired niche cruise operator into one of the industry's 'big names.'

The *Oriana* – P&O's 'retro' cruise ship

P&O Cruises, serving the UK domestic market (as opposed to the American and international clienteles of the P&O-owned Princess Cruises) had a similar problem to Holland America in needing to replace a much-loved flagship liner – but unlike the pristine old *Rotterdam*, the *Canberra* was badly run down and becoming life-expired. Yet, just as the new *Rotterdam* sought to evoke the vessel she replaced through similar external design and interior decorative references, so P&O too chose to create an *homage* to the past.

Initial negotiations took place with a consortium of the West German Bremer Vulkan and Lloyd Werft shipyards, which together produced a design concept known as 'Project Gemini'; this was unveiled at the 1991 Cruise and Ferry Conference in London. P&O decided, however, that the cost of proceeding would be prohibitive and so the idea was dropped. Early in 1992, however, P&O commenced negotiations instead with Meyer Werft and, thanks to the modern Papenburg yard's promise of an efficient construction process, these proved fruitful.[275] Early on, P&O announced that its new cruise ship would be named the *Oriana*, recalling the popular 1960s UK-Australia liner and cruise ship of that name.

The general dimensions and layout of the abortive 'Project Gemini' scheme were retained to form the basis for the new vessel, which would measure 69,153gt and accommodate 1,975 passengers. While 'Project Gemini' had been rather blandly streamlined, somewhat resembling Norwegian Cruise Line's the *Dreamward* and *Windward* in elongated form, as the *Oriana*'s design developed, a much more distinctive silhouette emerged. This was thanks to the early employment of the Swedish cruise ship design specialist Robert Tillberg, whose office re-styled the liner's exterior. Taking inspiration from the *Canberra*, Tillberg suggested forward-slanted lifeboat recesses and a funnel casing styled to hint at the *Canberra*'s characteristic twin stacks. Of course, the *Oriana* would have flat decks with none of the *Canberra*'s sheer or camber but, in emphasising horizontals, Tillberg made a virtue out of this necessity.[276]

In terms of performance, the *Oriana* was required to undertake similar types of lengthy cruises with long trans-oceanic segments as Holland America's *Rotterdam*. Therefore, a finer bow configuration was developed than was typical for cruise ships of her size and she was also rather more robustly constructed with thicker plates better to withstand the rigours of the open ocean. Thus, from a structural viewpoint, she was in essence a hybrid ocean liner and cruise ship. To maintain the high service speed necessary to carry out long voyages from Southampton with reserves of power to make up for storm delays, the *Oriana* was fitted with four 9-cyliner MAN-B&W diesels, generating 47,750 kW and enabling a speed of 24 knots to be maintained when necessary. (This output may be compared with the 24,000 kW generated by the *Star Princess*' four 8-cylinder main engines, but her speed was a mere 21 knots.) Unfortunately, whereas the *Rotterdam* was notable for her lack of vibration at speed, the *Oriana*'s aft hull was initially plagued by shaking (the retro-fitment of a sponson has since cured the problem).

In order to appeal to a diverse British clientele, a wide array of cabin types and sizes were specified – as well as no fewer than 26 different public rooms (as opposed to the mere 15 on the *Star Princess*). As was typical of new cruise ships, most of these were spread across two decks in the upper hull and lower superstructure with the dining rooms and galley aft and the theatre forward. A further subtle refinement on the *Oriana* was the positioning of the more elegant and exclusive public rooms aft of the mid-ships atrium with the more populist and fun-orientated, such as the disco and casino, placed forward. In some respects, this layout reflects the two-class structure of P&O liners of the past, albeit in a one-class ship – and of perceived differences in taste between the conservative lower and upper middle classes, who would form the bulk of her expected clientele.

The *Oriana*'s public rooms would be required to serve rather different purposes from those of her America-based contemporaries. Instead of the Las Vegas-style show lounge (or Copa Room) found on most recent cruise ships, there would be a theatre, staging plays and London West End musicals. Ballroom dancing, classical recitals, a cinema auditorium, a pub plus an elegant lounge suitable for hosting afternoon tea were all distinctly 'British' requirements, already well catered for on the *Canberra*.[277]

The *Oriana*'s interiors were largely the work of a London-based Scot, John McNeece, who was a mid-1960s graduate of the Glasgow School of Art's Interior Design department. McNeece had since established himself as a successful designer of cruise ship interiors. He worked alongside Robert Tillberg to realise the *Oriana*'s extensive and lavish public rooms, the themes of which not only recalled P&O vessels of the recent past, but also celebrated the company's nineteenth century imperialist origins. Particularly outstanding in these regards were The Anderson Room, named after P&O's co-founder, Arthur Anderson, and the adjacent library space, both of which were furnished by the cabinetmaker David Lindley, nephew of H.M. The Queen. The Curzon Room, named after the controversial Edwardian era Viceroy of India, Lord Curzon (1859-1925), was sumptuously furnished and specially designed acoustically for piano recitals, thereby reducing the problems and complexities of Curzon's legacy to pastel-shaded sofas and scatter-cushions. Just like the First Class interiors of historic P&O liners serving India and the Far East, the overall effects of McNeece's designs sought to reflect the traditionalism of English country houses and of Pall Mall gentlemen's clubs.[278]

McNeece took a more light-hearted approach when designing the Lord's Tavern pub, Harlequin's – which, by night, served as the ship's disco – and the Pacific Lounge. As the former was intended to replicate the role of the *Canberra*'s popular Cricketers' Tavern, McNeece, produced a witty post-modern take on the Marylebone Cricket Club's headquarters, featuring a green carpet in broad two-tone stripes, bar stools resembling cricket stumps and window blinds bordered in MCC 'ham and eggs' colours.[279] Elsewhere – notably in the restaurants and atrium – the *Oriana*'s colour palette tended towards the unchallenging pastel tones favoured in the era preceding her construction. Throughout, the standard of finish

Externally and inboard, the design of P&O Cruises' *Oriana* consciously sought to evoke elements of Britain's imperialist past and Commonwealth connections. The vessel's silhouette had similar detailing to the UK-Australia liner and cruise ship *Canberra* while some of the public rooms referenced P&O shipboard design of the early twentieth century. Here we see the Anderson Room (centre left), Lord's Tavern (centre right) and the Curzon Room (bottom left). The bottom right image shows the *Canberra* and *Oriana* together at Southampton, the latter's transom stern and fuller aft-body contrasting with the older liner's slimmer lines.

was exceptionally high, however.

Further public rooms – and extensive lido areas – were located on the *Oriana*'s topmost decks, but these spaces were rather more shaded than on the majority of cruise ships, it being expected that a greater proportion of her passengers would prefer to take the sea air than to sunbathe. A great many artworks adorned the passenger spaces – but, reflecting the predominant passenger demographic, these tended towards conservative taste and values. P&O's policy on shipboard art was to 'flatter and enlarge the cabins and public spaces where they are hung; nothing too disturbing, nothing gloomy… [Artworks] had to bridge the gap between those who know about art and those who do not, pleasing both.'[280] In practice, this specification translated into a combination of impressionistic, realist and Art Deco-style pieces with a strong sense of nostalgia for Britain's imperial past.

The *Oriana* was named by H.M. The Queen in Southampton in April 1995. At this event, P&O's Chairman, Lord Sterling, was interviewed by BBC Radio Solent, whose presenter questioned him on whether P&O had not made a terrible mistake in building the ship. Sterling's memorable response was 'our only mistake was not ordering two of her.'[281] Within only a few years, P&O would remedy this matter with the ordering from Meyer Werft of a near-sister, the 76,152gt, 1,878-passenger *Aurora*, which entered service in the year 2000.

When ordering the *Oriana* from Meyer Werft, P&O simultaneously placed contracts with the Fincantieri shipyard at Monfalcone for the first pair of what would eventually become a series of four 77,449-ton cruise ships for its Princess Cruises division. Fincantieri's naval architect Gianfranco Bertaglia decided to emulate aspects of their previous the *Crown Princess* and *Regal Princess* designs, albeit without the 'dolphin'-like domes on their superstructures. In place of the earlier vessels' vertical funnels, a parabolic design was selected, which Bertaglia thought more likely to disperse smoke successfully, as well as being less visually challenging. The *Sun Princess* entered service in 1995 and was followed less than two years later by the *Dawn Princess*. Two further examples – the *Sea Princess* and *Ocean Princess* – entered service in 1998 and 1999 respectively. These vessels could each carry 2,250 passengers, many in outside staterooms with balconies. There were, however, fewer public rooms than on the *Oriana* as the shipboard style reflected American tastes.

The interiors were designed by Teresa Anderson, an American of Peruvian birth who had studied interior design in Maryland in the 1970s. In the early 1990s, she was involved in designing parts of the *Crown Princess* and *Regal Princess* interiors and, consequently, she came to be employed full-time by Princess Cruises from 1994 onwards as its 'in house' designer, producing interiors for all of its subsequent new-buildings, commencing with the *Sun Princess*.[282] As the new Princess ships were Italian-built, Anderson was assisted in these projects by an Italian architect, Giacomo Mortola, whose previous work included spaces on Sitmar's the *Fairsky* of 1984.[283] In comparison with the glamorous light-toned Californian styling of previous Princess vessels, Anderson's *oeuvre* was conservative, her penchant being ornate mouldings, brown imitation wood panelling and marble slabs. Thus, the disjunction between the new Princess ships' slick exterior profiles, and their traditionalist interiors, was extreme. This notwithstanding, Princess' passengers evidently appreciated Anderson's approach as she has since designed numerous cruise ship interiors perpetuating the same design formula.

Several other new cruise ships in the same size category and serving similar market

Above: P&O Princess Cruises' *Sun Princess* (top) was designed and built by Fincantieri for the North American and international cruise markets. Celebrity Cruises' Meyer Werft-built *Mercury* was similarly dimensioned and laid out, though with much more rectilinear external styling by Jon Bannenberg. Inboard, both vessels followed the contemporary international approach of Americanised four-star hotels, as a lounge on the *Century* demonstrates.

Above: Royal Caribbean's *Legend of the Seas* (top) and *Rhapsody of the Seas* (above) were two of six large, new cruise ships in three different variations for the company, all of which featured extensive glazing of their public room decks, behind the nested lifeboats. This so-called 'Vision' concept emulated the approach first attempted on *Nordic Empress* to 'open up' key public rooms to the exterior.

segments as the newest Princess vessels entered service in the mid-1990s. Celebrity Cruises followed up the success of the *Horizon* and *Zenith* with the 76,522gt, 1,778-passenger *Century*, *Galaxy*, and *Mercury*, completed by Meyer Werft in 1995, 1996 and 1997 respectively.[284] As with the earlier pair, Jon Bannenberg designed their exterior silhouettes. Apart from them being of greater size overall, a significant change was the inclusion of cabins with balconies on the decks above the nested lifeboats. Inboard, the vessels were notably spacious – the most remarkable spaces being the mid-ships atrium, double-height restaurant and a glass-enclosed observation lounge above the bridge.

Three different interior designers were employed to design the interiors – the Greek Michael Katzourakis, London-based John McNeece and the American Birch Coffey, whose studio was located in Connecticut. As the latter had never previously carried out shipboard work, he did extensive research into liner interiors of the inter-war era to inform his approach. To make the vessels distinctive, the three consultants were asked to design different spaces on each one, meaning that there was an opportunity to compare from ship to ship a variety of approaches to decorating the same volumes. The restaurants, located aft, had extensive glazing on three sides, reflecting the precedent set by Royal Caribbean's the *Nordic Empress*.

As with previous Celebrity ships, the *Century*, *Galaxy* and *Mercury* were notable for their displays of contemporary art, including works by Damian Hirst, Ellsworth Kelly, Peter Halley and Michael Craig Martin. Indeed, they were among the last new cruise ships on which a ship owner personally selected the artworks. In future, as ownership slipped from established family-owned shipping companies to large conglomerates with international shareholders, specialist 'corporate art' suppliers came to the fore, extending their existing hotel and office work into the cruise sector. Names such as ICA (International Corporate Art), based in Oslo, and ArtLink, with offices in London and New York came to specialise in curating the many diverse pieces required to fill cruise ship interiors. These ranged from bespoke giant abstract glass, fabric and metal sculptures to fill the voids of atrium spaces, to smaller works for stairwells and lift lobbies – and well as hundreds of mass-produced framed prints for the cabins. To appeal to wide audiences, the types of work typically chosen were highly diverse and usually intended to form part of the scenography of the interior spaces, acting as a backdrop, rather than the focus of attention (as would be the case in gallery settings).

While Celebrity was developing the *Century*, *Galaxy* and *Mercury*, Royal Caribbean updated its Sovereign-class design by re-arranging the superstructure with a horizontal, rather than vertical segregation of cabins and public rooms to accommodate nested lifeboats while also providing some suites with balconies on the upper decks. An effect of this was to enable the sides of the restaurant and atrium in the lifeboat recesses to be fully-glazed, their expanses of tinted glass reflecting the approach previously tried on the *Nordic Empress*.

Using variations on this overall approach, Royal Caribbean ordered a series of six new cruise ships of three different designs. In all instances, the interior design was largely by Njål Eide and was in the same glitzy, pastel-shaded style as the *Nordic Empress*. The 69,130gt, 2,064-passenger *Legend of the Seas* and *Splendor of the Seas*, built by Chantiers de l'Atlantique St Nazaire and delivered in 1995 and 1996, were intended for cruising in regions other than the Caribbean and so had somewhat more enclosed upper decks than was typical of other members of the fleet. This was achieved by the installation of a light space-frame structure supporting a canopy of blue-tinted glass, designed by the Norwegian architect Per Høydahl, who was also responsible for styling the vessels' exteriors. Among the attractions beneath was the first shipboard miniature golf course, formed as a contoured landscape from sections of hardened foam and covered in various types of artificial turf to imitate rough, fairways and greens. Further aft, the 'Viking Crown' lounge was located at the base of the funnel, rather than being cantilevered out from its sides as on previous Royal Caribbean vessels, and this meant it could be much more commodious while saving construction costs.[285]

Chantiers de l'Atlantique subsequently built the 78,491gt, 2,417-passenger *Rhapsody of the Seas*, and *Vision of the Seas*, on which the Viking Crown was placed midway along the upper superstructure, entirely separate from the funnel; these entered service in 1997 and 1998. For the similar, though somewhat shorter, *Grandeur of the Seas* and *Enchantment of the Seas*, measuring 73,817gt and carrying 1,950 passengers, Royal Caribbean returned to its original favoured builder, the former-Wärtsilä shipyard in Helsinki, which delivered them in 1996 and 1997. Following a recent take-over by the

Norwegian Kværner engineering group, it and its sister yard in Turku were now known as Kværner Masa Yards. Altogether, these six cruise ships increased the capacity of the Royal Caribbean fleet by more than half.

These vessels' fairly uniform interiors were, when combined with similar Caribbean and Alaskan ports of call in which homogenous new retail and tourist infrastructure had been specially built to service cruise passengers' needs, likely to cause them to lose track of the passage of time. After all, a shopping centre in a vernacular Caribbean style on St Thomas in the Virgin Islands would be very similar to one at Freeport in the Bahamas. To mitigate against passengers forgetting which day of the week it was, Royal Caribbean henceforth placed carpets in the passenger elevators with the name of the day woven into the pattern; these were replaced by the crew at midnight with the next in sequence.

Desiring its own equivalents of the latest Royal Caribbean vessels, Costa Cruises placed orders for two new cruise ships with Bremer Vulkan at Vegesack, near Bremen in West Germany. Their design was based on the 'Project Gemini', which had been prepared jointly with Lloyd Werft and previously offered speculatively to P&O. Although the British company decided not to place an order with these yards Costa was more easily convinced. The final design, however, benefitted from significant changes demanded by Costa, who wanted vessels with aesthetic similarities to the recent *Costa Classica* and *Costa Romantica*.

The 75,051gt, 75,051gt 1,928-passenger the *Costa Victoria* and *Costa Olympia* were partly financed by Costa selling their 27-year-old former flagship, the *Eugenio Costa*, to a Bremer Vulkan subsidiary in part-exchange. With a deep recession affecting the Western World in the early 1990s, the yard's management were obviously keen to cut a deal just to keep going at a time when orders were few and far between. As Bremer Vulkan's steel fabrication facilities were unable alone to produce the sections necessary for so large a project within the required timeframe, it subcontracted some of this work to other shipyards in the vicinity, such as Schichau Unterweser of Bremerhaven. The interior fit-out was carried out by Lloyd Werft, whose yard was located nearby.

As with the *Costa Classica* and *Costa Romantica*, Pierluigi Cerri and Ivana Porfiri of Gregotti Associati were retained to style the exterior profile and to design some of the interiors, while the remainder were given to the Swedish cruise and ferry interior specialists, Tillberg Design. The forward superstructure had extensive glazing, behind which was located the tiered Concorde Plaza lounge, spanning four decks and giving passengers a spectacular view ahead, even in inclement weather (incidentally, this space also contained a seven-metre-high waterfall).[286]

Just as the *Costa Victoria* was being finished for delivery in July 1996, Bremer Vulkan, declared bankruptcy. Apart from recent losses in its shipbuilding division, the sprawling engineering group had accumulated too much debt and so the banks foreclosed. This meant that work had to stop on the *Costa Olympia*, which was only around 40% complete. Meanwhile, the *Costa Victoria* left for Venice to commence her maiden cruise through the Adriatic to Greece and Turkey. At that time – and only briefly – she could claim to be the largest cruise ship ever built for a European-headquartered shipping company. Although few could have predicted at that time, she was also to be Costa's final new ship delivered under the ownership of the founding family.

The incomplete *Costa Olympia* hull was sold in 1997 to Norwegian Cruise Line which badly needed larger, newer tonnage to compete with the Carnival and Royal Caribbean fleets. Completed by Lloyd Werft to a modified design which placed a greater emphasis on capacity than style, she entered service in 1998 as the 77,104gt, 2,002-passenger *Norwegian Sky* with interiors that were entirely the work of Tillberg Design. Her name's 'Norwegian' prefix reflected a growing tendency for cruise lines to emphasise at every opportunity their corporate brand by including it in vessels' nomenclature, followed by suffix relating either to the elements (Sea, Sky, Sun, Wind), female royalty (Queen, Princess, Countess), precious stones (Pearl, Diamond, Jewel) or temporal escapism (Dream, Fantasy). During ensuing decades, this homogenised approach of selling brands rather than particular vessels became generic across the mass market cruise industry.

So pleased were NCL with the *Norwegian Sky* that after a short interval, they ordered a further example, the slightly larger 78,309gt, 2,350-passenger *Norwegian Sun*. Her steelwork was built at Wismar in the former-East Germany by a shipyard recently purchased by the Norwegian-headquartered Aker engineering group – a situation made possible by German re-unification in 1990. Subsequently, outfitting was carried out by Lloyd Werft – whose employees and subcontractors had the requisite skills – and she entered service in 2001. A major difference

Below: Part of the double-height main dining room on Royal Caribbean's *Grandeur of the Seas* (below), designed by Njål Eide, showing how walls of tinted glass on either side with balconies set back within enabled the kinds of spatial relationship previously only seen in atrium spaces to be enjoyed in large public rooms such as this. Costa Cruises' *Costa Victoria* (bottom) likewise had some large areas of glazing between her lifeboats but, in addition, there was a much bigger expanse in the forward superstructure, behind which a four-deck-high lounge and event space, the Concorde Plaza, was located.

128 | Cruise Ships: A Design History

Above: Norwegian Cruise Line's *Norwegian Sky* was a modified near-sister of the *Costa Victoria*, the revised design of which eliminated the multi-deck forward lounge, but added balconies to the cabins on the upper decks.

Below: An example of Partnership Design's bright and informal approach to the interiors of the *Aida*, which sought to emulate the style found in a German or Mediterranean beach resort ashore.

between the *Costa Victoria* and the two NCL-owned near-sisters was the fitment of balconies on the exteriors of the upper superstructures of the latter pair. As more cruise passengers came to demand balconies, several other cruise lines subsequently used the same technique of simply welding these on.

The fall of the Iron Curtain and the re-unification of Germany led to profound changes in what had been the Communist German Democratic Republic. Throughout the Communist era, its principal shipping company, Deutsche Seereederei Rostock (DSR), had operated cruise ships – initially the 1948-vintage *Völkerfreundschaft* (originally the *Stockholm* of the Swedish American Line) and, latterly, the considerably more luxurious *Arkona*, which originally had been the *Astor* (described above); these were mainly chartered to West German travel agencies.

DSR's Chairman, Horst Rahne, correctly believed that, in future years, the cruise market in a prospering united Germany would have an exponential growth potential. After all, Germans have a strong maritime tradition and affinity with the sea and, just as in Britain and America, there was a relatively well-off post-war 'baby boom' generation approaching retirement age *en masse* and also a younger generation looking for value-for-money all-inclusive holidays in German-speaking environments. Aida Cruises would serve these markets with what were described as 'club ships' —essentially floating informal holiday resorts. In a German context, such facilities had first appeared ashore in the 1930s under Kraft durch Freude, the biggest resort of which was the Seebad Prora on Rügen Island. After the Second World War, commercial holiday centres appeared in the west while the East German Communist Party arranged its own such facilities. Moreover, Western Europeans in general took to the popular Mediterranean resorts run by Club Med and numerous other package holiday providers. Such approaches had not yet been attempted aboard cruise ships, however.

At first, DSR considered either chartering or purchasing the Baltic short-cruise ship and former ferry the *Sally Albatross*. One of her attractions was that all of her public rooms were grouped on the upper decks of the superstructure, surrounding a midships lido area; this was similar to the arrangement of a shore-based resort in which the pool was likewise a focus, around which the various bars and eating options were arranged. From a commercial viewpoint, this centralisation was attractive as it meant that every catering outlet could be supplied from a single central kitchen. On typical cruise ships, by contrast, there were usually two groupings of public rooms – one occupying two decks in the upper hull and lower superstructure and another atop the superstructure, adjacent to the lido areas.

Having failed to purchase the *Sally Albatross* and with no obvious alternatives available, DSR decided instead to order a purpose-built 38,531gt 1,230-passenger cruise ship from the Kværner Masa shipyard (formerly Wärtsilä) in Turku for delivery in 1996. DSR created a new brand, Aida Cruises, to operate the vessel, which was named the *Aida*. The influence of the *Sally Albatross* was felt in her layout with all public rooms located on the upper decks and in the consequently efficient utilisation of crew providing hotel services. Whereas traditional cruising involved a great deal of personal service from restaurant and cabin stewards, Aida Cruises' model more closely followed that of shore-based beach holiday resorts and large Baltic ferries, on which a majority of passengers preferred cafeteria and 'eat as much as you like' buffet dining to *à la carte* table service. A further influence was the type of buffet food provided in the so-called 'Food Markt' restaurants typically found in German shopping malls, with an emphasis on freshly chopped raw vegetables and salads, served in quantity. A single central galley provided a constant supply of food platters for the restaurant and lido buffets, as well as individual plated dishes for the small table service restaurant, which was included to please the expected minority of more traditionally-minded passengers. Whereas a typical cruise ship of the *Aida*'s size would have employed over 500 crew, thanks to her efficient layout and predominantly self-service catering, just 320 were needed. Reflecting another German tradition with origins in the inter-war era, the *Aida* had one sun deck reserved for nudist followers of so-called 'Frei Körper Kultur' (FKK).[287]

Upon completion, the *Aida* was painted in a distinctive livery, featuring red lips painted on her bow and eyes with trailing shadows on her hull's topsides, making her instantly recognisable. Inboard, her bright décor – featuring striped parasols, brightly-coloured awnings, reed-thatched pagoda roofs, imitation stone dressings and facsimile palm trees – was intended to create a festive resort-like atmosphere; this was the work of German interior designers, Kai Bunge and Siegfried Schindler of Hamburg-based Partnership Design, and thus provided a genuinely Teutonic image of holiday relaxation – a scrupulously ordered and absolutely punctual version of the vaguely exotic and primitive in

Above: The *Aida* as she appeared upon entry into service, with hull graphics by the German artist Feliks Büttner.

which German was the only language spoken.[288]

From the outset, Aida's 'club ship' concept was a great success and subsequently further vessels were planned – but DSR was short of the capital that their construction would require and so Rahn instituted negotiations with Britain's P&O to make Aida Cruises a joint venture. P&O's Lord Sterling, was convinced that Aida's business plan was a good one and so in 1999 P&O purchased the brand from DSR and immediately placed orders with Meyer Werft for two further ships, the *AIDAcara* and *AIDAaura* (the original Aida became *AIDAvita*).[289] P&O already had a strong relationship with German builders of ships of many different kinds and now, through the Aida brand, it was providing cruises for German holidaymakers too. Few of them would realise that a chameleon-like British owner was ultimately responsible for providing these highly tailored experiences.

The rise of Asian cruising

If Eastern Europe was one emerging market in which a new middle class was being encouraged to cruise, South East Asia was another offering even greater potential. Since the 1960s, a wide variety of ageing passenger liners had been based in Hong Kong for cruises to other destinations in the vicinity, mainly appealing to venturesome Australian, American and European passengers. The most successful of these was the China Navigation Company's 9,696gt *Coral Princess* (which originally had been the Brazilian coastal liner, the *Princesa Leopoldina* of 1961); from 1970 she operated for 20 years in the nascent Hong Kong cruise trade before old age finally caught up. Other less successful ventures included that of the Norwegian Thoresen & Bruusgaard, which from 1973 until 1977 operated the *Rasa Sayang* (ex-*Bergensfjord* of 1956), and the Danish J. Lauritzen's Pearl Cruises of Scandinavia, which between 1982 and 1987 ran the *Pearl of Scandinavia* (originally the Baltic ferry *Finlandia*, dating from 1967). Even the mainland Chinese Communist government-owned China Ocean Shipping Company (COSCO) chartered their flagship liner, the *Yaohua*, which had been built by Chantiers de l'Atlantique in 1967 for the China-East Africa service, for use as a cruise ship. Intriguingly for a Communist vessel, she had three classes of accommodation though, when cruising from 1982 onward, only the First and Second Class cabins were used. Her charterer was the Swedish Linblad organisation, which ran cruises between Beijing and Hong Kong, attracting an international clientele.[290]

At that time, Japan and Hong Kong were South East Asia's economic powerhouses, with Singapore, Taiwan and South Korea rapidly catching up. The demise in 1976 of the Chinese dictator Mao Zedong and the subsequent rise of Deng Xiaoping, who instituted market reforms, led to the emergence in China of a new middle class. China's new-found prosperity and rapid economic growth was echoed throughout the region.

Whereas Australian cruise passengers were tempted to sea primarily by the promise of cheap drink, for the Chinese market, the big attraction was shipboard gambling. Indeed, several passenger ships operated from Hong Kong on daytime or overnight casino 'junket' cruises. In 1993, a fast-growing Malaysian gaming company called Genting, which had been founded in 1965 by the business entrepreneur Tan Sri Lim Goh Tong, created a new Hong Kong-based subsidiary called Star Cruises. Having become personally wealthy from developing and operating the Genting Highlands gambling and entertainment resort, located in the mountains above Kuala Lumpur where the air was attractively cool and fresh, Tan Sri Lim Goh Tong became a frequent cruise passenger. His cruise experiences evidently gave him the idea of establishing his own cruise line.

Through an Isle of Man-based subsidiary, he bought a pair of large Baltic cruise ferries, the 40,012gt *Athena* and the *Kalypso*, which had been built in the late-1980s for the Swedish partner of the Viking Line ferry consortium. These were converted into cruise ships through the addition of extra outdoor deck space with a swimming pool and Jacuzzis while the car deck was converted into large casinos. As well as buying these two ships, Star Cruises wisely offered good terms of employment to their Swedish officers – meaning that those who chose to remain aboard could provide the new upstart with a great deal of operational expertise.

As the ferry routes between Sweden and Finland involved precise navigation in very constricted waters and as the

Above: Star Cruises' first purpose-built cruise ship, the *Superstar Leo*, was designed specifically for the Asian cruise market using ideas inherited from the company's existing converted ex-Scandinavian cruise ferries.

Below: A stern-quarter view of the *Superstar Virgo*, showing the three large dining room windows in her stern and the promenade deck rising upwards, indicating the rake of the main floor of her show lounge.

vessels used were of state-of-the-art design, their officers had developed some innovative navigation techniques to minimise the risk of making errors. Because the navigation bridges had four consoles, a 'conference' system was devised whereby, rather than simply issuing direct commands, the captain would solicit the advice of the other navigating officers and would confirm their agreement before a manoeuvre was executed; that way, four intellects rather than one would be brought to bear and any dissent would be heard, minimising the chance of an error being made. When Star Cruises introduced the *Athena* and *Kalypso* as the *Star Aquarius* and *Star Pisces* on cruises from Hong Kong and Singapore, these techniques continued to be applied – putting the company at the forefront of operational practices in the entire cruise industry.[291] Inboard, the vessels' ferry-style catering arrangements enabled types of informal service similar to those of Aida Cruises (described above) with a single galley simultaneously providing food *en masse* for a buffet and cafeteria, as well as smaller numbers of *a la carte* dishes. Star Cruises modified this by introducing a number of themed dining areas, each providing the typical dishes of a different Asian country or region – Indian, Thai, Malay, Indonesian, Cantonese and so on. That way, diners could come to eat whenever they felt hungry, rather than at the precisely set mealtimes typical at that time on most cruise ships. With gambling a key aim, such flexibility was advantageous in keeping the casinos in use at all times when at sea.

During the second half of the 1990s, Star Cruises expanded very rapidly – indeed, it seemed that nearly every second-hand cruise ship of fairly recent construction to appear on the market was snapped up. The outcome was a fleet encompassing vessels such as the former *Royal Viking Sky* of 1973, which in 1997 became the *Superstar Capricorn*, and Hapag-Lloyd's even more luxurious the *Europa* of 1982, which was renamed the *Superstar Europe* in 1999. As both of these were about as different as modern passenger ships could be from Star Cruises' initial converted ferries, it appears that their acquisition was opportunistic and the result of Tan Sri Lim Goh Tong's enthusiasm, rather than any strictly business-led strategy.

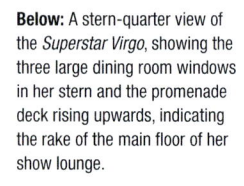

Soon, Star Cruises was contemplating its first new buildings, which were perhaps a necessary response to the South East Asian bourgeoisie's disdain for anything second hand. The basic design was produced by the Swedish naval architect, Bo Franzén, who, like Star Cruises' ships' officers, had been inherited from Viking Line. A decade previously, he had been involved in developing the *Athena* and *Kalypso* ferry projects, plus a design for a larger Baltic cruise ferry, the *Europa*, which upon completion was taken over by Viking Line's rival, Silja Line, entering service as the *Silja Europa*. The outcome of his concept development work for Star Cruises was a 75,904gt, Panamax-sized cruise ship design with a much higher than usual passenger capacity of 3,760, the layout of which owed a great deal to the *Europa/Silja Europa*.

Orders for two such new vessels, to be named *Superstar Leo* and *Superstar Virgo*, were placed with Meyer Werft, which had built the *Silja Europa*, with delivery scheduled for 1998 and 1999.[292] Although their predominant clientele would be Asian, the Swedish-based cruise ship specialists, Tillberg Design, were commissioned to create a majority of the internal spaces. Having recently produced sedate designs for P&O's the *Oriana* to please traditionalist Britons, as well as numerous flamboyant schemes for recent American-based vessels, Tillberg now needed to devise interiors resembling the latest casinos and hotels in Macau (the former Portuguese colony adjacent to Hong Kong which had become the region's equivalent of Las Vegas). The exceptionally rich and colourful interior décor made extensive use of colours considered auspicious in Chinese culture – such as red and gold. Even when compared with the vivid post-modernism of the interiors of the Carnival fleet in North America, the *Superstar Leo* and *Superstar Virgo* public rooms were eye-popping. The *Superstar Virgo*'s atrium, for example, was adorned with leaping golden horses and otherwise featured panels of Tiffany glass, chandeliers, ornate carpets, classical columns and a wide palette of saturated colours. Even the outside deck spaces had painted murals on seemingly every surface.

Star Cruises required several modifications from typical cruise ship layouts of the era in order make the vessels' facilities more suitable for local market conditions. The short duration of Star Cruises' itineraries with 3- or 4-night trips being the norm, meant that most passengers would happily occupy compact ferry-like cabins. Of course, there were also some very sumptuous multi-roomed suites for the 'high rollers' whom Star Cruises also planned to attract. Another change from recent cruise ship design for the western market was to make the areas dedicated to casino gaming larger and unusually prominent. As with all of the company's vessels, these were rather different from typical gaming spaces on cruise ships elsewhere in the world, in which the stakes are low to encourage non-habitual gamblers to enjoy a light-hearted flutter. Instead, Star Cruises' casinos are more like those for serious big money gamblers ashore, with higher stakes and with ceilings bristling with CCTV cameras. The main casino, the Star Club, was located in the forward superstructure where on any other cruise ship of the era a show lounge would inevitably have been. Like on the *Silja Europa*, this facility was placed aft, albeit above the main dining room, the latter making a virtue of the tiered arrangement with a deck head rising in steps towards three two-deck-high bow-headed windows, facing aft. Alongside this facility, the *Superstar Leo* and *Superstar Virgo* perpetuated the multi-restaurant dining concept so popular on the company's existing vessels.

The details of service provision were also modified according to local demand – such as late-night striptease shows in the theatre, obviously intended to attract voyeuristic male audiences of gamblers. Most remarkably in such a context was the display of extremely expensive and desirable modern artworks, which had been collected by Tan Sri Lim Goh Tong; these included paintings and drawings by Miró, Picasso – and, most notoriously, Lucien Freud's famous portrait of the supermodel Kate Moss when pregnant, which was hung amid the multi-coloured baroque and rococo enrichments of the *Superstar Virgo*'s extra-tariff restaurant.[293]

Before the *Superstar Leo* and *Superstar Virgo* even entered service, Star Cruises ordered a further pair from Meyer, expected to be named the *Superstar Scorpio* and *Superstar Libra*. Thus, within less than a decade, Star Cruises had gone from nothing to a projected ten-strong fleet by the early-2000s. Its exponential growth reflected that of South East Asia as a whole.

Family cruising from Florida

In Florida, meanwhile, one of America's biggest and best-known leisure brands, the Walt Disney Corporation, became another new entrant into the cruise industry via its British-based subsidiary, the Walt Disney Company. In 1996, it registered a new cruise line, Magical Cruise Company Ltd, the operational headquarters of which was located in the Disney-owned town of Celebration in Florida. Disney's plan was to offer family-orientated cruises and 'cruise and stay' vacations, involving a combination of shipboard days and a holiday in a Disney resort. Family-orientated cruising from Florida was not, however, a new idea; the concept was pioneered in 1983 by two former-Norwegian Caribbean Line executives, Bruce Nierenberg and Bjørnar Hermansen, who established Premier Cruise Line with finance from the Dial Corporation (makers of Dial soap and owners of the Greyhound long-distance bus service). They bought second-hand the 1957-vintage Costa Cruises vessel the *Federico C.* which was renovated with an entire deck for children's activities and named the *Starship Royale*.[294] Premier's bright red hull livery stood out from the other all-white vessels sailing regularly from Port Canaveral at that time. Although an

Above: An extra-tariff restaurant (top) and the atrium on the *Superstar Virgo*, featuring baroque-style enrichments and statues of gilded horses, all intended to appeal to Asian passengers' sense of what constitutes luxury.

132 | Cruise Ships: A Design History

Right: Disney Cruise Line's *Disney Wonder*, the exterior of which was styled and painted to resemble the public's idea of how a typical traditional ocean liner would have appeared.

Above: The *Disney Wonder*'s Animator's Palette restaurant (top) gradually transforms from black and white 'sketches' to full-colour 'animations' over the course of a meal. Elsewhere, the vessel contains very extensive facilities for the entertainment of children of all ages, including areas for 'creative play' (bottom).

obvious problem was managing fluctuating demand due to children being at school for much of the year, Premier found that parents would pay a premium on board to have them entertained and so on board revenue was high. Premier also solved the problem of gathering service charges for cabin and restaurant stewards by automatically adding fixed amounts to final accounts to be settled by credit card prior to disembarkation; this meant that passengers who were less accustomed to cruising's customary procedures would not have to worry about making appropriate payments.[295]

By the early-1990s, Premier had four so-called 'Big Red Boats' sailing between Florida ports and the Bahamas, the others being the *Starship Oceanic* and *Starship Atlantic* (both of which had belonged to Home Lines) and the *Starship Majestic*, formerly P&O's the *Spirit of London* and *Sun Princess*. Previously, Nierenberg had negotiated a deal with Disney whereby 'cruise and stay' vacations were offered involving several days at a Disney resort, plus a short cruise with costumed actors dressed as cartoon characters appearing on board – and this 'Disneyfication' was very successful in attracting families in even larger numbers. Soon Premier considered building new ships – though these plans were vetoed by Dial who refused to invest the necessary capital. Next, an attempt was made to sell Premier to Carnival, but it proved impossible to secure agreement between the parties.[296]

It was this situation that led Disney to establish its own cruise line instead, thereby taking control of the family cruise market from Florida and expanding the reach of its brand. Disney's 'imagineers' planned an entirely purpose-designed cruise operation from Port Canaveral, the overall aesthetic of which would mainly evoke the style of liner travel in the mid-twentieth century (or, at least the cartoon and comic-book image of how typical ocean liners might have looked during that period). In practice, this meant a black hull with a sheer line and gold strake and a superstructure capped by two slanted red funnels with black tops. Furthermore, the new Disney Cruises embarkation terminal was modelled on the streamlined Art Deco Ocean Terminal in Southampton which, ironically, had been demolished in the early-1980s at the very point when, thanks to calls by cruise ships, passenger travel by sea was beginning to experience a revival.

To build its initial two vessels, Disney signed a contract with Fincantieri. The *Disney Magic* and *Disney Wonder*, measuring 83,308gt and accommodating 2,834-passengers, were built at the company's Venice shipyard. Underpinning their retro-styled exteriors was the builder's by now considerable cruise ship design expertise, accumulated through its collaborations with Carnival and Holland America. From Premier Cruise Lines came the idea of devoting a single deck solely to children, with separate zones for toddlers through to teenagers, thereby allowing their parents and relatives a fairly child-free cruise experience elsewhere on board. Although Fincantieri's cruise ship design team, led by Maurizio Cergol, had very considerable technical, planning and aesthetic inputs into the convincingly well-proportioned vessels which resulted, the details of the passenger experience were almost entirely of Disney's own creation.

Inboard, perhaps the most surprising aspect of the Disney cruise concept was just how conventional so much of it appeared. Out with the children's areas, the predominant design style of the *Disney Magic* and *Disney Wonder* was revived Art Nouveau, perhaps inspired by images the 'imagineers' had seen of the Compagnie Générale Transatlantique's *Paris* as she had appeared in the 1920s. Disney, however, were shrewd enough to realise that its cruise line's biggest challenge would be adequately reflecting cruising's established traditions so as to attract passengers who might not be so attracted to cruise in a mere floating version of one of its shore-based theme parks. The most significant shipboard innovation was 'rotational dining', whereby passengers ate in a different themed restaurant every evening, the serving staff moving along with them to maintain continuity. Of the various themed eateries, the most remarkable was called 'Animator's Palette'; at the commencement of mealtimes, this was entirely black and white with all fixtures and fittings appearing to have been drawn in cartoon style. During the course of a sitting, these 'outlines' were gradually illuminated in colour, then began to come 'alive', thanks to back-projections. Throughout the passenger accommodation – but especially on the lido decks – Disney branded imagery was much in evidence – Mickey Mouse's head in silhouette on the funnels, his gloved hand supporting a water flume and Donald Duck emerging from the stern, apparently finishing painting the vessel's name and port of registry.

Euro cruising

So far as the European cruise market was concerned, the leading nations were Britain and Germany – countries with advanced commercial and industrial economies whose population demographics and spread of wealth were particularly affected by the legacies of the Second World War (meaning that the post-war population bulge was reaching retirement by the 1990s). Furthermore, these countries had strong maritime traditions with leading shipping lines such as P&O and Hapag-Lloyd that had pioneered cruising a century before. The other European countries contributed proportionately far fewer cruise passengers but the 1990s economic boom began to alter that situation. In particular, the nations of southern Europe – all net beneficiaries of EU membership – experienced a credit boom with a commensurate rise in holiday-making.

This situation led a Greek-born, Italian-based shipping entrepreneur, George Poulides, whose business career had begun in Genoa where, from the late-1960s onward, he acted as the agent for Corsica Ferries, to found Festival Cruises. In the early-1990s, Poulides developed Festival Cruises as a consciously pan-European cruise line, using the European Union's blue and yellow colours for its corporate brand identity and aiming to attract custom from all over the continent, rather from just a particular country, as was the case with most other European-based cruise operations.[297] In 1994, Festival Cruises commenced operations with a vessel originally built in the early-1970s for P&O as the UK-Spain car ferry the *Eagle* and subsequently converted for cruising under French, then Greek ownership as the *Azur*. A year later, another cruise ship, the *Bolero* (previously Norwegian Caribbean Line's the *Starward*) was acquired. In 1997, a third vessel was

Below: Festival Cruises' *European Stars* is seen at Barcelona, berthed alongside a ferry to the Balearic Islands.

134 | Cruise Ships: A Design History

The aesthetic resolution of the exterior of Festival Cruises' *Mistral* may have lacked finesse, but her blue and yellow livery and somewhat bland interiors were intended at attract a pan-European clientele. Here we see a lounge space (above left), her cocktail bar (above right), auditorium (left) and guest services desk (below).

added – the *Flamenco*, originally P&O's the *Spirit of London*, subsequently the *Sun Princess* and, later still, Premier Cruise Line's the *Starship Majestic*. Other than external repainting, little was done to make these hitherto American-based ships more European, the major differences being in the styles of cuisine served and entertainment provided. Even before they entered service, however, Poulides was planning new buildings, the fulfilment of his ambitions being made all the easier by the same ready availability of capital as was enabling the era's wider economic boom.

Poulides ordered the 47,276gt, 1,760-passenger *Mistral* from Chantiers de l'Atlantique at St Nazaire for delivery in 1999. While the vessel was under construction, he placed further orders with the same yard for a pair of bigger 58,625gt, 2,163-passenger cruise ships, the *European Stars* and *European Vision*, for completion in 2001 and 2002. Inboard, the vessels were designed by Michael Katzourakis, whose firm, AMK Design, had recently worked on the *Crown Odyssey* and, since then, had produced interiors for a number of new Greek-owned Adriatic ferries – all of which existed thanks to the same generous lending conditions as was giving rise to the new Festival Cruises fleet. Perhaps to save expense, or maybe in acknowledgement of Festival's mass-market concept, its three cruise ships were rather more ferry-like in terms of internal styling than Katzourakis' earlier projects had been. Throughout, there was a great deal of light wood-effect panelling, back-lit ceiling panels and a dearth of ornamentation. In such relatively large vessels, the overall effect was quite bland – but this might also have reflected a desire to avoid representing the cultural specifics of any particular European country (much in the way that Euro banknotes applied a consciously generic approach). The vessels' external appearances were equally undistinguished and, although they possessed all of the key features and layout characteristics of other cruise ships of their era, they looked utilitarian, as though engineers had had the final say, rather than the client's design consultant.

In the end, Festival Cruises' expansion was too ambitious for what could safely be afforded. In 2004, the company became unable to meet its obligations and therefore ceased to trade. Its fleet arrested, then auctioned at the behest of creditors.

The *European Vision* and *European Stars* were bought by the next major pan-European cruise operator to emerge: MSC Cruises. It was a division of the Mediterranean Shipping Company, which had been founded in 1970 by the Swiss-based, Neapolitan-born shipping entrepreneur, Captain Gianluigi Aponte, whose initial freight routes had linked southern Europe and Africa. In 1989, MSC bought the Flotta Lauro cruise business from Achille Lauro of Naples, renaming it Star Lauro. After the company's elderly flagship, the *Achille Lauro*, caught fire and sank in the Red Sea in 1994, the trading name was changed to MSC Cruises. During the 1990s, all aspects of MSC expanded greatly, driven by the exponential global growth in container shipping. Indeed, by the second decade of the twenty-first century, MSC was the world's second largest container ship operator and the fourth largest cruise line, owning one of the youngest fleets. In 2001, MSC renamed the two former Festival cruise ships as the *MSC Armonia* and *MSC Sinfonia*; it then commissioned two further examples of the type from Chantiers de l'Atlantique, the *MSC Lirica* and *MSC Opera*, which entered service in 2003 and 2004 respectively. Where Festival Cruises had been financially stretched, MSC was wealthy from its burgeoning container business and soon it managed to fulfil George Poulides' unrealised ambition for a pan-European mass-market cruise operation.

Smaller cruise ships of the millennium period

Alongside the many large new cruise ships in the 60-90,000gt size range entering service in the late-1990s and early-2000s, a new generation of smaller vessels appeared. Perceptions of size in cruise ships are, however, relative and so, in comparison with typical historic examples, these were actually fairly average in terms of tonnage, measuring in the 20-30,000gt range. Also, they tended to attract a conservative clientele who wished to enjoy 'old world' shipboard hospitality and tranquillity, rather than the constant entertainment and retail opportunities of the big, new mass market resort ships.

Following the sale of Sitmar Cruises to P&O in 1988, the parent Vlasov Group was renamed V-Ships. Headquartered in Monaco, it remained active in the cruise industry as partners in new cruise projects as providers of naval architecture and technical expertise and as ship managers for other companies. One venture was to co-found a new upmarket cruise line, Silversea Cruises, in partnership with the former-Sitmar Cruises owner, Manfredi Lefebvre d'Ovidio. The aim was to operate slightly larger and more seaworthy vessels than those of the 1980s 'Yacht Cruiser' generation while maintaining a sense of intimacy and attracting wealthy and traditionally-minded predominantly American passengers. In line with other upscale cruise operations, Silversea's relatively expensive fares included gratuities and beverages, the company describing itself as a 'boutique' cruise line and thereby referencing trendy boutique hotels, such as the Philippe Starck-designed Royalton and Paramount in New York.

Silversea placed orders for a pair of 16,927gt, 314-passenger vessels which were designed by V-Ships' naval architects, with the T. Mariotti shipyard in Genoa as builder, though it subcontracted the construction of the hull and superstructure steelwork to a different yard, F. Vinsentini of Donada. The *Silver Cloud* and *Silver Wind* were completed in 1994-1995 and featured an unremarkable slightly streamlined external design, which emphasised the private balconies that were a feature of all cabins. These ships were followed by two slightly larger examples, the 28,258gt, 388-passenger *Silver Shadow* and *Silver Whisper*, also designed by V-Ships' naval architects and

Below: Silversea Cruises' 'boutique' cruise ship *Silver Wind* was in terms of layout and appearance a further development of the 'yacht cruisers' of the previous decade, albeit with a large provision of cabins with balconies.

Right: The 'second generation' Silversea cruise ship *Silver Whisper*, the superstructure of which was somewhat bigger than that of the company's initial vessels.

completed at the same builders in 2000 and 2001 respectively. (It cannot be coincidental that these vessels' names are identical to those of types of Rolls Royce limousine.) Inboard, the Silversea fleet was as bland as external appearances suggested, lest any 'memorable' design features should jar with their clientele's preconceptions of what constituted high-end shipboard luxury. The quirky visual characteristics of shore-based boutique hotels – which were intended to set these premises apart from those of the big chains – were notable by their absence.

Between the first and second pair of Silversea ships, V-Ships designed a conversion into a cruise ship of what had been intended as a Soviet satellite tracking vessel, the *Akademik Nikolay Pilyugin*. Its construction had begun in Leningrad in the latter-1980s but, upon the collapse of the Soviet Union, it remained unfinished. This time, the client was Radisson Seven Seas Cruises (operator of the catamaran-hulled *Radisson Diamond*) with T. Mariotti carrying out the transformation. Its outcome in 2001 was the 28,550gt, 504-passenger *Seven Seas Navigator*, a vessel which, notwithstanding its unlikely origins, had much in common in terms of layout, appearance and facilities with those of the Silversea fleet. For V-Ships and T. Mariotti, this was not, however, such a unique project as, shortly after, in 1996, another incomplete former-Soviet research vessel, the *Okean*, was rebuilt by the same partnership for charter to Swan Hellenic Cruises (which by that time was a P&O subsidiary) as the 12,500gt, 350-passenger cruise ship *Minerva*. Since its establishment in the 1950s, Swan Hellenic had evolved into a specialised niche operator of cruises centred on visits to ancient sites of archaeological and religious interest, attracting a discerning, largely British clientele, for whom the *Minerva*'s design was specially tailored. Just like the First Class accommodation of British colonial liners of the past, inboard, the vessel most resembled a floating version of a traditional English country house. The Oxbridge dons and Anglican bishops who formed the core of Swan Hellenic's regular clientele apparently appreciated the possibility of visiting foreign places in a type of shipboard ambience which, aside from advances in technology, had changed little over the course of the past century.

Perhaps the most remarkable example of this return to tradition was the *Deutschland*, a 22,496gt cruise ship ordered in the mid-1990s by Peter Deilmann, a specialist German niche cruise operator targeting a mature, wealthy and conservative German-speaking clientele. Since the 1980s, Deilmann's cruise operations had steadily built up a loyal following with the *Regina Maris* and *Berlin* (described above) and, subsequently, also with river cruise vessels. Delivered in 1998, the *Deutschland* was designed and built in Germany by Howaldtswerke Deutsche Werft of Kiel. To make the

Right: The *Minerva* was converted from an incomplete Soviet research vessel to serve a niche British market.

The mid-1990s generation | 137

The *Seven Seas Navigator* (top left) was likewise converted from an unwanted research ship, while the *R Two* (top right and upper centre left) was one of a series of eight practically identical 'boutique' cruise ships. Inboard, these were decorated in the manner of luxury passenger ships of the Edwardian era, as the hallway and dining room on *R Five* demonstrate (above right and right). The German-flagged *Deutschland* (lower centre left) was similarly treated inboard, albeit to a higher quality level, as her Kaisersaal (above) demonstrates.

Above: The *Olympic Voyager* and *Olympia Explorer* are seen while under construction at the Blohm & Voss shipyard in Hamburg.

Below: The sleek *Olympic Voyager* is seen at Piraeus during her brief career with Royal Olympic Cruises.

Teutonic experience complete, she flew the Germany flag, rather than a flag of convenience, and had a German-speaking crew. While the vessel's exterior was particularly undemonstrative with a complete lack of the applied 'styling' so typical of a majority of 1990s cruise ships, inboard, her 620 passengers were surrounded by an astonishingly convincing extravaganza of finely-crafted baroque such as would have been found on German passenger ships of the early-twentieth century 'gilded age.' This was the work of Kai Bunge and Siegfried Schindler of Hamburg-based Partnership Design and it bore no resemblance whatsoever to their concurrent rather populist and colourful interiors for Aida Cruises. The *Deutschland*'s main ballroom and entertainment space was called the Kaisersaal and, apart from up-to-date stage equipment and slightly terraced floor, it really did resemble a Hamburg-Amerika Linie interior of the kind Albert Ballin would approve. Even in the lido buffet – a quintessentially modern cruise ship facility – the baroque fantasy was maintained.

Serving an even more exclusive mainly German-speaking market with a minority of wealthy international passengers was Hapag-Lloyd's latest the *Europa*, completed in 1999 by Kværner Masa Yards in Helsinki. Measuring 28,437gt and accommodating just 410 passengers, her smaller dimensions and capacity than those of her 1981 namesake reflected her owner's decision to move into an even more specialised niche, in which space, tranquillity and highly attentive service were the major attractions. Unlike the *Deutschland*, every one of the *Europa*'s cabins had a balcony and particular attention was paid to sound insulation. Decoratively, the *Europa*'s interiors, designed by Yran & Storbraaten of Oslo, were rather muted in terms of colour and style, but, throughout, they were finished using high quality materials, such as might also be found in a contemporary five-star hotel. Finnish construction and Norwegian interior design by a firm with previous 'yacht-cruiser' expertise reflected Hapag-Lloyd's long-standing tradition of selecting suitable international 'ingredients' for its vessels and lent the *Europa* a more cosmopolitan atmosphere than its closest rival, the more overtly German *Deutschland*.

Renaissance Cruises – for the past decade an operator of yacht cruise ships – was re-capitalised in the mid-1990s by Edward Rudner, an American businessman best known for having founded the Alamo car rental company. The decision was then taken to supersede the existing fleet, which was regarded as too small to earn a decent return, with a series of somewhat bigger cruise ships, each measuring 30,277gt and accommodating 702 passengers. Ordered from Chantiers de l'Atlantique at St Nazaire, their design was developed from that of an earlier French Polynesian cruise ship, the 19,170gt *Paul Gauguin*, which the yard had completed in 1997. All of these vessels were designed by the Finnish naval architecture firm, Deltamarin, founded in 1990 by a group of six naval architects – Alf Björkman, Markku Kanerva, Jukka Laiterä, Kyösti Herrala, Jaakko Järvinen and Juhani Kivi – most of whom had previously worked in Wärtsilä's drawing offices. As we shall see, Deltamarin would thereafter become a major force in cruise ship design. Initially, Renaissance commissioned two examples – named the *R One* and *R Two* – but, following an attractive offer from Chantiers de l'Atlantique, eventually no fewer than eight were built. The rather utilitarian nomenclature reflected both the name style of some large private superyachts and Renaissance's ongoing desire to emphasise a uniform brand, rather than individual vessels.

As Renaissance sought to attract a mainly American and European clientele of similar age and outlook to those of Peter Deilmann, a very similar interior aesthetic approach was adopted. Externally and within, the *R One* to *R Eight* were styled by John McNeece who took as his inspiration British trans-Atlantic liner interiors of the Edwardian era – including Cunard's the *Mauretania* and White Star's the *Olympic*, sister of the notorious *Titanic*. By coincidence, shortly before the *R One* entered service in 1998, the 'Titanic' blockbuster film, starring Leonardo DiCaprio and Kate Winslet, was an international cinema hit and featured scenes in a replica of the same hallway space as McNeece had attempted to replicate on the *R One*; his design work for the cruise ship, however, pre-dated the film set. The eight vessels were not only identical in terms of external appearance (which McNeece styled) but their interiors were also undistinguishable with even the same reproduction artworks in the same locations throughout and, regrettably, areas of generic marine suspended ceiling system. Thus, although the R-ships' interiors appeared sufficiently convincing at a cursory glance, they did not withstand such close and detailed scrutiny as those of the *Deutschland*, in which even the cabin corridor ceilings and lighting were detailed like those of passenger ships of the 1900s. Unlike the *Deutschland*, the R-ships' design had the advantage of including significant numbers of cabins with balconies (by contrast, the *Deutschland* subsequently required retro-fitting with these once passengers paying higher rates came to expect them as standard).

Renaissance sought to offer the elements of an upmarket cruise at prices closer to those of the mass market and did so by standardising as many elements as possible, including the itineraries with each R-ship following one of two schedules from a single embarkation port, thereby enabling stores and fuel to be provided in bulk by the same suppliers. The advent of the Internet also made it possible to sell cruises directly to clients, rather than via travel agents – and Renaissance was a pioneer of what subsequently became a common approach across the travel and hospitality industries.

Renaissance unfortunately soon suffered from expanding too quickly using borrowed money. By 2001, when the final example of the R-ship series, the *R Eight*, was delivered, the company was teetering on the verge of bankruptcy; the attacks on the World Trade Centre in New York and on the Pentagon on 11th September 2001 were the final straw, leading Renaissance cruises to declare bankruptcy. Its fleet was arrested and eventually sold by the major creditor – Chantiers de l'Atlantique – to other, better capitalised operators. In the longer run, the eight vessels became highly successful for subsequent owners and greatly sought after on the second hand market. Clearly, the Renaissance concept was a good one, but merely launched too quickly at an unpropitious moment.

The historicist interior design styles of the *Deutschland* and the R-ships were reflective of a growing romantic interest in a supposedly 'golden age' of liner travel and were much more difficult to realise convincingly than the more abstract homages to liners of the recent past, represented by the *Oriana* and *Rotterdam*. However, in the ensuing decade ocean liner-themed cruise ship designs would continue to be produced, enabling passengers to enjoy fantasy environments redolent of past eras of sea travel associated with great glamour.

Above: A stern-quarter view of the *Olympia Explorer*, berthed at San Juan in Puerto Rico.

In 1998, Greece's Royal Olympic Cruises – created through the merger of Epirotiki Lines and Sun Cruises – was listed on the NASDAQ in New York, raising $91 Million. The constituent companies' founding families – Potamianos and Kioscoglou – kept a controlling interest in the business, however. With fresh capital, they announced a plan to build two new cruise ships measuring 24,391gt with the unique ability to sail at up to 33 knots. The idea was that they would be able to cruise from Piraeus, visiting ports in North Africa, Asia and Southern Europe and sailing at high speed overnight between. A 'three continents' itinerary was thought to be a unique and attractive proposition – and one not offered by any other cruise line.

The vessels' builder was Blohm & Voss in Hamburg, a company with a historic pedigree of constructing fast passenger and naval vessels and it was from warship design research that the design solution emerged. The secret of the vessels' great speed potential was their innovative hull design with an unusually slender entry and an aft-body configuration in which the twin propeller shafts were unusually deeply submerged and located very close together with the blade tips nearly touching. The hull steelwork above formed a semi-tunnel, thereby intensifying the thrust while minimising vibration. The wave-making resistance of this design was significantly lower than for conventional hull forms intended for high-speed operation and allowed for an undisturbed flow of water to the propellers. Propulsion was from four 9-cylinder Wärtsilä engines, any two of which could together maintain a 22-knot speed.

Although Blohm & Voss was responsible for the hull form, the superstructure and interior layout was devised by the Danish naval architects, Knud E. Hansen A/S, who had originally designed many of the cruise ships that had been acquired second-hand by Royal Olympic and which formed the bulk of its existing fleet. The superstructure was low with a strong horizontal emphasis, capped by a large streamlined funnel, the entire ensemble appearing more like an up-to-date ferry than other typical cruise ships of the era.

Inboard, Michael Katzourakis' AMK Design was responsible for the passenger accommodation. As with the Festival Cruises vessels, this was rather understated with Greek and Aegean-inspired shades of blue predominating. Due to the vessels' speed, only 12 so-called 'sky suites', set back from the topsides, had balconies and, instead, the other superior ones were fitted with bay windows.

The *Olympic Voyager* was delivered in 2000, as expected, but Royal Olympic refused to accept the *Olympic Explorer* upon her completion in 2001. While the company cited technical issues, many cruise industry observers suspected that the real problem was that experience with the *Olympic Voyager* was causing it to have second thoughts. Indeed, as subsequent events would prove, the entire commercial concept underpinning the vessels' design proved to be flawed. From a business perspective, there was no imperative for high-speed cruising with its ensuing high fuel burn and less tenable outdoor spaces due to stronger head-winds. The vessels' low passenger capacity of just 800 tightened margins, while their lack of balconies deterred passengers who could pay similar prices for these on larger, slower vessels with more extensive leisure and entertainment facilities. When transferred to the Caribbean for the winter season, the *Olympic Voyager*'s name and, indeed, that of her owner incurred the wrath of the International Olympic Committee who demanded modification under threat of legal action. Indeed, when the second of the ships belatedly entered service in 2002, her name had been altered to the *Olympia Explorer*.

Royal Olympia Cruises, as their operator was now known for the same reason, went bankrupt in 2003 and its fleet was sold. The company's great error had been to focus upon speed at the expense of capacity and shipboard revenue.[298] Indeed, the New York-based travel writer and cruise aficionado, Ted Scull, subsequently recalled to the author about cruising in the Mediterranean aboard a much larger, slower cruise ship and being overhauled by the *Olympia Explorer*, doing at least twice her speed. Scull and his fellow passengers were impressed by this show of energy as they gazed down from the upper decks – but were nonetheless glad to be moving in a more sedate and relaxing fashion, surrounded by superior comfort-giving facilities.[299]

Chapter 14

Post-Panamax cruise ships

In the early-1990s, Carnival Corporation began planning the first ever post-Panamax cruise ships; these would measure over 100,000gt and provide berths for over 3,000 passengers. At around the same time, elsewhere in the world, designs the first post-Panamax container ships were also on shipyards' drawing boards. Hitherto, it had been considered vital that all examples of both ship types should be able to transit the Panama Canal – but by the last decade of the twentieth century, that was no longer the case. In the container trade, the trans-Pacific routes to the Far East increasingly used U.S. West Coast ports, accessed from the rest of the North American continent by rail, rather than sailing from the East Coast, where America's traditional industrial heartlands had lain. For cruise ships, meanwhile, the idea that all vessels should be able to operate from ports on either seaboard depending on the time of year was no longer the case. Quite simply, the Caribbean market had grown so greatly that there was a strong demand for cruises from Miami throughout the year. Besides, an exceptionally large mass market Caribbean cruise ship would be unlikely ever to be required to carry out itineraries requiring Panama Canal passages for a subsequent owner. Indeed, in future, new cruise ships of all categories would come increasingly to be optimised for specific markets.

The great advantage of building a cruise ship to post-Panamax dimensions was that by significantly increasing the width of the hull, it would be possible to build a much taller superstructure with many more decks of cabins equipped with balconies. A similar advantage was also found in post-Panamax container ships, upon which much higher container stacks could be loaded on deck without a loss of stability due to the wider hull giving greater reserve buoyancy and a lower centre of gravity. The parallel development of so-called 'Finite Element Analysis' programmes for three-dimensional structural modelling enabled the optimal use of steel or aluminium alloy to achieve the greatest integrity with the thinnest possible materials. As understanding of the stresses experienced by cruise ship superstructures grew, it became possible to make additional weight savings, which meant that yet more decks of cabins could be piled on.

For Carnival's initial post-Panamax cruise ships, the company requested that its in-house naval architects, Technical Marine Planning, and Fincantieri's cruise ship design department, which by this point was led by Maurizio Cergol, should each produce a competitive design, from which Carnival would select the one it preferred. While TMP's solution was in essence a greatly enlarged *Fantasy*-class, the Fincantieri design was entirely new and it was this much more original solution that Carnival's senior management most liked.[300]

At this point, Carnival's technical organisation was restructured. Instead of Technical Marine Planning producing designs in-house, as had been the case with the Fantasy-class, it would henceforth mostly be left to shipyard design departments to generate concepts. In 1995, TMP was renamed Carnival Corporate Shipbuilding and became Carnival Corporation's representative in project development processes, liaising with the shipyards to develop their schemes according to Carnival Corporation's operating subsidiaries' requirements.[301]

Fincantieri's post-Panamax cruise ship design was very well conceived in terms of layout, technical, operational and aesthetic characteristics. Measuring 272.35m x 35.54m, it contained eleven passenger decks, four of which were devoted to public circulation space. There were a total of 3,400 berths, of which 2,966 were lowers. Approximately a third of cabins had balconies – a first for a Carnival Cruise Line vessel but very necessary for 'future-proofing' the design. While the overall disposition of public rooms and service spaces was typical of nearly all recent cruise ships with entertainment forward and dining aft, their scale was unprecedented. The show lounge was three decks high, as was the central 'plaza', the width of which created a spectacular impression with sweeping staircases and lifts adding constant horizontal and vertical movement; this was much more impressive than the narrower atria of other recent cruise ships, the predominantly vertical emphasis of which gave insufficient distance to take in more than a small part at any one time. The two dining rooms also had voids, surrounded by balconies much like the ones on Fincantieri's recent cruise ships for Holland America. The very generous dimensions of the circulation, dining and entertainment spaces enabled Joe Farcus to use his great imagination to produce vivid and flamboyant interiors representing the epitome of shipboard post-modernism.

One challenge on a vessel of such a scale was to muster passengers for emergencies requiring evacuation into the lifeboats. The solution was to include deep lifeboat embarkation decks, running one deck above the length of the lifeboat promenades with enough space for everyone to gather and an ability to step straight into the boats (rather than embarking only once they had been swung outboard of the hull, as was the case on all other passenger ships). Potentially, this solution should have made the design the safest yet in this regard.[302]

Aesthetically, the Maurizio Cergol's treatment of the exterior was very successful, being at once harmonious and futuristic, while making a virtue of the massive bulk of hull and superstructure. As with the Statendam-class, Cergol used wedge-shapes in combination with large areas of tinted glazing, the sloped but faceted steelwork of the forward and aft superstructure creating a powerful impression. Carnival's trademark 'winged' funnel was rendered at a very large size and, to save weight, this was fabricated as a single GRP moulding. The cabin balconies, with their unbroken tinted balustrades, added to an impression of length. In common with the *Rotterdam*, the hull had significant tumblehome and, as well as increasing buoyancy, this also mitigated against the overall appearance being too rectilinear. Mechanically, the design used a six-engine diesel-electric power plant, comprising four 16-cylinder Sulzer diesels plus two 12-cylinder examples with conventional shafted propulsion.

The first of the new series was the 101,353gt *Carnival Destiny*, delivered in 1996 from Fincantieri's Monfalcone shipyard. While under construction, Carnival ordered further examples – the *Carnival Triumph*, completed in 1999, and

Post-Panamax cruise ships | 141

The Carnival Cruise Line 'Destiny'-class cruise ship *Carnival Triumph* (top), the vessel's South Beach Club and 'Big Easy' bar (upper left and right) and the Rotunda (atrium) on the *Carnival Destiny* (above); the interior designs by Joe Farcus made effective use of the vessels' generously-dimensioned spaces to produce spectacular effects.

Right: An aerial view of the *Costa Atlantica*, the first of a series of six Finnish-built near-sisters for the Costa Cruises and Carnival Cruise Line fleets.

Below: The *Costa Atlantica*'s Caffe Florian was created by photographing the decorative panels of the real café in Venice, then printing these on marine wall panelling.

the *Carnival Victory*, finished in 2000; all were for operation from Miami, from which Carnival now had multiple daily departures, all year round. Their names – and those of subsequent Carnival Cruise Line new buildings – were, however, rather jingoistic and perhaps reflected Middle America's sense of pride in the wake of the military defeat of Iraq in the Gulf War. Although the vessels were Panamanian registered and crewed by multi-national staffs, Carnival's red, white and blue livery and 'all American' shipboard offer in terms of cuisine and entertainment was intended to stir patriotic feelings in the popular demographic forming the bulk of its clientele. Over the ensuing decade, mass-market cruise ships increasingly came to exemplify what might be termed as 'banal nationalism' – or jingoistic flag-waving. (In the 1930s, of course, the German Kraft durch Freude cruise operation sought to encourage similar feelings).

While the first members of what became known as the Destiny-class were under construction in Italy, Carnival Corporation and Carnival Corporate Shipbuilding were simultaneously involved in developing a new class of smaller Panamax-sized cruise ship with the objective of forming a standard design 'platform' for use by all current and future sub-brands, replacing their existing, less efficiently optimised tonnage. In the wake of Carnival's successful Fantasy-class, the concept, code-named 'Project 800', was developed jointly with Kværner Masa Yards in Helsinki. The aim was to achieve a high proportion of outside cabins with balconies (the '800' referred to 80% being outside of which a further 80% would have balconies). The Carnival/Kværner Masa standard design measured 85,619gt, accommodated 2,680 passengers and was 292.56 metres in length with a beam of 32.2 metres. Power was provided by six 9-cylinder Wärtsilä diesels, coupled to two generators with propulsion from two ABB Azipods. The difference between each Carnival sub-brands vessels would be largely decorative.[303]

While the first example was under construction, early in 2000, Carnival Corporation purchased Costa Cruises, giving the company a major presence in the Mediterranean as well as the Caribbean. Carnival Corporation decided slightly to reposition Costa as an Italian-themed, but mainly European and American mass market-orientated operator, effectively a European-headquartered equivalent of Carnival Cruise Line itself. It was therefore decided that the initial 'Project 800' cruise ship would be delivered to the Costa fleet as the *Costa Atlantica*. She would be by far the largest vessel in Costa's history.

Both Carnival Corporation and Costa's own management agreed that, rather than utilising contemporary Italian architects and designers to decorate her, instead, Carnival's Joe Farcus would be given the task and, perhaps unsurprisingly, the resulting interiors were distinctly Las Vegas-flavoured renditions of 'Italian traditions.' Throughout, Farcus' theme for her interiors was Italian cinema, in particular taking inspiration from Fellini's 'La Dolce Vita.' She even had a 'Sala Papparazzi', perhaps reflecting the present-day fascination with the lives of celebrities as conveyed through the popular media. Perhaps her most remarkable space, however, was the Caffe Florian – a near-perfect replica of the real café of that name in Venice, cleverly achieved by carefully photographing each of the decorative panels inside the original and printing the images out on marine wall board. The centrepiece of the interiors was a very tall but narrow ten-deck-high atrium, cutting through all of the cabin and public room decks, the summit of which had a glazed cupola.

Of the six examples of the 'Project 800' type that were ordered, one further example was for Costa: the *Costa Mediterrannea* of 2002 with interiors themed by Farcus around Italian Renaissance palaces. The remaining four were for Carnival Cruise Line and were named the *Carnival Spirit* (2001), *Carnival Pride* (2001), *Carnival Legend* (2002) and *Carnival Miracle* (2004). The Costa examples had a vertical funnel of similar appearance to the one on the *Costa Victoria*. Henceforth, this design would be used as a central element in Costa Cruises' brand image. On the four Carnival Cruises examples, the topmost deck of the atrium extended into the front of the slanted funnel, which was glazed in red tinted glass

Post-Panamax cruise ships | 143

to match the paintwork of the remainder of the funnel casing.

While Carnival Cruise Line and Costa Cruises were largely satisfied with the 'Project 800' design, Holland America's management had strong reservations. The entire internal layout had a retail focus and was intended to extract as much on board revenue as possible from the passengers, whereas Holland America's clientele paid a premium for lots of quiet space in which to relax undisturbed. Holland America, therefore, strongly encouraged the development of an alternative solution and Maurizio Cergol and his colleagues at Fincantieri were only too glad to oblige with what became known as the Vista-class, described below. At the same time, there were allegedly some strains in relations between Carnival Corporate Shipbuilding and Kværner Masa Yards over the choice of suppliers for the 'Project 800' technical specification – and this only encouraged Carnival Corporation's relationship with Fincantieri to grow ever closer.[304]

Britain's P&O, meanwhile, was set on a course to expand its cruise operations. To finance this, it sold off its construction and international property interests, which generated £2 billion, just over half of which they re-invested in new cruise ships for Princess Cruises which were of a size and technical specification commensurate with Carnival's Destiny-class.

The *Grand Princess* and *Golden Princess*, delivered by Fincantieri in 1998 and 1999, measured 108,806gt, making them briefly the world's largest passenger ships yet seen. Accommodating up to 3,209 passengers, they were among the first cruise ships with an external superstructure that was composed entirely of cabin balconies, engendering more the appearance of a tropical resort hotel than a conventional passenger ship. To give a unique design identity, Fincantieri's naval architect Gianfranco Bertaglia designed a convex-shaped bow profile with a swan-neck and a whale-back form above the mooring deck. A passenger promenade continued round the forepeak, enabling guests to enact a famous romantic scene from the film 'Titanic.' The aft profile comprised a transom stern, from which the superstructure rose vertically with aft-facing staterooms. High above, a large aluminium 'pod' was held aloft by broad aluminium box-sections, which was meant to resemble the spoiler of a racing car but which many observers thought gave more the appearance of a shopping trolley. The pod contained a discotheque, accessed from abaft the funnel by a 'travelator' in a blue tinted glass tube. Copious additional use of the same blue glazing for cabin balcony balustrades and deck screens gave the *Grand Princess* and *Golden Princess* a futuristic aura, which was further enhanced by their parabola-shaped funnel casings.[305] The small-scale detailing of their exteriors was, however, much less well resolved than that of Carnival's Destiny-class, there being many infelicitous protrusions which, from a distance, looked rather fiddly.

Inboard, the contrast could hardly have been greater; Princess Cruises' interior designers Teresa Anderson and Giacomo Mortola employed a traditionalist approach, using many ornate mouldings and expanses of brown wood-effect panelling. Considering the vessels' great size, their atria were remarkably small and bland. Yet, the rather bland and derivative stylistic formula was apparently successful, so much so that during the ensuing decade, a further seven slightly varied examples of the type were built for Princess plus two for P&O Cruises. Existing Princess ships displaced by this new armada were mainly shifted either to P&O Cruises Australia, or to other newly established P&O cruise brands.

To enable passengers a degree of flexibility with regard to when they dined and were entertained, there were two show lounges and three main restaurants; these were also unmemorable in scale and décor but they enabled staggered opening times to be offered. The idea for this arrangement originated with a Princess Cruises executive, Colin Veitch, who was Senior Vice President of Marketing and Corporate Development in Los Angeles. Subsequently in his career, as noted below, Veitch further developed the idea of shipboard flexibility of choice, particularly with regard to dining options.

Royal Caribbean, meanwhile, had developed its own plans for post-Panamax cruise ships that were significantly bigger and more sophisticated in terms of layout and

Above: The *Carnival Spirit*, an example of Carnival Cruise Line's variation of the same design; externally, the winged funnel and red, white and blue livery are the only major changes from the Costa Cruises versions.

Below: The Bar Veneto on the *Costa Atlantica*; the interior design approach on Costa Cruises' ships following Carnival's take-over was very different from that under Italian ownership and represented an Americanised, popular view of the nation's visual culture.

144 | Cruise Ships: A Design History

Above: The *Golden Princess* is seen at New York; note the 'pod' aft of her funnel, which contained a nightclub, the glazed access passage and interior of which are shown above. Despite her futuristic external design, throughout, the interiors were rather blandly coloured and of fairly conservative design.

specification than those of either Carnival or P&O/Princess. In the winter of 1995, while Royal Caribbean's *Grandeur of the Seas* and *Enchantment of the Seas* were under construction, the company's CEO, Richard Fain, took part in a brainstorming meeting in a remote chalet in Lapland, owned by Kværner Masa Yards' CEO, Martin Saarikangas. The other participants were Gert Wilhelmsen, CEO of Royal Caribbean's parent company, Anders Wilhelmsen, the naval architect Harri Kulovaara – who had recently been appointed by Royal Caribbean as its Senior Vice President of Marine Operations but who previously had been employed by the Baltic ferry operator, Silja Line – and long-serving Kværner Masa senior naval architect Kai Levander. There, in between skiing sessions, they discussed the development of a new type of Royal Caribbean cruise ship, code-named 'Project Eagle.'[306]

With Kulovaara and Levander involved, it is hardly surprising that an earlier design they had produced in the late-1980s for a pair of Baltic cruise ferries – the *Silja Serenade* and *Silja Symphony* – should prove highly influential. These ferries, which operated overnight between Stockholm and Helsinki, pioneered the concept of an end-to-end internal mall, lined with shops, bars and restaurants. Above on either side were six-deck-high hotel blocks containing a majority of passenger cabins, which all had large windows, either overlooking the mall, or facing outward to sea. This design solution necessitated the development of innovative solutions to fire containment, involving the extensive use of sprinklers, fire-resistant glazing and the lateral division of fire zones.[307]

Richard Fain's only doubt about the Silja Line mall concept was its initial manifestation in a design for a ferry (cruise executives tend to be snobbish about ferries as a 'lower' form of passenger ship than theirs –although, in reality, the two genres have many commonalities). Having been persuaded by Kulovaara and Saarikangas, he probably realised that a mall was in fact the ideal type-form for a mass-market cruise ship, intended to maximise revenue-generating opportunities. Since the 1960s, edge-of-town shopping malls had become an integral part of North American car and consumer culture. Writing about the West Edmonton Mall in Canada – which, in the 1990s, was the world's largest – the sociologist Margaret Crawford observed how its post-modern interior presented users with:

'…A dizzying spectacle of attractions and diversions: a replica of Columbus's *Santa Maria* floats in an artificial lagoon, where real submarines move through an impossible seascape of imported coral and plastic seaweed inhabited by live penguins and electronically-controlled rubber sharks.' [308]

Measuring around 137,276gt (more than twice the size of the Silja ferries) with a hull nearly a third of a kilometre in length and with a capacity for 3,840 passengers in 1,557 cabins, 69% of which either faced the sea or the internal promenade, 'Project Eagle' would be a cruise ship of superlatives. In Miami, the scheme was further developed by Royal Caribbean's senior commercial and technical staff with expertise in particular aspects of cruise ship operation – such as hotel services, entertainment and revenue generation. They liased with engineers from Anders Wilhelmsen's Newbuilding Department in Oslo, led by Technical Director, Olav Eftedal. The Finnish naval architecture consultancy Deltamarin was also retained to design the machinery spaces, where six 12-cylinder Wärtsilä diesel engines would generate power for three pods, the outer of which were Azimuthing (capable of rotating through 360 degrees) while the centre pod was fixed (triple-screw propulsion was necessitated by the broad 38.6-metre-wide hull). To reduce the stern wave and the drag it would create in the hull's wake, a lip was added at the stern to lengthen the profile aft of the pods. The stern was otherwise curved, rather than of the transom variety used for a majority of recent cruise ships and its smooth forms

Post-Panamax cruise ships | 145

Royal Caribbean's impressive *Voyager of the Seas* represented a new paradigm shift in the development of giant 'mass market' cruise ships. The interior images show the multi-level main dining room on *Explorer of the Seas* (above) and that vessel's theatre (above right) and internal mall (right).

Right: A bow-quarter view of the *Explorer of the Seas* which, despite her great size, possesses a high degree of visual unity, her multiple curves make her distinct from the 'faceted' appearance of Carnival's 'Destiny'-class, which were major competitors.

Below: The 'Flowrider' surf simulator aboard *Explorer of the Seas*; in recent years, sports facilities for active people have become major attractions on large cruise ships such as this – indeed, for increasing numbers of passengers, the availability of such attractions can be a deciding factor when booking a cruise on one ship instead of another.

were replicated in the styling of the superstructure. Consequently, although much bulkier than previous Royal Caribbean vessels, the overall effect remained within the company's established design tradition and was distinct from the angular appearance of the most recent units of the rival Carnival fleet.

Inboard, just like malls ashore, 'Project Eagle' would provide a wide variety of themes, atmospheres and diversions. To design these, twelve different firms of interior architects – most of which had previous cruise ship project experience – were employed and the designs ranged from a 'Windjammer' bar recalling the days of sail with canvas and rigging hung from masts, brass lanterns and portholes, to a multi-tiered restaurant with a giant chandelier, supposedly recalling the days of liner travel in the early-twentieth century. In the mall itself, a restored vintage car was prominently situated as a 'talking point' for passengers to examine. Martin Saarikangas – who played ice hockey – suggested including a half-size ice rink for sport and for skating shows.[309] Another feature not previously seen on a cruise ship was a rock-climbing wall, mounted on the rear of the funnel casing. Indeed, there would be space for so many diverse features that the vessel, rather than its destinations, would now be the prime attraction.

The lead ship of the class, named the *Voyager of the Seas,* was built over a two-year period at Kværner Masa Yards' Turku shipyard with delivery in October 1999. While she was under construction, Royal Caribbean ordered further examples, the *Explorer of the Seas* (2000) and *Adventure of the Seas* (2001), followed by the slightly larger 138,279gt *Navigator of the Seas* (2002) and *Mariner of the Seas* (2003). Whereas the cabin balconies of the first three were within the shell of the superstructure, on the last two examples, to increase the internal volume, they were attached to its exterior as long horizontal strips.[310] All of these vessels were placed in Caribbean service from Miami, where they displaced existing large Royal Caribbean cruise ships for use in other cruising regions and where they competed with units of Carnival's Fantasy- and Destiny-classes.

Next, in November 2003, Royal Caribbean ordered the first of a new class of cruise ship derived from 'Project Eagle' but bigger still. Measuring 154,407gt, the *Freedom of the Seas*, completed in 2006, and her sisters *Liberty of the Seas* (2007) and the *Independence of the Seas* (2008) had space for 4,375 passengers as well as yet more attractions – such as a children's water park on deck with sculptures modelled after the manner of the sculptor, Nikki de Saint Phalle, and a 'Flow Rider' surf simulator, enabling passengers to enjoy surfing on an artificial wave.[311]

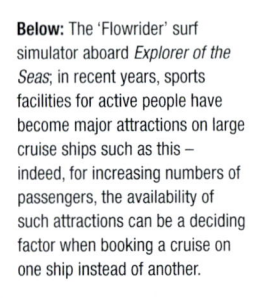

Gas turbine cruise ships

In 1997 Royal Caribbean's purchased Celebrity Cruises from Chandris, providing it with a more upmarket cruise brand to compete with the Carnival-owned Holland America Cruises and P&O's Princess Cruises. Royal Caribbean had access to the necessary financial resources to further develop the Celebrity brand, which the family-owned Chandris company lacked. Shortly, both Celebrity Cruises and Royal Caribbean took delivery of new classes of Panamax-dimensioned cruise ships from Chantiers de l'Atlantique and Meyer Werft respectively for deployment in various cruise regions around the world. Apart from their similarities of size and capacity, what both types had in common was gas turbine power, generating electricity for podded propulsion.

During the 1960s and 1970s, various largely unsuccessful experiments had taken place with gas turbine plants on merchant ships of various types and sizes, the most prominent of which was the Finland-West Germany ferry the *Finnjet*. None of these vessels proved economic in operation and most had curtailed existences due to the very high cost of kerosene relative to marine diesel. Since then, both gas turbine technology and ship propulsion systems had developed greatly. The great advantage over diesel solutions was much cleaner exhaust and, particularly when sailing in environmentally-sensitive areas such as Alaska or the Norwegian fjords, the choice of a 'greener' option was seen as a good way of future-proofing designs as ever more stringent emissions regulations were expected to be put into effect over the course of their projected 30-40-year lifespans.

The new Celebrity cruise ships would be equipped with two aero-derivative gas turbines supplied by General Electric's Marine Engines Division, augmented with a single steam turbine, each of which would drive an electric generator, supplying power to drive a pair of Mermaid podded propulsion units. These were devised by Cegelic-Kamewa to compete with the Finnish-made Azipod type, as installed on several recent cruise ships. The inclusion of a steam turbine would enable the recovery of heat from the exhaust gases, returning it for conversion back to electricity. Burning only clean distillate fuel, this state-of-the-art power plant design would produce significantly less pollution than any diesel installation. The project was developed with considerable input from Chantiers de l'Atlantique's naval architects and engineers, who could draw on the expertise of its parent Alstom engineering group, as well as those of Kamewa and General Electric.

The first member of the new class was the 90,228gt, 2,460-passenger *Millennium* – a highly appropriate choice for a state-of-the-art cruise ship scheduled to enter service in the year 2000. The vessel's exterior styling and a large part of the interior were designed by AMK of Athens, with other designers – Birch Coffey Design Associates of New York and French-based Architectes Ingénieurs Associés – designing the restaurants and atrium respectively. The external silhouette was criticised for being much less coherently resolved than the earlier Celebrity schemes by Jon Bannenberg, there being too many inelegantly resolved elements and an overly-complicated livery application with red and yellow accents in addition to the operator's blue and white house colours; the use of external-facing glass lifts on each side of the superstructure was, however, a new innovation. Inboard, a variety of hotel-like design schemes predominated – though one intriguing feature was an extra-tariff grill restaurant lined with ornate panelling rescued from the 1911 White Star trans-Atlantic liner the *Olympic*. Since the mid-1930s, when the *Olympic* was scrapped, this had been installed in a house in Liverpool and, by a lucky coincidence, came up for sale when the *Millennium*'s interiors were being planned. The recent success of the film 'Titanic' made purchasing it irresistible and so Birch Coffey re-integrated it into the new cruise ship, almost ninety years since it had first gone to sea. Of course, fire-proofing to the latest standards was a requirement. Rather than a central galley, as was typical of other recent cruise ships, each of the five dining spaces had a galley of its own, ensuring that dishes would arrive promptly and fresh at the tables.

Three further units of the Millennium-class – named the *Infinity*, *Summit* and *Constellation* – entered service in 2001-2002. After some initial teething troubles with the reliability of their Mermaid pods, resulting in a lawsuit against the supplier, the vessels eventually came to be widely regarded as successful.

To develop cruise ships of equivalent size, capacity and propulsion for Royal Caribbean's own fleet, an alliance was entered into with Meyer Werft in Papenburg, the outcome of which was a class of four 90,090gt, 2,100-passenger vessels – the *Radiance of the Seas*, *Brilliance of the Seas*, *Serenade of the Seas* and *Jewel of the Seas* – which entered service between 2001 and 2004.[312] Topsides, they had many similarities to Royal Caribbean's other recent additions while, mechanically, they used combined gas and steam turbine plants, powering generators. On this occasion, General Electric turbines and generators were married to Azipods with more reliable initial results than the Cegelic-Kamewa type installed on the Millennium-class. Upon completion in 2001, the *Radiance of the Seas* was the largest passenger vessel yet built in Germany but, as Meyer Werft received yet more orders for cruise ships that were bigger still, she maintained that distinction only briefly.

P&O Princess Cruises also built gas turbine/diesel hybrid cruise ships during the same period. Having come under pressure from institutional investors, in 2000, the P&O Group had de-merged its cruise businesses – comprising 22 vessels in the Princess Cruises, P&O Cruises, P&O Cruises Australia and Aida Cruises fleets. A new company, P&O Princess Cruises PLC, was thus created with a separate stock market listing. Following this move, orders for two new cruise ships for Princess Cruises were placed with Mitsubishi in Japan – a most unusual choice as the builder had never previously built any cruise ships for European or American owners. Mitsubishi's senior management had, however, been eyeing the major European cruise ship builders' recent successes with envy and therefore wished their company also to play a part in what appeared to be a lucrative area of activity. Gaining the requisite skills was felt to be important, as the Asian cruise market was expected to grow greatly in future years and further orders might therefore be gained.

Mitsubishi therefore gave a more competitive tender than Fincantieri could match as, although Japanese labour costs were high, making a loss was thought to be an acceptable price to pay for gaining an opportunity to demonstrate willing and know-how, hopefully leading to subsequent profitable contracts. Fincantieri's Grand-class design was used as the basis for these vessels, which were intended for operation in Pacific waters where a turbine supplied by General Electric augmenting the four main Wärtsilä diesel engines would enable high-speed sailing to shorten voyage times between the more distant ports of call.

Above: Celebrity Cruises' *Millennium* (above), her Olympic Restaurant featuring panelling originally installed in the famous White Star trans-Atlantic liner of that name (below) and her atrium, featuring cascading translucent curtains lit from above (bottom).

Right: A stern-quarter view of Celebrity Cruises' *Infinity*, with slanting light emphasising the many overhanging protrusions from her superstructure; unlike previous Celebrity ships, the 'Millennium'-class vessels privileged interior features over external harmony.

Most unfortunately, during fitting out, the first of the pair, the 115,906gt 3,100-passenger *Diamond Princess*, suffered a very serious fire which gutted and distorted a large part of her superstructure, necessitating scrapping it down to hull level and rebuilding afresh from there. This caused a two-year delay, during which completion of the sister ship proceeded according to schedule and so she instead was given the *Diamond Princess* name. The rebuilt original subsequently was completed as the *Sapphire Princess*, both vessels entering service in 2004. As a result of an unexpectedly difficult and costly construction process, Mitsubishi decided not to become a major cruise ship builder after all.[313]

While P&O Princess' two Japanese new builds were under construction, a further two somewhat smaller gas turbine/diesel vessels were being constructed for the company at Chantiers de l'Atlantique in France. The 91,627gt *Coral Princess* and *Island Princess* entered service in 2002 and 2003. All four of Princess's hybrid ships signalled their use of gas turbine power externally through having aviation jet engine-shaped tubes mounted horizontally on each side of their funnel casings – though these were in fact empty and the ones on the *Island Princess* were subsequently removed.[314]

A fresh round of consolidation

Early in 2000, Carnival Corporation attempted to buy Norwegian Cruise Line but soon found that there was an unexpected rival bidder – the Malaysian Genting Corporation, owner of Star Cruises, which purchased a 60% shareholding. This process coincided with the appointment of a new Chief Executive Officer, Colin Veitch, who had previously held senior positions at P&O Cruises and at P&O Princess Cruises. With the expansionist Star Cruises in control of NCL, Veitch could begin a major programme of expansion, which commenced by taking over two Panamax-sized 91,740gt cruise ships under construction at Meyer Werft for Star. These were to have been the *Superstar Libra* and *Superstar Capricorn* but instead they entered service in 2001 and 2002 as the *Norwegian Star* and *Norwegian Dawn*.[315] Although their interior design by Tillberg had been intended for the South-East Asian market, being practically identical to that of Star's own recent *Superstar Virgo* and *Superstar Leo*, with only the most superficial modification, it seemed to work just as well in North American waters.

NCL inherited from Star Cruises its open-seating, multi-restaurant dining concept which was extensively marketed as 'Freestyle Dining.' The appropriation of this approach was Veitch's behest as, when at Princess Cruises, he had overseen the introduction of a primitive version of the concept on the Grand-class ships, described above. For NCL, 'Freestyle Dining' became a major selling point in the American and European cruise markets as it enabled passengers to appear for dinner whenever and wherever they wished within a window of opportunity lasting several hours. This informality proved highly

Right: P&O Princess Cruises' *Island Princess*, featuring facsimile 'jets' on either side of her funnel casing to indicate the advanced propulsion technology within.

attractive and brought the company's dining offer into line with approaches in shore-based resorts. The large size of the new vessels, offering repetitive weekly itineraries, enabled demand to be accurately predicted each evening and, thus, approximately the correct numbers of each dish to be prepared on an on-going basis.

Having failed to take over NCL, Carnival Corporation eyed up other tempting opportunities. When in 2001, P&O Princess Cruises Plc became the subject of a take-over attempt by Royal Caribbean, Carnival Corporation entered the fray with a rival offer and, after the best part of a year of corporate wrangling, in late-2002, it was Carnival who prevailed, giving the Miami-based giant control over a second famous British cruise operator alongside its earlier acquisition of Cunard.[316]

In a context of growth across the cruise industry, the management of P&O Princess Cruises' British subsidiary, P&O Cruises, was by this point aware that the brand was perceived as rather conservative and therefore had limited potential to saturate the UK cruising market. Without losing its loyal existing clientele, P&O Cruises wished to emulate the success of mass-market operators such as Aida and NCL which had succeeded in presenting less formal, more youthful images, more attractive to thirty- and forty-somethings. In 2003, the company therefore experimentally launched Ocean Village, seeking to do for the British market what Aida had so successfully achieved in Germany. Its slogan was 'the cruise line for people who don't do cruises.' P&O Cruises' the *Arcadia* (the former *Star Princess* of 1988) was refitted in an informal style, repainted in a pink, red and orange colour scheme – featuring coloured hoops along her hull and stripes around the superstructure – and renamed the *Ocean Village*. As with Aida's vessels, the emphasis was on entertainment, buffet dining and, at ports of call, cycles were provided by the gangway for passengers to use at will. In the end, however, P&O found that too few 'people who don't do cruises' could be persuaded to change their non-cruising habits. Ocean Village's self-defeating slogan therefore failed to connect with whatever potential new market might have existed.

The consequences of 9/11 and the 'Homeland Cruising' concept

The terrorist attacks of 11th September 2001 abruptly ended a decade-long interlude of apparent freedom, safety and stability since the ending of the Cold War. The effects of these events on the cruise industry were immediate, there being a sudden drop in bookings and many cancellations by Americans who had planned to cruise overseas. Under-capitalised and financially over-stretched operators who had recently introduced expensive new tonnage – such as Renaissance Cruises, Royal Olympic Cruises and Festival Cruises – went bankrupt in 2001, 2003 and 2004 respectively (although the latter depended almost exclusively on a European clientele, rather than American, here too the fall-off in bookings was enough to cause a severe shortage of liquidity).

The cruise industry's giants – Carnival, Royal Caribbean and Norwegian Cruise Line/Star Cruises – were all sufficiently well-capitalised to weather the 9/11 storm and as each served its core market by sailing from US ports without any need for international flights, it was perhaps easier to persuade would-be passengers that this was a more secure holiday choice (although the 9/11 hijacked flights were all on American domestic routes on which security tended to be rather minimal).

In the wake of the attacks, cargo ships were perceived by the American government as a major threat as these might be acquired by terrorists, loaded with explosives, sailed into coastal cities and detonated. The administration therefore forced the international acceptance of new 'International Ship Protection System' (ISPS) regulations, requiring, among other things, that all port facilities handling tonnage in international service to be secured to the same standard as airports, meaning complete enclosure with security fences and CCTV. No unauthorised persons would be allowed pier-side and certainly not aboard any ships. This ruling affected all cruise ports – including those in fairly remote and picturesque settings, such as Flåm in Norway, where the village pier was secured to resemble the environs of a maximum-security prison; as a result, locals could no longer promenade along their own waterfront during cruise ship calls.

Hitherto, the cruise industry had only ever suffered one terrorist incident when in 1985 the Italian *Achille Lauro* was seized in the Mediterranean by Palestinian separatists, who murdered one American passenger before escaping. Since then, security measures had gradually been enhanced but, post-9/11, there was a major re-think and shipboard security became highly professionalised. In preceding years, the use of digital technologies had grown in various shipboard

Below: Royal Caribbean's *Jewel of the Seas* was one of a series built by Meyer Werft, likewise utilising gas turbine power.

applications, one of which was the issuing of combined passenger identification and shipboard credit cards, which everyone swiped at the gangway to record whether they were aboard or ashore and which also enabled shipboard purchases to be made, the total bill being settled prior to disembarkation. Cruise ships also made increasingly extensive use of CCTV for the surveillance of all passenger and crew spaces (except for cabins, which nonetheless, had heat and smoke sensors). Indeed, despite cruise publicists' claims of holidays offering great freedom, cruise ships became the most surveyed and subtly controlled leisure environments imaginable, every passenger's movements potentially being scrutinised for anything 'suspicious.' In that sense, for all their lavish décor, cruise ship interiors arguably now had much in common with Jeremy Bentham's notorious eighteenth century 'panopticon' design for prisons.

With popular sentiment in the USA hardening against the Islamic world and Iraq framed as culpable for the 9/11 attacks by the US Government with a war there in the offing, Carnival Cruise Line gave its latest Destiny-class new buildings particularly jingoistic names – the *Carnival Conquest* (2002), *Carnival Glory* (2003) and *Carnival Valor* (2004). When victory in the Iraq War was announced by President George W. Bush, these were followed by the *Carnival Liberty* (2005) and *Carnival Freedom* (2007). The fact that France refused to participate militarily in what its Government argued was an illegal and unwarranted attack on a sovereign country caused the widespread renaming of French fries to 'freedom fries' in the USA – and this also applied throughout the Carnival Cruise Line fleet, though not on the more upmarket and cosmopolitan vessels of its sister companies, Holland America and Costa Cruises. The nomenclature of Royal Caribbean's the *Freedom of the Seas*, *Liberty of the Seas* and *Independence of the Seas*, while slightly less overtly jingoistic than that of some of Carnival's latest new buildings nonetheless reflected the same spirit of patriotism stirred up in the wake of 9/11.

Above: The initial hull and superstructure sections for NCL's *Pride of America* were built in the USA, then towed to Lloyd Werft in Germany for completion. The top image of Lloyd Werft's dry dock shows the extent of the American work. Above, the completed ship is seen at sea, shortly after entering service. Patriotic hull graphics were added to what was otherwise a fairly typical 'economy of scale' design.

NCL, meanwhile, introduced what it termed as 'Homeland Cruising' – the emphasis being on departures from US ports visiting other American ports in the US Virgin Islands, Costa Rica, Alaska and Hawaii. Of course, as practically all cruise ships were all built in Europe and flew the Bahamian flag while employing with international crews, it was necessary to intersperse ports in US territory with ones that were not in order to get around restrictive Jones Act legislation which debarred foreign vessels from sailing between any two US ports in succession. (In the instance of cruises between Hawaiian Islands, this meant 1,000-kilometer diversions to ports in Canada or Mexico.)

Since the early-1980s, the Hawaiian cruise market had been served by American Hawaii Cruises, using the 1951-vintage former trans-Atlantic liner the *Independence* which, being American built, flagged and crewed was acceptable under Jones Act strictures. By the 1990s, this elderly steam turbine-powered vessel was on her last legs and so the operator, by then trading as American Classic Voyages, launched an ambitious project to build two state-of-the-art replacements, the basic design for which was provided by the long-established cruise ship naval architects, Knud E. Hansen A/S of Copenhagen. These vessels, code-named 'Project America 1' and 'Project America 2', would be the first US-built passenger ships for half-a-century. To bring them to fruition, extensive political lobbying was required to argue that shipbuilding capacity that was orientated towards naval vessels should, in the era after the Cold War, be re-directed to build commercial ships instead. Indeed, a one billion dollar Federal programme was launched of which the 'Project America' vessels formed only one part of a wider strategy.

In 2000, construction of the first of the pair began at Ingalls Shipbuilding in Pasagoula but, one year in, American Classic Voyages went bankrupt while, at the shipyard, construction costs for the first 'Project America' vessel began to spiral out of control. American politicians may have imagined that anybody could build a large cruise ship but, in reality, their specifications had advanced to such a level of sophistication that they could only be constructed economically by a few highly specialised builders in Europe.

After 9/11, Norwegian Cruise Line's Colin Veitch spotted an opportunity to take control of the Hawaii cruise market by purchasing the incomplete 'Project America 1' – but, to finish her to the required standard at an acceptable cost would necessitate sending her to a European yard. The *New York Times* records what happened thereafter:

'With platoons of lobbyists, including a former senator from Washington State, Norwegian Cruise persuaded Congress to approve its entry into a protected American market. The company's competitors, long eager for the privileges, are fuming. In Congress, Norwegian Cruise's biggest friend was the Hawaiian delegation, drawn by the company's promise that it would create 10,000 jobs in Hawaii – on the ships and in the tourist trade… It cost the company $880,000 to lobby for the provision this year, according to federal lobbying records… In addition, even though foreign companies are barred from making political contributions in the United States, the president of Norwegian Cruise, Colin Veitch, who is an American based in Miami, gave a total of $20,000 to the Democratic Party of Hawaii and to Representative Abercrombie, who led the fight for the company.'[317]

The incomplete hull was towed across the Atlantic to Lloyd Werft in Bremerhaven with completion scheduled for 2005. Meantime, NCL increased the size for the vessel from around 70,000gt to 80,439gt by adding an extra deck of cabins, bringing her capacity up to 2,500; this was necessary to offset the greater cost of sailing with an all-American crew. While the overall design and diesel-electric propulsion were – as one would expect from Knud E. Hansen A/S – typical of cruise ships of the period, the detailing of the construction, which was largely by Ingalls' naval architects, appeared chunkier than that of other cruise ships of the era – indeed, it was more reflective of the approach used in American shipyard drawing offices for naval and cargo vessels.

Riding America's post-9/11 sense of patriotism and injured pride, NCL announced that the vessel would be named the *Pride of America*. As with previous NCL cruise ships, the interiors were the work of Tillberg Design's office in Weston, Florida. There, the Swedish designer Tomas Tillberg and his assistants produced a feast of Yankee imagery, evoking famous and heroic episodes in American history, bald eagles, the Stars and Stripes and so on. Externally, even the hull topsides were emblazoned with decorative swirls and stars abstracted from the national flag.[318] In anticipation of the *Pride of America*'s entry into service, the *New York Times* reported:

'For the first time in 50 years, a [new] cruise ship flying the American flag will soon be sailing the seas. There will be no mistaking it for anything but an all-American vessel… Red and white stripes, blue stars and a huge bald eagle will decorate its hull. Its public rooms will strike a patriotic theme: the Liberty restaurant, the Capitol Atrium, Jefferson's Bistro, the John Adams Coffee Bar… But the *Pride of America* is not what it seems. The ship is actually being built in a German shipyard and is owned by Norwegian Cruise Line, a subsidiary of Star Cruises, which has its headquarters in Hong Kong and is run out of its offices in Malaysia; Star Cruises is in turn a unit of Genting Berhad, a holding company in Kuala Lumpur, Malaysia.'[319]

The *New York Times* conceded, however that '…in an industry where most cruise ship companies maintain foreign registry so they can hire employees from poor countries and pay them lower wages, Norwegian Cruise Line will have to play by American rules and… pay American taxes.'[320]

As part of NCL's deal to circumvent to an extent the Jones Act in return for investing in the Hawaiian cruise sector, it was allowed to transfer an existing entirely German-built cruise ship, the *Norwegian Sky*, to the US flag as the *Pride of Aloha* and, furthermore, to introduce one of a series of new builds under construction at Meyer Werft to a design derived from Star Cruises' *Superstar Leo/Virgo*-type as the *Pride of Hawaii*.[321] Thus, only some of the steelwork of one out of three cruise ships forming NCL's Hawaiian operation was actually 'born in the USA.'

Three sisters of the *Pride of Hawaii* were subsequently delivered by Meyer to NCL for international cruise service between 2005 and 2007; these were the *Norwegian Dawn*, *Norwegian Star*, *Norwegian Jewel*, *Norwegian Pearl* and *Norwegian Gem*.[322] At the same time, Star Cruises' the *Superstar Leo* was transferred to NCL as the *Norwegian Spirit* in exchange for older NCL ships, such as the *Seaward* and *Windward* which were deemed suitable for less discriminating Asian casino cruise passengers. Each of NCL's new acquisitions featured hull decorations based on suns, stars or gemstones and thereby reflecting both their names and a possible relationship between aspiring to cruise and owning glamorous-looking costume jewellery. Thereafter, hull decorations became an increasingly common feature of new cruise ships with other lines seeking to emulate NCL and Aida Cruises. Typically, designs consisted of swirling ribbons, stars and other such easily-decoded imagery, the idea being to break up the monolithic bulk of typical new cruise ships' silhouettes while making the operating brands appear a little distinct from each other in a context of increasingly homogenised ship design solutions.

The idea of hull decoration – or 'hull art', as it is often known – was not new, however, as, back in the late 1960s, the liner *Independence*, referenced above, had briefly been chartered to a Fugazi Tours, a New York travel agency, which had repainted the vessel's hull with a giant yellow

Below: The interiors of the *Pride of America* continued the patriotic theme with a variety of renditions of 'typical' American public and commercial interiors, as shown by the guest services counter (top) and burger bar (above).

Right: Norwegian Cruise Line's *Norwegian Spirit* was formerly Star Cruises' *Superstar Leo*. NCL introduced so-called 'hull art' to distinguish its fleet from those of competitors.

sun setting on each side, featuring the eyes of the Hollywood 'movie queen' Jean Harlow, surrounded by orange and red rays that spread all over the superstructure. While the effect was attention-grabbing, it hardly flattered the otherwise traditionally-styled liner. Fugazi obviously wanted to associate its 'Go-Go Cruises' with a youthful, fashionable and fun-seeking clientele – but only had limited success as its sought-after demographic was not attracted by the idea of taking a cruise. Fifty years later, NCL's hull decorations were more conservative in terms of subject matter than Fugazi's 1960s psychedelia and, in any case, they were conceived in a context of a greatly expanded mass cruise market, attracting a far broader demographic than had been the case back in the 1960s.[323]

As for NCL's 'Homeland Cruising' concept, very soon it became clear that Hawaii was a limited market and that operating three vessels under the US flag was, at best, only marginally profitable. After a few years, the *Pride of Hawaii* and *Pride of Aloha* were returned to the main NCL fleet with Bahamian registry as the *Norwegian Jade* and *Norwegian Sky*, leaving only the *Pride of America* to continue with Hawaiian itineraries. As Americans who cruised came to realise that their initial post-9/11 fearfulness of taking overseas trips was unwarranted, the cruise industry made a rapid recovery and, indeed, began to expand with even greater vigour than before.

The *Queen Mary 2* – a ship apart

Of the many large cruise ships completed in the first decade of the new millennium, one stood apart from all the rest. While practically all mass market cruise ships are essentially 'fair weather' craft, designed mainly for calm and unchallenging conditions, Cunard's 148,258gt the *Queen Mary 2*, completed in 2003, was the first 'thoroughbred' trans-Atlantic liner to be built since the *Queen Elizabeth 2* back in 1969. In the 1990s, Cunard had produced various design concepts for an eventual *QE2* replacement but because its then-owner, Trafalgar House, was unwilling to invest, these never progressed beyond the 'idea' stage.[324] Following Carnival Corporation's take-over, there was a new determination to invest in the Cunard brand and so serious discussions commenced regarding a new flagship. At first, Carnival's CEO, Micky Arison, reputedly thought that it would be possible to modify an existing cruise ship design with thicker hull plates and extra strengthening – but he was dissuaded from this view by Carnival Corporate Shipbuilding's naval architect, Stephen Payne.[325] Payne showed him 1960s film footage of the Italian trans-Atlantic liner the *Michelangelo* arriving in New York with a severely damaged bow and forward superstructure, resulting from an encounter with a ferocious storm

Right: The *Norwegian Jade* (ex-*Pride of Hawaii*) is seen on the Clyde at Greenock during a round-Britain cruise, a very different type of itinerary from Star Cruises' short trips from Hong Kong and Singapore, or NCL's Hawaii circuits. These various deployments illustrate the design's inherent flexibility.

Cunard's unique trans-Atlantic liner and cruise ship *Queen Mary 2* required a bespoke design approach to enable her to withstand the worst weather on the open ocean. Inboard, retro-design is used to evoke First Class liner travel in the early-twentieth century, as demonstrated by a Grill Room (centre left), the Commodore Club (centre right), the Winter Garden (above) and the Britannia Restaurant (right).

en route. The clear message was that, such can be the strength of an Atlantic tempest that the only safe option would be to build a bespoke vessel with similar characteristics to the finest ocean liners of the past.[326] Rather than the rather bluff hull configurations of practically all purpose-built cruise ships with superstructure piled up forward and aft, a fine-lined profile would be needed to slice through the ocean with adequate protection from high waves. Yet, in an era when most travellers demanding speed would fly, it would also be necessary to make the voyage cruise-like and therefore to include all of the facilities expected by passengers used to the biggest mass market cruise ships. Furthermore, to make the project viable, the vessel would need to accommodate in style no fewer than 3,000 passengers. To fit in these requirements, the vessel would need an internal volume more akin to that of the *Voyager of the Seas* than to the *QE2*.[327]

As nobody had ever previously designed a liner hull measuring nigh-on 150,000gt, a great deal of research would be required. Stephen Payne – whose childhood ambition had been one day to design an Atlantic liner – took charge of the project and his starting point was to find out what had worked well on the last generation of liners built in the 1960s. While the whale-back bow design appeared to have much in common with that of the *QE2*, a long bulb was fitted to improve efficiency and to provide additional buoyancy, offsetting the loss of volume resulting from the slim profile. Aft, the stern configuration was developed from that of 1960s Italian liners, such as the *Oceanic* and *Eugenio C.*, the sterns of which combined a transom at the waterline with a spoon-shape above; this would enable the fitment of four Azipod propulsion units across the width of the transom while retaining a curving shape above, advantageous in following seas.[328]

To enable a speed of nearly 30 knots, as well as providing power for the vast array of onboard services, machinery capable of generating 110,200 kW would be necessary, the solution being to install four 16-cylinder Wärtsilä diesels and two General Electric gas turbines, the latter unusually placed atop the superstructure in a housing to the rear of the funnel. (For comparison, the power requirement of Celebrity Cruises' 24.5-knot the *Millennium* was a mere 50,000 kW.) The order to build the vessel was won by Chantiers de l'Atlantique – which in the distant past had built the famous French Atlantic liners – but never one flying the British flag.

Externally and inboard, the *Queen Mary 2*'s design emerged as the ultimate ocean liner theme park. The exterior detailing referenced elements of past Cunard liners such as the *Queen Mary* in the double-curvature of the forward superstructure and the *QE2* in the hull, bridge, mast and funnel – though, as the vessel needed to sail beneath the Verrazano Narrows Bridge at the entrance to New York harbour, the latter two elements were rather short and stumpy. Where the *Queen Mary 2* differed markedly from any liner of the past was in her five decks of superstructure with cruise ship-style cabins and staterooms featuring balconies. In addition, cabins in the upper hull also had verandas with holes cut in the topsides – a feature not previously seen on any passenger ship.[329]

Inboard, the *Queen Mary 2*'s public circulation used an axial plan, inspired by the famous 1930s trans-Atlantic liner *Normandie*, and benefitting from exceptionally generous deck heights to create a sense of grandeur not typically found on recent cruise ships. Reflecting the vessel's transoceanic routing with consecutive days at sea, an inward focus was advantageous and also enabled best use to be made of the 41-metre beam with smaller public rooms on either side. The interior design was co-ordinated by Tillberg Design – which had opened an office in Weston, Florida, presided over by Robert Tillberg's son, Tomas – with inputs from the London firms of SMC and Designteam. What they produced together was all essentially nostalgic. As on most flagship Atlantic liners of the past, a key space was the main dining saloon and, on the *Queen Mary 2*, this was a three-deck-high affair, named the Britannia Restaurant and, like much of the rest of the interiors, decorated in pastiche Art Deco style. The balcony fronts were double-curved, again using the motif from the *Queen Mary*'s superstructure. Those occupying the more expensive staterooms instead dined in one of two grill restaurants, located towards the stern on Boat Deck. In addition, there was an extra-tariff option, operated under the brand of the American 'celebrity' chef, Todd English – an early instance of what would subsequently become a common approach on many large cruise ships of using tie-ins with famous names. A Cunard press release reported 'His restaurant, Olives, in Charlestown, MA, opened in May of 1989, and has drawn national and international acclaim ever since… However, it was in 2001 that English's face became as renowned as his cooking when he was named one of People magazine's "50 Most Beautiful People."'[330]

Of the *Queen Mary 2*'s many other public rooms, the bars ranged from a curved, forward-facing cocktail lounge named the 'Commodore Club', reminiscent of the famous one on the *Queen Mary*, the midships-located Chart Room, an Art Deco champagne lounge and an 'English Pub' called 'The Golden Lion', which was conceptually and decoratively reminiscent of a branch of Wetherspoon's ashore. For entertainment, popular features of the old *QE2* – such as the Queen's Room ballroom and the library – were replicated in enlarged form, albeit decorated with mixed Edwardiana and 1930s styling. There was also a theatre and a separate lecture auditorium called 'Illuminations' with a planetarium installed in the ceiling dome. Less successful was the Winter Garden, featuring a trompe l'oeil ceiling, grottoes and rattan furniture. While the aim may have been to emulate an Edwardian-era shipboard winter garden, in actuality, the overall effect was decidedly tacky, the space being subsequently entirely re-configured.

Technically, operationally and economically, the *Queen Mary 2* was fortunately a resounding success overall and her hull form and propulsion system were magnificent engineering achievements – but aesthetically she was arguably a missed opportunity. At the time of her construction, Britain was undergoing a design renaissance, arguably comparable with that which in the 1960s had given rise to the *QE2*'s futuristic styling. In architecture and industrial design ashore, Norman Foster, Zaha Hadid and Thomas Heatherwick, to name but three, were high-profile celebrities of the creative industries. Although Cunard might have employed any of these or other prominent British designers of the era to work on the *Queen Mary 2*'s silhouette and interiors, instead extreme design conservatism dominated thinking. Nonetheless, the liner's great size (upon entry into service, she was briefly the world's biggest ever passenger ship) and her high media profile drew crowds wherever she sailed.

Chapter 15
A globalising cruise market

In the first decade of the twenty-first century, the largest cruise operators realised the potential of an emerging global middle class and the opportunity of breaking out of their traditional American and European markets this presented. The new target nations for growth were some of the so-called 'BRIC' countries (Brazil, Russia, India and China), all of which were showing unprecedented growth at that time. Carnival Corporation decided that, in future, its global mass-market brand would be Costa Cruises and that the Destiny-class cruise ship design would be the ideal platform for Costa to be expanded with a special focus on the Chinese and Brazilian markets (the latter being a traditional territory for brand, dating back to 1950s liner days). Under CEO Pier Luigi Foschi, the company ordered five examples of the Destiny-class, all to be built at Fincantieri's Sestri Ponente shipyard. The first of these, the 102,587gt, 3,470-passenger *Costa Fortuna*, was delivered in 2003, followed by the *Costa Magica* in 2004.

Inboard on the *Costa Fortuna*, Joe Farcus' vivid and visually rich post-modern design paid homage to Italian ocean liners of the past. The deckhead at the top of the atrium was painted to resemble a sea on which was mounted a series of large illuminated waterline models of most of Costa's famous liners of the past, as well as members of their present day cruise fleet. The restaurants took their names from the Italian Line's famous but short-lived 1965-built trans-Atlantic liners the *Michelangelo* and *Raffaello*, while their earlier 1930s flagships, the *Rex* and *Conte di Savoia*, were commemorated respectively in the theatre and Grand Bar. In contrast, the *Costa Magica* was a more general homage by Farcus to 'the magic of Italy' with themes inspired by various Italian holiday locations. As Italian food and culture are much loved around the world, Farcus' referencing of Costa's Italian background made effective use of these positive associations in a context of globalisation.

The next trio, named the *Costa Concordia*, *Costa Serena* and *Costa Pacifica* were slightly enlarged versions of the Destiny-class, each measuring 112,000 tons and with 3,800 berths. The first of this trio took as her theme the grand architectural styles of Europe's capital cities, rendered with Farcus' usual whimsy and keen eye for detail.[331] The *Costa Serena* highlighted Greek and Roman mythology, while the *Costa Pacifica* had a musically inspired theme. A further example of the type was delivered in 2008 to Carnival Cruise Line, named the *Carnival Splendor*.

In Mediterranean mass-market cruising, Costa's rapidly emerging rival was MSC Cruises, owned by Mediterranean Shipping Company, which was otherwise a global operator of container ships and which, as a private company, could divert its profits into purchasing large cruise ships. As well as the Mediterranean, MSC Cruises sought to enter the so-called BRIC markets, principally Brazil, and also to increase its presence in South Africa. Between 2006 and 2013, MSC Cruises introduced no fewer than eight very large new cruise ships, split between two classes. All were built by STX France, which was the former Chantiers de l'Atlantique at St Nazaire, renamed following partial sale by the Alsthom engineering group to South Korea's STX Corporation. The hull design for the 92,409gt, 2550-passenger *MSC Musica*, *MSC Orchestra*, *MSC Poesia* and *MSC Magnifica*, which entered service between 2006 and 2010, was based upon that developed for P&O Princess Cruises' the *Coral Princess* and *Island Princess*.[332] The larger, post-Panamax 137,936gt, 3,887-passenger *MSC Fantasia*, *MSC Splendida*, *MSC Divina* and *MSC Preziosa* appeared between 2008 and 2013. All of these vessels had diesel-electric propulsion, employing five Wärtsilä 16-cylinder diesels.

With their entry into service, MSC's capacity grew by 25,748 berths in just five years.[333] To fill this capacity, the company began selling cruises on the basis of one passenger paying the full fare and another paying just 1 Euro with children included free-of-charge. This strategy broadened the market, getting younger people 'hooked' on cruising yet, with an increased focus on shipboard revenue, all of these extra passengers were profitable once they embarked and began spending. To keep children entertained, MSC Cruises offered 'Formula 1 simulators, full-size outdoor tennis and basketball courts, bowling alleys, mini-golf, kids and teenagers clubs and 4D cinema.'[334]

Perhaps responding to Joe Farcus' showy designs for Costa Cruises, MSC's Italian-based designers, Studio De Jorio, likewise produced flamboyant themed designs, comprising shiny and glittering surfaces, ornate drapes, deep upholstery and expanses of marble and granite slabs. The amount of internal space requiring filling with visually-distracting and profit-generating imagery across the new fleet was immense. In the ships' atria, curving feature stairs with Swarovski diamond-inlaid treads became a 'signature feature', reflecting a general strategy of emphasising symbols and materials associated with popular conceptions of aspirational luxury.[335] Such designs were, however, merely the latest manifestations of a trajectory begun in the early-1980s with Carnival's the *Tropicale* and, although the size of mass market vessels had since grown six-fold and new types of large internal space had been opened up, so far as surface finishes were concerned, the need for obvious glitz and glamour had remained much the same.

Yet, quickly generating designs to fill so many linear kilometres of shipboard space with attention-grabbing dining, retail and entertainment distractions while working within the limitations of a strict commercial budget inevitably led to qualitative compromises. As the cruise writer Matthew Sudders cruelly observed of the *MSC Fantasia*'s interiors:

> 'The actual implementation is really quite awful. For instance, in the Transatlantico Bar, all the décor features are in shiny plastic; in the Piazza San Georgio, there are amateurishly painted bricks and similar effects; the atrium in 1980s Joan Collins bling and the La Cantina Toscana wine bar and El Sombrero Tex Mex restaurant are pale imitations of the settings that their names conjure up. I was trying to think what the standard of finish reminded me of and then it came to me: my student hall of residence (not the crystals and marble stuff but the rest). It looks for all the world as if amateurs had watched a home decorating programme and then tried to create particular

156 | Cruise Ships: A Design History

The *Costa Concordia* was one of a series of derivations of Carnival's 'Destiny'-class, built to greatly expand Costa Cruises' fleet into a major global brand. Carnival's Joe Farcus designed her interiors in his typically ornate manner. These included the 'Lisbona' disco (centre left), 'Riviera Magica' lido (centre right), 'Europe' atrium (above) and 'Athens' theatre (right).

effects or ideas on the cheap. Much of the furniture is colourful but seems covered in an artificial plastic-like material when the sought after effect was, I suspect, leather…'[336]

Such 'scenography', more reminiscent of stage and film sets than highly crafted passenger ship interiors of the past, looked most appealing in low-resolution web images or when glanced at but it evidently failed to withstand further, closer scrutiny by discerning eyes and intellects. Yet, in the ensuing period, economic forces would ensure that the approach became increasingly commonplace on large mass market cruise ships. The sheer speed at which these giant vessels were built alone prevented any more thorough attention being paid to the felicitous resolution of design details. Perhaps this situation merely reflected the aesthetic and qualitative compromises needed to bring the cost of cruises down sufficiently to enable new demographics to indulge.

As Sudders went on to observe, the need to limit costs also led to tight planning of the seating in main dining room which was 'so crowded with tables and chairs that passengers must arrive and depart in formation in order to access their seats… in some parts, the waiters simply cannot reach to put your plate in front of you.'[337] For more space and a less frenetic atmosphere, it was necessary to book one of the extra-tariff speciality restaurants – but, unlike Sudders, 'first timers' would probably have lacked knowledge of cruise ship precedents or points of reference with which to form comparisons. Instead, their reference points would be more likely to be malls, retail parks or multiplex cinemas, sharing similar design values to cruise ships such as the *MSC Fantasia*. For a majority of passengers like them, vessels such as this appeared to offer really good value for money.

The Vista-class

Since the mid-1990s, Carnival Corporation had desired a standard cruise ship design which could be decorated in various ways to suit each of its brands' requirements. The Finnish-built 'Project 800' series, described above, was one attempt that did not meet with universal approval among the various managements of Carnival's various subsidiaries. Holland America executives were particularly sceptical and therefore took the lead in commissioning Fincantieri's naval architects, led by Maurizio Cergol, to produce a superior alternative. The outcome of their efforts was the so-called Vista-class which was to prove arguably the most successful design of passenger ship ever conceived in terms of layout, economy and flexibility. This Panamax design could be used equally for repetitive week-long circuits of the Mediterranean, or lengthy world-cruises, lasting well over a month.[338]

Measuring 81,769gt and with a 2,388-passenger capacity, the class was powered by a combination of three 16-cylinder and two 12-cylinder Wärtsilä diesels, augmented by a single General Electric gas turbine to push the maximum speed from 20 to 24 knots when it was necessary to traverse long stretches of open ocean during world cruises. Initially Holland America ordered four examples, constructed at Fincantieri's Marghera shipyard near Venice and delivered at annual intervals from 2002 onwards; these were the *Zuiderdam*, *Oosterdam*, *Westerdam* and *Noordam*. Shortly after, there followed two more slightly enlarged versions, the 86,273gt, 2,671-passenger *Eurodam* and *Nieuw Amsterdam* of 2008 and 2010. Externally, Maurizio Cergol's design was crisply detailed with continuous cabin balcony balustrades in dark tinted glass and matching external lifts, the funnels being a pair of closely-spaced vertical cylinders, somewhat reminiscent of the treatments of Costa Cruises' recent vessels. Inboard, they were essentially enlarged versions of previous Holland America projects by the Dutch architect Franz Dingemans.[339] One major innovation of members of the class from *Oosterdam* onward was the fitment of air blowers inside the stern to produce a 'carpet' of small bubbles above the propellers, reducing the transfer of noise and vibration to the hull. Developed by Danish engineers, the system was thereafter used on numerous cruise ships. A decade later, the use of air bubbles was expanded to 'lubricate' the entire underside of ships' hulls, reducing drag and improving fuel economy.[340]

Shortly, a fifth example of the Vista-class was ordered for Cunard, to be named the *Queen Victoria*, but while she was under construction, it was decided that her hull was insufficiently long to accommodate the required range of facilities nor was it engineered robust enough to make even occasional winter crossings of the North Atlantic. The solution was to transfer her to P&O Cruises, for whom she was completed as the *Arcadia*, albeit with a modified Cunard-style funnel and mast (both of which were derived from the distinctive designs on the company's ageing but popular 1969-vintage liner, the *Queen Elizabeth 2*). Subsequently, Cunard received modified versions of the Vista-class with longer, stronger hulls; these were the *Queen Victoria* (2007) and *Queen Elizabeth* (2010).[341] Four more of another variation were built for Costa Cruises – the *Costa Luminosa* (2009), *Costa Deliziosa* (2010), *Costa Favolosa* (2011) and *Costa Facinosa* (2012).[342] The Cunard examples were decorated internally by Teresa Anderson and Giancomo Mortola in a style mixing Edwardiana and Art Deco, recalling Cunard's great trans-Atlantic liners of the past, while Joe Farcus decorated the two Costa sisters in his typically vivid manner.[343]

Celebrity's Solstice-class

The Royal Caribbean-owned Celebrity Cruises' response to Carnival's Vista-class was a new series of four 121,878gt, 2,850-passenger cruise ships, incorporating a great many diverse innovations; these were the *Celebrity Solstice*, *Celebrity Equinox*, *Celebrity Eclipse* and *Celebrity Silhouette*, built by Meyer Werft and delivered at yearly intervals from 2008 onwards.[344]

Celebrity's passenger demographic was on average slightly younger and was thought to be a little more progressive in taste with regard to design matters than that of Holland America at whom the initial examples of the Vista-class were aimed. With hindsight, the Royal Caribbean and Celebrity managements viewed the company's first five German-built cruise ships as being its most successful, the subsequent Millennium-class allegedly being considered somewhat retrograde both in external appearance and in terms of internal style. It was decided therefore to return to Meyer Werft for

The *Celebrity Silhouette* is one of a series of large cruise ships, the design process of which involved unusually progressive thinking. The vessel's 'Blu' clean food restaurant (centre left), 'Grand Epernay' main dining room, 'Hideaway' sitting lounge and lido deck all demonstrate the contemporary overall approach.

A globalising cruise market | 159

The exterior of the *MSC Musica* and interiors of the *MSC Fantasia*, showing the Manhattan Bar (centre left), El Sombrero Tex Mex Restaurant (centre right), Liquid Disco (above) and Teatro Avanguardia (right); the flamboyant thematic styles somewhat echo those of Costa Cruises recent tonnage, albeit with less attention to decorative detail.

Above: The mighty *MSC Splendida* is seen ploughing her way through the Mediterranean Sea (top) while Holland America's 'Vista'-class cruise ship *Zuiderdam* is pictured at anchor (above).

the development and construction of the new series. By the early-2000s, Meyer had invested substantial sums to create arguably the most advanced and sophisticated commercial shipbuilding facility in the world. In 2002, a second, much larger fully-enclosed building hall was inaugurated, enabling even bigger vessels to be built, and shortly thereafter a laser welding hall was also completed, its state-of-the-art equipment enabling substantial improvements in precision and productivity.

As with the recent Finnish-built vessels for Royal Caribbean, the design development for Celebrity's new series was overseen by Harri Kulovaara, although the design itself was developed by Meyer Werft, working alongside external consultants, such as Deltamarin. With a view to enhanced damage survivability requirements relating to forthcoming SOLAS 2010 legislation, the hull was divided into no fewer than 18 compartments and the machinery space was divided into fully isolated fire zones to enable a so-called 'Safe Return to Port' to be made in the event of one or more of the four 16-cylinder Wärtsilä diesels engines, or one of the electric generators, catching fire. Twin Azipods of the largest available dimension enabled a 24-knot maximum speed. On the bridge, separate areas were devoted to navigation and to a safety command centre, immediately to the rear. The hull form was highly advanced, incorporating several developments to minimise drag. As with the *Voyager of the Seas* and her sisters, the aft-body featured a wide 'lip' to increase hull length and cancel out the stern wave. A so-called 'interceptor plate' on its underside forced the propeller wake water downward. In combination with an unusually long bulbous bow to reduce the bow wave, this had the effect of reducing total resistance by four per cent. To cut resistance even more, all hull welds below the water line were ground flush and the entire surface was then silicon-coated.[345] The smoothness and precision of the steel finish achieved by Meyer Werft's laser welding techniques were, indeed, unprecedented for large commercial ship hulls.

Technical innovation extended also to the provision of service infrastructure in the passenger accommodation. For example, rather than there being a central air conditioning plant located around the base of the funnels, as was the case on all other large passenger ships, instead a decentralised system was fitted alongside the plumbing in the cabin corridor walls and between the deck heads and suspended ceilings throughout the passenger accommodation. Not only did this save space and weight, but it also allowed the level of cooling and ventilation to be sensed and varied locally with a consequent a 25 per cent reduction in energy use over a conventional solution. Atop the superstructure, 500 square metres of solar panels were installed to power the elevators. All shipboard services were controlled by an energy management system, NAPA Power.[346]

As with Celebrity's initial ships, a well-known yacht designer was commissioned to style the exterior. Martin Francis was a specialist in designing mega-yachts – the ultimate symbols of globalised, off-shore wealth in the early twenty-first century. Celebrity briefed him that 'we wanted the ship to have the quality of an iPod… a design quality that makes you go 'wow'… a masculine design, from the sexy shape of the bow to the slant of the superstructure, much like a mega-yacht.'[347] Much of this desired effect was achieved through particular attention being paid to the forward ten per cent of the hull and superstructure, the bow having a pronounced curving knuckle-joint and the bridge being encased in a continuous case with chamfered edges, lending a futuristic quality. Further aft were the generic decks of projecting balconies found on every cruise ship of the era. The slanting forward superstructure was matched at the stern, which was sloped at the same angle. As with Carnival's Vista-class for Holland America, two closely-spaced funnels were fitted and these too were slanted to match the overall design. The topmost decks were enclosed with extensive areas of what appeared from the outside to be frameless tinted blue glazing, which added to the futuristic overall effect.

For the interiors, Celebrity took the unusual step of engaging an all-female team to help advise on the commissioning of suitable designs; this comprised professional women in Celebrity's target 48-64 age range who were respectively a travel agent, a travel writer, a hotelier, a frequent traveller who had never previously cruised and one who had sailed on over 30 cruise ships. Celebrity gave each a digital camera and took them on visits to a variety of stylish and aspirational environments, such as a mega yacht and boutique hotels where they were asked to photograph things they liked. Celebrity's reasoning for this approach was that, just as in the days of liner travel, women were more likely than men to select a brand, ship or cruise itinerary and, furthermore, women were believed to be generally more discerning and sensitive to the details of their surroundings than men, particularly with regard to cabin and stateroom design and layout. Recently,

Cunard's enlarged 'Vista'-class derivation *Queen Elizabeth* has a more extensive superstructure at the stern than the Holland America versions. Inboard, she reflects the 'ocean liner'-themed design approach previously seen on the *Queen Mary 2* and on Renaissance Cruises' *R One* to *R Eight*, as her atrium (above left and right), ballroom (above right) and Grill Room (above) demonstrate.

162 | Cruise Ships: A Design History

The *AIDAdiva* is seen leaving Barcelona on a Mediterranean cruise; her 'Theatrium', amidships on the upper decks (above left and bottom right), is enclosed by curving walls of glass with stairways behind. Elsewhere, eating at a variety of themed buffet counters (above right) and sunbathing (above) are the major attractions.

Above: The *AIDAluna* is seen arriving at Stavanger on a Norwegian fjords cruise.

the Swedish car maker Volvo had used a women-led design approach and had found this highly beneficial. Celebrity's female commissioning team concluded that the interiors should be 'stylish but not trendy, sophisticated but not over-smart, elegant but not formal, playful but not juvenile.'[348] There was a strongly-expressed desire to avoid the post-modern fantasy-worlds of large mass-market cruise ships. Instead, the aim was to develop a more soothing and refined approach, reviving the more glamorous aspects of mid-twentieth century international modernism, as found, for example, in post-war Hilton hotels and, more recently, in new urban boutique hotels and resorts. Although the overall design for the new class was recognisably up-to-date, its combination of a 'masculine'-looking, high-tech exterior and a 'feminine' comfortable interior was a familiar one from passenger ships built throughout the twentieth century.

Rather than using any of the established cruise ship interior design specialists, Celebrity instead selected US-based architects better known for hospitality design ashore – Boston-based Wilson Butler Architects, BG Studio International and Tihany Design of New York and the Miami office of RTKL. The atrium, though tall, was rather sedate in comparison with those of other recent cruise ships, its centrepiece being a mature tree suspended in mid-air. Of six different themed restaurants, Adam Tihany's design for the two-deck-high Grand Epernay main dining room was the most remarkable. Located immediately aft of the atrium, it was entirely white but with extensive concealed LED lighting to enable the colour to be changed as desired. An oval void in the centre was surrounded with exposed ribs, vaguely suggestive of flying buttresses and supposedly inspired equally by the work of the early twentieth century Barcelona architect, Antoni Gaudi, and the contemporary structural engineer, Santiago Calatrava (these elements were, however, also reminiscent of the structural ribs forming sailing ships' hulls). At one end was a glass tower of wine bottles – a feature of several Tihany restaurant interiors ashore – and the ceiling featured matching glass chandeliers. Further aft, various smaller speciality restaurants had more conventional themed interiors of the type found on numerous cruise ships – Murano and the Tuscan Grill served Italian food while Silk Harvest provided Asian cuisine. More unusual was the Blu Restaurant for 'Aqua Class' passengers, occupying the more costly staterooms, serving 'clean cuisine' (ie organic low-fat and low-sugar dishes) in an interior with equally clean-looking blue and white décor.[349] Above the bridge, the Sky observation lounge, which was largely enclosed by large panels of blue tinted glass, featured white leather Arne Jacobsen egg chairs, this combination creating a retro-futuristic impression. Throughout the public areas, Celebrity's 'Starring You' strapline was reflected through what appeared to be curtained off and roped off areas to create sense of exclusivity so that passengers there would be made to feel superior and 'on the inside.'

The cabins and staterooms were designed by the Miami-based architects RTKL Associates. Their unusual interlocking layouts, which were wider at the bed but narrower at the sofa with alternate cabins having one or other adjacent to the window, gave 15 per cent more floor space than was typical of other recent cruise ships in the same size and price category. Their décor was, however, rather more conservative than in many of the public spaces. A small detail suggested by Celebrity's all-female commissioning team was a foot rest in the shower for use when shaving one's legs.

One of the most remarkable features was outdoors – an expanse of outdoor deck covered in real grass, known as 'the lawn' and requiring the employment of a 'green keeper' to keep it manicured. Achieving this on a ship was a major technical and horticultural undertaking, requiring a protective layer over the steelwork, a layer of drainage board, a filter layer, a mineral lightweight soil layer incorporating a network of irrigation pipes and, finally, salt water-resistant Bermuda grass. Elsewhere topsides were an indoor adults-only indoor pool, surrounded with cascades of pink bougainvillea flowers and a hot glass show with professional glass-makers demonstrating the making of glass ornaments, which passengers could then purchase. There were also extensive spa facilities offering a wide range of treatments and thereby reflecting a widespread cultural trend aspiring to health and beauty, which itself reflected contemporary celebrity culture. Both this aspect and the 'Blu' clean food restaurant enabled passengers to at least pretend to be 'detoxing.'

Of the many large cruise ships to have entered service in the first decade of the twenty first century, the four Solstice-class were among the most attention-grabbing on account of their many ground-breaking design elements. This was especially so at the upper end of the mass market which had hitherto been distinguished by design conservatism. The new approach perhaps reflected a generational shift with the 'baby boomers', hitherto cruising's core audience, giving

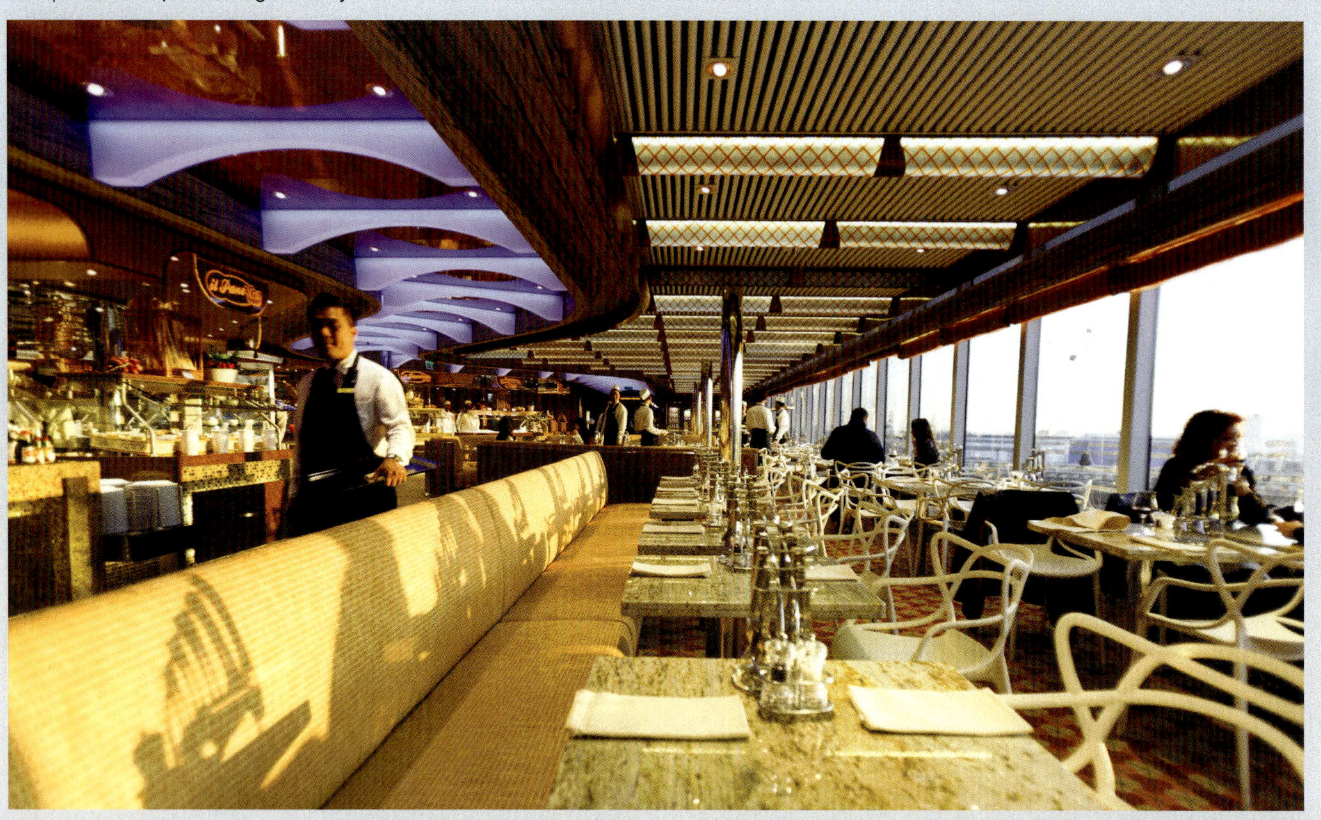

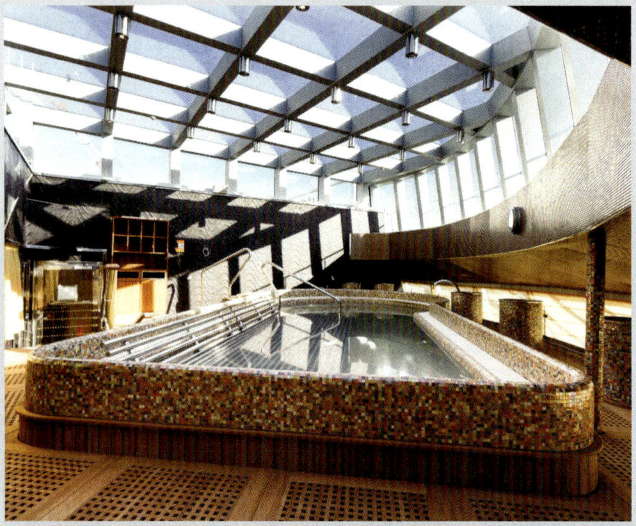

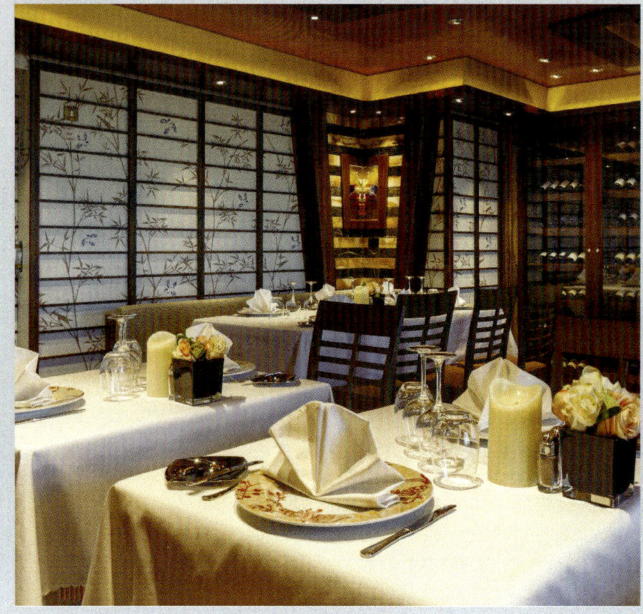

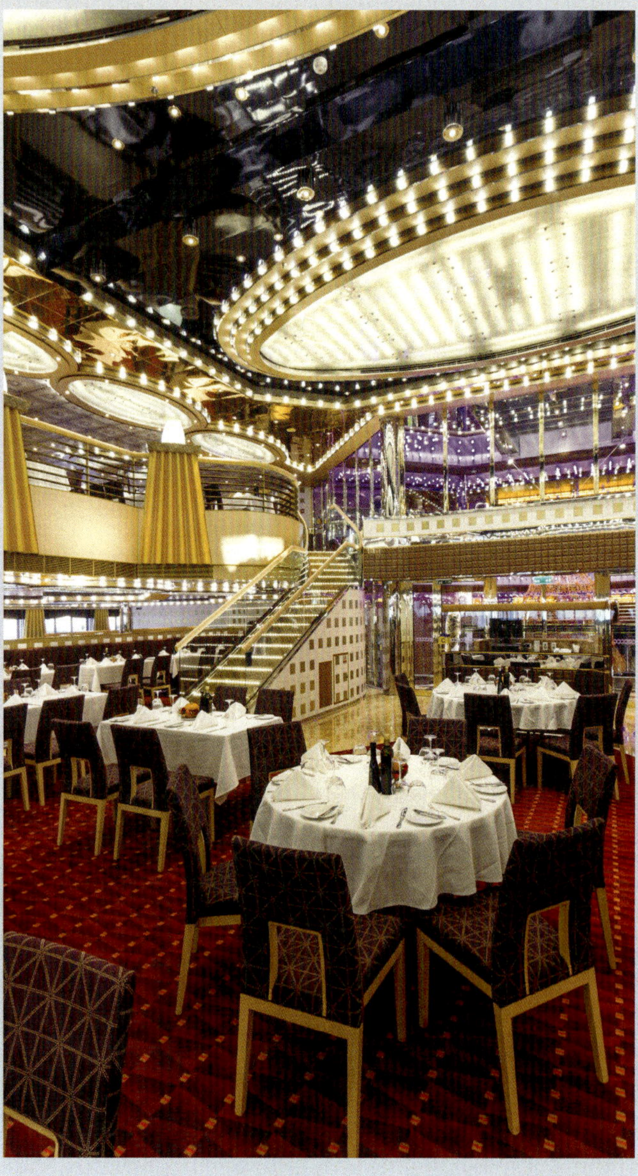

way to more style-conscious Generations X and Y.

In 2012, a fifth, somewhat enlarged, example of the type was completed: the *Celebrity Reflection*, which had an extra half-deck of cabins, giving a capacity for 3,609 passengers and a bigger tonnage measurement of 125,366gt. Below the waterline, her hull was innovatively fitted with a row of glands on the bottom under the bow, producing a constant 'carpet' of tiny air bubbles (or micro-bubbles, as they are referred to in technical descriptions). This installation would reduce surface tension between hull and water, thereby lowering drag and greatly increasing energy efficiency. Earlier on, as previously mentioned, a more primitive version of 'air bubbling' technology had been fitted towards the stern on some of Holland America's Vista-class vessels, where the bubbles were found to disrupt the transfer of vibrations caused by the propellers. In Japan, meanwhile, Mitsubishi had developed its own version of the same concept which had been successfully demonstrated on ferries it had built for Japanese coastal service.

The Aida Sphinx-class

Following Carnival's take-over of P&O Cruises, there was a reorganisation which placed the successful German Aida brand under the Italian management of Costa Cruises, albeit with many decisions still being made by lower-ranking managers in Hamburg. For Aida's clientele, it was felt necessary to continue building vessels in Germany, notwithstanding the greater cost this entailed to ensure that a sufficiently distinct level of Teutonic quality and detail was achieved. The plan was for Aida to receive from Meyer Werft a new series of no fewer than seven new cruise ships between 2007 and 2013 to accommodate expected growth; Code-named the Sphinx-class, these were the *AIDAdiva*, *AIDAbella*, *AIDAluna*, *AIDAblu*, *AIDAsol*, *AIDAmar* and *AIDAstella*.[350] Measuring 69,203gt and accommodating 2,030 passengers, they were larger by a third than its existing fleet. Due to the number of ships on order world-wide during the boom years of the early-2000s, it was impossible for the major marine engine builders to keep pace with demand and so, rather than the typical Wärtsilä units favoured for most new cruise ships, each Aida vessel was fitted with four MaK engines. Subsequently, the marque would be widely used for such vessels' diesel-electric propulsion systems.[351]

The interiors and external silhouettes were styled by Partnership Design of Hamburg and, as with Aida's earlier fleet members, the unusual solution of locating public rooms above cabins to group all activity around the topmost lido decks was perpetuated. A major layout innovation, however, was to combine the atrium and theatre functions into a single centrally-located, three-deck-high 'Theatrium.' This was intended as a place of high activity around the clock in the prime central location and was enclosed on either side by gently curved expanses of tinted glazing, on the inside of which were sweeping staircases connecting the various levels. The balconies around the void were surrounded with two rows of theatre seats, behind which was circulation space.[352] At the lower level, the designers attempted to create the 'more casual atmosphere of a modern airport terminal with benches instead of comfy chairs – a revealing statement about the hidden priorities of modern mass market cruise ship design to keep passengers moving and spending.[353] One side-effect of combining public circulation and staged performance was that it was necessary for rehearsals to take place in front of the public, but rather than spoiling the 'magic' of a theatre show, this was considered as an additional attraction during daytime hours. Moving the theatre function amidships enabled the inclusion of a large, forward-facing lounge space giving views ahead through panoramic windows.

Dining was mainly of the buffet variety, augmented by three surcharge a la carte restaurants (whereas on the earlier Aida ships there was only one of these). Of the two main buffet restaurants – named 'Markt' and 'Weite Welt' – the latter had themed areas serving food inspired by various styles from around the world – including Moroccan, Japanese, Dutch and Norwegian, the latter two respectively serving mainly cheeses and fish dishes. Of course, the décor combined all of the obvious clichés of these various countries and cultures: tiles with Islamic patterns, pagoda roofs, clapboard wall finishes and so on. As beer and table wine were included in the tariff, large storage tanks were located 'below decks' from which these were pumped. Among the other notable facilities was a television studio where interviews were performed with staff and passengers for broadcast over the ship's media system. In addition, extensive spa facilities included special variations for the German market, such as naked sunbathing areas and three types of mix-sex sauna.

Concurrently with the Aida series, Carnival Cruise Line also employed Partnership Design to produce interiors for the last of a series of three new vessels from Fincantieri, comprising the *Carnival Dream*, *Carnival Magic* and *Carnival Breeze*. These were developed from the commercially-successful Destiny-class, but enlarged to measure 128,251gt with accommodation for 3,652 passengers. Perhaps Carnival's management felt that the overtly post-modern work of its long-serving interior architect, Joe Farcus, was becoming dated – or maybe its high level of bespoke detail was becoming too costly to realise. The three vessels were delivered between 2009 and 2012 for Caribbean and Mediterranean itineraries.[354] Perhaps it was with a view to an operation there, attracting larger numbers of Europeans, that finally swayed Carnival towards an Aida-style design aesthetic for the *Carnival Breeze*, albeit married with a fully American-style level of shipboard service. A fourth example of the class for Costa Cruises, the 133,019gt, 3,724-passenger *Costa Diadema*,

Opposite: Interiors of the *Costa Diadema*, one of the last cruise ship interior projects conceived by Joe Farcus, include the Corona Blu Café (top), Samsara Spa and Samsara Restaurant (centre and bottom left) and Audularia Restaurant (right).

Below: The *Carnival Breeze* is seen at anchor; although her design was developed from that of the earlier 'Destiny'-class, more decks have been added and the lifeboats have been pushed outboard of the superstructure, freeing more space on the main public room decks for revenue-generating activities.

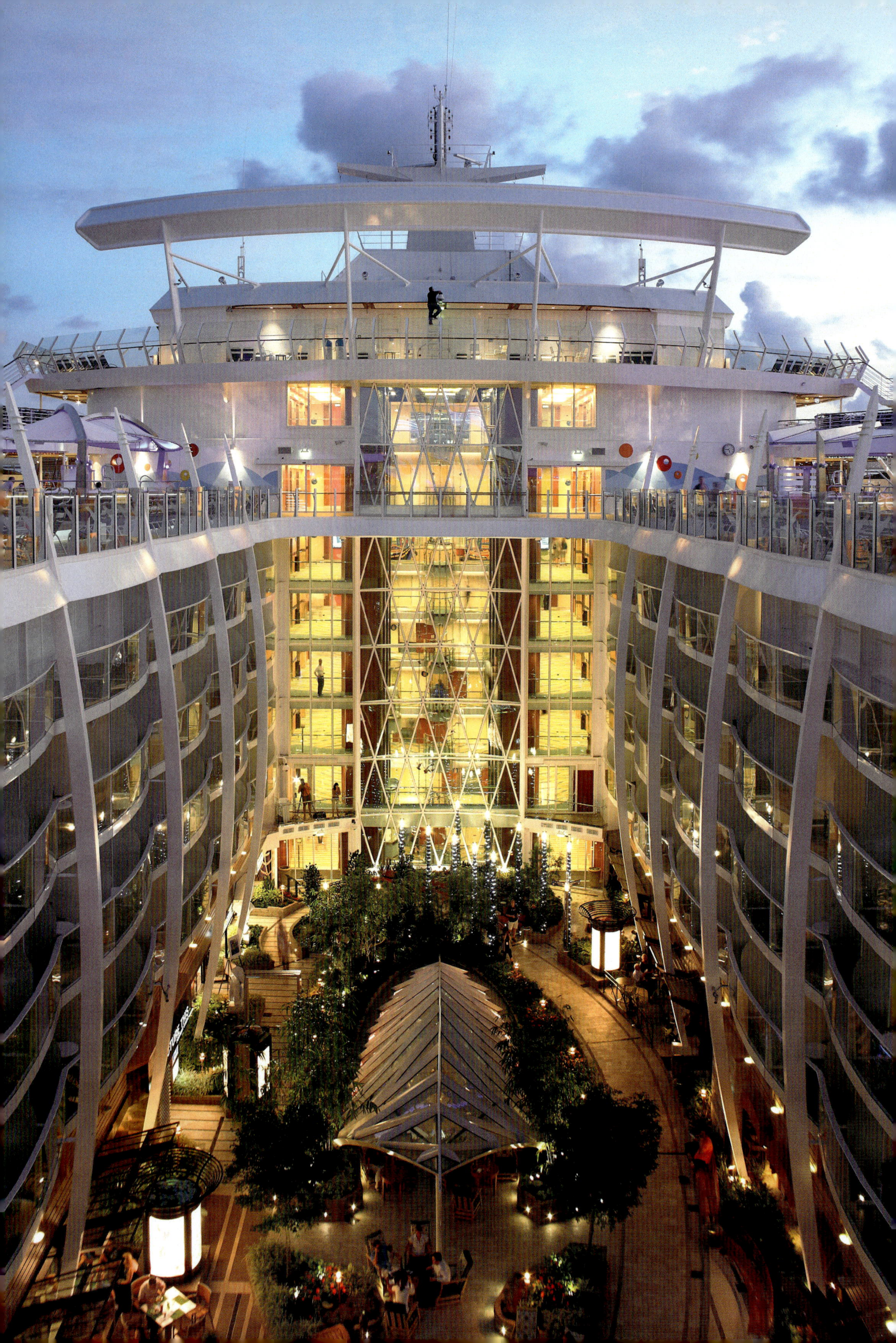

was completed by Fincantieri in the summer of 2014 and, for this project, Farcus was employed.[355] Subsequently, in 2016 Carnival added a further, slightly bigger variation – the 133,5596gt 3,936-passenger *Carnival Vista* – for which Partnership Design again produced the interiors.[356] The fact that a European interior designer was employed by an American brand and an American designer by a sister European brand demonstrates how, in a globalising market, the managements of Carnival Corporation's main mass market subsidiaries felt a need to commission design that would reach beyond their traditional core markets.

The biggest yet: the *Oasis of the Seas* and *Allure of the Seas*

By the millennium, Royal Caribbean and its Finnish shipbuilding partner had commenced development work for a Caribbean cruise ship almost twice the size of the existing Voyager and Freedom classes (which were themselves the world's biggest cruise ships at that time). In this period, the builder had undergone several changes of ownership due to financial difficulties being experienced elsewhere in successive parent companies' wider empires. Having traded since the early-1990s as Kværner Masa Yards, the company passed in 2005 to another Norwegian owner, the Aker group, and then in 2008 to the South Korean STX Corporation, which had also bought a substantial shareholding in the French cruise ship builder, Chantiers de l'Atlantique.

The entry into service of the *Voyager of the Seas* had convincingly demonstrated the desirability of a wide post-Panamax hull with space for many more passenger facilities. Subsequently, these initial ideas coalesced into what became known within Royal Caribbean as 'Project Genesis' As the company's Senior Vice President of Marine Operations, Harri Kulovaara, recalled:

> 'Our goal was to create a new project using available knowledge [and] the competence that was already there but creating a new ship providing a guest experience which was totally unparalleled to anything existing at that time. We made some 15 different ship designs… and we analysed them carefully, putting the best minds and brains together [to achieve the best solution]. Quite soon we zoomed down to quite a wide ship. We found that if we drastically increased the ship's width, then we [could] make its centre more attractive [with] a lot of inward-facing areas… and to be able to organise [the layout] in such a way as to provide several 'neighbourhoods' – [distinct zones] for people who have certain mind sets.[357]

Thanks to the increased stability of a wide hull, more decks of superstructure could be added and, by further developing the 'mall' concept from the Voyager-class, it would still be possible to retain a majority of cabins with windows. Making the hull significantly longer would however be undesirable, leading to a decline in manoeuvrability and an inability to fit existing port infrastructure.

As with the earlier 'Project Eagle' design process, for 'Project Genisis', Royal Caribbean used the accumulated experience of its own senior department managers to refine the design to ensure that its various aspects would function smoothly and inter-relate well with each other. Their work was co-ordinated by Harri Kulovaara and Kelly Gonzalez, Royal Caribbean's Associate Vice President of Architectural Design in the New Building Department, who was responsible for architecture, aesthetics and 'passenger interfaces.' On a project of such unprecedented complexity, it was necessary to employ the two leading Finnish consulting naval architecture practices, Deltamarin and Elomatic, to work in consort with the shipbuilder's design office in Turku, where the vessel would eventually be constructed. Each of the three teams of naval architects was given responsibility for devising approximately a third of the steelwork and servicing, the vessel being split vertically into three equal parts – bow, mid-body and stern. Initially, a core team of 30 naval architects and engineers began work in 2003 and this rose to 70 once detailed design was commenced.

The design that emerged was for a 225,282gt behemoth, 360 metres long by 47 metres wide and capable of accommodating no fewer than 6,360 passengers. A majority of cabins would have balconies facing the sea or overlooking outdoor voids between two longitudinal superstructure blocks, while other 'inside' cabins on the lower decks would have windows overlooking a four-deck-high internal mall, top-lit by skylights.

To maximise revenue-generating deck surface area to the greatest possible extent, the superstructure blocks slightly overhung the hull topsides with the lifeboats tucked underneath so that they could be launched vertically into the sea directly beneath (rather than down davits placed at

Above: The outdoor multi-functional performance 'Aquatheatre' space at the stern of Royal Caribbean's *Harmony of the Seas*, with rock-climbing walls mounted on the splayed bulkheads aft of the cabin blocks.

Opposite: The open-air 'Central Park' area on *Harmony of the Seas* is overlooked by deck upon deck of cabin balconies.

Below: Royal Caribbean's *Allure of the Seas*, the second of a series of 'Oasis'-class cruise ships, is pictured at sea; in appearance, the vessel is essentially a super-sized version of the company's earlier post-Panamax vessels.

Above: NCL's Meyer Werft-built *Norwegian Breakaway*, the hull of which features pop art decorations by the New York-based artist Peter Max. Waterslides are installed forward and aft of her comparatively small funnel casing.

a 45 degree angle, as on all other recent cruise ships with 'nested' lifeboats). Although this solution freed up a great deal of space, it nonetheless left the lifeboats very exposed to damage on the rare occasions when the vessel would encounter high waves. Furthermore, should the system fail, an uncontrolled vertical drop of such massive and heavy items might be hazardous for those standing on the quay underneath. Such a solution demonstrated Royal desire to embrace new technologies, but also the extent to which profitability had become a prime driver, even if that meant such a large vessel would be less sea-strong. (It is however the case that, with few exceptions and despite their great size, most modern cruise ships are essentially 'fair weather' craft with many delicate design features unable to withstand the rigours of the open ocean at its most tempestuous.)

In the outdoor spaces between the superstructure blocks, two different themed environments, known as 'neighbourhoods', were developed. One of these was the 'Central Park' neighbourhood, which was planted with trees and lush foliage and surrounded by 'upmarket' cocktail bars and speciality restaurants with seating spilling outdoors into the 'parkland' setting. Aft of this was a neighbourhood known as the 'Boardwalk', in which an attempt was made to replicate the seaside atmosphere of Coney Island with an amusement park, burger stalls, a pizzeria and ice cream parlour. Towards the stern was a multi-functional amphitheatre with water displays, known as the 'Aquatheater.' In addition to these outdoor neighbourhoods, there were several major indoor shopping, dining, entertainment and fitness zones. The internal 'Royal Promenade' was a mall surrounded by shops, bars and restaurants, similar to those found on the Voyager and Freedom classes, albeit considerably wider. The 'Vitality Spa and Fitness Center' contained spas of various types and 29 treatment rooms, the 'Entertainment Place' was a 'hub' of themed bars, nightclubs, a casino and the 'Youth Zone' was for children and teenagers, including a science laboratory, jewellery workshop and a small theatre. Finally, on the topmost decks was the 'Pool and Sports Zone.'[358]

Whereas one might have thought that attempts would be made to give the world's biggest cruise ship a unique 'personality', instead, Royal Caribbean's in-house design team insisted upon the same detailing in the main public circulation areas as had been applied to other recent members of the fleet. Furthermore, many of the same architecture and interior design firms as had worked on the Voyager-class were employed to execute the designs according to these predetermined specifications. They included, among others, the UK-based Atkins Global and the American practices Wilson Butler Architects, RTKL and Waterfield Design Group. This approach reflected the extent to which a perceived need for rigorous brand homogeneity had come to affect mass market cruise ship design. Having begun in the 1960s with corporate logos, the approach had now been extended to nearly every aspect of their internal and external appearances. Thus, apart from their cavernous size, the main interiors would be entirely recognisable to regular Royal Caribbean passengers.

Mechanically, 'Project Genesis' used a somewhat scaled-up but otherwise conventional diesel-electric plant, consisting of three 12-cylinder and three 16-cylinder Wärtsilä diesels, powering three 20 mW ABB Azipods to enable a 22.6-knot cruising speed. Towards the bow, four lateral thrusters – the largest in the world – were fitted to enable the vessel to move sideways easily. Yet, the main propulsion was only one aspect of an unprecedentedly complex and sophisticated technical solution. Everything from the checking-in of passengers in Miami to internal 'flows' of food, beverages, luggage, laundry and waste removal for over 6,000 passengers required re-thinking or at least up-scaling from solutions developed

A globalising cruise market | 169

The mighty *Norwegian Epic* is seen departing from Barcelona; the application of bands of dark blue paint to the fronts of the four decks piled above her bridge does little to conceal their impact. Inboard, the vessel's cabins (centre left) are of a so-called 'New Wave' design by Tillberg, featuring padded walls, LED lighting, sliding shutters over the window and a glazed bathroom cubicle. Also shown is one of her lido areas (centre right) The *Norwegian Breakaway*'s atrium (left) features an LED chandelier while her 'Spiegel Tent' dining and performance space (above) supposedly resembles a circus arena.

for previous vessel classes. Having 4,030 toilets and a similar number of showers, for example, meant that waste water and sewage purification needed to be state-of-the-art, using a moving bed bioreactor, capable of treating liquid waste to a level twice as stringent as the US Federal standard. The many restaurants needed no fewer than 20 galleys, staffed by a crew of 1,100 to prepare and serve food.

The contract to build the first example of the 'Project Genesis' type was signed in February 2006 and it was announced that she would be named the *Oasis of the Seas*. Notwithstanding the great many challenges to be overcome, completion was achieved a week ahead of schedule in October 2009. Upon the vessel's entry into service, Harri Kulovaara explained:

> 'The ship is very complex… it's a huge infrastructure, full of technology. It required two million design hours, half a million [of which were expended] on interior design and decoration and about 1.5 million on bringing the design and engineering together [to create] something that could be built. The building required some ten million working hours as well as half a million individual pieces of steel… This kind of project is only possible if there is a good understanding from the beginning, a good vision and trust and a seamless collaborative partnership.'[359]

By then a sister, to be named the *Allure of the Seas*, was already under construction with delivery scheduled for October 2010. Both giant cruise ships operated from Miami, where they undertook mainly week-long Caribbean itineraries. For many passengers, the ports of call were incidental; the ships themselves were the main attraction.

Norwegian Cruise Line's response to the *Oasis of the Seas* and *Allure of the Seas* was to commission its own giant cruise ship design from STX France at St Nazaire. Measuring 155,873gt and with a mere 4,200-passenger capacity, the outcome was not only smaller but also conceptually somewhat more conservative than Royal Caribbean's remarkable sisters. However, the facilities provided were expected to depart from convention, the initial intention being that there would be neither a main dining room, nor a buffet and, in their place, passengers would be expected to dine in one of a number of speciality restaurants – perhaps the ultimate development of NCL's 'Freestyle' concept. Nor was there even a conventional show lounge, entertainment being provided instead in other types of smaller venue.

In November 2006, NCL placed orders for two sisters with an option for a third example. Less than a year later, however, half of the company's shares were acquired by a new owner, the New York-based private equity firm Apollo Global Management. Founded in 1990, its specialities were 'leveraged buyout transactions and purchases of distressed securities, involving corporate restructuring, special situations and industry consolidations.'[360] Genting was consequently relegated to a minority interest, retaining just 12 per cent of NCL's capital. Apollo allegedly took fright at the lack of main restaurant, buffet and show lounge, and demanded that fundamental changes be made to the design to include these. The outcome of the necessary modifications was that the first vessel would cost much more than had been budgeted. The construction of both ships was therefore placed on hold until a new agreement could be reached. In the end, after tense negotiations, the less bad option appeared to be to proceed with building the first vessel to a modified design and to cancel the order for the second.

Completed in 2010 as the *Norwegian Epic*, more than any other recent cruise ship, her exterior appeared to have been designed by accountants, there being a great mass of identikit cabin balconies stacked high from bow to stern and with four additional decks piled vertically above the bridge, lending a distinctly top-heavy appearance. Within, NCL's usual interior designers, Tillberg, produced what publicity material described optimistically as a 'New Wave' interior – but one which in fact merely followed the themed decorative approaches found on so many other recent large cruise ships. The cabin wet room cubicles had curved walls – a feature perpetuated in subsequent NCL new buildings – and entertainment options included the world's first Ice Bar at sea. For those occupying 60 premium staterooms, the topmost two decks were imagined as a small boutique cruise ship within a large mass market, one with a 'private' swimming and spa facility, an indoor/outdoor restaurant, lounge and bar.[361] Although most cruise ships built since the 1960s had their most exclusive staterooms forward on the topmost decks, the idea of a small, exclusive 'ship within a ship' was otherwise new, though perpetuated in numerous subsequent large, essentially mass market vessels introduced in the *Norwegian Epic*'s wake. For those willing to pay, the concept offered the twin benefits of tranquillity with access to a very broad range of entertainments in what were effectively the 'second class' areas. The 'first class' signalled its exclusivity through a more restrained colour palette and stylish detailing than was found in the remainder, thereby engendering what many would hopefully recognise as an 'upmarket' atmosphere.

The lingering bitterness resulting from NCL's tough negotiations with STX France led to it ordering subsequent cruise ships from Meyer Werft instead. Indeed, from 2010 onward, Meyer became a production line for one giant cruise ship after another; it seemed as if the 2008 economic downturn had failed to affect the mass market cruise industry whatsoever. In 2010 and 2012, it completed the 129,630gt, 2,500-passenger *Disney Dream* and *Disney Fantasy* for Disney Cruise Line; inboard and out, these were in essence enlarged versions of Disney's existing pair of Italian-built vessels. Next, Meyer built the 144,017gt, 4,000-passenger *Norwegian Breakaway* and *Norwegian Getaway* which were delivered in 2013 and 2014, followed by the enlarged, though otherwise broadly similar 165,157gt, 4266-passenger the *Norwegian Escape* in 2015, which had two extra decks of cabins. All five of these vessels were intended for short cruises from US ports (in the instance of the *Norwegian Breakaway*, sailing year-round from New York).[362] Inboard, the NCL pair retained much of the thematic styling found on the *Norwegian Epic* and, indeed, all of NCL's ships introduced in the period since Star Cruises had first become a shareholder. One ingenious development was an indoor-outdoor arrangement of bars and restaurants along the length of the promenade decks, known as the 'Waterfront', thereby bringing 'street life' and pleasant new shipboard experiences to areas that on most other recent cruise ships were under-used as anything other than 'smokers' corners.'[363] Commenting on the *Norwegian Breakaway*, NCL's CEO, Kevin Sheehan observed that the design intention was:

> '…Taking the best of New York and bringing it out to sea… With the expansive Waterfront area, three Broadway shows, special fitness classes designed by the Rockettes [the Radio City Music Hall dance troupe], Geoffrey Zakarian's new restaurant Ocean Blue and incredible nightlife venues like Spice H20 and an Ice Bar with Gotham-

Above: The tragic *Costa Concordia* lies on her side on the coast of the Italian island of Giglio; clearly evident is the great hole ripped by a boulder in her underwater hull.

inspired ice sculptures, guests will get the feel of the Big Apple with the world-class amenities and service that Norwegian is known for.'[364]

Sheehan's marketing spiel reveals a great deal about the ways in which mass-market cruise lines plunder and 'enhance' what they perceive to be the most popular and desirable aspects of culture ashore, repackaging these in hybridised form to suit their own commercial ends. Needless to say, inboard, the slick and shiny *Norwegian Breakaway* was about as different from the glamour and grit of the 'real' New York as it is possible to imagine.

The loss of the *Costa Concordia*

The *Oasis of the Seas* and *Allure of the Seas* had crews of 2,394 each while the *Norwegian Epic*'s crew numbered a mere 1,724. Training so many seafarers so quickly required the development of special training schools in the countries from which the majority were drawn, namely the Philippines, Indonesia and India. Finding officers with enough experience to command the many new cruise ships was another challenge – and inculcating any sense of shipboard camaraderie among so many diverse individuals could be more challenging still. In his 1998 collection of essays *A Supposedly Fun Thing I'll Never Do Again*, the late American writer David Foster Wallace took a Caribbean cruise aboard an up-to-date, mass market ship, on which he observed how the Greek officers appeared as a bunch of uniformed gangsters with sunshades, whose mere appearance seemed to strike fear into their third world underlings forming the deck and hotel staff.[365] Wallace worried that those in the lower ranks might fear using initiative or reporting upward when they spotted something wrong. Nonetheless, the cruise industry had an enviably good safety record.

Then, on the evening of 13th January 2012, disaster struck spectacularly when Costa Cruises' very large five-year-old Mediterranean cruise ship the *Costa Concordia* partially capsized and sank on the rocky coast of the Italian island of Giglio. Rather than remaining on the bridge to command the necessary evacuation and rescue operation, the captain, Francesco Schettino, saved himself by launching a lifeboat and motoring ashore. Schettino had been a Costa employee for ten years, during which time he had risen from being a security officer to first officer, then captain in 2006. His rapid elevation through the ranks was fairly typical of the contemporary cruise industry – but nobody had checked that in an emergency he would have the necessary calm and brave demeanour required of one responsible for so large a passenger ship.

Having been sailed too close to the coast at too great a speed by Schettino, an enormous gash had been torn in the *Costa Concordia*'s port side. The vessel had then circled round, drifting ashore on her starboard side. Had an evacuation order been given promptly, all of her passengers would have been saved – but the fact that nothing happened for more than an hour meant that, by the time attempts to launch the lifeboats were made, there was such a severe list that most of them could not be used and so around 300 had to await rescue by helicopter. Of the 3,229 passengers and 1,023 crew known to have been aboard, 32 died.

It was subsequently revealed that Costa Cruises' captains not infrequently spontaneously diverted their vessels from the pre-ordained route to carry out so-called 'sail-pasts' of scenic sections of coastline (the *Costa Concordia*'s diversion on the evening of the sinking was to show the vessel off to a retired officer colleague of the captain who lived on Giglio); these changes were alleged to have been tacitly approved by the company's senior management. The fact that a captain would put at risk so many lives to make an attention-grabbing gesture – and the fact that the shipboard chain of command appeared to disintegrate so quickly in an emergency situation – shone a very unflattering light on at least part of the mass market cruise industry's operational practices.

Although alike situations could have occurred on other similar ships, the disaster did surprisingly little to dent passengers' confidence and, thereafter, demand for cruises remained high (the reasoning that it is often safest after a tragedy because everyone is more careful may have partly accounted for this). The sad irony was that, of all recently-built cruise ships, the *Costa Concordia* should have been among the easiest to evacuate quickly and safely as, from the outset, Carnival's naval architects had included a deep lifeboat embarkation deck on all examples of her class, meaning that there was plenty of dedicated space to muster and disembark in a quick but orderly fashion. Cruise ships built in the wake

Right: P&O Cruises' *Britannia*, featuring a new NCL-style livery with dark blue funnels and with a stylised Union flags emblazoned on her bow.

of the *Costa Concordia* sinking have tended to eschew outdoor mustering in favour of gathering passengers in the main public rooms, which double as muster stations, the theory being that these are more comfortable particularly for the elderly and infirm. In the event of fire, affected areas should be isolated through the closure of bulkhead doors, meaning that the remainder of the passenger accommodation would still be safe. The history of disasters at sea, however, suggests that when things go wrong, they go multiply wrong and so designers and regulators of cruise ships may be unduly optimistic that procedures will always work as intended.

More and more, contemporary mass market cruise ship design is driven by a desire on the part of owners to leverage the maximum profit and this has resulted in an ongoing trend whereby lifeboats are placed relatively lower on vessels' sides and also further outboard to increase the amount of shipboard space for commerce. The proportion of exterior surface area devoted to cabin balconies has been constantly increased since the mid-1980s and now these cover a majority of the outside of every vessel. From a distance, the repetitive pattern of open-sided square boxes reflects modern cruising's mass standardisation, the resemblance from a distance being closest to the stacked pens of livestock carriers. Topsides, funnels have shrunk and sometimes are buried among water-slides and rock climbing walls, but, notwithstanding the undesirability of giving prominence to smoke-production in an environmentally-conscious age, they have not disappeared altogether as naval architects and ship owners alike still consider their presence *de rigeur*. Without a funnel, a modern cruise ship would really be just a floating apartment block.

Princess Cruises' new 142,714gt, 4,380-passenger the *Royal Princess*, completed by Fincantieri at Monfalcone in 2013, evidenced this situation and demonstrated the development of cruise ship design since the completion of her predecessor of the same name 29 years before.[366] Whereas the 1984 *Royal Princess* had a mere two decks of cabins with balconies in a vessel with seven passenger decks, her namesake has 14 passenger decks, seven of which have balcony cabins. A sister ship, the *Regal Princess*, was delivered in 2014 and a third, broadly similar example, named the *Britannia*, was finished for P&O Cruises the year after. Intriguingly, whereas Carnival has built standard designs of cruise ship for each of its other brands, P&O Cruises has been given single or twin examples of these, rather than anything purpose-designed. Prior to the *Britannia*, P&O Cruises' most recent units were the 116,017gt *Ventura* and *Azura* of 2008 and 2010, derived from Princess Cruises' Grand-class.[367]

Cruise industry commentators – and the travel trade – meanwhile criticised the brand for its lack of homogeneity, its vessels ranging from the rather 'posh' (but middle-aged) *Oriana* and *Aurora* to much larger, more recent and obviously mass-market-orientated units. This situation reflected the make-up of P&O Cruises' clientele which, for the past half-century had tended to consist of a conservative upper middle class and an equally conservative lower middle class, each of whom was attracted by different facets of P&O Cruises' broad offer. For both groups, senses of tradition and patriotism to an established idea of 'Britishness' were important constants – evenings devoted to listening or singing along to patriotic music, similar to the 'Last Night of the Proms' in London, waving the Union flag, or relaxing amid ambiences reminiscent of idealised British life ashore, such as 'traditional'-looking pubs or spaces decorated like gentlemen's clubs.[368] This conservative image of Britishness was enriched by references to Britain's colonial legacy, such as P&O's tradition of serving curry and employing large numbers of Indian hotel staff (rather than the predominantly South-East Asian crew of other cruise brands). On the *Azura*, P&O had even introduced what it described as a 'contemporary Indian' restaurant, operated by the Michelin-starred celebrity chef Atul Kochhar (proprieter of the Tamarin and Benares restaurants in London's Mayfair).

Since the 1980s, the image of Britishness had changed considerably, thanks in part to the phenomenon of 'Cool Britannia', involving the foregrounding of popular music, fashion and sporting celebrities and the creative industries. In the wake of London's subsequent success in hosting the 2012 Olympic Games, a new kind of more inclusive patriotism was established (as opposed to the imperialistic kind of past decades – though it still lingered too). In this context – and wishing to 'strengthen' its brand identity, P&O Cruises decided for the *Britannia* to launch a new visual identity, replacing its existing livery, which dated back to the mid-1930s. In doing do, however, P&O Cruises appears, more than anything else, to have copied Norwegian Cruise Line, adopting a similar royal blue funnel colour, augmented with a stylised Union Flag emblazoned on the bow (though this perhaps also referenced British Airways' ubiquitous tailfin design). Yet, ashore, in the short period since the *Britannia*'s debut, a nostalgic English nationalist sentiment has become ever more obvious, with Britain's vote by a narrow majority to leave the European Union in June 2016 placing the union itself under strain. Thus, the arguably 'banal nationalism' of P&O Cruises identity now represents more problematic and divisive issues than had been intended upon its launch. In any case, such an overtly nationalistic approach to visual identity on vessels flying flags of convenience (the P&O Cruises fleet is registered in Bermuda) and staffed with international crews is surely highly questionable. Today, as in the past, cruise passengers are discouraged from thinking about such paradoxes while relaxing on holiday. On a P&O cruise ship, the fantasy idea of Britain as a still-important world power can be maintained.

In contrast with P&O Cruises which serve a single nation, international cruise brands, serving multiple markets, have continued to align brand identity and perceptions with those of the large American-owned but globally-operative hotel chains, such as Marriott, Hilton or Holiday Inn (within the Carnival Corporation 'family' of brands, Princess Cruises particularly exemplifies this fairly bland and homogenous approach). Royal Caribbean too has sought to negate its earlier identification as a Norwegian-controlled company and, instead, to present itself as a global brand. More than those of other operators, its vessels exemplify the design values of such internationalised constants of leisure and consumerism as the corporate chain hotel, the shopping mall and the theme park.

The company's next series of vessels, the 168,666gt 4,905-passenger *Quantum of the Seas*, *Anthem of the Seas* and *Ovation of the Seas* ordered from Meyer Werft for delivery in 2014-2016, clearly exemplified this strategy. (The name of the lead ship of the series was reminiscent of the James Bond action film 'Quantum of Solace' which was an international cinema hit while construction was under way.) The three were intended for service both in Western markets and in South-East Asia, where Royal Caribbean's operations were rapidly expanding.[369] With cruising in various climatic areas and tropical monsoon weather to be contended with, a greater proportion of indoor activities were provided than on other recent members of the Royal Caribbean fleet. Apart from an indoor pool, elsewhere on the upper decks was a twin-level 'Seaplex' – a multi-function space containing bumper cars, a roller skating rink and roller disco, trampolines plus basketball courts. It allowed diverse energetic activities to be enjoyed throughout the day, none of which were weather dependent.

Following Disney Cruise Line's 'rotational dining' system, which obviated any need for a main dining room, Royal Caribbean introduced a so-called 'dynamic dining' concept, through which passengers would use a mobile phone APP to make their own bookings in one of the various themed restaurants on different nights. In the aft location where a dining room would otherwise have been located on decks five through to seven, instead there was a vast three-deck-high entertainment space named Two70°. This was enclosed by a three-story-high, 270-degree panoramic expanse of glazing. Remarkably, given its size and the many decks piled above, there were few structural supports, the engineering resolution demonstrating the 'magical' effects achievable by finite 3D modelling. The glazing could be entirely blanked out by automatic window screens, on to which a 13-projector audio-visual system projected imagery. Retractable furniture, dividers and chandeliers enabled the space to be reconfigured in the evening as a performance venue. Elsewhere inboard, digital technology and robotics were applied in a 'Bionic Bar' in which mechanical arms mixed the drinks.[370]

In the inside cabins a 'virtual porthole' concept was installed, whereby circular LED screens created a simulation of the seascape out with. (Previously, this had been applied on the recent Meyer-built sisters for Disney.) Out on deck, meanwhile, there was a sky-diving simulator, set in a vertical wind tunnel, and a zip-wire across the pool area. At the forward end of the topmost deck, the 'North Star' was a glass-walled observation capsule, hung on the end of a 41-meter-long crane arm to lift groups of up to 14 upwards and over the edge of the ship, 300 feet above the sea. These entertainments were, however, fairly superficial additions to what was in most other respects a well-tried overall design and decorative concept, centred upon an internal mall similar to those found on numerous Royal Caribbean vessels of the previous decade.[371] As with the *Celebrity Reflection*, described above, the Quantum-class' hull bottoms were fitted with air-bubbling technology to reduce drag.

Upon delivery, the *Quantum of the Seas* was launched in the US market from New Jersey, but subsequently shifted to China to cruise from Shanghai. *En route*, several areas were modified for an Asian clientele – for example, the size of the casino was increased to include an additional area for 'high-rollers' and a 'Kung Fu Panda'-themed noodle bar was added

Left: Princess Cruises' *Regal Princess*, a vessel of similar design to the *Britannia*, catches evening sunlight during a Mediterranean cruise.

174 | Cruise Ships: A Design History

adjacent to the pool deck. While the *Anthem of the Seas* was also initially American-based, the third of the series, the *Ovation of the Seas*, was delivered directly to Tianjin in China, where she became the first brand new cruise ship for Chinese passengers. By then, two further examples of were already on order for delivery in 2019 and 2020.

Back in the summer of 2012, Royal Caribbean announced plans to commission a further sister to the *Oasis of the Seas* and *Allure of the Seas*, the expectation being that this vessel would, like the initial pair, be built at the STX Finland Turku shipyard. Following the 2008 downturn, the South Korean STX parent company suffered economic difficulties resulting from over-expansion and the consequent accumulation of debt. STX Finland consequently found that lenders were unwilling to loan the necessary sums to enable construction there and so, instead, Royal Caribbean placed the order with STX France, which being partly French Government-owned did not have the same problem of demonstrating financial resilience.

This news – which was somewhat reminiscent of the loss of the *Sovereign of the Seas* contract to the French back in the mid-1980s – caused considerable political turmoil in Finland where the government was criticised for doing too little to help the shipbuilding industry. Shortly after, however, a recently-formed German cruise operator, Mein Schiff, owned jointly by Royal Caribbean and the TUI travel agency, placed an order at the Turku shipyard for two 99,500gt, 2,500-passenger the *Mein Schiff 3* and *Mein Schiff 4*. Mein Schiff's operations had begun in 2009, its initial vessel, the *Mein Schiff 1*, being the former *Galaxy* of Celebrity Cruises. The concept was to serve the German market with an offer upmarket of Aida Cruises in terms of style and service, the latter otherwise being the major competitor. Mein Schiff's decision to name all of its vessels with the brand, suffixed by a number, took cruise industry corporate uniformity to an extreme not seen since the demise of Renaissance Cruises a decade previously. Once again, the romantic or cultural potential of past passenger ship nomenclature was dismissed in favour of an utterly homogenised approach. With regard to livery, the Mein Schiff vessels had dark blue hulls with words in German relating to the experience of sea travel and onboard lifestyle, repeated at different sizes all over in a font resembling a hand-written signature (to an English ear, the word 'Fahrtwind' does not have particularly positive connotations, however). For supposedly 'superior' cruise brands – and many other corporate organisations besides, the idea of a 'signature' (of authenticity) or of promoting 'signature features', distinct from those of competitors, had been widely applied since the 1980s. Mein Schiff's emphasis of this type of strategy not only in brochures and on websites, but on the exteriors of the vessels, was enabled by contemporary printing technology, enabling weather-resistant decals to be produced at a scale sufficient to make an impact on so large an object as a cruise ship.

While the *Mein Schiff 3* and *Mein Schiff 4* were under construction, in August 2014 the Turku shipyard was bought from STX by the German Meyer Werft. The Turku yard had both a larger building dock and direct access to sea, which Meyer's existing, long-established yard at Papenburg lacked. It was then renamed as Meyer Turku Shipyard Oy. When this was announced, two further cruise ship orders were also revealed; these were for the *Mein Schiff 5* and *Mein Schiff 6*.

The *Mein Schiff 3*, *Mein Schiff 4* and *Mein Schiff 5* entered service in 2014, 2015 and 2016 respectively. Inboard, these vessels were largely the work of the Boston-based architects Wilson Butler Associates, whose previous work included spaces on Royal Caribbean's Oasis-class and Celebrity Cruises' Solstice-class. Many of the public areas were, however, designed by CM Design, based in Hamburg, and some others by the prolific cruise ship specialists, Tillberg Design. Alongside the conventional features of vessels of their size and market segment, there are some unique and notable differences. Overlooking the stern is a suite of bars and restaurants, collectively known as the 'Grosse Freiheit' (Great Freedom). These are located beneath an atrium, the glazing of which references deconstructivism in architecture – an approach initially associated with 1990s 'starchitects' such as Frank Gehry, Zaha Hadid or Daniel Liebeskind. While much emulated ashore, desconstructivist aesthetics had never previously been attempted on a ship. On the *Mein Schiff* sisters, faceted triangular panels of glass form an abstract pattern above diners but, viewed from the exterior, this excrescence forms only a small part of an otherwise fairly conventional overall silhouette.[372]

The Klanghaus, by CM Design, located near to amidships, is the first ever chamber concert hall at sea. In appearance, it resembles a contemporary hall or rehearsal space for classical music ashore, having a clean-lined, rather formal appearance and making extensive use of

Opposite: Royal Caribbean's *Anthem of the Seas* is seen with the pole arm holding the 'North Star' observation capsule in the raised position. Within, the vessel and her sisters feature a rink with dodgems (centre left), the Two70° multi-use entertainment lounge (centre right), an indoor pool (bottom left) and a mall (bottom right).

Below: A novel feature of the German TUI-operated cruise ship *Mein Schiff 4* is her collection of bars and restaurants, known as the 'Grosse Freiheit', which face aft and are enclosed by a faceted glass structure, referencing architectural deconstructivism.

Above: The Japanese-built *AIDAprima*, which was intended to make regular cruises from Hamburg, features a novel hull design with a straight stem to enable her builder's 'air bubbling' hull lubrication system to work most optimally. Inboard, there is a larger than usual amount of enclosed deck space, reflecting her North Sea and Channel itineraries.

panelling resembling oak. The choice of the name 'Klanghaus' is interesting; 'klang' means 'treble' – but it also infers a big noise and so obviously avoids sounding too refined and exclusive in the way 'Konserthalle' might have felt. Thus, while existing classical music lovers would attend anyway, those who might like to try something new (and aspirational) by attending a chamber concert would hopefully be less likely to be dissuaded.

While the *Mein Schiff 3* and *Mein Schiff 4* were being built in Finland, at STX France in St Nazaire, Royal Caribbean's giant 226,963gt, 6,780-passenger the *Harmony of the Seas* was gradually taking shape with completion scheduled for the summer of 2016. Upon delivery, the vessel took the title of being the world's biggest cruise ship from her Finnish-built near-sisters.[373] By then, two further examples of the series were also under construction at STX France for delivery in 2018 and 2019.[374]

Fresh Japanese attempts

With an expected further increase in the numbers of orders for large cruise ships being placed, in 2011 Japan's Mitsubishi decided to make another attempt to enter the cruise construction market. This was welcomed by Carnival Corporation, which felt that the involvement of an additional builder could only be advantageous in improving competition and thereby potentially lowering costs. The two orders won by Mitsubishi were – perhaps surprisingly – for operation under the German Aida Cruises brand which in Carnival Corporation's hierarchy was at that time under the management of Costa Cruises. Hitherto, nearly all Aida ships had been German-built by Meyer Werft and, given their clientele, this was considered as a useful selling point.

Since the *Diamond Princess* and *Sapphire Princess* projects for Princess Cruises, Mitsubishi had developed new energy-saving technologies for passenger ships, initially for Japanese coastal ferries. The new Aida sisters, to be named the *AIDAPrima* and *AIDAPerla*, would be the first cruise ships fitted with its sophisticated version of air-bubbling hull lubrication technology, the Mitsubishi Air Lubrication System (MALS). To enable the MALS system to work most optimally, rather than a highly flared bow and long bulb of the type used on nearly all other large cruise ships, a straight stem and bow topsides perpendicular to the water was found to be optimal, thereby returning to a type of forward hull profile more commonly found on ships built a century previously. In addition, MaK dual-fuel engines would be fitted, capable of running on diesel or liquid natural gas.

The plan was that the 125,572gt *AIDAprima* and *AIDAperla* would offer week-long cruises from Hamburg, all year round, calling at the same North Sea and Channel ports on each cruise. They would, therefore, require considerably more enclosure than other large cruise ships to keep out the North Sea chill. They would offer Germans an 'immediate' holiday, rather than one involving airport transfers and flights at each end. There, the Baltic, and North Sea coasts and the Frisian Islands were well established holiday destinations – and, of course, for those visiting such places out with the summer season, bracing sea air was a large part of the attraction.

Accommodating 3,300 passengers but with only 900 crew, the Aida sisters' ratio was much more like that of European cruise ferries than typical cruise ships and it reflected Aida's extensive use of self-service catering. In addition, numerous small speciality restaurants, at which an extra tariff was payable, were serviced by the same centralised galleys. In terms of layout, however, Aida's tradition of grouping all public rooms atop the superstructure was abandoned in favour of a conventional mass market cruise ship arrangement with these spaces sandwiched between the hull and superstructure cabin decks. Nonetheless, the design retained the 'Theatrium' and other features of the previous Meyer-built class and the public rooms extended nearly to the forepeak, where a cocktail lounge was located. Up top, the most remarkable feature was The Beach Club, enclosed by a huge transparent UV-permeable membrane dome and enabling passengers to relax in a warm pool-side setting with natural light, even during inclement weather. By night, this could be transformed into a concert venue or disco with LED lighting mounted on the arcs supporting the dome and a laser show. Further aft was another enclosed entertainment area, this time panelled in glass. Known as The Four Elements, it featured a 'jungle gym' for adults with ropes, zip-wires and what was claimed to be the world's longest indoor water slide.

On the exterior, the edges of the cabin balconies were also fitted with an LED lighting system, enabling the vessel to present at night a spectacular multi-coloured visual display. As the Port of Hamburg hosts cruise ship parades with fireworks, the Aida vessels would be able to contribute to the spectacle. The approach of outlining a leisure-orientated passenger ship with effects lighting, however, could be traced back to the Mississippi river steamers of the early-twentieth century, the 'fairground' lighting and baroque visual enrichments reflecting their status as venues for eating, drinking, dancing and romance, as well as means of transport. Ever since, excursion ships have employed variations of this approach, but never on the scale of the *AIDAprima* and *AIDAperla*.

Unfortunately, the construction of these technically advanced vessels proved more complex and costly than Mitsubishi's Nagasaki shipyard had imagined and, although the first of the pair was floated out May 2014, it required a further two years to complete her. Mitsubishi therefore decided not to solicit further cruise ship orders and so, once again, European shipyards completely dominated the cruise ship construction market.

Above: The *Genting Dream* is the first of a number of very large new cruise ships planned for the South-East Asian market, which is expected to grow greatly in coming years. The vessel's décor, which is largely by Tillberg, blends Western cruise ship design features with colours and imagery intended to appeal to a predominantly Chinese clientele, as the bar in her 'Silk Road' cabaret lounge shows.

Genting's bold return

Since 2007, when Star Cruises' founder, Tan Sri Lim Goh Tong, died the company's parent Genting Group had instead prioritised the development of a global casino gaming empire ashore over further investments in cruise ships – indeed, as we have seen, its shareholding in NCL was reduced to a mere 12 per cent. All that changed in 2015 when Genting bought Crystal Cruises from the struggling Japanese shipping conglomerate, Nippon Yusen Kaisha. The new owner announced major plans for expansion into river cruising, a cruise yacht and the use of dedicated airliners for 'world cruises' by plane. Shortly after, Genting's Star Cruises announced orders for its first new cruise ships since the *Superstar Virgo* and, as with that vessel, the contracts for two 151,300gt, 3,352-passenger vessels specifically for the South East Asian market were signed with Meyer Werft.

Shortly after this announcement, the shipbuilding industry and its observers were astonished to learn that Genting had purchased a number of German shipyards, comprising Lloyd Werft at Bremerhaven and the Nordic Yards at Wismar, Warnemünde and Stralsund in order to build new large cruise ships for its Star Cruises and Crystal Cruises fleets. (The Nordic Yards acquisition alone cost Genting 230.6 million Euros.) For a casino operator to become a shipbuilder was indeed a remarkable turn of events and the decision reflected the lack of capacity at the existing major yards, whose order books

178 | Cruise Ships: A Design History

Above: An impression of one of a series of new giant cruise ships to be built by Lloyd Werft Group for Star Cruises for operation in the fast-expanding Chinese market.

were filled with cruise ship projects to beyond 2020. Henceforth, Genting's yards would be collectively known as Lloyd Werft Group and, together, they would build cruise ships and river cruise ships of various sizes for Genting's brands. As both the Wismar and Warnemünde yards' dry docks measured over 320 metres in length, each was capable of building cruise ships larger than the biggest examples currently afloat.

To return to Genting's Meyer Werft new buildings, during construction of the first of the two vessels, the future owner announced a change of plan whereby, rather than operating for Star Cruises, she would instead fall under a new Star Cruises-associated brand, Dream Cruises. (Incidentally, in the past, this name had been used quite separately by various downmarket Israeli, Greek and American cruise entrepreneurs, none of whom were successful in the long-run, but this situation, nonetheless shows how cruise marketeers liked to promote cruising to first-time passengers as a potentially 'dream-like' experience.) Dream Cruises' vessels would be named the *Genting Dream* and *World Dream* (the latter name being particularly vague-sounding, yet simultaneously suggestive of corporate megalomania).

Completed in the autumn of 2016 the *Genting Dream* was claimed to be the first 'mega cruise ship' purpose-built for the Chinese market though, in many respects, her design, layout and some of her decoration was fairly similar to that of NCL's Meyer-built the *Norwegian Breakaway/Getaway* type and, likewise, with Tillberg interiors. As with previous cruise ships for the Asian market, a preponderance of auspicious red and gold tones were used – including for the ornate enrichments applied to her bow.

Again, in common with recent NCL tonnage, her uppermost decks formed a 'ship within a ship', comprising what was promoted as the Genting Palace, where 400 top-paying passengers occupied their own set of lounges, dining rooms, a high-stakes casino and an outdoor swimming pool area. As would have been expected of a Hong Kong luxury hotel, the use of European brands of luxury goods was widespread in this area, there being Frette linens and Ferragamo toiletries in the suites, which had their own private butlers. Unlike on the *AIDAPrima*, the *Genting Dream* had a large crew, numbering 1,999; in part, this was accounted for by there being larger than usual numbers of casino workers, but it also reflected Hong Kong expectations of service provision.

For a majority of passengers, the Genting Palace was off limits. Their experience instead was of a vessel fine-tuned in every respect to part them from their money in the numerous themed bars, lounges, retail opportunities and extensive casino areas. Most unusually, the main restaurant was capable of accommodating only half the total number of passengers meaning that, for those who failed to find seats there, the options were the self-service buffet by the pool, where only a basic level of catering was available, or paying extra to dine in one of numerous additional tariff speciality restaurants. As well as the many of these dedicated to Asian regional cuisines, there was one taking the name of the British celebrity chef, Mark Best. The approach of limiting the supply of inclusive dining forcibly to leverage shipboard revenue perhaps marks the beginning of a new trend for mass market cruise ships, but as the lure of abundant 'free' food of high quality has been one of cruising's main attractions for as long as cruise ships have existed, it is unlikely to be a popular one.

On deck, the *Genting Dream* features an outdoor sports complex with zip-lines, rope courses, mini-golf and a water park with five thrilling water slides. Features such as these reflect cultural and generational shifts in the cruise market away from smoking, drinking and lounging and towards fitness activities. With increasing numbers of passengers being children of the 1970s, eighties and nineties, this change presented a challenge for long-established cruise operators such as Holland America. As its existing 'brand values' were designed to be most attractive to an older clientele who would eventually decline in number and perhaps disappear altogether, there was a need to re-position in order to connect with

Right: The 'Lincoln Center Stage' on Holland America's *Koningsdam*, one of a number of tie-ins with brands ashore thought suitable for the 'culturally-engaged' demographic the operator seeks to attract.

Left: The *Koningsdam* features a piled-up forward superstructure while the sides of her funnel casing are supposed to resemble billowing flags; there is less aesthetic harmony evident than on the operator's earlier vessels.

the next generations of potential passengers.

To do so, Holland America developed the Pinnacle-class, the first example of which, the 99,836gt, 2,650-passenger *Koningsdam*, built by Fincantieri, entered service in the summer of 2016 with a sister, the *Nieuw Statendam*, to follow in 2018. Conceptually, the design represented a hybrid between existing Holland America cruise ships and Celebrity Cruises' Solstice-class; the *Koningsdam* even features an Adam Tihany-designed dining room close in appearance to his schemes for these vessels. In addition, Holland America has followed the recent trend of cruise ship operators 'buying in' well-known brands from ashore – in this instance Lincoln Centre in New York, which provides classical musicians to perform on a 'Lincoln Centre Stage' in a large lounge space designed by Yran & Storbraaten with various bandstands for different types of music (though, presumably, not simultaneously). Much attention has been paid to the possibility of generating revenue through 'enrichment' activities, one feature being a 'Culinary Arts Center' with an open galley where passengers can watch, take part in and eat the results of professional cookery demonstrations. Nearby is a winery, branded through Chateau Ste Michelle, where they can learn to blend their own wines (which can then be drunk).[375]

Holland America's President, Orlando Ashford, who was appointed in 2014, has explained these features as responding to cultural changes that are 'less about age or demographic… more about a psychographic or attitude, an approach to things you are interested in.'[376] Ashford, whose vision the *Kongingsdam* largely represents, has, in a short time, become a well-known public figurehead for the cruise industry, about which he seems passionate. At the vessel's inauguration, he argued optimistically and in a way not often heard from a cruise executive in support of cruise travel's cultural benefits:

> 'Travel changes us and how we experience the world from the inside-out. As Mark Twain observed 150 years ago, "travel is fatal to prejudice, bigotry and narrow-mindedness and many of our people need it sorely on these accounts." When we have met people from other cultures… we become ambassadors for their culture and they of ours. Travel really does have the power to change the world.'[377]

Ashford's positivity, however well intentioned, arguably ignores the issue of very large mass market cruise ships tending to be experienced as floating self-referential worlds, cocooning their passengers in an alternative reality, far removed from the realities of those living ashore in third world countries, or even the lives of their crews, below decks. Nor does this stance reflect the very real anxieties in popular cruise destinations – particularly Venice or certain Caribbean ports – where historic environments are arguably over-run by tens of thousands of visiting cruise passengers. In fairness, Holland America is probably one of the less offending cruise lines, given that none of its fleet measures over 100,000gt or accommodates many more than two and-a-half thousand passengers.

To take the idea of involving passengers in creative and constructive activities a stage further, in 2015, Carnival Corporation launched Fathom Cruises as a new experimental brand in the American market. Its aim was to attract a clientele who wished to volunteer to engage in what were described as social impact-focused activities ashore in the Dominican Republic, namely 'teaching English in schools, helping to cultivate cacao plants and building water filtration systems.' As Fathom's CEO, Tara Russell put it, 'Fathom resonates with travellers as the best way to travel with intention, to culturally immerse, to experience and to see more… helping the Dominican Republic to flourish and making history through human connections and immersive experiences.'[378] The vessel selected was one of the former-Renaissance cruises 'R-ships', the *Adonia*, ex-*R Eight*, which latterly had been a member of the P&O Cruises fleet. (The name *Adonia* had been chosen as a compression of 'Adults Only' reflecting the fact that P&O Cruises had previously used the vessel for child-free cruises from the UK).

Despite Russell's evident passion about Fathom Cruises' potential, the ethical problems inherent in mixing

Below: The atrium on the *Koningsdam* contains a giant chromed metal sculpture, supposedly representing the playing of classical music with strings, arches and bow-forms. The artwork was inserted before the surrounding decks could be completed.

Above: Silversea's *Silver Spirit* represents a further development of the 'boutique' cruise ship concept into a vessel commensurate in scale with some of the largest cruise ships of the early-1980s.

leisure for the privileged with intervention into the lives of those less fortunate via the corporate filtration of a cruise run by a giant profit-focused multinational such as Carnival Corporation were, unsurprisingly, glossed over. To an extent, the Fathom Cruises sought to realise ideas which the Norwegian founder of NCL, Knut Kloster, had had in the early-1970s about using cruise ships for social engagement (though Kloster had apparently wished to bring Caribbean locals on board to meet the passengers in a luxury shipboard setting). Unsurprisingly in the circumstances, the types of American who were attracted to involve themselves in social development work in their free time were not the same as ones who took cruises. Thus, instead of focusing on the Dominican Republic, Fathom instead ran trips to Cuba, where U.S. President Barrack Obama had recently eased sanctions that had been in force for the previous 55 years. These were a success – but the 'social engagement' element was subsumed by the more conventional attractions of visiting Havana, which was a new experience for nearly all but the oldest American passengers. Having opened Cuba to the American cruise market and gained access for its fleet, in November 2016 Carnival Corporation announced the abandonment of its Fathom Cruises operation, though elements of the idea would continue for the planning of some shore excursions for its other brands.

As *Koningsdam* demonstrated, the size and capacity of a typical average mass market cruise ship in 2016 was about five times that of its equivalent in the mid-1980s; tonnages of between 100,000gt and 150,000gt had become 'the new normal' while vessels of up to 200,000gt were hardly exceptional. Meanwhile, at the expensive end of the cruise market, new cruise ships now considered rather small and exclusive were actually commensurate in tonnage terms with the larger examples of the 1980s generation. Seabourn Cruises' 32,000gt, 450-passenger the *Seabourn Odyssey*, *Seabourn Sojourn* and *Seabourn Quest*, built by T. Mariotti of Genoa and introduced in 2009-2011, exemplified this situation, as did Silversea Cruises' 36,009gt, 564-passenger the *Silver Spirit*, delivered in 2009 from Fincantieri in Ancona.[379] In 2013, Hapag-Lloyd introduced the *Europa 2*, measuring 42,830gt and accommodating 516 passengers as a companion for its existing Finnish-build the *Europa*. Built by STX France at St Nazaire, the vessel was bigger by a third than her 1999 fleet mate.[380] More recently, Regent Seven Seas Cruises' 54,000gt, 750-passenger the *Seven Seas Explorer*, completed by Fincantieri 2016, showed how big the size envelope of a supposedly intimate cruise ship could be pushed. The order followed a take-over by NCL, for whom Regent Seven Seas Cruises would henceforth be the premium brand. The intention of CEO Frank Del Rio was that the *Seven Seas Explorer* should be 'the most luxurious cruise ship ever built.'[381] Employing NCL's regular interior architects, Tillberg Design, this aim would be achieved through the deployment of considerable ostentation:

> 'Grand entryways, gold leaf, exquisite inlaid marble floors, hand-blown crystal chandeliers, vast private balconies, a $10,000-a-night suite with its own spa… *Seven Seas Explorer* has nearly an acre of marble, half of it from Carrara, Italy, and nearly an acre of granite. All the stones were individually selected. There are 473 crystal chandeliers throughout the ship… 'A classic core with a modern twist,' is how Michal Jackiewicz of Tillberg Design, the ship's coordinating architectural firm, described *Seven Seas Explorer*. Tillberg created the atrium with its monumental Chelsom chandelier and curving staircases, backed by a lobby brightened by more chandeliers that leads to the main restaurant, Compass Rose, also designed by Tillberg. Compass Rose is dripping in four types of marble, with metal inlays. Inspired by the sea, the room's centerpiece is a stunning aqua and cobalt Preciosa chandelier of hand-blown crystal droplets evoking an underwater feeling. Other golden chandeliers suggest sea urchins, and columns are finished in handcrafted mother of pearl… While luxury means different things to different people, rarity or uniqueness is certainly a key factor… The $500,000, cast-bronze Tibetan prayer wheel his firm commissioned from UAP of Australia for the vestibule of Pacific Rim, the pan-Asian restaurant: 'you're not going to find anywhere else. It is luxury because it is the only one in the world,' Walton said. The prayer wheel weighs about two tons…'[382]

The *Seven Seas Explorer* and the other recent smaller cruise ships listed above – 'smaller' being a relative term – were all the products of Italian builders. Fincantieri in Ancona also produced a series of genuinely intimate cruise ships for the recently-established French cruise operator, Compagnie de Ponant. The 10,944gt, 268-passenger *L'Austral*, *Le Boreal*, *Le Soléal* and *Le Lyrial*, which entered service in 2010-2015, were aimed at an exclusive, mainly French-speaking clientele and were distinguished from all others by their external and interior styling by the French architect Jean-Philippe

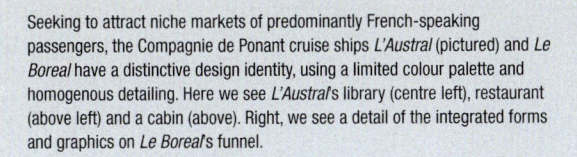

A globalising cruise market | **181**

Seeking to attract niche markets of predominantly French-speaking passengers, the Compagnie de Ponant cruise ships *L'Austral* (pictured) and *Le Boreal* have a distinctive design identity, using a limited colour palette and homogenous detailing. Here we see *L'Austral*'s library (centre left), restaurant (above left) and a cabin (above). Right, we see a detail of the integrated forms and graphics on *Le Boreal*'s funnel.

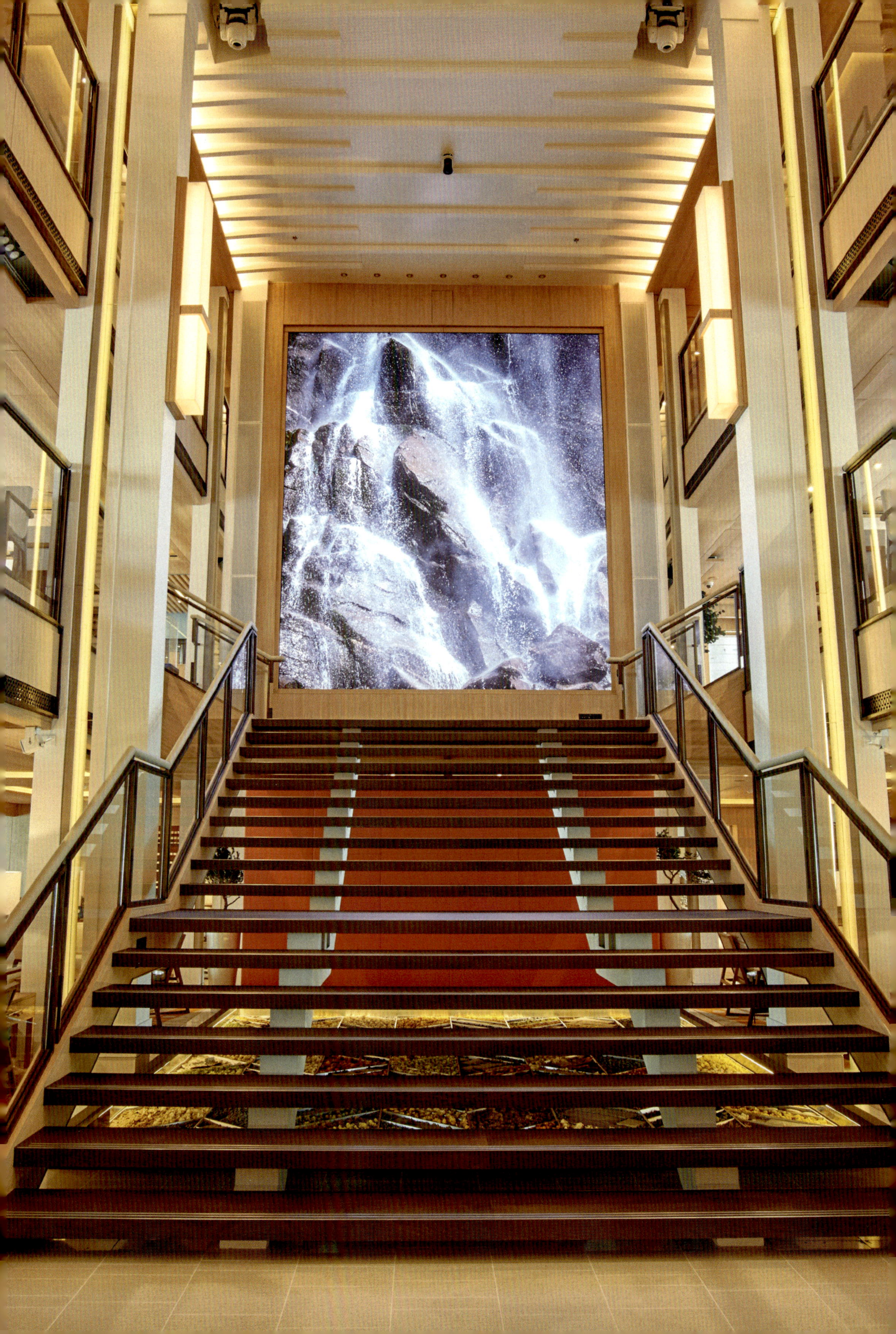

Nuel, who was a newcomer to the cruise sector, having previously specialised in the design of boutique hotels. The scheme was based around grey, red and white colours – a variation of the Tricolour flag. The exterior featured twin parabola-shaped funnel casings and other quirky details, bringing to mind French automotive design traditions, as found in classic Citroen cars, for example. Overall, the vessels were considerably more 'designerly' than most others of their generation, the bright, fresh approach being more analogous to recent critically acclaimed work in the leisure and hospitality sectors ashore, rather than existing cruise ship practices.[383]

Another recently-established cruise operator to distinguish itself by commissioning recognisably contemporary design was Viking Ocean Cruises, a new entrant into the upper end of the 'deep sea' market with an interesting pedigree. This Norwegian company was established by Torstein Hagen, who had many years previously been the CEO of Royal Viking Line. Hagen was very sorry when, in the mid-1980s, that company was sold to Kloster Cruise International and, ever since, had fondly imagined re-creating it. In the period since, Hagen had formed Viking River Cruises in 1997, operating on the European river network. In this sector, Hagen's best initiative was to sponsor an American PBS television series of English costume dramas called 'PBS Masterpiece', which included the Downton Abbey, Sherlock and Mr Selfridge series'. Just as 'The Love Boat' made Princess Cruises' reputation on TV back in the 1970s, so sponsorship of PBS Masterpiece caused a wide yet carefully targeted American audience, numbering tens of millions, to consider Viking River Cruises as synonymous with European river cruising. Indeed, so many Americans were persuaded by this means to take trips on the Rhine, Mosel, Loire and Rhône that, by 2015, Viking River Cruises' fleet numbered 64 vessels. The main limit to further growth was finding space for them all within the confines of riverside wharves. Hagen's company thus generated a large database of loyal, repeat passengers, increasing numbers of whom, having sailed on all of the river itineraries, next might be persuaded to enjoy similar experiences on purpose-designed deep-sea cruise vessels. By this means, Hagen found his opportunity to re-create Royal Viking Line in twenty-first century form.

At first, Hagen held discussions with an ex-Lloyd's of London naval architect of his acquaintance, Richard Goodwin, who drew up initial design proposals, based closely on the characteristics and layout of the *Royal Viking Star*, *Royal Viking Sea* and *Royal Viking Sky* of 1972-73. When Hagen showed these to Fincantieri's naval architect, Maurizio Cergol, with a view to getting quotations for their construction, the latter was allegedly politely dismissive, warning that such an approach would be unlikely to generate sufficient profits in present and future markets. Cergol's team at Fincantieri thus produced proposals of their own which, after some discussion, Hagen accepted. Conceptually and in terms of exterior aesthetics, these had

Opposite and above: The *Viking Star* of Viking Ocean Cruises attempts to marry an up-to-date hotelier aesthetic to a 'traditional' cruise experience with an emphasis on relaxation. The vessel's main circulation space features a panel with a screen showing a Norwegian waterfall in spate. The vessel's Winter Garden, meanwhile, evokes the type of shipboard environment found on Edwardian era cruise yachts, albeit using contemporary forms, materials and technologies (above).

Below: The Nordic Spa on the *Viking Star* continues the theme of understated elegance and precision of detail to create a soothing, spacious atmosphere.

Right: Externally, the *Viking Star* is broadly similar to other recent Italian-built upmarket cruise ships of her size category. Her short bow and forward-facing cabin balconies appear to offer little protection from head-on seas, however, suggesting that she was designed mainly for operation in fairly sheltered waters and calm conditions.

Below: An aerial view of Regent Seven Seas Cruises' *Seven Seas Explorer*, which is, according to her owners, the world's finest cruise ship. The design, construction and operation of vessels such as this demonstrate the taste preferences of today's international wealth elite. Yet, in some senses, they are merely looking for cruise holiday experiences of a kind broadly similar to those offered by the most exclusive cruise ships of the past. The vessel's external appearance is rather understated, however, and avoids drawing attention to the opulence found within.

a little more in common with the *Royal Viking Sun* of 1988 and, even more so, with other recent Fincantieri new buildings, such as the *Seven Seas Explorer*.

Viking Ocean Cruises' 47,842gt, 944-passenger the *Viking Star*, *Viking Sea* and *Viking Sky* entered service between 2015 and 2016. Although Norwegian-owned and even Norwegian-registered, just like the original Royal Viking Line, the bulk of their clientele was American. Thus, an American interior design company, Rottet Studio, based in Houston, Texas was employed to design a majority of their interiors, the aim being to provide an American 'take' on contemporary Scandinavian design. Rottet Studio had been founded in 2008 by a Texan architect, Lauren Rottet, whose speciality was designing boutique hotels around the world and who was 'an inductee of the Interior Design Hall of Fame.' Her studio worked alongside SMC Design of London, established experts in cruise ship interiors with numerous projects to their credit.[384]

The outcome of their work was very refreshing, with clean lines, precise detailing and a sense of 'architecture' as well as 'decoration' thanks to the clear, rectilinear design of the three-storey-high atrium, off which numerous small and quiet spaces were located. Indeed, in complete contrast with a majority of recent cruise ships, the Viking Ocean Cruises trio reverted wholly to an idea of relaxation at sea, rather than frenetic organised activity. Other notable spaces included a 'winter garden'-type lounge, with a trellis formed of precisely laminated bent timber verticals and horizontals beneath a glazed deck head, and a Scandinavian-inspired spa with thermal pools, saunas and a 'snow grotto', in which flakes fall gently from the ceiling.[385] Viking Ocean Cruises' blending together of tranquil space for quiet recuperation – a shipboard ideal as old as cruising itself – with cutting-edge hospitality design attracted widespread attention and admiration from cruise industry observers more used to themed décor and an emphasis upon maximising shipboard revenue streams. Apparently, the relaxation-orientated formula that had worked on Viking River Cruises' vessels was found to be equally desirable at sea, at least so far as the type of audience who, back home, watched 'PBS Masterpiece' was concerned.

The differences of decorative approach between the *Seven Seas Explorer*, on the one hand, and the fleets of Compagnie de Ponant and Viking Ocean Cruises on the other, reflect a schism in conceptions of what constitutes 'luxury' dating back to the nineteenth century. The *Seven Seas Explorer* perpetuates a tradition of decorative excess that originated in the so-called 'floating palaces' operating in liner service in the Edwardian era. The Ponant and Viking ships, by contrast, reflect a more intellectualised tradition of design debate calling for decorative moderation, the theory being that in a world of great complexity and seemingly lacking in control, visual restraint represents true luxury. Because restrained designs evidence a disciplined mind-set, the egos of users who believe that they have superior taste are flattered. In the history of cruising, it is an approach that has only ever been used for a small minority of vessels.

Presently on Order

At the time of going to press, there are 57 cruise ships on order – an unprecedented quantity. The biggest single number are for MSC Cruises which, by 2020, aims to have 85 per cent more capacity than its existing fleet provides, amounting to a total of 75,000 berths. At the end of 2016, the company's orders comprised three so-called Seaside-class cruise ships, measuring 154,000gt and accommodating 4,140 passengers to be built by Fincantieri, two 167,600gt, 5,714-passenger Meraviglia-class plus two 177,100gt, 6,297-passenger Meraviglia Plus-class ordered from STX France and up to four 200,000gt World-class, also from STX France, the latter to be fuelled with liquid natural gas. When the *MSC Merivaglia* was ordered in the summer of 2016, MSC announced that, among her features, there would be:

> '…The first and only classic and contemporary fine art museums at sea. This industry-first feature will enable guests to discover world culture on board by experiencing masterpieces from around the globe in collaboration with the world's premier cultural centres, classic and modern art museums as well as public and private institutions. The public spaces [will be] filled with boutiques, restaurants and spots for shopping, eating and relaxing as well as socialising. The ships will have a 111-metre-long interior promenade comparable to what is available on Royal Caribbean ships. However, the innovation will be an impressive LED sky screen from Samsung in the ceiling (96m x 6m). This will beam out visual events and vistas around the clock, animating the entire promenade from above and creating a unique atmospheric experience… The recently-announced partnership with Samsung brings next-generation technology with everything from the latest displays and mobile solutions to medical equipment, as well as products for enhanced reality experiences…'[386]

MSC Cruises recorded a 10 per cent growth rate in 2015 with 1.7 million passengers carried aboard the existing 12-strong fleet. In Europe, demand was strongest in Italy, Germany, Spain and France. Out with Europe, MSC found heavy custom from South America and South Africa and saw great potential for expansion in China, Dubai, Abu Dhabi and Oman. With its many new ships, the company expected six per cent year-over-year growth from 2016 onward.[387]

So far as Carnival Corporation was concerned, orders were placed with Fincantieri for one 135,000gt, 3,954-passenger cruise ship for Carnival Cruise Line plus two near sisters for Costa Cruises, the latter both for the Asian cruise market. In addition, orders for Costa were placed with Meyer Turku for two 183,200gt, 4,200-passenger vessels for the Asian market and with Meyer Werft for a further pair measuring 180,000gt and accommodating 6,600 passengers for Aida Cruises. Carnival's Princess Cruises subsidiary, meanwhile, booked three additional examples of the *Royal Princess* type with Fincantieri, plus one 135,000gt, 4,200 passenger cruise ship for P&O Australia (which hitherto had used only second-hand tonnage). For the upmarket Seabourn brand, the 40,350gt, 604-passenger *Seabourn Encore* and *Seabourn Ovation* were also to be built by Fincantieri.

Royal Caribbean commissioned two more Quantum-class, plus one more Oasis-class; Celebrity Cruises ordered two 117,000gt 2,900-passenger ships of a new design from STX France, TUI Cruises ordered the *Mein Schiff 5-Mein Schiff 8* from Meyer Turku and NCL requested three further examples of the *Norwegian Escape* type from Meyer Werft, the first to be named the *Norwegian Joy*. Genting-owned Star Cruises placed orders with its own builder, Lloyd Werft Group, for two 201,000gt Global-class cruise ships and, for Crystal Cruises, three vessels measuring 117,000gt and accommodating a mere 1,000 passengers were ordered, plus a smaller 25,000gt ice-strengthened 'adventure' cruise ship, the *Crystal Endeavour*.

Other orders for smaller operators included Silversea's 40,700gt, 596-passenger the *Silver Muse* from Fincantieri, three further cruise ships for Viking Ocean Cruises to the same design as the existing trio, yet again from Fincantieri, and a single 55,900gt, 999-passenger ship for Saga Cruises, a British niche operator specialising in holidays for the over-50s and hitherto running only second-hand cruise tonnage; this from Meyer Werft.

What is one to make of this unprecedented glut of cruise ship orders and of the design values a majority of the vessels will represent? In the 1990s, the French anthropologist Marc Augé introduced the concept of 'non-place' to describe contemporary 'globalised' corporate environments, assembled in excessive quantities from standard factory-produced

Above: The 3,785 square foot 'Regent Suite' on the *Seven Seas Explorer* is claimed to be the most exclusive on any cruise ship in terms of space, comfort and cost. The bed alone reputedly represents and expenditure of 150,000 dollars. Cruise ship accommodation such as this is sold on the promise of perfection and an excess of comfort with the fluffiest towels imaginable, the finest bed linen and very attentive service to provide for almost every whim.

Right: The 'Regent Suite' even includes a private 'Relaxation Chamber' with spa treatments and a sauna. The decoration makes extensive use of marble and gold leaf. The opulent materials and restricted colour palette can be related to 'expensive' design found in a broad range of contemporary boutique retail and hospitality environments.

Opposite: The *Seven Seas Explorer*'s main hallway combines curving grand staircases, a crystal chandelier and an inlaid marble floor – the traditional ingredients of the lobbies of grand hotels and of First Class passenger ship interiors since the latter-nineteenth century. In many respects, the vessel represents an up-to-date, technologically-advanced rendition of the same type of shipboard environment as found on the early cruise yacht *Prinzessin Victoria Luise*, described near the beginning of this book.

elements and filled with 'formulaic' fixtures and fittings to generate profits. Whereas Augé sees 'place' as filled with accumulations of 'authentic' objects and images, understood by users in terms of history and locale, 'non-places' at best present selected elements of the past in decontextualised form as a kind-of theme-park spectacle. Furthermore, they are designed subtly to control their users' behaviours.[388] The many kilometres of glitzy, yet banal atria, lounges, bars, casinos, restaurants, fitness centres, theatres and cabin corridors found across the fleets of current and future cruise ships, mostly designed by the same circumscribed ranges of specialist interior architect, surely exemplify Augé's observations. Even cruise ship names such as the *Celebrity Silhouette*, *World Dream* and *Silver Muse* seem to have been deliberately drained of meaningful cultural content.

A more recent, related phenomenon is that of Hypermodernity, a term initiated by the French philosopher Gilles Lipovetsky who has observed that we live in an era characterized by hyper-consumption, which absorbs and integrates more and more spheres of social life, yet paradoxically distances consumers more than ever from traditional or collective social structures.[389] The British documentary film-maker Adam Curtis, meanwhile, has used the term 'hyper normalisation' to suggest that the types of corporate and aspirational imagery and environment promoted by the media and experienced by a majority of consumers on a daily basis have combined to destroy critical faculties, enabling the normalisation of a false 'reality.' While there is arguably more than an element of truth in the positions of Augé, Lipovetsky and Curtis, cultural critics have made similar observations about modern consumer culture since the mid-nineteenth century.

It would be unfair, moreover, to characterise such a very large and diverse industry as the cruise business in relation to cultural criticisms most applicable to the newest and biggest vessels. Remarkably, at the present moment, there are cruise ships in operation from every generation since the early-1970s. As they tend to be scrupulously well maintained, such vessels usually have long lives and, as they age, they begin to accumulate the very aura of history and use wished for by Augé and others to represent a greater level of 'placedness.' Vessels such as Fred. Olsen Cruise Lines' the *Black Watch* and *Boudicca* – the former *Royal Viking Star* and *Royal Viking Sky* of 1972-73 – are now 44 years old and have passed through several owners, each of whom has added to their sense of character. As we have seen, the cruise ships built in subsequent eras have come in many shapes and sizes and, despite the compromises inevitable in the creation of such large and capital-intensive objects; they form a fascinating and remarkable genre.

All ships, no matter how well maintained, are ephemeral, however, and old cruise vessels are no exception. When the final passengers and most of the crew have disembarked, a cruise ship's true age becomes sadly apparent. Layers of paint, dented hull plates, worn fixtures and fittings from which passengers were distracted by endless food and entertainment now become most obvious. After a period of lay-up, with the air conditioning switched off, the mustiness of old carpet, bedding and pipe-work fills the air and mould begins to grow in damp corners. Past the point of no return, the ship is next taken over by a scrap delivery crew for a one-way voyage, ended by being driven ashore on an Indian or Turkish beach for demolition. The final end is squalid; some of the world's poorest-paid and worst-treated workers are set the dangerous task of dismantling decaying interiors, filthy pipes, rusty steelwork and oily engine blocks. Far from their glamorous images in service, every cruise ship's career ends in abjection. It is then that nostalgia asserts itself among former passengers and crew who recall with fondness the many vanished vessels described in the earlier chapters of this book.

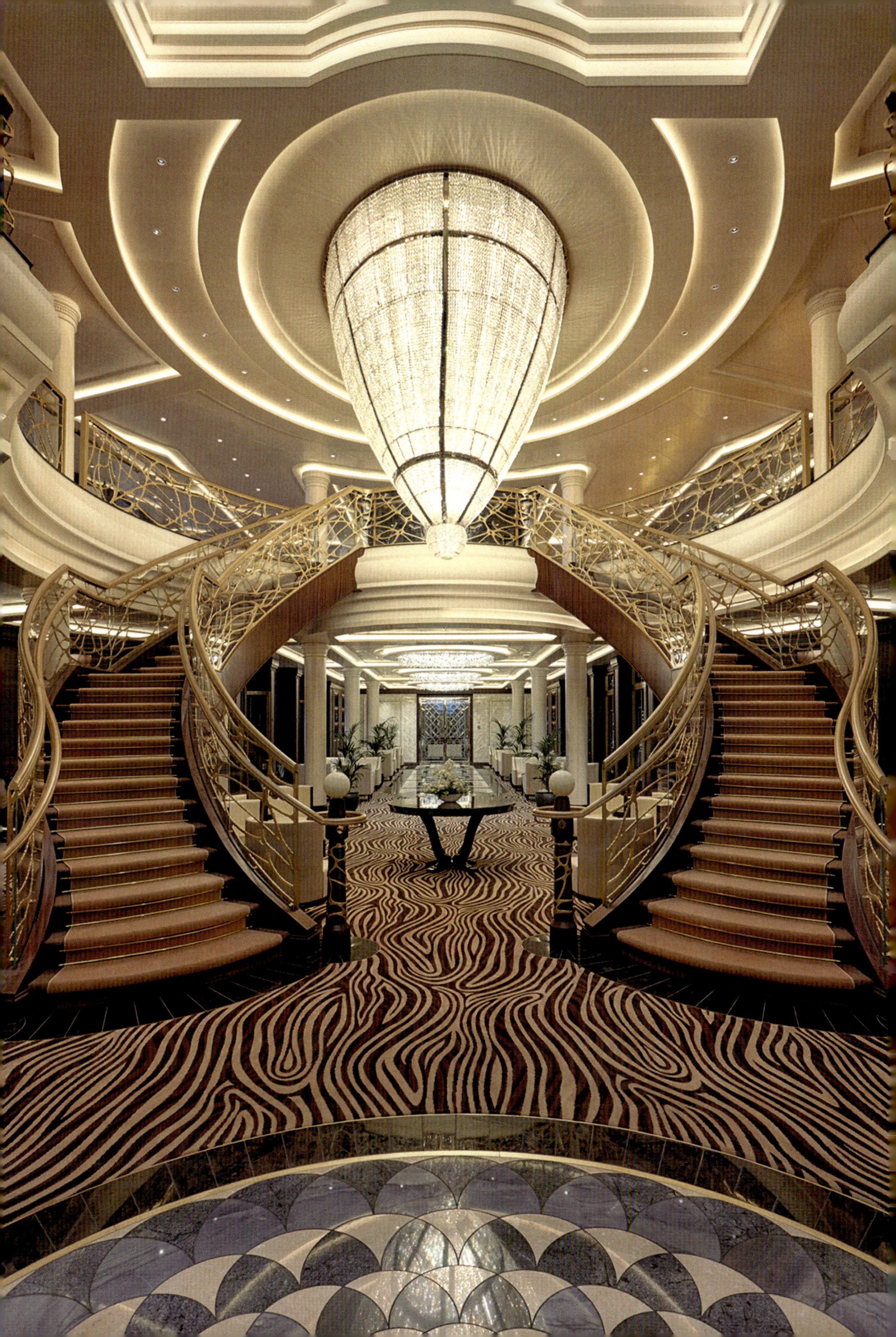

ENDNOTES

1. http://www.cruising.org/docs/default-source/research/2016_clia_sotci.pdf?sfvrsn=0
2. Cruise on order, ShipPax CFI, July-August 2016, pp.40-41.
3. http://www.cruising.org/docs/default-source/research/2016_clia_sotci.pdf?sfvrsn=0
4. See Peter Quartermaine, Building on the Sea: Form and meaning in Ship Architecture, Academy Editions, London, 1996, pp.34-53 for a detailed discussion of the implications of post-modernism for naval architecture and ship design.
5. Pierre Bourdieu, Distinction: A Social Critique of the Judgement of Taste, Harvard University Press, Cambridge, Mass, 1984, p.65.
6. John Maxtone-Graham, Liners to the Sun, Macmillan, New York, 1985, p.226.
7. Dick Hebdige, Towards a Cartography of Taste in Hiding in the Light: On images and things, Psychology Press, London, 1988, p.45.
8. Anon, 'The Middlebrow', Punch 169, December 1925, p.673.
9. William Makepeace Thackeray, Notes of a Journey from Cornhill to Grand Cairo, https://archive.org/details/notesajourneyfr00thacgoog.
10. William Makepeace Thackeray, Notes of a Journey from Cornhill to Grand Cairo, https://archive.org/details/notesajourneyfr00thacgoog.
11. William Makepeace Thackeray, Notes of a Journey from Cornhill to Grand Cairo, https://archive.org/details/notesajourneyfr00thacgoog.
12. Advertisement in *The Scotsman*, 8 June 1886, p.1.
13. http://www.wirksworth.org.uk/A04value.htm#1710 records that in 1881, teachers earned on average £133 per annum and civil servants £215.
14. The Hamburg American yacht *Prinzessin Victoria Louise*, Scientific American, 9 February 1901, p.86.
15. The Hamburg American yacht *Prinzessin Victoria Louise*, Scientific American, 9 February 1901, p.86.
16. The Hamburg American yacht *Prinzessin Victoria Louise*, Scientific American, 9 February 1901, p.86.
17. The Hamburg American yacht *Prinzessin Victoria Louise*, Scientific American, 9 February 1901, p.86.
18. The Hamburg American yacht *Prinzessin Victoria Louise*, Scientific American, 9 February 1901, p.86.
19. The Hamburg American yacht *Prinzessin Victoria Louise*, Scientific American, 9 February 1901, p.86.
20. The Illustrated London News, 26 December 1905, p??
21. A 6,000-ton Passenger Yacht: *Stella Polaris*, the Bergen S.S. Co's new yacht for cruising in the Mediterranean and Norwegian fjords, The Motor Ship, October 1926, pp.229-231.
22. A. L. Chapman and R. Knight, Wages and Salaries in the United Kingdom, 1920–38, Cambridge University Press, Cambridge, 1953, pp. 26-30, 154, 201-2; J. Burnett, A History of the Cost of Living, Penguin, Harmondsworth, 1969, pp. 297-310; G. Routh, Occupation and Pay in Great Britain, 1906-79, Palgrave, London, 1980, pp. 120-1.
23. R. Stone and D. A. Rowe, The Measurement of Consumer Behaviour in the United Kingdom, 1920-38, Vol. 2, Cambridge University Press, Cambridge, 1966, p. 92.
24. 'A Fine Romance' was written by Jermone Kern with lyrics by Dorothy Fields and published in 1936 for the RKO musical film *Swing Time*, starring Fred Astaire and Ginger Rodgers.
25. See John K. Galbraith, The Great Crash 1929, Penguin, London, 1954 for a detailed description of the circumstances leading to and consequences of the Wall Street Crash.
26. A New Luxury Liner: The alterations to the Blue Star liner *Arandora Star*, Shipbuilding and Shipping Record, 21 June 1929, pp.704-707.
27. The Blue Star Line: Reconditioned liner for luxury cruising, The Shipping World, 12 June 1929, pp.917-919.
28. Shipbuilding and Shipping Record, 17 March 1938, pp.323 and 335 ; and 21 April 1938, p.524.
29. 'Passenger Liners For German Workmen: 25,000-ton Ships, One with Diesel-electric Machinery, Designed for Economical Cruising', The Motor Ship, March 1937, p.460.
30. 25,000-ton German Motor-Cruising Liners, The Motor Ship, April 1937, p.26. See also A Cruising Liner For Workmen: The 24,000-ton 15½-knot Geared Diesel M.S. *Wilhelm Gustloff*, The Motor Ship, April 1938, p.24.
31. R. Keine, Schiffbau, Schiffahrt und Hafenbau, 1939, pp.206-216.
32. Launch of the *Andes*, Shipbuilding and Shipping Record, 16 March 1939, pp.339-341.
33. The Latest Royal Mail Liner: General description of the *Andes*, Shipping World & Shipbuilder, 27 September 1929, pp.27-38.
34. The Swedish trans-Atlantic liner *Stockholm*, The Shipbuilder and Marine Engine Builder, London, May 1940, p.206-7. See also The trans-Atlantic liner *Stockholm* of the Swedish American Line, Shipbuilding and Shipping Record, London, 2 June 1938, p.722.
35. Ian Johnston, Ships for a Nation: John Brown & Company Clydebank, West Dunbartonshire Libraries and Museums, 2000, p.238.
36. John Maxtone-Graham, Liners to the Sun, Macmillan, New York, 1985, p.159.
37. Philip Dawson, Cruise Ships: An Evolution in Design, Conway Maritime Press, 2000, p.37.
38. John Maxtone-Graham, Liners to the Sun, Macmillan, New York, 1985, p.163.
39. John Maxtone-Graham, Liners to the Sun, Macmillan, New York, 1985, p.165.
40. Peter C. Kohler, The Green Goddess R.M.S. *Caronia*, Sea Lines, No. 17, Winter 2000, pp.9-12 p.10.
41. The *Rotterdam*, Shipbuilding and Shipping Record, 8 October 1959, pp270-276.
42. 'The Secret Staircase', The New Flagship *Rotterdam*, Holland-America Line, guide booklet, Rotterdam, 1959, p.3.
43. Stephen Payne, Grand Dame: Holland America Line and the S.S. *Rotterdam*, RINA, London, 1990, pp.37-38.
44. The New Flagship *Rotterdam*, Holland-America Line, guide booklet, Rotterdam, 1959, p.9.
45. Paul Groenendijk, Piet Vollaard, Guide to Modern Architecture in Rotterdam, Uitgeverij 010 Publishers, Rotterdam, 1996.
46. The New Flagship *Rotterdam*, Holland-America Line, guide booklet, Rotterdam, 1959, p.9.
47. Donato Riccesi, Gustavo Pulitzer Finali: Il Disegno della Nave, Marsilio Editori, Venice, 1985, p.204 and p.206.
48. A Caribbean cruise ship, Shipbuilding and Shipping Record, 21 January 1960, pp75-77.
49. A Caribbean cruise ship, Shipbuilding and Shipping Record, 21 January 1960, pp75-77.
50. R. P. Bonsor, North Atlantic Seaway, T. Stephenson & Sons Ltd, Prescot, 1955 p.541.
51. *Oceanic*: CRDA-built for Home Lines: The largest ever purely cruising vessel, Shipbuilding and Shipping Record, April 1965, pp.438-446.
52. Stephen Payne, 'Drawing up an efficient design', special supplement to The Naval Architect, 2004, p.25.
53. See Philip Dawson, British Superliners of the Sixties, Conway Maritime Press, London, 1990, pp.41-78 for a detailed description of

the *Canberra*'s design. See also Features of the *Canberra*, Shipbuilding and Shipping Record, 24 March 1960, pp374-381.
54. *Oceanic*: CRDA-built for Home Lines: The largest ever purely cruising vessel, Shipbuilding and Shipping Record, April 1965, pp.438-446.
55. '*Oceanic*: CRDA-built for Home Lines: The largest ever purely cruising vessel, Shipbuilding and Shipping Record, April 1965, pp.438-446.
56. *Oceanic*: CRDA-built for Home Lines: The largest ever purely cruising vessel, Shipbuilding and Shipping Record, April 1965, pp.438-446.
57. K. Haug, Some considerations leading to the design and construction of the *Sagafjord*, The Motor Ship, April 1966, pp17-19.
58. *Sagafjord*: A New Norwegian America Liner, Shipbuilding and Shipping Record, October 1965, pp.519-526 and pp.555-557.
59. K. Haug, Conception and design of the new flagship *Sagafjord*, The Motor Ship, November 1965, pp340-341.
60. The £7 million Swedish American Line passenger ship *Kungsholm*, The Motor Ship, May 1966, pp53-63.
61. Ian Johnston, Ships for a Nation: John Brown & Company Clydebank, West Dunbartonshire Libraries and Museums, 2000, pp.260-262.
62. The £7 million Swedish American Line passenger ship *Kungsholm*, The Motor Ship, May 1966, pp53-63.
63. Ian Johnston, Ships for a Nation: John Brown & Company Clydebank, West Dumbartonshire Libraries and Museums, 2000, p.262. See also 'Most Disastrous Contract', Shipbuilding and Shipping Record, 4 August 1966, p144.
64. *Kungsholm*: Public rooms on new Swedish liner, Shipbuilding and Shipping Record, 12 May 1966, pp418-428.
65. *Kungsholm*: Public rooms on new Swedish liner, Shipbuilding and Shipping Record, 12 May 1966, pp418-428.
66. http://www.bbc.co.uk/blogs/adamcurtis/entries/e2da64b6-4921-3ce5-b05f-beec93cf3b7f.
67. *Andes* in a new role, Shipbuilding and Shipping Record, 16 June 1960, p776.
68. Ian Johnston, Ships for a Nation: John Brown & Company Clydebank, West Dunbartonshire Libraries and Museums, 2000, p.254 and pp.270-280.
69. Neil Potter & Jack frost, Queen Elizabeth 2: The Authorised Story, George G. Harrap, London, 1969, p.49.
70. *Queen Elizabeth 2*: a ship with a past and a future, Shipbuilding and Shipping Record, 31 January 1969, pp.146-161.
71. Kenneth Agnew, 'Concept to Cunarder', The Architectural Review, London, June 1969, p.418. See also The P&O-Orient liner *Oriana*, Shipbuilding and Shipping Record, 1 December 1960, pp699-708.
72. *Queen Elizabeth 2*: a ship with a past and a future, Shipbuilding and Shipping Record, 31 January 1969, pp.146-161.
73. D.N. Wallace, *Queen Elizabeth 2*: some design considerations, Shipping World and Shipbuilder, January 1969, pp.87-88.
74. Neil Potter & Jack Frost, Queen Elizabeth 2: The Authorised Story, George G. Harrap & Co. Ltd. London, 1969, p.124-5.
75. *Queen Elizabeth 2*: a ship with a past and a future, Shipbuilding and Shipping Record, 31 January 1969, pp.146-161.
76. *Queen Elizabeth 2*: a ship with a past and a future, Shipbuilding and Shipping Record, 31 January 1969, pp.146-161.
77. Cunard Line inaugural season brochure for *Queen Elizabeth 2*.
78. Anthony Cooke, Liners and Cruise Ships-2: some more notable smaller vessels, Carmania Press, London, 2000, pp.89-90.
79. Anthony Cooke, Liners and Cruise Ships-2: some more notable smaller vessels, Carmania Press, London, 2000, pp.90-91.
80. Donato Riccesi, Gustavo Pulitzer Finali: Il Disegno della Nave, Marsilio Editori, Venice,1985, p.217.
81. Interview with Tage Wandborg, formerly naval architect of Knud E. Hansen A/S, by Bruce Peter at his home in Snekkersten, Denmark on 14 August 2012.
82. Clive Harvey, The Tragedy of the Yarmouth Castle, Sea Lines, Winter 2006, pp.19-21 p.21.
83. *Nili* – a £2.5 million passenger/vehicle liner: second Swiss-Israeli ship runs trials. Twin Sulzer engines of 11,000 bhp provide 20 knots service speed, The Motor Ship, July 1965, pp.146-147.
84. Another UK-based Scandinavian-owned ferry service, The Motor Ship, August 1966, pp207-211.
85. Interview with Tage Wandborg, formerly naval architect of Knud E. Hansen A/S, by Bruce Peter at his home in Snekkersten, Denmark on 20th February 2000.
86. Interview with Tage Wandborg, formerly naval architect of Knud E. Hansen A/S, by Bruce Peter at his home in Snekkersten, Denmark on 20th February 2000. See also *Sunward*: A long-haul passenger ferry, Shipbuilding and Shipping Record, 4 August 1966, pp155-157.
87. C. Barclay, *Sunward*: Design considerations, Shipping World & Shipbuilder, January 1967, pp.247-253.
88. Interview with Tage Wandborg, formerly naval architect of Knud E. Hansen A/S, by Bruce Peter at his home in Snekkersten, Denmark on 20th February 2000.
89. Interview with Tage Wandborg, formerly naval architect of Knud E. Hansen A/S, by Bruce Peter at his home in Snekkersten, Denmark on 20th February 2000.
90. Interview with Tage Wandborg, formerly naval architect of Knud E. Hansen A/S, by Bruce Peter at his home in Snekkersten, Denmark on 20th February 2000.
91. *Starward*: a 13,100 gross ton cruise liner enters service in the Caribbean, The Motor Ship, March 1969, pp.613-616.
92. Interview with Tage Wandborg, formerly naval architect of Knud E. Hansen A/S, by Bruce Peter at his home in Snekkersten, Denmark on 20th February 2000.
93. *Starward*: a 13,100 gross ton cruise liner enters service in the Caribbean, The Motor Ship, March 1969, pp.613-616.
94. Clive Harvey (ed), Denny Bond Beattie, Dear Bliss…, Sea Lines, Spring 2001, pp.19-21.
95. *Starward*: a 13,100 gross ton cruise liner enters service in the Caribbean, The Motor Ship, March 1969, pp.613-616.
96. Interview with Tage Wandborg, formerly naval architect of Knud E. Hansen A/S, by Bruce Peter at his home in Snekkersten, Denmark on 20th February 2000.
97. Interview with Tage Wandborg, formerly naval architect of Knud E. Hansen A/S, by Bruce Peter at his home in Snekkersten, Denmark on 20th February 2000.
98. Interview with Tage Wandborg, formerly naval architect of Knud E. Hansen A/S, by Bruce Peter at his home in Snekkersten, Denmark on 20th February 2000.
99. *Bohème*: a Finnish-built cruise liner for Wallenius Group, The Motor Ship, December 1968, p.415.
100. Interview with Christian Landtman, formerly Managing Director of Wärtsilä Shipbuilding, by Bruce Peter by telephone on 29th June 2015.
101. Anders Bergenek and Klas Brogren, Passagerare till sjöss: Den svenska färjesjöfartens historia, ShipPax, Halmstad, 2006, pp.220-221.
102. Bård Kolltveit, Fra Verdens Ende mot de syv hav: Anders Wilhelmsen & Co. 1939-1989, Merkur Trykk, Oslo, 1989, pp.131-132.

103. Interview with Christian Landtman, formerly Managing Director of Wärtsilä Shipbuilding, by Bruce Peter by telephone on 29th June 2015.
104. Interview with Martin Saarikangas, formerly Managing Director of Wärtsilä Shipbuilding and CEO of Masa Yards, by Bruce Peter and Kalle Id at the Hotel Pasila in Helsinki on 11th December 2014.
105. Wärtsilä-built cruise liner *Song of Norway*, Shipbuilding and Shipping Record, 30th October 1970, pp.21-22.
106. Bård Kolltveit, Fra Verdens Ende mot de syv hav: Anders Wilhelmsen & Co. 1939-1989, Merkur Trykk, Oslo, 1989, pp.136-137.
107. Interview with Heikki Sorvali, industrial designer of ferry and cruise ship exteriors and interiors by Bruce Peter and Kalle Id at his home in Helsinki on 11th December 2014.
108. http://www.prnewswire.com/news-releases/royal-caribbean-founder-edwin-w-stephan-retires-from-board-after-35-years-with-company-55659442.htm
109. Bård Kolltveit, Fra Verdens Ende mot de syv hav: Anders Wilhelmsen & Co. 1939-1989, Merkur Trykk, Oslo, 1989, p.137.
110. Interview with Tage Wandborg, formerly naval architect of Knud E. Hansen A/S, by Bruce Peter at his home in Snekkersten, Denmark on 20th February 2000.
111. Interview with Martin Saarikangas, formerly Managing Director of Wärtsilä Shipbuilding and CEO of Masa Yards, by Bruce Peter and Kalle Id at the Hotel Pasila in Helsinki on 11th December 2014.
112. Interview with Vuokko Laakso, interior designer of Finnish-built passenger ships, by Bruce Peter in Helsinki on 28th February 2012.
113. Wärtsilä-built cruise liner *Song of Norway*, Shipbuilding and Shipping Record, 30th October 1970, pp.21-22.
114. Interview with Tage Wandborg, formerly naval architect of Knud E. Hansen A/S, by Bruce Peter at his home in Snekkersten, Denmark on 20th February 2000.
115. Interview with Tage Wandborg, formerly naval architect of Knud E. Hansen A/S, by Bruce Peter at his home in Snekkersten, Denmark on 20th February 2000.
116. Interview with Jim Davis, Former P&O Lines director, by Bruce Peter at The Baltic Exchange in London on 8th August 2011.
117. Interview with Hans Kjærgaard, formerly of Knud E. Hansen A/S, by Bruce Peter in Copenhagen on 5th November 2005.
118. Interview with Bruce Nierenberg, formerly NCL manager, by Bruce Peter in Helsinki on 14th April 2016.
119. Interview with Bruce Nierenberg, formerly NCL manager, by Bruce Peter in Helsinki on 14th April 2016.
120. Clive Harvey, The Last White Empresses, Carmania Press, London, 2004, pp.76-77.
121. Interview with Stephen Payne, formerly a Senior Naval Architect in Technical Marine Planning and Carnival Corporate Shipbuilding, by Bruce Peter by telephone on 10th April 2015.
122. Interview with Bruce Nierenberg, formerly NCL manager, by Bruce Peter in Helsinki on 14th April 2016.
123. Clive Harvey, The Last White Empresses, Carmania Press, London, 2004, p.78.
124. Interview with Hans Kjærgaard, formerly of Knud E. Hansen A/S, by Bruce Peter in Copenhagen on 5th November 2005.
125. Interview with Albert Hinckley, interior designer and son of Steedman Hinckley, by Bruce Peter by telephone on 24th July 2008.
126. Interview with Joel Schalit, son of the shipbroker Ellie Schalit, by Bruce Peter by telephone on 3rd August 2008.
127. Interview with Jan Erik Wahl, former Technical Director of Øivind Lorentzen's Rederi by Bruce Peter by telephone on 2nd May 2007.
128. Interview with Jan Erik Wahl, former Technical Director of Øivind Lorentzen's Rederi by Bruce Peter by telephone on 2nd May 2007.
129. Interview with Jan Erik Wahl, former Technical Director of Øivind Lorentzen's Rederi by Bruce Peter by telephone on 2nd May 2007.
130. Interview with Jan Erik Wahl, former Technical Director of Øivind Lorentzen's Rederi by Bruce Peter by telephone on 2nd May 2007.
131. Interview with Jim Davis, Former P&O Lines director, by Bruce Peter at The Baltic Exchange in London on 8th August 2011.
132. Interview with Jim Davis, Former P&O Lines director, by Bruce Peter at The Baltic Exchange in London on 8th August 2011.
133. William H. Miller, Going Dutch: The Holland America Line Story, Carmania Press, London, 1998, pp.78-83.
134. Anthony Cooke, Liners and Cruise Ships: some notable smaller vessels, Carmania Press, London, 1996, pp.109-110.
135. Dag Bakka Jr.: Bergenske – Byen og Selskapet, Seagull, Bergen 1993, pp. 160-193.
136. Interview with Christian Landtman, formerly Managing Director of Wärtsilä Shipbuilding, by Bruce Peter by telephone on 29th June 2015.
137. William H. Miller, Passenger Liners Italian Style, Carmania Press, London, 1996, pp.41-48, pp.63-68, pp.72-76 and p.89.
138. Maurizio Eliseo, The Sitmar Liners & the V Ships, Carmania Press, London, 1998, pp.11-20.
139. Maurizio Eliseo, The Sitmar Liners & the V Ships, Carmania Press, London, 1998, pp.113-133.
140. Maurizio Eliseo, The Sitmar Liners & the V Ships, Carmania Press, London, 1998, pp.113-133.
141. Georgios M. Foustanos, Greek Coastal Service 1945-1995, Argo Publishing, Athens, 2010, p.23. See also Lawrence Dunn, Lawrence Dunn's Mediterranean Shipping, Carmania Press, London, 1999, pp.70-76.
142. Georgios M. Foustanos, Greek Coastal Service 1945-1995, Argo Publishing, Athens, 2010, pp.138-139.
143. William H. Miller, Passenger Liners French Style, Carmania Press, London, 2001, pp.92-100.
144. Philip Dawson, Cruise Ships: An Evolution in Design, Conway Maritime Press, London, 2000, pp.138-140.
145. Interview with Hans Kjærgaard, formerly of Knud E. Hansen A/S, by Bruce Peter in Copenhagen on 5th November 2005.
146. Interview with Hans Kjærgaard, formerly of Knud E. Hansen A/S, by Bruce Peter in Copenhagen on 5th November 2005.
147. Anthony Cooke, Liners and Cruise Ships: some notable smaller vessels, Carmania Press, London, 1996, pp.116-118.
148. Interview with Costis Stamboulelis, former Technical Manager of Royal Cruise Line, by Bruce Peter in Piraeus on 4th September 2012.
149. Interview with Tage Wandborg, formerly naval architect of Knud E. Hansen A/S, by Bruce Peter at his home in Snekkersten, Denmark on 14th August 2012.
150. Interview with Hans Kjærgaard, formerly of Knud E. Hansen A/S, by Bruce Peter in Copenhagen on 5th November 2005.
151. *Cunard Princess* Ceremony, The Times, 3rd March 1977, p.4.
152. Interview with Tage Wandborg, formerly naval architect of Knud E. Hansen A/S, by Bruce Peter at his home in Snekkersten, Denmark on 20th February 2000.
153. Interview with Bruce Nierenberg, formerly NCL manager, by Bruce Peter in Helsinki on 14th April 2016.
154. Interview with Christian Landtman, formerly Managing Director of Wärtsilä Shipbuilding, by Bruce Peter by telephone on 29th

June 2015.
155. Interview with Hans Kjærgaard, formerly of Knud E. Hansen A/S, by Bruce Peter in Copenhagen on 5th November 2005.
156. Interview with Christian Landtman, formerly Managing Director of Wärtsilä Shipbuilding, by Bruce Peter by telephone on 29th June 2015.
157. Interview with Kai Levander, formerly Project Manager of Wärtsilä Shipbuilders, by Bruce Peter in London on 25th January 2010.
158. Anthony Cooke, Liners and Cruise Ships: some notable smaller vessels, Carmania Press, London, 1996, pp.119-120.
159. Interview with Tage Wandborg, formerly naval architect of Knud E. Hansen A/S, by Bruce Peter at his home in Snekkersten, Denmark on 14th August 2012.
160. Interview with Bruce Nierenberg, formerly NCL manager, by Bruce Peter in Helsinki on 14th April 2016.
161. Interview with Tage Wandborg, formerly naval architect of Knud E. Hansen A/S, by Bruce Peter at his home in Snekkersten, Denmark on 20th February 2000.
162. Interview with Bruce Nierenberg, formerly NCL manager, by Bruce Peter in Helsinki on 14th April 2016.
163. Interview with Tage Wandborg, formerly naval architect of Knud E. Hansen A/S, by Bruce Peter at his home in Snekkersten, Denmark on 20th February 2000.
164. Interview with Tage Wandborg, formerly naval architect of Knud E. Hansen A/S, by Bruce Peter at his home in Snekkersten, Denmark on 20th February 2000.
165. Interview with Bruce Nierenberg, formerly NCL manager, by Bruce Peter in Helsinki on 14th April 2016.
166. Interview with Bruce Nierenberg, formerly NCL manager, by Bruce Peter in Helsinki on 14th April 2016.
167. Interview with Bruce Nierenberg, formerly NCL manager, by Bruce Peter in Helsinki on 14th April 2016.
168. Interview with Bruce Nierenberg, formerly NCL manager, by Bruce Peter in Helsinki on 14th April 2016.
169. Interview with Hans Kjærgaard, formerly of Knud E. Hansen A/S, by Bruce Peter in Copenhagen on 5th November 2005.
170. Interview with Bruce Nierenberg, formerly NCL manager, by Bruce Peter in Helsinki on 14th April 2016.
171. Interview with Tage Wandborg, formerly naval architect of Knud E. Hansen A/S, by Bruce Peter at his home in Snekkersten, Denmark on 20th February 2000.
172. Interview with Knud Erik Bengtsen, former Managing Director of Aalborg Værft, by Bruce Peter at his home in Aalborg on 25th July 2005.
173. Interview with Knud Erik Bengtsen, former Managing Director of Aalborg Værft, by Bruce Peter at his home in Aalborg on 25th July 2005.
174. Philip Dawson, Cruise Ships: An Evolution in Design, Conway Maritime Press, London, 2000, p.130.
175. Interview with Knud Erik Bengtsen, former Managing Director of Aalborg Værft, by Bruce Peter at his home in Aalborg on 25th July 2005.
176. Interview with Stephen Payne, formerly a Senior Naval Architect in Technical Marine Planning and Carnival Corporate Shipbuilding, by Bruce Peter by telephone on 10th April 2015.
177. Interview with Stephen Payne, formerly a Senior Naval Architect in Technical Marine Planning and Carnival Corporate Shipbuilding, by Bruce Peter by telephone on 10th April 2015.
178. Interview with Martin Saarikangas, formerly Managing Director of Wärtsilä Shipbuilding and CEO of Masa Yards, by Bruce Peter and Kalle Id at the Hotel Pasila in Helsinki on 11th December 2014.
179. Philip Dawson, Cruise Ships: An Evolution in Design, Conway Maritime Press, London, 2000, p.130.
180. Bård Kolltveit, Fra Verdens Ende mot de syv hav: Anders Wilhelmsen & Co. 1939-1989, Merkur Trykk, Oslo, 1989, pp.196-197.
181. Philip Dawson, Cruise Ships: An Evolution in Design, Conway Maritime Press, London, 2000, p.131-132.
182. Bård Kolltveit, Fra Verdens Ende mot de syv hav: Anders Wilhelmsen & Co. 1939-1989, Merkur Trykk, Oslo, 1989, p.197.
183. Philip Dawson, Cruise Ships: An Evolution in Design, Conway Maritime Press, London, 2000, pp.133-134.
184. I am grateful to the American cruise ship historian Allan Jordan for providing detailed information about the *Atlantic*'s interior design in an email dated 24th September 2016.
185. Interview with Bruce Nierenberg, formerly NCL manager, by Bruce Peter in Helsinki on 14th April 2016.
186. Anthony Cooke, Liners and Cruise Ships: some notable smaller vessels, Carmania Press, London, 1996, p.110.
187. Philip Dawson, Cruise Ships: An Evolution in Design, Conway Maritime Press, London, 2000, p.112.
188. Stephen Payne, Grand Dame: Holland America Line and the S.S. *Rotterdam*, RINA, London, 1990, p.68.
189. I am grateful to the American cruise ship historian Allan Jordan for providing detailed information about the *Fairsky*'s interior design in an email dated 24th September 2016.
190. Maurizio Eliseo, The Sitmar Liners & the V Ships, Carmania Press, London, 1998, pp.137-140.
191. Interview with Bruce Nierenberg, formerly NCL manager, by Bruce Peter in Helsinki on 14th April 2016.
192. See Bruce Peter, DFDS 150, Nautilus Forlag, 2015, pp.300-305 and pp.317-320 for a detailed description of the *Scandinavia* and of Scandinavian World Cruises.
193. Kai Levander, Increasing Profitability for Passenger Ships, Hellenic Institute of Maritime Technology conference, Athens, 1982, p.9.
194. Interview with Kai Levander, formerly project manager of Wärtsilä, by Bruce Peter in London on 25th January 2010.
195. Interview with Kai Levander, formerly Project Manager at Wärtsilä, by Bruce Peter in London on 25th January 2010.
196. Interview with Heikki Sorvali, industrial designer of ferry and cruise ship exteriors and interiors at his home in Helsinki on 11th December 2014.
197. Interview with Kai Levander, formerly Project Manager at Wärtsilä, by Bruce Peter in London on 25th January 2010.
198. Philip Dawson, The Development of an Ideal: The AOC Ship, Guide 85, ShipPax, Halmstad, 1985, pp.23-25.
199. Seks skips-arkitekter, Byggekunst, No. 4, 1991, p.186.
200. Philip Dawson, Cruise Ships: An Evolution in Design, Conway Maritime Press, London, 2000, p.160.
201. Ivar Moltke, Cabin Standards of the Future, Guide 85, ShipPax, Halmstad, 1985, pp.19-21.
202. Philip Dawson, Cruise Ships: An Evolution in Design, Conway Maritime Press, London, 2000, p.162.
203. Klas Brogren, The World's Most Advanced Cruise Ship Onboard Report, Guide 85, ShipPax, Halmstad, 1985, pp.7-9.
204. Michael Bally, *Royal Princess*, The Times, 17 February 1984, p.1.
205. Interview with Hans Kjærgaard, formerly of Knud E. Hansen A/S, by Bruce Peter in Copenhagen on 5th November 2005.
206. Interview with Hans Kjærgaard, formerly of Knud E. Hansen A/S, by Bruce Peter in Copenhagen on 5th November 2005.
207. Interview with Kai Levander, formerly Project Manager at Wärtsilä, by Bruce Peter in London on 25th January 2010.
208. Kai Levander, Increasing Profitability for Passenger Ships, Hellenic Institute of Maritime Technology conference, Athens, 1982, p.11.

The bow and forward superstructure of the *AIDAprima* on the River Elbe near Hamburg.

209. John Maxtone-Graham, Liners to the Sun, Sheridan House, New York, 2000, pp. 441-445.
210. Interview with Hans Kjærgaard, formerly of Knud E. Hansen A/S, by Bruce Peter in Copenhagen on 5th November 2005.
211. Anthony Cooke, Liners and Cruise Ships: some notable smaller vessels, Carmania Press, London, 1996, pp.124-125.
212. Seks skips-arkitekter, Byggekunst, No. 4, 1991, p.186.
213. Mikko Uola: "Meidän isä töissä telakalla" – Rauma-Repolan laivanrakennus 1945-1991, Otava, Helsinki 1996, p. 516.
214. Anttila, Arto, Purjeristeilijä Rakennetaankin Ranskassa, Navigator No. 2, 1985, p. 43.
215. Interview with Kai Levander, formerly Project Manager at Wärtsilä, by Bruce Peter in London on 25th January 2010.
216. Philip Dawson, Cruise Ships: An Evolution in Design, Conway Maritime Press, London, 2000, p.211.
217. Philip Dawson, Cruise Ships: An Evolution in Design, Conway Maritime Press, London, 2000, p.210
218. Philip Dawson, Cruise Ships: An Evolution in Design, Conway Maritime Press, London, 2000, p.213.
219. Interview with Johan Snellman, Sales Manager at Meyer Turku and previously employed by Rauma-Repola, by Bruce Peter by telephone on 4th June 2015.
220. Interview with Johan Snellman, Sales Manager at Meyer Turku and previously employed by Rauma-Repola, by Bruce Peter by telephone on 4th June 2015.
221. Interview with Johan Snellman, Sales Manager at Meyer Turku and previously employed by Rauma-Repola, by Bruce Peter by telephone on 4th June 2015.
222. Interview with Kai Levander, formerly project manager of Wärtsilä, by Bruce Peter in London on 25th January 2010.
223. Philip Dawson, Cruise Ships: An Evolution in Design, Conway Maritime Press, London, 2000, pp.167-168.
224. Seks skips-arkitekter, Byggekunst, No. 4, 1991, p.186.
225. Philip Dawson, Cruise Ships: An Evolution in Design, Conway Maritime Press, London, 2000, pp.168-169.
226. Seks skips-arkitekter, Byggekunst, No. 4, 1991, p.186.
227. Interview with Kai Levander, formerly project manager of Wärtsilä, by Bruce Peter in London on 25th January 2010.
228. Philip Dawson, Cruise Ships: An Evolution in Design, Conway Maritime Press, London, 2000, pp.177-178.
229. Philip Dawson, Cruise Ships: An Evolution in Design, Conway Maritime Press, London, 2000, p.175.
230. Seks skips-arkitekter, Byggekunst, No. 4, 1991, p.194.
231. Bård Kolltveit, Fra Verdens Ende mot de syv hav: Anders Wilhelmsen & Co. 1939-1989, Merkur Trykk, Oslo, 1989, pp.206-207.
232. Bård Kolltveit, Fra Verdens Ende mot de syv hav: Anders Wilhelmsen & Co. 1939-1989, Merkur Trykk, Oslo, 1989, pp.204-205.
233. Hans Jörgen Witthöft, Meyer Werft: Innovativer Schiffbau aus Papenburg, Koehlers Verlag, Hamburg, 2005, pp.98-110.
234. Hans Jörgen Witthöft, Meyer Werft: Innovativer Schiffbau aus Papenburg, Koehlers Verlag, Hamburg, 2005, p.164.
235. Hans Jörgen Witthöft, Meyer Werft: Innovativer Schiffbau aus Papenburg, Koehlers Verlag, Hamburg, 2005, pp.110-116.
236. Hans Jörgen Witthöft, Meyer Werft: Innovativer Schiffbau aus Papenburg, Koehlers Verlag, Hamburg, 2005, p.165.
237. Interview with Hans Kjærgaard, formerly of Knud E. Hansen A/S, by Bruce Peter in Copenhagen on 5th November 2005.
238. Interview with Hans Kjærgaard, formerly of Knud E. Hansen A/S, by Bruce Peter in Copenhagen on 5th November 2005.
239. William H. Miller, The Chandris Liners, Carmania Press, Greenwich, 1993, p.74.
240. Hans Jörgen Witthöft, Meyer Werft: Innovativer Schiffbau aus Papenburg, Koehlers Verlag, Hamburg, 2005, p.165
241. William H. Miller, The Chandris Liners, Carmania Press, Greenwich, 1993, p.74.
242. Maurizio Eliseo, The Sitmar Liners & the V Ships, Carmania Press, London, 1998. Pp.142-144.
243. Philip Dawson, Cruise Ships: An Evolution in Design, Conway Maritime Press, London, 2000, pp.146-150.
244. Maurizio Eliseo, The Sitmar Liners & the V Ships, Carmania Press, London, 1998, pp.141-144.
245. Maurizio Eliseo, The Sitmar Liners & the V Ships, Carmania Press, London, 1998, pp.145-148.
246. Maurizio Eliseo, The Sitmar Liners & the V Ships, Carmania Press, London, 1998, p.130 and p.142.
247. Maurizio Eliseo, The Sitmar liners & The V Ships, Carmania Press, London, 1998, pp.107-140.
248. Maurizio Eliseo, The Sitmar liners & The V Ships, Carmania Press, London, 1998, pp.141-149.
249. Paolo Piccione and Gian Paolo Cesarani, Costa Crociere: Cinquant'anni di stile, Silvana Editoriale, Genoa, 1998, pp.132-133.
250. Maurizio Eliseo, Queen Elizabeth: More than a Ship, Fincantieri, Genoa and Trieste, 2010, pp.72-73.
251. Paolo Piccione and Gian Paolo Cesarani, Costa Crociere: Cinquant'anni di stile, Silvana Editoriale, Genoa, 1998, pp.126-131.
252. Paolo Piccione and Gian Paolo Cesarani, Costa Crociere: Cinquant'anni di stile, Silvana Editoriale, Genoa, 1998, pp.135-139.
253. Interview with Stephen Payne, formerly a Senior Naval Architect in Technical Marine Planning and Carnival Corporate Shipbuilding, by Bruce Peter by telephone on 10th April 2015.
254. Philip Dawson, Cruise Ships: An Evolution in Design, Conway Maritime Press, London, 2000, pp.180-181.
255. Interview with Stephen Payne, formerly a Senior Naval Architect in Technical Marine Planning and Carnival Corporate Shipbuilding, by Bruce Peter by telephone on 10th April 2015.
256. Interview with Martin Saarikangas, formerly Managing Director of Wärtsilä Shipbuilding and CEO of Masa Yards, by Bruce Peter and Kalle Id at the Hotel Pasila in Helsinki on 11th December 2014.
257. Interview with Stephen Payne, formerly a Senior Naval Architect in Technical Marine Planning and Carnival Corporate Shipbuilding, by Bruce Peter by telephone on 10th April 2015.
258. Interview with Stephen Payne, formerly a Senior Naval Architect in Technical Marine Planning and Carnival Corporate Shipbuilding, by Bruce Peter by telephone on 10th April 2015.
259. Interview with Martin Saarikangas, formerly Managing Director of Wärtsilä Shipbuilding and CEO of Masa Yards, by Bruce Peter and Kalle Id at the Hotel Pasila in Helsinki on 11th December 2014.
260. Interview with Martin Saarikangas, formerly Managing Director of Wärtsilä Shipbuilding and CEO of Masa Yards, by Bruce Peter and Kalle Id at the Hotel Pasila in Helsinki on 11th December 2014.
261. Bård Kolltveit, Fra Verdens Ende mot de syv hav: Anders Wilhelmsen & Co. 1939-1989, Merkur Trykk, Oslo, 1989, pp.215-216.
262. Seks skips-arkitekter, Byggekunst, No. 4, 1991, p.194.
263. Seks skips-arkitekter, Byggekunst, No. 4, 1991, p.186.
264. Bruce Peter, Passenger Liners Scandinavian Style, Carmania Press, London, pp.148-150.
265. Eric Flounders and Michael Gallagher, The Story of Cunard's 175 Years, Ferry Publications, Ramsey, 2014, p.176.
266. Eric Flounders and Michael Gallagher, The Story of Cunard's 175 Years, Ferry Publications, Ramsey, 2014, p.179.
267. SOLAS (Safety of Life At Sea) Chapter III Regulation 13.1.2, 1996.
268. Interview with Stephen Payne, formerly a Senior Naval Architect in Technical Marine Planning and Carnival Corporate Shipbuilding, by Bruce Peter by telephone on 10th April 2015.

269. Interview with Stephen Payne, formerly a Senior Naval Architect in Technical Marine Planning and Carnival Corporate Shipbuilding, by Bruce Peter by telephone on 10th April 2015.
270. Interview with Stephen Payne, formerly a Senior Naval Architect in Technical Marine Planning and Carnival Corporate Shipbuilding, by Bruce Peter by telephone on 10th April 2015.
271. Interview with Stephen Payne, formerly a Senior Naval Architect in Technical Marine Planning and Carnival Corporate Shipbuilding, by Bruce Peter by telephone on 10th April 2015.
272. Interview with Stephen Payne, formerly a Senior Naval Architect in Technical Marine Planning and Carnival Corporate Shipbuilding, by Bruce Peter by telephone on 10th April 2015.
273. Interview with Stephen Payne, formerly a Senior Naval Architect in Technical Marine Planning and Carnival Corporate Shipbuilding, by Bruce Peter by telephone on 10th April 2015.
274. Interview with Stephen Payne, formerly a Senior Naval Architect in Technical Marine Planning and Carnival Corporate Shipbuilding, by Bruce Peter by telephone on 10th April 2015.
275. Hans Jörgen Witthöft, Meyer Werft: Innovativer Schiffbau aus Papenburg, Koehlers Verlag, Hamburg, 2005, p.167.
276. Philip Dawson, Cruise Ships: An evolution in design, Conway, London, 2000, pp.226-232.
277. Interview with John McNeece by Bruce Peter at his home in Edinburgh on 16th May 2008.
278. Interview with John McNeece by Bruce Peter at his home in Edinburgh on 16th May 2008.
279. Interview with John McNeece, McNeece Design, by Bruce Peter, Edinburgh, 16th May 2008.
280. Theo Hodges and Gary Pownall, *Aurora*: Dawn of a New Era, P&O, London, 2000, p.22.
281. Bruce Peter and Philip Dawson, P&O at 175, Ferry Publications, Ramsey, 2012, p.141.
282. Maurizio Eliseo, *Queen Elizabeth*: More than a Ship, Fincantieri, Genoa and Trieste, 2010, p.77.
283. Maurizio Eliseo, *Queen Elizabeth*: More than a Ship, Fincantieri, Genoa and Trieste, 2010, p.78.
284. Hans Jörgen Witthöft, Meyer Werft: Innovativer Schiffbau aus Papenburg, Koehlers Verlag, Hamburg, 2005, p.166.
285. Jim Shaw, *Legend of the Seas*: Envisioned with the world, Cruise & Ferry Info, August 1995, pp.18-19.
286. Paolo Piccione and Gian Paolo Cesarani, Costa Crociere: Cinquant'anni di stile, Silvana Editoriale, Genoa, 1998, pp.143-148.
287. Daniel Cooper, German cruising & the *Aida*, Cruise & Ferry Info, March 2007, pp.20-21.
288. Ralf Schröder and Michael Thamm, AIDA: Die Erfolgsstory, Delius Klasing Verlag, Bielefeld, 2008, pp.96-101.
289. Ralf Schröder and Michael Thamm, AIDA: Die Erfolgsstory, Delius Klasing Verlag, Bielefeld, 2008, pp.96-101.
290. William H. Miller, The Cruise Ships, Conway Maritime Press, London, 1988, pp.162-168.
291. Information from Captain Magnus Gottberg, master for Star Cruises' cruise ship *Superstar Virgo*, whom the author met in May 2010.
292. Hans Jörgen Witthöft, Meyer Werft: Innovativer Schiffbau aus Papenburg, Koehlers Verlag, Hamburg, 2005, pp.170-171.
293. Bruce Peter, Cruising on a Super Star, Cruise & Ferry Info, November 2010, pp.44-46.
294. Interview with Bruce Nierenberg, formerly NCL manager, by Bruce Peter in Helsinki on 14th April 2016.
295. Interview with Bruce Nierenberg, formerly NCL manager, by Bruce Peter in Helsinki on 14th April 2016.
296. Interview with Bruce Nierenberg, formerly NCL manager, by Bruce Peter in Helsinki on 14th April 2016.
297. Angelo Scorza, Festival: Distinctly European, Cruise & Ferry Info, May 2003, pp.49-52.
298. David Glass, ROC demise rocks Greece, Cruise & Ferry Info, February 2004, pp.7-8.
299. Information supplied to the author by Ted Scull in an email dated 25 May 2010.
300. Interview with Stephen Payne, formerly a Senior Naval Architect in Technical Marine Planning and Carnival Corporate Shipbuilding, by Bruce Peter by telephone on 10th April 2015.
301. Interview with Stephen Payne, formerly a Senior Naval Architect in Technical Marine Planning and Carnival Corporate Shipbuilding, by Bruce Peter by telephone on 10th April 2015.
302. Interview with Stephen Payne, formerly a Senior Naval Architect in Technical Marine Planning and Carnival Corporate Shipbuilding, by Bruce Peter by telephone on 10th April 2015.
303. Interview with Stephen Payne, formerly a Senior Naval Architect in Technical Marine Planning and Carnival Corporate Shipbuilding, by Bruce Peter by telephone on 10th April 2015.
304. Interview with Stephen Payne, formerly a Senior Naval Architect in Technical Marine Planning and Carnival Corporate Shipbuilding, by Bruce Peter by telephone on 10th April 2015.
305. See Fulvio Roiter, *Grand Princess*, Fincantieri, Trieste, 1999 for a detailed illustrated record of the vessel's construction and outfitting.
306. Interview with Martin Saarikangas, formerly Managing Director of Wärtsilä Shipbuilding and CEO of Masa Yards, by Bruce Peter and Kalle Id at the Hotel Pasila in Helsinki on 11th December 2014.
307. Interview with Kai Levander, formerly Project Manager at Wärtsilä, by Bruce Peter in London on 25th January 2010.
308. Michael Sorkin (ed) Variations on a Theme-Park: The New American City and the End of Public Space, Hill and Wang, New York, 1992, p.3.
309. Interview with Martin Saarikangas, formerly Managing Director of Wärtsilä Shipbuilding and CEO of Masa Yards, by Bruce Peter and Kalle Id at the Hotel Pasila in Helsinki on 11th December 2014.
310. Klas Brogren, A Voyage to Freedom, Cruise & Ferry Info, March 2006, pp.13-20.
311. Frank Behling, A shipload of possibilities, Cruise & Ferry Info, June 2006, pp.46-49.
312. Hans Jörgen Witthöft, Meyer Werft: Innovativer Schiffbau aus Papenburg, Koehlers Verlag, Hamburg, 2005, pp.174-177.
313. Ralph Grizzle, Princess gets its gem, Cruise & Ferry Info, April 2004, pp.52-53.
314. David Mott, Pan-American Princess, Cruise & Ferry Info, January 2003, pp.46-47.
315. Hans Jörgen Witthöft, Meyer Werft: Innovativer Schiffbau aus Papenburg, Koehlers Verlag, Hamburg, 2005, pp.173-174.
316. Ralph Grizzle, Let the Honeymoon Begin?, Cruise & Ferry Info, January 2003, pp.6-7.
317. Leslie Wayne, Political Savvy Gets U.S. Flags on Foreign Ship, The New York Times, 14th December 2003, http://www.nytimes.com/2003/12/14/us/political-savvy-gets-us-flags-on-foreign-ship.html?_r=0
318. Philip Dawson, The Patriot, Cruise & Ferry Info, November 2005, pp.55-56.
319. Leslie Wayne, Political Savvy Gets U.S. Flags on Foreign Ship, The New York Times, 14th December 2003, http://www.nytimes.com/2003/12/14/us/political-savvy-gets-us-flags-on-foreign-ship.html?_r=0
320. Leslie Wayne, Political Savvy Gets U.S. Flags on Foreign Ship, The New York Times, 14th December 2003, http://www.nytimes.com/2003/12/14/us/political-savvy-gets-us-flags-on-foreign-ship.html?_r=0
321. Philip Dawson, New ship diversifies NCL's Hawaiian offer, Cruise & Ferry Info, July/August 2006, pp.49-50.
322. Klas Brogren, A Jewel show-off, Cruise & Ferry Info, November 2005, pp.51-52.

323. Bruce Peter, Dazzling Ships: The explosion of cruise and ferry 'hull art', Cruise & Ferry Info, April 2008, pp.16-23.
324. Eric Flounders and Michael Gallagher, The Story of Cunard's 175 Years, Ferry Publications, Ramsey, 2014, pp.186-188.
325. Interview with Stephen Payne, formerly a Senior Naval Architect in Technical Marine Planning and Carnival Corporate Shipbuilding, by Bruce Peter by telephone on 10th April 2015.
326. Interview with Stephen Payne, formerly a Senior Naval Architect in Technical Marine Planning and Carnival Corporate Shipbuilding, by Bruce Peter by telephone on 10 April 2015.
327. Philip Dawson, *Queen Mary 2*, Ferry Publications, Ramsey, 2011, pp.34-39.
328. Interview with Stephen Payne, formerly a Senior Naval Architect in Technical Marine Planning and Carnival Corporate Shipbuilding, by Bruce Peter by telephone on 10th April 2015.
329. Philip Dawson, *Queen Mary 2*, Ferry Publications, Ramsey, 2011, pp.42-66.
330. http://www.cunard.co.uk/documents/press%20kits/usa/queen%20mary%202/qm2%20todd%20english.pdf
331. Angelo Scorza, Costa goes pan-European, Cruise & Ferry Info, September 2006, pp.61-62.
332. Mike Louagie, Mediterranean maturity, Cruise & Ferry Info, September 2006, pp.59-60.
333. Mike Louagie, MSC steps it up with Fantasia, Cruise & Ferry Info, February 2009, pp.43-45. See also Philippe Holthof, Precious Preziosa debuts for MSC, ShipPax CFI, May 2013, pp.58-60.
334. Mike Louagie, E=MSC2: growth at the speed of light, Cruise & Ferry Info, November 2010, pp.55-56.
335. See Michael Benis, Cruising in Style, teNeues, Kempten, 2009 for comprehensive interior images of the MSC Cruises fleet at that time.
336. Matthew Sudders, *MSC Fantasia*: The most beautiful ship in the world?, Sea Lines No. 59, Summer 2010, pp.6-7.
337. Matthew Sudders, *MSC Fantasia*: The most beautiful ship in the world?, Sea Lines No. 59, Summer 2010, p.7.
338. Interview with Stephen Payne, formerly a Senior Naval Architect in Technical Marine Planning and Carnival Corporate Shipbuilding, by Bruce Peter by telephone on 10th April 2015.
339. Angelo Scorza, Cruise with a view, Cruise & Ferry Info, January 2003, pp.43-45.
340. Air cushion results in less vibration for HAL, Cruise & Ferry Info, September 2004, p.44.
341. See Philip Dawson, *Queen Victoria*, Ferry Publications, Ramsey, 2010 and Philip Dawson, *Queen Elizabeth*, Ferry Publications, Ramsey, 2010 for detailed descriptions of these vessels. See also Philip Dawson, Tradition trumps contemporary at Cunard, Cruise & Ferry Info, May 2006, pp.8-9.
342. Mike Louagie, Delightful *Costa Luminosa*, Cruise & Ferry Info, June 2009, pp.44-46.
343. Mike Louagie, A Fabulous Moneymaker, Cruise & Ferry Info, September 2011, pp.58-59.
344. Mike Louagie, A bright Eclipse, Cruise & Ferry Info, June 2010, pp.50-51. See also Mike Louagie, Celebrity's Green ship, Cruise & Ferry Info, December 2008, pp.53-55.
345. Jon Boyce, Celebrity Innovation, ShipPax Designs 09, ShipPax, Halmstad, 2009, pp.86-87.
346. Jon Boyce, Celebrity Innovation, ShipPax Designs 09, ShipPax, Halmstad, 2009, pp.89-90.
347. Sue Bryant, Feminine Intuition, ShipPax Designs 09, ShipPax, Halmstad, 2009, p.96.
348. Sue Bryant, Feminine Intuition, ShipPax Designs 09, ShipPax, Halmstad, 2009, pp.94-95.
349. Mike Louagie, *Celebrity Silhouette*: What is new?, Cruise & Ferry Info, October 2011, pp.45-47.
350. Hans Jörgen Witthöft, Meyer Werft: Innovativer Schiffbau aus Papenburg, Koehlers Verlag, Hamburg, 2005, p.179.
351. Klas Brogren, A smiling Diva, Cruise & Ferry Info, July/August 2007, p.53.
352. Ralf Schröder and Michael Thamm, AIDA: Die Erfolgsstory, Delius Klasing Verlag, Bielefeld, 2008, pp.116-117.
353. Klas Brogren, *AIDAdiva*: all the details, ShipPax Designs 07, ShipPax, Halmstad, 2007, p.28
354. Mike Louagie, *Carnival Dream*: Awesome!, Cruise & Ferry Info, December 2009, pp.47-48. See also Art Sbarsky, Carnival's Newest Ship: It's a Breeze, Cruise & Ferry Info, October 2012, pp.47-49.
355. Susan Parker, *Costa Diadema* launches a new era, ShipPax CFI, March 2015, pp.55-57.
356. Mike Louagie, *Carnival Vista*: Surprise of the year, ShipPax CFI, September 2016, pp.56-61.
357. Mike Louagie, Team Quotes: The design team at a conference, Guide 10, ShipPax, Halmstad, 2010, p.96.
358. Mike Louagie, Mission Accomplished: The WOW has been delivered, ShipPax Guide 10, ShipPax, Halmstad, 2010, pp.14-47.
359. Mike Louagie, Team Quotes: The design team at a conference, Guide 10, ShipPax, Halmstad, 2010, p.97.
360. https://en.wikipedia.org/wiki/Apollo_Global_Management
361. Mike Louagie, Surprises of an Epic kind, Cruise & Ferry Info, September 2010, pp.49-52.
362. Susan Parker, *Norwegian Breakaway*, al fresco with ocean view, ShipPax CFI, July-August 2013, pp.44-48.
363. Susan Parker, Passenger flow is key on *Norwegian Breakaway*, ShipPax Designs 2013, ShipPax, Halmstad, 2013, pp.41-50.
364. Art Sbarsky, Kevin Sheehan: Heading up the new Norwegian Cruise Line, Cruise & Ferry Info, December 2012, pp.7-8.
365. David Foster Wallace, A Supposedly Fun Thing I'll Never Do Again, Abacus, New York, 1998.
366. Art Sbarsky, *Royal Princess*: Truly Royal, ShipPax CFI, October 2013, pp.54-57.
367. *Britannia*, Breaking the Mould, ShipPax CFI, June 2015, pp.4-9.
368. Keith Ellis, Essential British Kit, Cruise & Ferry Info, April 2008, pp.53-54.
369. China: A Quantum Leap, ShipPax CFI, December 2014, pp.11-15.
370. Susan Parker, Meyer Werft takes Quantum leap in its stride, ShipPax CFI, November 2014, pp.4-7.
371. Anthem of the Seas: High-tech on the high seas, ShipPax CFI, June 2015, pp.16-18.
372. Eero Mäkinen, *Mein Schiff 3* – TUI's huge stride into the future, ShipPax CFI, March 2015, pp.58-62.
373. David Mott, 'Victory of the Seas' for St Nazaire, ShipPax CFI, February 2013, p.19.
374. Mike Louagie, Measuring the stress factor in a world of Harmony, ShipPax CFI, July-August 2016, pp.10-15.
375. Susan Parker, Hitting the High notes, ShipPax CFI, November 2016, pp.52-58.
376. Susan Parker, Orlando Ashford, passionate about Holland America Line, ShipPax CFI, October 2016, p.6.
377. Susan Parker, Orlando Ashford, passionate about Holland America Line, ShipPax CFI, October 2016, p.6.
378. Rebecca Gibson, Fathom adds 2017 dates for Cuban and Dominican Republic cruises, Cruise & Ferry.net, http://www.cruiseandferry.net/articles/fathom-adds-2017-dates-for-cuba-and-dominican-republic-cruises#.WDgtANKLTIU
379. Mike Louagie, The Spirit of Luxury, Cruise & Ferry Info, February 2010, pp.47-51. See also Art Sbarsky, *Seabourn Odyssey* debuts, Cruise & Ferry Info, September 2009, pp.51-52.
380. Susan Parker, *Europa 2*: 21 knots without a tie, ShipPax CFI, September 2013, pp.48-52.
381. http://www.seatrade-cruise.com/news/news-headlines/a-look-inside-whats-touted-as-the-most-luxurious-ship-ever-built.html

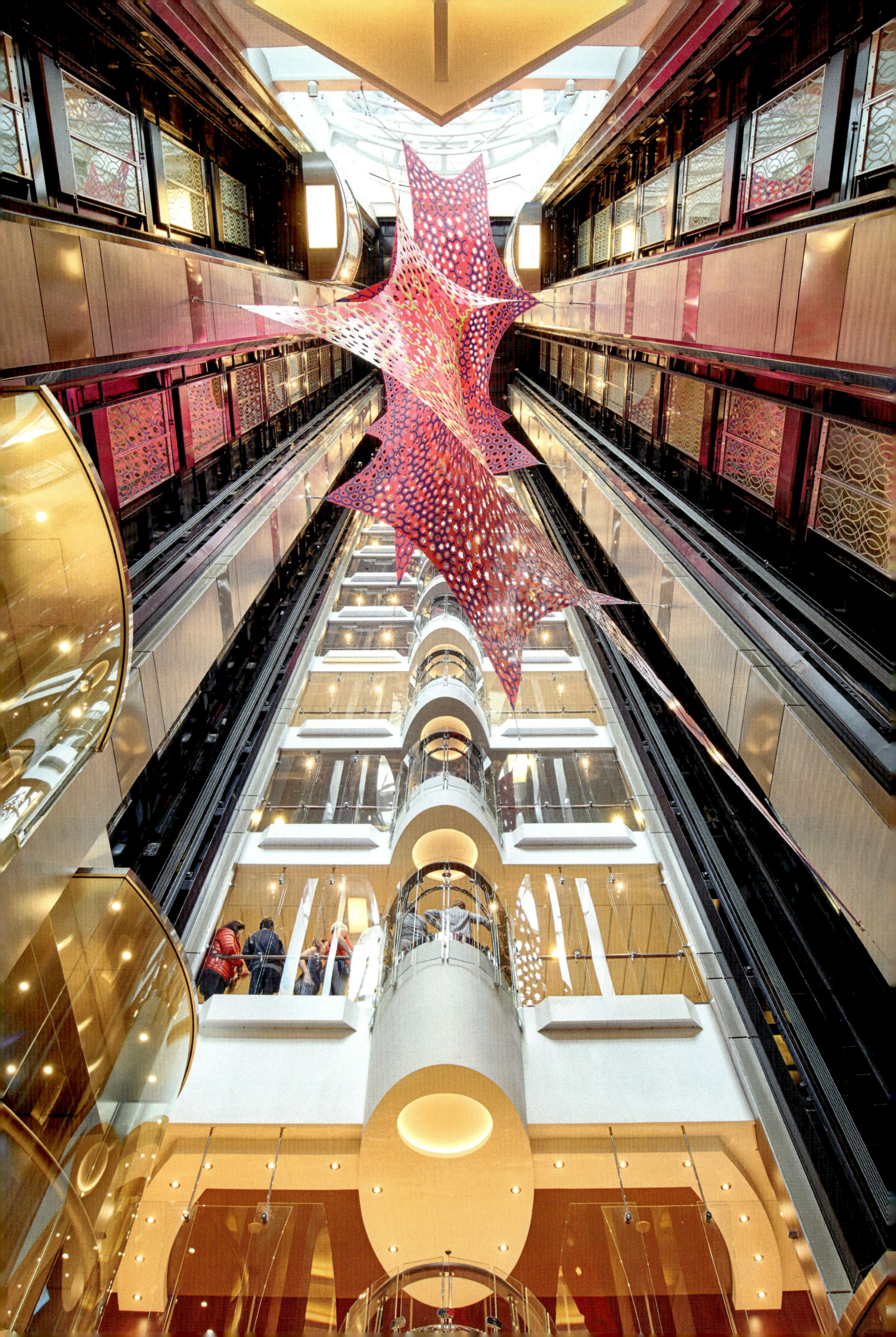

382. http://www.seatrade-cruise.com/news/news-headlines/a-look-inside-whats-touted-as-the-most-luxurious-ship-ever-built.html
383. Mike Louagie, A tricolour trendy expedition, Cruise & Ferry Info, October 2010, pp.43-45.
384. Aaron Saunders, A new star is born, ShipPax CFI, June 2013, pp.14018.
385. Aaron Saunders, Viking's Newest Star, ShipPax CFI, September 2015, pp.13-17.
386. Mike Louagie, A multi-billion day in Saint-Nazaire, ShipPax CFI, March 2016, pp.62-63.
387. Mike Louagie, A multi-billion day in Saint-Nazaire, ShipPax CFI, March 2016, p.63.
388. Marc Augé, Non-places: An introduction to the anthropology of supermodernity, Verso, London, 1993.
389. Gilles Lypovetsky, Hypermodern Times, Polity, London, 2005.

BIBLIOGRAPHY

Interviews
Interview with Knud Erik Bengtsen, former Managing Director of Aalborg Værft, by Bruce Peter at his home in Aalborg on 25th July 2005.
Interview with Jim Davis, Former P&O Lines director, by Bruce Peter at The Baltic Exchange in London on 8th August 2011.
Interview with Albert Hinckley, interior designer and son of Steedman Hinckley, by Bruce Peter by telephone on 24th July 2008.
Interview with Hans Kjærgaard, formerly of Knud E. Hansen A/S, by Bruce Peter in Copenhagen on 5th November 2005.
Interview with Vuokko Laakso, interior designer of Finnish-built passenger ships, by Bruce Peter in Helsinki on 28th February 2012.
Interview with Christian Landtman, formerly Managing Director of Wärtsilä Shipbuilding, by Bruce Peter by telephone on 29th June 2015.
Interview with Kai Levander, formerly Project Manager at Wärtsilä, by Bruce Peter in London on 25th January 2010.
Interview with John McNeece by Bruce Peter at his home in Edinburgh on 16th May 2008.
Interview with Bruce Nierenberg, formerly NCL manager, by Bruce Peter in Helsinki on 14th April 2016.
Interview with Stephen Payne, formerly a Senior Naval Architect in Technical Marine Planning and Carnival Corporate Shipbuilding, by Bruce Peter by telephone on 10th April 2015.
Interview with Martin Saarikangas, formerly Managing Director of Wärtsilä Shipbuilding and CEO of Masa Yards, by Bruce Peter and Kalle Id at the Hotel Pasila in Helsinki on 11th December 2014.
Interview with Joel Schalit, son of the shipbroker Ellie Schalit, by Bruce Peter by telephone on 3rd August 2008.
Interview with Johan Snellman, Sales Manager at Meyer Turku and previously employed by STX Europe, Aker Finnyards and Rauma-Repola, by Bruce Peter by telephone on 4th June 2015.
Interview with Heikki Sorvali, industrial designer of ferry and cruise ship exteriors and interiors by Bruce Peter and Kalle Id at his home in Helsinki on 11th December 2014.
Interview with Costis Stamboulelis, former Technical Manager of Royal Cruise Line, by Bruce Peter in Piraeus on 4th September 2012.
Interview with Holger Terpet, formerly naval architect of Knud E. Hansen A/S, by Bruce Peter in Copenhagen on 6th November 2005.
Interview with Jan Erik Wahl, former Technical Director of Øivind Lorentzen's Rederi by Bruce Peter by telephone on 2nd May 2007.
Interviews with Tage Wandborg, formerly naval architect of Knud E. Hansen A/S, by Bruce Peter at his home in Snekkersten, Denmark on several occasions between 20th February 2000 and 14th August 2012.

Books
Augé, Marc, Non-places: An introduction to the anthropology of supermodernity, Verso, London, 1993.
Bakka, Dag Jr.: Bergenske – Byen og Selskapet, Seagull, Bergen, 1993.
Benis, Michael, Cruising in Style, teNeues, Kempten, 2009.
Bergenek, Anders and Brogren, Klas, Passagerare till Sjöss: Den svenska färjesjöfartens historia, ShipPax, Halmstad, 2006.
Bonsor, R.P., North Atlantic Seaway, T. Stephenson & Sons Ltd, Prescot, 1955
Bourdieu, Pierre, Distinction: A Social Critique of the Judgement of Taste, Cambridge: Harvard University Press, 1984.
Burnett, J., A History of the Cost of Living, Penguin, Harmondsworth, 1969.
Chapman, A. L. and Knight, R., Wages and Salaries in the United Kingdom, 1920–38, Cambridge University Press, Cambridge, 1953.
Cooke, Anthony, Liners and Cruise Ships: some notable smaller vessels, Carmania Press, London, 1996.
Cooke, Anthony, Liners and Cruise Ships-2: some more notable smaller vessels, Carmania Press, London, 2000.
Corlett, Ewan, The Ship: The Revolution in Merchant Shipping, National Maritime Museum, London, 1981.
Dawson, Philip, British Superliners of the Sixties, Conway Maritime Press, London, 1990.
Dawson, Philip, Cruise Ships: An Evolution in Design, Conway Maritime Press, London, 2000.
Dawson, Philip, *Queen Victoria*, Ferry Publications, Ramsey, 2010.
Dawson, Philip, *Queen Elizabeth*, Ferry Publications, Ramsey, 2010.
Dawson, Philip, *Queen Mary 2*, Ferry Publications, Ramsey, 2011.
Dunn, Lawrence, Lawrence Dunn's Mediterranean Shipping, Carmania Press, London, 1999.
Eliseo, Maurizio, The Sitmar Liners & the V Ships, Carmania Press, London, 1998.
Eliseo, Maurizio, *Queen Elizabeth*: More than a Ship, Fincantieri, Genoa and Trieste, 2010.
Flounders, Eric and Gallagher, Michael, The Story of Cunard's 175 Years, Ferry Publications, Ramsey, 2014.
Foster Wallace, David, A Supposedly Fun Thing I'll Never Do Again, Abacus, New York, 1998.
Foustanos, Georgios M., Greek Coastal Service 1945-1995, Argo Publishing, Athens, 2010.
Galbraith, John K., The Great Crash 1929, Penguin, London, 1954.
Groenendijk, Paul and Vollaard, Piet, Guide to Modern Architecture in Rotterdam, Uitgeverij 010 Publishers, Rotterdam, 1996.
Harvey, Clive, The Last White Empresses, Carmania Press, London, 2004.
Hebdige, Dick, Towards a Cartography of Taste in Hiding in the Light: On images and things, London, Psychology Press, 1988.
Hodges, Theo and Pownall, Gary, *Aurora*: Dawn of a New Era, P&O, London, 2000.
Johnston, Ian, Ships for a Nation: John Brown & Company Clydebank, West Dunbartonshire Libraries and Museums, 2000.
Kolltveit, Bård, Fra Verdens Ende mot de syv hav: Anders Wilhelmsen & Co. 1939-1989, Merkur Trykk, Oslo, 1989, pp. 131-132.
Lypovetsky, Gilles, Hypermodern Times, Polity, London, 2005.
Maxtone-Graham, John, Liners to the Sun, Macmillan, New York, 1985.
Miller, William H., The Cruise Ships, Conway Maritime Press, London, 1988.

Opposite: Looking upwards through many decks between the shafts for the glass lifts on Royal Caribbean's *Harmony of the Seas*. An artwork is suspended in the space between.

Miller, William H., The Chandris Liners, Carmania Press, Greenwich, 1993.
Miller, William H., Passenger Liners Italian Style, Carmania Press, London, 1996.
Miller, William H., Going Dutch: The Holland America Line Story, Carmania Press, London, 1998.
Miller, William H., Passenger Liners French Style, Carmania Press, London, 2001.
Pakkala, Eero (ed.), Suomi ja meri, Meriliitto – Sjöfartsförbundet ry, Porvoo 1981.
Payne, Stephen, Grand Dame: Holland America Line and the S.S. *Rotterdam*, RINA, London, 1990.
Peter, Bruce, Passenger Liners Scandinavian Style, Carmania Press, London, 2001.
Peter, Bruce, Knud E. Hansen A/S: Ship Design through Seven Decades, Forlaget Nautilus, Copenhagen, 2007.
Peter, Bruce and Dawson, Philip, P&O at 175, Ferry Publications, Ramsey, 2012.
Peter, Bruce, DFDS 150, Nautilus Forlag, Lyngby, 2015.
Piccione, Paolo and Cesarani, Gian Paolo, Costa Crociere: Cinquant'anni di stile, Silvana Editoriale, Genoa, 1998.
Potter, Neil and Frost, Jack, *Queen Elizabeth 2*: The Authorised Story, George G; Harrap, London, 1969.
Quartermaine, Peter, Building on the Sea: Form and meaning in Ship Architecture, Academy Editions, London, 1996.
Riccesi, Donato, Gustavo Pulitzer Finali: Il Disegno della Nave, Marsilio Editori, Venice, 1985.
Roiter, Fulvio, *Grand Princess*, Fincantieri, Trieste, 1999.
Routh, Guy, Occupation and Pay in Great Britain, 1906–79, Palgrave, London, 1980.
Schröder, Ralf and Thamm, Michael, AIDA: Die Erfolgsstory, Delius Klasing Verlag, Bielefeld, 2008.
Sorkin, Michael (ed), Variations on a Theme-Park: The New American City and the End of Public Space, Hill and Wang, New York, 1992.
Stone, R. and Rowe, D. A., The Measurement of Consumer Behaviour in the United Kingdom, 1920–38, II, Cambridge University Press, Cambridge, 1966.
Uola, Mikko, 'Meidän isä töissä telakalla' – Rauma-Repolan laivanrakennus 1945-1991, Otava, Helsinki 1996.
Witthöft, Hans Jörgen, Meyer Werft: Innovativer Schiffbau aus Papenburg, Koehlers Verlag, Hamburg, 2005.

Journals and magazines
The Architectural Review
Agnew, Kenneth, Concept to Cunarder, June 1969, p. 418.

Byggekunst
Seks Skibsarkitekter, No 4, 1991, pp. 182-186.

Cruise & Ferry Info/ShipPax CFI
Shaw, Jim, *Legend of the Seas*: Envisioned with the world, August 1995, pp. 18-19.
Grizzle, Ralph, Let the Honeymoon Begin?, January 2003, pp. 6-7.
Angelo Scorza, Cruise with a view, January 2003, pp. 43-45.
Mott, David, Pan-American Princess, January 2003, pp. 46-47.
Scorza, Angelo, Festival: Distinctly European, May 2003, pp. 49-52.
Glass, David, ROC demise rocks Greece, February 2004, pp. 7-8.
Grizzle, Ralph, Princess gets its gem, April 2004, pp. 52-53.
Air cushion results in less vibration for HAL, September 2004, p. 44.
Brogren, Klas, A Jewel show-off, November 2005, pp. 51-52.
Brogren, Klas, A Voyage to Freedom, March 2006, pp. 13-20.
Tradition trumps contemporary at Cunard, May 2006, pp. 8-9.
Behling, Frank, A shipload of possibilities, June 2006, pp. 46-49.
Dawson, Philip, New ship diversifies NCL's Hawaiian offer, July/August 2006, pp. 49-50.
Louagie, Mike, Mediterranean maturity, September 2006, pp. 59-60.
Scorza, Angelo, Costa goes pan-European, September 2006, pp. 61-62.
Cooper, Daniel, German cruising & the *Aida*, March 2007, pp. 20-21.
Brogren, Klas, A smiling Diva, July/August 2007, p. 53.
Peter, Bruce, Dazzling Ships: The explosion of cruise and ferry 'hull art', April 2008, pp. 16-23.
Ellis, Keith, Essential British Kit, April 2008, pp. 53-54.
Louagie, Mike, Celebrity's Green ship, December 2008, pp. 53-55.
Louagie, Mike, MSC steps it up with Fantasia, February 2009, pp. 43-45.
Louagie, Mike, Delightful *Costa Luminosa*, June 2009, pp. 44-46.
Art Sbarsky, *Seabourn Odyssey* debuts, September 2009, pp. 51-52.
Louagie, Mike, *Carnival Dream*: Awesome!, December 2009, pp. 47-48.
Louagie, Mike, The Spirit of Luxury, February 2010, pp. 47-51.
Louagie, Mike, A bright Eclipse, June 2010, pp. 50-51.
Louagie, Mike, Surprises of an Epic kind, September 2010, pp. 49-52.
Louagie, Mike, A tricolour trendy expedition, October 2010, pp. 43-45.
Peter, Bruce, Cruising on a Super Star, November 2010, pp. 44-46.
Louagie, Mike, E=MSC2: growth at the speed of light, November 2010, pp. 55-56.
Louagie, Mike, A Fabulous Moneymaker, September 2011, pp. 58-59.
Louagie, Mike, *Celebrity Silhouette*: What is new?, October 2011, pp. 45-47.
Sbarsky, Art, Carnival's Newest Ship: It's a Breeze, October 2012, pp. 47-49.
Sbarsky, Art, Kevin Sheehan: Heading up the new Norwegian Cruise Line, December 2012, pp. 7-8.
Mott, David, 'Victory of the Seas' for St Nazaire, February 2013, p. 19.
Holthof, Philippe, Precious Preziosa debuts for MSC, May 2013, pp. 58-60.
Saunders, Aaron, A new star is born, June 2013, pp. 14-18.
Parker, Susan, *Norwegian Breakaway*, al fresco with ocean view, July-August 2013, pp. 44-48.
Parker, Susan, *Europa 2*: 21 knots without a tie, September 2013, pp. 48-52.
Sbarsky, Art, *Royal Princess*: Truly Royal, October 2013, pp. 54-57.

Parker, Susan, Meyer Werft takes Quantum leap in its stride, November 2014, pp. 4-7.
China: A Quantum Leap, December 2014, pp. 11-15.
Parker, Susan, *Costa Diadema* launches a new era, March 2015, pp. 55-57.
Mäkinen, Eero, *Mein Schiff 3* – TUI's huge stride into the future, March 2015, pp. 58-62.
Britannia, Breaking the Mould, June 2015, pp. 4-9.
Anthem of the Seas: High-tech on the high seas, June 2015, pp. 16-18.
Saunders, Aaron, Viking's Newest Star, September 2015, pp. 13-17.
Cruise on order, July-August 2016, pp. 40-41.
Louagie, Mike, A multi-billion day in Saint-Nazaire, March 2016, pp. 62-63.
Louagie, Mike, Measuring the stress factor in a world of Harmony, July-August 2016, pp. 10-15.
Louagie, Mike, *Carnival Vista*: Surprise of the year, September 2016, pp. 56-61.
Parker, Susan, Orlando Ashford, passionate about Holland America Line, October 2016, p. 6.
Parker, Susan, Hitting the High notes, November 2016, pp. 52-58.

Designs/ShipPax Designs
Brogren, Klas, The AIDAvita Story, ShipPax Designs 02, ShipPax, Halmstad, 2002, pp. 16-40.
Dawson, Philip, 'Robert Tillberg: Reflections on a remarkable career', Designs 04, ShipPax, Halmstad, 2004, pp. 90-95.
Klas Brogren, AIDAdiva: all the details, ShipPax Designs 07, ShipPax, Halmstad, 2007, p. 28.
Boyce, Jon, Celebrity Innovation, ShipPax Designs 09, ShipPax, Halmstad, 2009, pp. 86-90.
Bryant, Sue, Feminine Intuition, ShipPax Designs 09, ShipPax, Halmstad, 2009, pp. 94-96.
Parker, Susan, Passenger flow is key on *Norwegian Breakaway*, ShipPax Designs 13, ShipPax, Halmstad, 2013, pp. 41-50.
Parez, Patrick, *Quantum of the Seas*: A Fusion of Technology and Entertainment, ShipPax Designs 15, ShipPax, Halmstad, 2015, pp. 60-82.
Saunders, Aaron, *Viking Star* sails into the future, ShipPax Designs 15, ShipPax, Halmstad, 2015, pp. 88-104.

Guide/ShipPax Guide
Brogren, Klas, The World's Most Advanced Cruise Ship Onboard Report, Guide 85, ShipPax, Halmstad, 1985, pp. 7-9.
Dawson, Philip, The Development of an Ideal: The AOC Ship, Guide 85, ShipPax, Halmstad, 1985, pp. 23-25.
Moltke, Ivar, Cabin Standards of the Future, Guide 85, ShipPax, Halmstad, 1985, pp. 19-21.
Brogren, Klas, From a Star to a Star: Onboard Report *Norwegian Star*, Guide 10, ShipPax, Halmstad, 2010, pp. 16-43.
Brogren, Klas, Menu a la Minute: The Freestyle Cruise Concept, Guide 10, ShipPax, Halmstad, 2010, pp. 50-55.
Louagie, Mike, Mission Accomplished: The WOW has been delivered, ShipPax Guide 10, ShipPax, Halmstad, 2010, pp. 14-47.
Louagie, Mike, Team Quotes: The design team at a conference, ShipPax Guide 10, ShipPax, Halmstad, 2010, p. 96.

The Illustrated London News
Loss of the *Prinzessin Victoria Louise*, 26 December 1905, p. 12.

The Motor Ship
A 6,000-ton Passenger Yacht: *Stella Polaris*, the Bergen S.S. Co's new yacht for cruising in the Mediterranean and Norwegian fjords, October 1926, pp. 229-231.
Passenger Liners For German Workmen: 25,000-ton Ships, One with Diesel-electric Machinery, Designed for Economical Cruising', March 1937, p. 460.
25,000-ton German Motor-Cruising Liners, April 1937, p. 26.
A Cruising Liner For Workmen: The 24,000-ton 15 ½-knot Geared Diesel M.S. *Wilhelm Gustloff* – The First of a Series of New Liners', April 1938, p. 24.
Nili – a £2.5 million passenger/vehicle liner: second Swiss-Israeli ship runs trials. Twin Sulzer engines of 11,000 bhp provide 20 knots service speed, July 1965, pp. 146-147.
Haug, K., Some considerations leading to the design and construction of the *Sagafjord*, April 1966, pp. 17-19.
The £7 million Swedish American Line passenger ship *Kungsholm*, May 1966, pp. 53-63.
Another UK-based Scandinavian-owned ferry service, August 1966, pp. 207-211.
Bohème: a Finnish-built cruise liner for Wallenius Group, December 1968, p. 415.
Starward: a 13,100 gross ton cruise liner enters service in the Caribbean, March 1969, pp. 613-616.
Song of Norway, November 1970, pp. 368-374.
Royal Viking Star: a luxury class cruise liner, August 1972, pp. 207-213.

The Naval Architect
Stephen Payne, 'Drawing up an efficient design', special supplement, 2004, p. 25.

Navigator
Anttila, Arto, Purjeristeilijä Rakennetaankin Ranskassa, Navigator No. 2, 1985, p. 43.

The New York Times
Wayne, Leslie, Political Savvy Gets U.S. Flags on Foreign Ship, The New York Times, 14th December 2003, http://www.nytimes.com/2003/12/14/us/political-savvy-gets-us-flags-on-foreign-ship.html?_r=0

Punch
'The Middlebrow', 169, December 1925, p. 673.

The Scientific American
The Hamburg American yacht *Prinzessin Victoria Louise*, 9 February 1901, p. 86.

Representing 1980s and 1990s generations of cruise ship design, the *AIDAcara* and the *Thomson Spirit* (ex-*Nieuw Amsterdam*) are seen at dusk in Genoa.

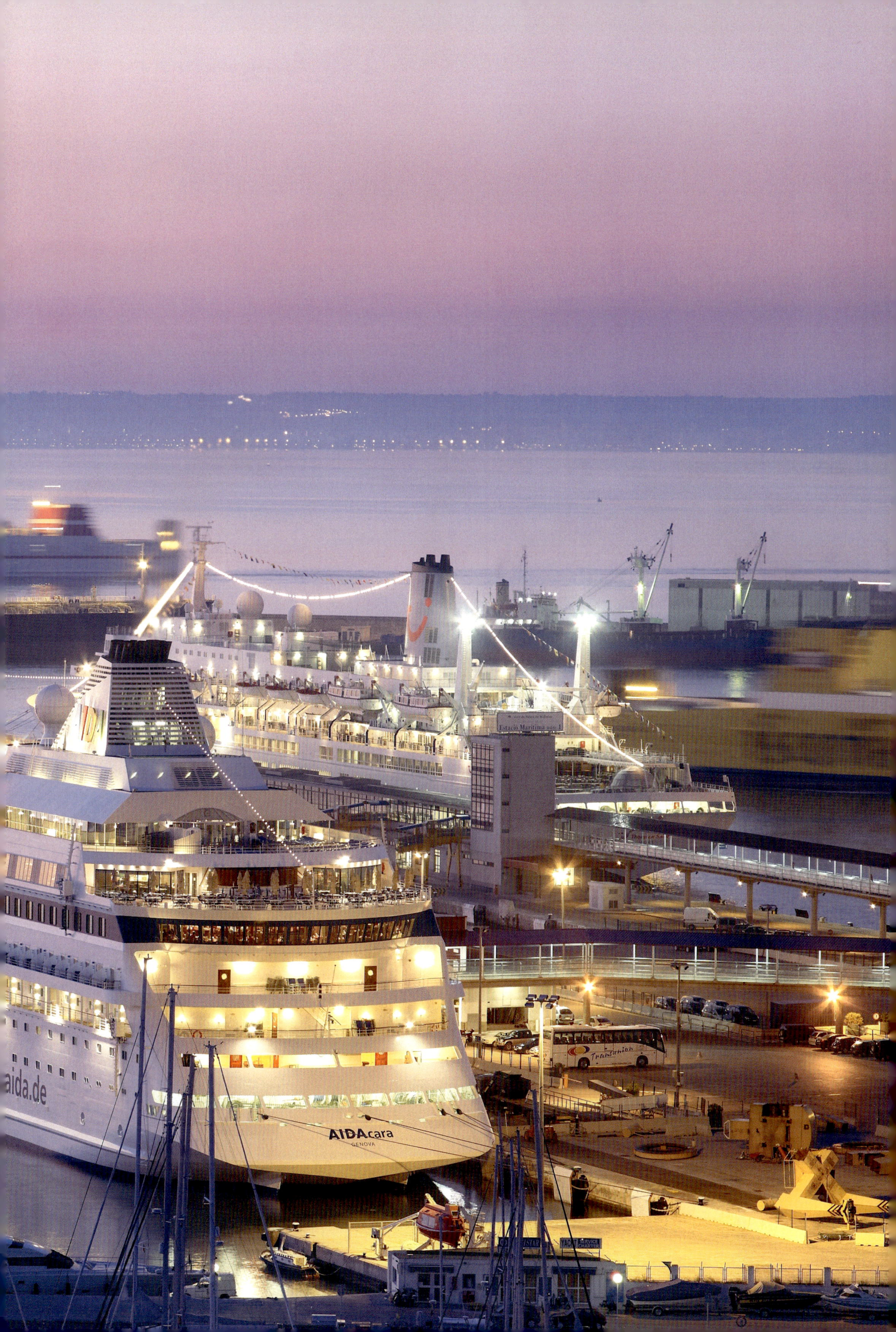
aida.de
AIDAcara

Schiffahrt und Hafenbau
R. Keine, Schiffbau, 1939, pp. 206-216.

The Scotsman
Advertisement in The Scotsman, 8 June 1886, p. 1.

Sea Lines
Kohler, Peter C., The Green Goddess R.M.S. Caronia, winter 2000, pp. 9-12 p. 10.
Harvey, Clive (ed), Bond Beattie, Denny, Dear Bliss…, Sea Lines, Spring 2001, pp. 19-21.
Harvey, Clive, The Tragedy of the Yarmouth Castle, winter 2006, pp. 19-21 p. 21.
Matthew Sudders, *MSC Fantasia*: The most beautiful ship in the world?, Summer 2010, pp. 6-7.

Shipbuilder and Marine Engine Builder
The Swedish trans-Atlantic liner *Stockholm*, May 1940, p. 206-7.

Shipbuilding and Shipping Record
A New Luxury Liner: The alterations to the Blue Star liner *Arandora Star*, 21st June 1929, pp. 704-707.
The German worker cruise ship *Wilhelm Gustloff*, 17th March 1938, pp. 323 and 335.
The delivery of the *Wilhelm Gutloff*, 21 April 1938, p. 524.
Launch of the *Andes*, Shipbuilding and Shipping Record, 16th March 1939, pp. 339-341.
The trans-Atlantic liner *Stockholm* of the Swedish American Line, 2nd June 1938, p. 722.
The *Rotterdam*, 8th October 1959, pp. 270-276.
A Caribbean cruise ship, 21st January 1960, pp. 75-77.
Features of the *Canberra*, 24th March 1960, pp. 374-381.
Andes in a new role, 16th June 1960, p. 776.
The P&O-Orient liner *Oriana*, 1st December 1960, pp. 699-708.
Oceanic: CRDA-built for Home Lines: The largest ever purely cruising vessel, April 1965, pp. 438-446.
Sagafjord: A New Norwegian America Liner, October 1965, pp. 519-526 and pp. 555-557.
Kungsholm: Public rooms on new Swedish liner, 12th May 1966, pp. 418-428.
Most Disastrous Contract, 4th August 1966, p. 144.
Sunward: A long-haul passenger ferry, Shipbuilding and Shipping Record, 4th August 1966, pp. 155-157.
Wallace, D.N., *Queen Elizabeth 2*: some design considerations, 31st January 1969, pp. 87-88.
Queen Elizabeth 2: a ship with a past and a future, 31st January 1969, pp. 146-161.
Wärtsilä-built cruise liner *Song of Norway*, 30th October 1970, pp. 21-22.
Royal Viking Star – first of new luxury cruise liner series from Wärtsilä, 21st July 1972, pp. 17-23.

Shipping World & Shipbuilder
The Blue Star Line: Reconditioned liner for luxury cruising, 12th June 1929, pp. 917-919.
Barclay, C., *Sunward*: Design considerations, January 1967, pp. 247-253.

The Times
Cunard Princess Ceremony, 3rd March 1977, p. 4.
Michael Bally, *Royal Princess*, 17th February 1984, p. 1.

Other documents and sources
The New Flagship *Rotterdam*, Holland-America Line, guide booklet, 1959.
Cunard Line inaugural season brochure for *Queen Elizabeth 2*, 1969.
Kai Levander, Increasing Profitability for Passenger Ships, Proceedings of the Hellenic Institute of Maritime Technology Conference, Athens, 1982, p. 9.
SOLAS (Safety of Life At Sea) Chapter III Regulation 13.1.2, 1996.
Information from Captain Magnus Gottberg, master for Star Cruises' cruise ship *Superstar Virgo*, whom the author met in May 2010.
Information supplied to the author by Ted Scull in an email dated 25th May 2010.

Web sources
http://www.cruising.org/docs/default-source/research/2016_clia_sotci.pdf?sfvrsn=0
https://archive.org/details/notesajourneyfr00thacgoog
http://www.wirksworth.org.uk/A04value.htm#1710
http://www.bbc.co.uk/blogs/adamcurtis/entries/e2da64b6-4921-3ce5-b05f-beec93cf3b7f.
http://www.prnewswire.com/news-releases/royal-caribbean-founder-edwin-w-stephan-retires-from-board-after-35-years-with-company-55659442.htm
http://www.cunard.co.uk/documents/press%20kits/usa/queen%20mary%202/qm2%20todd%20english.pdf
https://en.wikipedia.org/wiki/Apollo_Global_Management
http://www.cruiseandferry.net/articles/fathom-adds-2017-dates-for-cuba-and-dominican-republic-cruises#.WDgtANKLTIU
http://www.seatrade-cruise.com/news/news-headlines/a-look-inside-whats-touted-as-the-most-luxurious-ship-ever-built.html
http://www.seatrade-cruise.com/news/news-headlines/a-look-inside-whats-touted-as-the-most-luxurious-ship-ever-built.html

Index | 203

Aalborg Værft, 86, 88
Abdul Aziz, 98, 99
Achille Lauro, 72, 99, 135, 149
Admiral Cruises, 117
Adonia, 180
Adventure of the Seas, 146
Ahberg, Rolf, 32
Aida, 128
Aida Cruises, 128, 129, 130, 138, 147, 151, 165, 175, 176, 185
AIDAaura, 129
AIDAbella, 165
AIDAblu, 165
AIDAcara, 129
AIDAdiva, 165
AIDAluna, 165
AIDAmar, 165
AIDAperla, 176, 177
AIDAprima, 176, 177, 178
AIDAsol, 165
AIDAstella, 165
AIDAvita, 129
Akademik Nikolay Pilyugin, 136
Al Mansur, 98
Alde, Gustav, 29
Alexandra, 19
Alexandra, H.M. Queen, 19
Allure of the Seas, 6, 167, 170, 171, 175
Al-Mansur, 99
American International Travel Services, 62
AMK Design, 107, 108, 135, 139
Amsterdam, 122
Andern, Karl Gösta, 101
Anderson, Teresa, 125, 143, 156
Andes (I), 23
Andes (II), 26, 29, 32, 45
Angelina Lauro, 72
Ankara, 72
Annie Johnson, 112, 113
Ansaldo Shipbuilders, 32
Anthem of the Seas, 173
Apollo Global Management, 170
Aponte, Gianluigi, 135
Aquitania, 22, 30
Arandora, 23, 26
Arandora Star, 23, 26, 53
Arcadia, 149, 156
Arcadian, 23
Architectes Ingénieurs Associés, 147
Argentina, 40, 69
Ariadne, 55
Arison Shipping Company, 57, 59, 61
Arison, Micky, 152
Arison, Ted, 57, 58, 61, 62, 64, 86
ArtLink, 126
Ashford, Orlando, 179
Astor (I), 81, 82, 107, 128
Astor (II), 82
Asturias, 23
Asuka, 98
Atalante, 74
Athena, 129, 130
Atkins Global, 168
Atlantic, 91, 92, 106, 109
Atlantis, 23
Atlas, 74
Augusta Victoria, 17
Aurora, 125, 172
Axel Johnson, 112
Azerbaizhan, 79
Azipod, 116, 142, 147, 154, 160, 168
Azur, 133
Azura, 172

Bahama Star, 55
Ballin, Albert, 17, 18, 138
Bannenberg, Jon, 50, 108, 126, 147
Beattie, Denny Bond, 55, 58, 68
Bell, Henry, 13
Belorussiya, 79
Berengaria, 23
Bergens Mekaniske Verksteder, 57
Bergensfjord, 39, 129
Bergsten, Carl, 22
Berlin, 80, 82
Berlitz Guides, 11
Bernadotte, Count Sigvard, 40
Bertaglia, Gianfranco, 109, 125, 143
BG Studio International, 163
Bilu, 55, 57
Birch Coffey Associates, 126, 147
Bitsch-Christensen, Axel, 35, 40
Björkman, Alf, 138
Black Sea Steamship Company, 78, 79
Black Watch, 186
Blohm & Voss, 17, 19, 22, 25, 139
Blue Star Line, 23, 53
Bohème, 59, 119
Borinquen, 55
Boudicca, 186
Brasil, 40, 69
Bremen, 42
Bremer Vulkan A.G, 81, 121, 123, 127
Brilliance of the Seas, 147
Brinkmann, Woldemar, 25, 26
Britannia, 172
British Overseas Airline Corporation, 49
Brocklebank, Sir John, 49
Broström AB, 22, 33, 69, 76
Brynestad, Atle, 99
Buchwald, Joachim, 81
Bunge, Kai, 128, 138
Burmeister & Wain, 21, 32, 76
Calabar, 74
Cambodge, 74
Canadian Pacific, 62, 64, 68, 77
Canali, Guido, 112
Canberra, 36, 76, 109, 123
Cantiere San Marco, Trieste, 72
Cantieri Navali e Riuniti Riva Trigoso, 61
Cantieri Riuniti dell'Adriatico, 29, 35
Cantu, Ennio, 91
Carinthia, 72
Carla C., 68
Carmania, 49, 62, 72, 78
Carnival Breeze, 165
Carnival Conquest, 150
Carnival Corporate Shipbuilding, 140, 142, 143, 152
Carnival Corporation, 106, 119, 121, 122, 140, 142, 143, 148, 149, 152, 155, 156, 167, 173, 176, 180, 185
Carnival Cruise Line, 6, 12, 77, 78, 86, 102, 106, 114, 117, 121, 140, 142, 143, 150, 155, 165, 185
Carnival Destiny, 12, 140
Carnival Dream, 165
Carnival Freedom, 150
Carnival Glory, 150
Carnival Legend, 142
Carnival Liberty, 150
Carnival Magic, 165
Carnival Miracle, 142
Carnival Pride, 142
Carnival Spirit, 142
Carnival Splendor, 155
Carnival Triumph, 140
Carnival Valor, 150
Carnival Victory, 142

Carnival Vista, 167
Caronia, 30, 32, 49, 67
Celebration, 88, 102, 106, 114
Celebrity Cruises, 107, 108, 126, 146, 154, 156, 163, 175, 179, 185
Celebrity Eclipse, 156
Celebrity Equinox, 156
Celebrity Reflection, 165, 173
Celebrity Silhouette, 156, 186
Celebrity Solstice, 156
Century, 126
Cergol, Maurizio, 113, 121, 133, 140, 143, 156, 183
Cernobori, Fulvio, 109, 113, 121
Cerri, Pierluigi, 113, 127
Chandris Cruises, 74, 107, 108, 112, 114, 146
Chandris, John D., 72, 107, 112
Chantiers de France, 74
Chantiers de l'Atlantique, 83, 91, 92, 103, 105, 108, 109, 117, 118, 126, 129, 135, 138, 139, 146, 147, 148, 154, 155, 167
Chantiers du Nord et de la Méditeranée, 91
Chimborazo, 17
China Ocean Shipping Company, 129
Chobol, Sanford, 59
Christiansson, Eric, 29, 39
Clarke Steamship Company, 53
Clipper Cruises, 100
Clipper Line, 51
Club Med, 101
Club Med 1, 101
Club Med 2, 101
Clyde Line, 72
CM Design, 175
Cockerill of Hoboken, 55
Cogedar Line, 72
Comet, 13
Commodore Cruise Line, 59, 119
Compagnie de Ponant, 180
Compagnie Générale Transatlantique, 17, 101, 133
Constellation, 147
Constructions Navales et Industrielles de la Méditerrannée, 91
Conte di Savoia, 155
Copenhagen, 79
Coral Princess (I), 129
Coral Princess (II), 148, 155
Costa Allegra, 113
Costa Atlantica, 142
Costa Classica, 113, 114, 121, 127
Costa Concordia, 155, 171
Costa Cruises, 109, 112, 113, 127, 131, 142, 143, 150, 155, 156, 165, 171, 176, 185
Costa Deliziosa, 156
Costa Diadema, 165
Costa Favolosa, 156
Costa Fortuna, 155
Costa Line, 68, 72
Costa Luminosa, 156
Costa Magica, 155
Costa Marina, 112, 113
Costa Mediterrannea, 142
Costa Pacifica, 155
Costa Riviera, 112
Costa Romantica, 113, 114, 121, 127
Costa Serena, 155
Costa Victoria, 127, 128, 142
Costa, Angelo, 72
Costanzi, Nicolò, 35, 36, 51, 61, 113
Cosulich Line, 33, 35, 36
Council of Industrial Design, 50
Craxi, Bettino, 109
Crosby, Fletcher, Forbes, 50
Crown Cruise Line, 118, 119

Crown Del Mar, 119
Crown Dynasty, 118, 119
Crown Jewel, 118, 119
Crown Monarch, 119
Crown Odyssey, 107, 108, 109, 114, 135
Crown Princess, 112, 113, 114, 120, 125
Crystal Cruises, 97, 98, 177, 185
Crystal Endeavour, 185
Crystal Harmony, 97, 98, 109
Crystal Symphony, 98
CTC Cruises, 79
Cunard, 10, 22, 23, 30, 32, 35, 39, 49, 50, 62, 67, 68, 69, 71, 72, 76, 77, 78, 97, 98, 99, 100, 102, 108, 109, 119, 138, 149, 152, 154, 156
Cunard Adventurer, 67, 76, 77
Cunard Ambassador, 67, 76, 77
Cunard Conquest, 76
Cunard Countess, 76, 77, 119
Cunard Crown Dynasty, 119
Cunard Crown Jewel, 119
Cunard Crown Monarch, 119
Cunard Princess, 76, 77, 119
Curtis, Adam, 186
Dana Anglia, 86
Danae, 75
Daphne, 75
Dawn Princess, 125
Dawson, Philip, 12, 30
De Merwede van Vliet, 69
De Vlaming, Fennis, Dingemans, 92, 122
Deilmann, Peter, 80, 82, 136, 138
Del Rio, Frank, 180
Delfin Caravelle, 100, 101
Delfin Clipper, 100, 101
Delfin Cruises, 100
Deltamarin, 138, 144, 160, 167
Det Bergenske Dampskipsselskap, 19, 21, 67, 69, 71, 102
Det Forenede Dampskibs-Selskab, 93
Det Nordenfjeldske Dampskipsselskap, 19, 71, 77
Deutsche Arbeitsfront, 23
Deutsche Atlantik Linie, 40, 45
Deutsche Seereederei Rostock, 128
Deutsche Werft A.G., 40
Deutsche-Atlantik Linie, 78
Deutschland, 136, 138, 139
Diamond Cruise, 101
Diamond Princess, 148, 176
Dingemans, Franz, 156
Discoverer Reederei, 100
Disney Cruise Line, 170
Disney Dream, 170
Disney Fantasy, 170
Disney Magic, 132, 133
Disney Wonder, 132
Donghia, Angelo, 84
Doric, 91
Dream Cruises, 178
Dreamward, 118, 123
Dubigeon Normandie Nantes, 93
Dunnottar Castle, 35, 74
Eagle, 133
East India Company, 11
Eastern Shipping Corporation, 53, 55
Eastern Steamship Lines, 53, 77, 117
Ecstasy, 116, 117
Effjohn, 119
Eftedal, Olav, 103, 144
Efthymiades Lines, 74
Eide, Njål, 39, 89, 96, 97, 102, 105, 117, 126
Elation, 117, 122
Elder Dempster Lines, 74
Elffers, Cornelius, 33
Emerald Seas, 77

Empress of Britain, 77
Empress of Canada, 62, 64
Empress of England, 76
Empress of Scotland, 40, 55
Enchantment of the Seas, 126, 144
Engströmer, Margaretha, 32
Epirotiki Cruises, 74, 139
Eriksson, Nils Einar, 29
Eugenides, Eugen, 33, 35, 74, 75
Eugenides, Nicolaos Veronicos, 35, 40
Eugenio C., 154
Eurodam, 156
Europa (ex-Rimutaka), 35
Europa (II), 69, 80
Europa (III), 81, 82, 89, 92, 102, 130
Europa (IV), 138, 180
Europa 2, 180
European Stars, 135
European Vision, 135
Evangeline, 53, 55, 72
Explorer, 52
Explorer of the Seas, 146
Exposition des Arts Décoratifs et Industriels Modernes, 22
F.W. Hollming Shipbuilders, 99, 100
Fain, Richard, 103, 120, 144
Fairfield Shipbuilding & Engineering Company, 55
Fairland, 72
Fairsea, 72, 92, 108
Fairsky, 91, 92, 93, 108, 112, 125
Fairwind, 72, 92, 108
Fantasy, 109, 114, 116, 117, 118, 127, 140, 142
Farcus, Joe, 78, 88, 116, 122, 140, 142, 155, 156, 165, 167
Fascination, 116, 117
Fathom Cruises, 180
Fearnley & Eger, 59, 67, 68, 69, 100
Federico C., 131
Fedor Shalyapin, 78
Ferdinand de Lesseps, 74
Festival Cruises, 133, 135, 139, 149
Festivale, 78, 88
Fincantieri, 109, 112, 113, 121, 122, 123, 125, 132, 133, 140, 143, 147, 155, 156, 165, 167, 172, 179, 180, 183, 184, 185
Finnhansa, 59
Finnjet, 80, 81, 89, 146
Finnpartner, 59
Flagler, Henry, 53
Flagship Cruises, 67, 68, 69, 76
Flamenco, 135
Flavia, 72
Flender Werke, 51
Flota Mercante Dominicana, 53
France, 6, 40, 49, 83, 84, 85, 103
Franconia, 49, 62, 72, 78
Fraser, Frank Leslie, 53, 55, 57
Fraser, Leslie, 57
Freedom of the Seas, 146, 150
Freeport, 59
French Line, 10, 22, 26, 32, 42, 83, 85
Fugazi Tours, 152
Fuji Maru, 98
Furness Withy, 67
Galaxy, 126, 175
Galileo, 108, 112
Galileo Galilei, 108
Gardiner, James, 49
Garonne, 17
Genting Corporation, 129, 148, 151, 170, 177, 178, 185
Genting Dream, 178
Golden Odyssey, 75
Golden Princess, 143

Gonzalez, Kelly, 167
Gotaas-Larsen, 59, 77, 103, 117
Götaverken, 21
Grand Princess, 12, 143
Grandeur of the Seas, 126, 144
Great Liverpool, 13
Greek Line, 78
Grimaldi, Aldo, 72
Grimaldi, Guido, 72
Gripsholm, 32, 76
Groupe 3, 91
Grundstad, Oddmund, 118, 119
Grung, Gier, 60, 89, 105
Gruziya, 79
Guglielmo Marconi, 112
Gustav VI, H.M. King, 40
Haakon VII, 19
Hafen-Dampfschiffahrt A.G., 81
Hagen, Torstein, 102, 183
Hallen, Martin, 59, 103
Hamburg, 40, 42, 45, 49, 50, 78
Hamburg-Amerika Linie, 17, 69, 138
Hamburg-Atlantik Linie, 40
Hammer, Mogens, 57, 58, 60, 89
Hanseatic, 55
Hanseatic (I), 40
Hanseatic (II), 40, 45
Hanseatic Tours, 100
Hanseatic(III), 100
Hapag-Lloyd, 69, 80, 81, 82, 84, 89, 92, 102, 130, 133, 138, 180
Harland & Wolff, 26, 45, 74
Harmony of the Seas, 6, 176
Harsia, Pirjo, 95
Haug, Kaare, 39
Held, Marc, 101
Helsingør Skibsværft, 75
Hermansen, Bjørnar, 83, 131
Hicks, David, 50
Hinckley, Steedman, 64
Hirsch-Bender Associates, 97, 112
Hohenzollern, 17
Holiday, 6, 88, 102, 106, 114
Holland America Cruises, 32, 33, 69, 74, 91, 92, 106, 121, 122, 123, 132, 140, 143, 146, 150, 156, 160, 165, 178, 179, 180
Home Lines, 33, 35, 36, 40, 62, 67, 74, 75, 91, 92, 93, 106, 109, 132
Homeland Cruising, 149, 150, 152
Homeric, 106, 107
Hopkins, John, 114
Horizon, 107, 108, 126
Howaldtswerke A.G., 25
Howaldtswerke Deutsche Werft, 80, 82, 107, 138
Høydahl, Per, 105, 117, 126
Hurtigrute, 69, 71
Iberia, 13
Ile de France, 22
Imagination, 116, 117
Imperator, 23
Inchbald, Michael, 49, 50
Incres Line, 33, 35
Independence, 150, 151
Independence of the Seas, 146, 150
Industrie Navali Merchaniche Affine, 76
Infinity, 147
Inspiration, 116, 117
International Corporate Art, 126
International Ship Protection System (ISPS), 149
Iroquois, 72
Ishikawajima-Harima Heavy Industries, 98
Island Escape, 93
Island Princess (I), 96
Island Princess (II), 148, 155

Island Venture, 67, 68, 88
Italia, 51, 61
Ivernia, 49, 72
J. Lauritzen A/S, 129
J.P. Smit & Son, 67
Japan Cruise Line, 98
Jean Laborde, 74
Jewel of the Seas, 147
John Brown & Co, 30, 39, 40, 49
Jones Act, The, 93
Jubilee, 88, 102, 106, 114
Kalypso, 129, 130
Kanerva, Markku, 138
Karras, John C., 75
Katzourakis, Michael, 75, 107, 108, 126, 135, 139
Kingo, Jan, 95
Kioscoglou, Haralambos, 74, 139
Klaveness & Co, 71, 102
Kloster Cruise International, 102, 118, 183
Kloster, Knut, 57, 58, 59, 61, 83, 84, 85, 86, 102, 118, 180
Knud E. Hansen A/S, 52, 57, 59, 67, 75, 76, 77, 79, 84, 85, 95, 96, 97, 98, 99, 107, 139, 150, 151
Kohler, Peter C., 30
Köhnemann, Wilfred, 81
Kommanditselskabet A/S Norske Cruise, 99
Koningsdam, 179, 180
Koninklijke Mij. De Schelde, 32
Kørbing, Kay, 39
Kraft durch Freude, 23, 25, 29, 60, 95, 128, 142
Kulovaara, Harri, 144, 160, 167, 170
Kungsholm (I), 22, 29, 32, 35
Kungsholm (II), 32, 39, 80
Kungsholm (III), 39, 40, 42, 45, 49, 68, 76
Kværner Masa Yards, 98, 127, 138, 142, 143, 144, 167
L'Atlantique, 95
L'Austral, 180
La Perla, 74
Laakso, Vuokko, 60
Lady Mary Wood, 13
Laiterä, Jukka, 138
Lapidus, Morris, 78
Lauro Line, 72, 135
Laviosier, 55
Le Boreal, 180
Le Lyrial, 180
Le Soléal, 180
Lefebvre d'Ovidio, Manfredi, 109, 135
Legend of the Seas, 126
Lelakis, Antonis, 112, 113
Lennon, Dennis, 50, 93
Leonardo da Vinci, 40
Leonid Sobinov, 78
Levander, Kai, 95, 96, 98, 100, 101, 103, 144
Liberty of the Seas, 146, 150
Linblad Explorer, 99
Lindblad Explorer, 51, 52
Lindblad Travel, 52
Lindblad, Lars-Eric, 52
Lindfors, Per, 32
Lindley, David, 123
Lion Ferry, 59
Lloyd Triestino, 35, 108
Lloyd Werft, 108, 123, 127, 151, 177, 178, 185
London & Glasgow Shipbuilding Company, 53
Lorentzen, Øivind, 67, 68, 69, 76
Love Boat, The, 79, 82
Lovett, William R., 55
Lübeck Linie, 51
Luzzati, Emanuele, 39
Maasdam, 122
Majesty of the Seas, 106
Manner, Georg, 42

Mardi Gras, 64, 77, 86, 88
Mariella, 102
Mariner of the Seas, 146
Masters, Mildred, 68
Matthews, Victor, 62, 77
Mauretania (I), 22, 23, 138
Mauretania (II), 49
Maxim Gorkiy, 78, 79, 80
Maxtone-Graham, John, 8, 10, 30
McDonald, Stanley, 68
McNeece, John, 123, 126, 138
Med Sun Line, 74
Media, 72
Mein Schiff 1, 175
Mein Schiff 3, 175, 176
Mein Schiff 4, 175, 176
Mein Schiff 5, 175, 185
Mein Schiff 6, 175
Mercury, 126
Meridian, 108, 112
Meteor, 19, 69
Meteor (II), 69
Meyer Turku, 175
Meyer Werft Papenburg, 80, 106, 107, 123, 125, 126, 129, 131, 146, 147, 148, 151, 156, 160, 165, 170, 173, 175, 176, 177, 178, 185
Miaoulis, 72
Michelangelo, 40, 42, 83, 152, 155
Millennium, 147, 154
Minerva, 136
Mistral, 135
Mitsubishi Shipbuilders, 97, 98, 147, 148, 165, 176, 177
Mitsui O.S.K. Line, 98, 101
Monarch of Bermuda, 67
Monarch of the Seas, 106
Mongolia, 35
Monro, Jean, 49
Moore-McCormack Line, 40, 69
Morris, William, 17
Mortola, Giacomo, 93, 125, 143, 156
MSC Armonia, 135
MSC Cruises, 135, 155, 184, 185
MSC Divina, 155
MSC Fantasia, 155, 156
MSC Lirica, 135
MSC Magnifica, 155
MSC Merivaglia, 184
MSC Musica, 155
MSC Opera, 135
MSC Poesia, 155
MSC Preziosa, 155
MSC Sinfonia, 135
MSC Splendida, 155
Mutters & Zoon, 32, 33
Naarstad, Helge, 98, 99
Nassau, 35
National Physical Laboratory, 49
Navigator of the Seas, 146
New Northland, 53
New York World Fair, 35
New Zealand Shipping Company, 35
Nierenberg, Bruce, 62, 85, 131, 132
Nieuw Amsterdam (I), 91, 92, 121, 122
Nieuw Amsterdam (II), 156
Nili, 55, 57, 62
Nilsson, Finn, 39, 68, 71, 89
Nippon Maru, 98
Nippon Yusen Kaisha, 98, 177
Nomikos Lines, 72, 74
Noordam, 91, 92, 93, 108, 121, 122, 156
Norddeutscher Lloyd, 17, 23, 42, 69
Nordic Empress, 117, 118, 119, 126
Nordic Prince, 59, 61, 77

Nordio, Umberto, 72
Nordline K/S, 79
Normandie, 26, 103, 154
North of Scotland Steam Navigation Company, 17, 19
North Star, 53
Northern Star, 76
Norway, 6, 83, 84, 85, 88, 103
Norwegian America Cruises, 82
Norwegian America Line, 39
Norwegian Breakaway, 170, 171, 178
Norwegian Caribbean Line, 57, 59, 61, 64, 77, 91, 95, 98, 102, 131, 133
Norwegian Cruise Line, 102, 121, 123, 127, 148, 149, 150, 151, 152, 170, 172
Norwegian Dawn, 148, 151
Norwegian Epic, 170, 171
Norwegian Escape, 170, 185
Norwegian Gem, 151
Norwegian Getaway, 170
Norwegian Jade, 152
Norwegian Jewel, 151
Norwegian Pearl, 151
Norwegian Sky, 127, 151, 152
Norwegian Spirit, 151
Norwegian Star, 148, 151
Norwegian Sun, 127
Nuevo Dominicano, 53
Nystads Varv AB, 52
Oasis of the Seas, 6, 167, 170, 171, 175
Ocean Monarch, 67, 76
Ocean Princess, 125
Ocean Village, 149
Oceanic, 35, 36, 39, 40, 42, 45, 49, 51, 61, 62, 67, 74, 91, 93, 106, 107, 109, 154
Oceanos, 74
Odessa, 79
Ojjeh, Akram, 83
Olau Britannia, 81
Olau Hollandia, 81
Olympia Explorer, 139
Olympic Voyager, 139
Oosterdam, 156
Oranje, 72
Orenstein & Koppel, 59
Oriana (I), 49
Oriana (II), 123, 125, 139, 172
Orient Line, 17, 49
Orient Venus, 98
Oriental, 13
Oslofjord, 39
Ovation of the Seas, 173
Overseas National Airways, 64, 67, 76
P&O, 11, 12, 13, 17, 26, 35, 36, 53, 61, 68, 76, 79, 96, 97, 102, 105, 109, 112, 114, 120, 123, 125, 127, 129, 131, 132, 133, 135, 136, 143, 144, 146, 147, 148, 149, 155, 156, 165, 172, 173, 180, 185
Pacific Princess, 68, 96
Pacific Steam Navigation Company, 45
Pan American Cruise Lines, 57
Panagopoulos, Pericles, 75, 107
Paradise, 117, 122
Paris, 133
Partnership Design, 128, 138, 165, 167
Pasteur, 42
Paul Gauguin, 138
Payne, Stephen, 35, 122, 152, 154
Pearl Cruises of Scandinavia, 129
Pearl of Scandinavia, 129
Peninsular & Occidental Steamship Company, 53
Penttinen, Ilkka, 95
Peter Pan, 51
Phoenix World City, 85, 86, 95, 99, 118
Piano, Renzo, 96, 109, 112

Platou, Fritjof S., 39, 71
Ponti, Giò, 36
Porfiri, Ivana, 113, 127
Port Line, 74
Port Melbourne, 74
Port Sydney, 74
Portman, John, 105
Potamianos, George, 74, 139
Poulides, George, 133, 135
Premier Cruise Line, 131, 132, 135
Pride of Aloha, 151, 152
Pride of America, 151
Pride of Hawaii, 151, 152
Princesa Leopoldina, 129
Princess Carla, 68
Princess Cruises, 12, 68, 79, 96, 97, 109, 112, 120, 123, 125, 143, 146, 147, 148, 149, 155, 172, 173, 176, 183, 185
Princess Leopoldina, 59
Princess Patricia, 68
Prins Hamlet, 59
Prins Olav, 19, 21
Prinsendam (I), 69
Prinzessin Victoria Luise, 17, 18, 98
Pulitzer Finali, Gustavo, 35, 36, 42, 51
Qidissiyat Al Saddam, 98
Quantum of the Seas, 173
Queen Anna Maria, 77
Queen Elizabeth, 49, 156
Queen Elizabeth 2, 6, 49, 50, 67, 69, 71, 74, 77, 93, 108, 109, 119, 152, 154, 156
Queen Mary, 30, 49, 154
Queen Mary 2, 35, 152, 154
Queen of Bermuda, 67
Queen of Nassau, 53
Queen Victoria, 156
Quirconi, Bruno, 112
R Eight, 138, 139, 180
R One, 138
Radiance of the Seas, 147
Radisson Corporation, 101
Radisson Diamond, 101, 136
Radisson Seven Seas Cruises, 136
Raffaello, 40, 42, 83, 155
Rahne, Horst, 128
Rasa Sayang, 129
Rauma-Repola Shipbuilders, 100, 101
Reemtsma Tobacco A.G., 81
Regal Princess (I), 112, 113, 114, 120, 125
Regal Princess (II), 172
Regent Seven Seas Cruises, 180
Regina Maris, 51, 136
Reina Del Mar, 45
Renaissance Cruises, 99, 100, 138, 149, 175
Renaissance Four, 100
Renaissance One, 100
Renaissance Three, 100
Renaissance Two, 100
Revnes, Richard, 75
Rex, 155
Rhapsody of the Seas, 126
Rheinstahl Nordseewerke, 67
Riklis, Meshulam, 62
Rimutaka, 35
Robert Ley, 25, 26, 95
Rome, 13
Rotterdam (I), 32, 33, 40, 68, 92, 122, 123
Rotterdam (II), 122, 123, 139, 140
Rotterdam Lloyd, 36
Rotterdamsche Droggdok Mij, 32, 67
Rottet Studio, 184
Royal Caribbean, 6, 11, 59, 60, 61, 64, 67, 68, 69, 71, 75, 76, 77, 78, 79, 81, 86, 88, 89, 93, 97, 102, 103, 105, 106, 108, 112, 114, 117, 118, 119, 120, 121, 126, 127, 143, 144, 146, 147, 149, 150, 156, 160, 167, 168, 170, 173, 175, 176, 185
Royal Cruise Line, 75, 107
Royal Mail Lines, 17, 23, 26, 32, 45
Royal Olympia Cruises, 139
Royal Olympic Cruises, 139, 149
Royal Princess (I), 96, 97, 98, 102, 105, 106, 107, 109, 112
Royal Princess (II), 172, 185
Royal Viking Line, 11, 69, 71, 75, 77, 79, 81, 82, 98, 99, 100, 102, 103, 117, 183, 184
Royal Viking Queen, 100
Royal Viking Sea, 71, 183
Royal Viking Sky, 71, 77, 130, 183, 186
Royal Viking Star, 71, 183, 186
Royal Viking Sun, 102, 184
RTKL Associates, 163
Ryndam (I), 74
Ryndam (II), 122
S.A. Vaal, 78
Saarikangas, Martin, 117, 144, 146
Saga Cruises, 185
Sagafjord, 39, 40, 42, 45, 50, 68, 102, 119
Sally Albatross, 128
Sapphire Princess, 148, 176
Saturnia, 35, 36
Saxonia, 49, 72
Scandinavia, 93, 107
Scandinavian World Cruises, 93
Schalit, Ellie, 62, 64, 67, 76
Schettino, Captain Francesco, 171
Schichau Seebeckwerft, 99
Schindler, Siegfried, 128, 138
Sea Goddess Cruises, 99
Sea Goddess I, 99, 102, 119
Sea Goddess II, 99, 102, 119
Sea Princess, 125
Sea Venture, 67, 68, 88
Seabourn Cruises, 99, 180
Seabourn Pride, 99
Seabourn Spirit, 99
Seaward, 102, 119, 151
Seebeckwerft, Bremerhaven, 102
Sensation, 116, 117
Sensation,, 117
Serenade of the Seas, 147
Sessanlinjen, 86
Seven Seas Explorer, 180, 184
Shalom, 40
Shaw Savill, 76
Silja Europa, 131
Silja Serenade, 144
Silja Symphony, 144
Silver Cloud, 135
Silver Muse, 185, 186
Silver Shadow, 136
Silver Whisper, 136
Silver Wind, 135
Silversea Cruises, 135, 136, 180, 185
Sitmar Cruises, 72, 91, 92, 93, 108, 109, 112, 113, 114, 120, 125, 135
Sitmar Fair Majesty, 112
Sitmar Line, 72
Skaugen, I.M., 59, 103
Skyward, 59, 60, 61, 67
Smallpeice, Sir Basil, 49, 50
SMC Design, 184
Société des Forges et Chantiers de la Méditerranée, 39
Société Nouvelle des Ateliers et Chantiers du Havre, 100
Society Adventurer, 100
Society Advenurer, 101
SOLAS (Safety of Life At Sea), 55, 120, 160

Somerfin Lines, 55, 62
Song of America, 89, 91, 96, 97, 102, 103, 105, 106, 118
Song of Norway, 59, 61, 75, 77, 89
Sorvali, Heikki, 60, 95
Southward, 61
Sovereign of the Seas, 103, 105, 106, 108, 114, 118, 175
Speer, Albert, 26
Spirit of London, 61, 68, 132, 135
Splendor of the Seas, 126
St Rognvald, 17
St Sunniva, 17
Stamboulelis, Costis, 107
Star Aquarius, 130
Star Cruises, 129, 130, 131, 148, 149, 151, 170, 177, 178, 185
Star Lauro, 135
Star Pisces, 130
Star Princess, 112, 123, 149
Stardancer, 93
Starship Atlantic, 132
Starship Majestic, 132
Starship Oceanic, 132
Starship Royale, 131
Starward, 58, 59, 61, 64, 79, 88, 133
Statendam (I), 69, 122
Statendam (II), 122
Stella Polaris, 21, 23, 51, 69
Stella Solaris, 74, 75
Stephan, Edwin, 59, 60
Sterling, Jeffrey, 109, 125, 129
Stockholm, 29, 39, 95
Studio Bertolotii, 91
Studio DeJorio, 91, 112
STX Corporation, 155
Sulzer, 21, 29, 60, 88, 89, 97, 114, 122, 140
Summit, 147
Sun Line, 74
Sun Princess (I), 68, 96, 132
Sun Princess (II), 125
Sun Viking, 59, 61
Sunward, 57, 58, 59, 61, 62, 77
Sunward Car Ferries, 57
Sunward II, 77
Superstar Capricorn, 130
Superstar Europe, 130
Superstar Leo, 131, 148, 151
Superstar Virgo, 131, 148, 177
Swan Hellenic Cruises, 50, 69, 72, 74, 79, 136
Swan, Hunter & Wigham Richardson, 50, 69, 74, 79
Swedish American Line, 22, 29, 32, 33, 35, 39, 40, 42, 69, 76, 80, 95, 128
Swiss Cruise Lines Ltd, 55
Sylvania, 72
T. Mariotti Genoa, 112, 113, 135, 136, 180
Tahitien, 74
Tan Sri Lim Goh Tong, 129, 130, 131, 177
Technical Marine Planning, 62, 78, 86, 88, 114, 116, 121, 122, 140
Thackeray, William Makepeace, 13
Thomas Cook Ltd, 17
Thoresen & Bruusgaard A/S, 129
Tihany, Adam, 163, 179
Tillberg Design, 40, 68, 98, 102, 106, 123, 127, 131, 148, 151, 154, 170, 175, 178, 180
Trafalgar House Plc, 97, 102, 109, 119, 152
Transvaal Castle, 78
Travel Savings Ltd, 45
Troost, Paul Ludwig, 25, 26
Tropicale, 86, 88, 89, 91, 93, 114, 155
Trygge, Birger, 95
TUI A.G., 81, 175, 185
Union Naval de Levante, 119

The *AIDAdiva* and the *Costa Favolosa*, viewed from the deck of Viking Ocean Cruises' *Viking Star* at Warnemünde.

United States, 40, 83
United States Line, 10
Upper Clyde Shipbuilders, 49
US Freight Corporation, 59
Valmet Shipbuilders, 117
van den Steene, Cuno, 33
van Tienhoven, J.A., 33
Vectis, 13
Veendam, 69
Veitch, Colin, 143, 148, 150, 151
Ventura, 172
Venus, 69
Viceroy of India, 26, 29
Vickers Barrow-in-Furness, 79
Vickers-Armstrong Ltd, 49
Victoria, 33, 35, 74
Victoria and Albert, 19
Viking Ocean Cruises, 183, 184, 185
Viking Princess, 55
Viking River Cruises, 183, 184
Viking Sally, 80
Viking Sea, 184
Viking Sky, 184
Viking Star, 184

Viktor, Jacob, 62
Vision of the Seas, 126
Vistafjord, 50, 79, 82, 102, 119
Vlasov, Alexandre, 72, 108, 109, 112, 135
Volendam (I), 69
Volendam (II), 123
Voyager of the Seas, 146, 154, 160, 167
V-Ships, 135, 136
Vulcania, 36
Wall Street Crash, 1, 23
Wallace, Dan, 49
Wallenius, Olof, 59
Walt Disney Corporation, 131
Wandborg, Tage, 57, 58, 59, 61, 75, 83, 84, 85, 86, 95
Warneke, Horst, 81
Wärtsilä Shipbuilders, 1, 8, 59, 60, 69, 71, 79, 86, 89, 91, 95, 96, 97, 98, 99, 100, 101, 102, 103, 105, 107, 114, 116, 117, 126, 128, 138, 139, 142, 144, 147, 154, 155, 156, 160, 165, 168
Welton Becket Associates, 112
Weser Seebeckwerft, 58
Westerdam, 106, 107, 156
Whicker, Alan, 45

Wilhelm Gustloff, 25, 26, 29
Wilhelmsen, Anders, 59, 60, 144
Wilhelmsen, Gert, 144
Willem Ruys, 36, 72, 109
Wilson Butler Associates, 163, 168, 175
Wilstar, 60
Wilton Fijenoord, 35, 74
Wind Song, 100, 101
Wind Star, 100, 101
Windstar Cruises, 100, 101, 106
Windward, 118, 123, 151
Wirtz, Carel L., 33
World Dream, 186
Yaohua, 129
Yarmouth, 53, 55, 72
Yarmouth Castle, 55
Yarmouth Cruise Lines, 55, 59
Yran & Storbraaten, 102, 118, 138, 179
Yran, Petter, 85, 99, 102, 118, 138, 179
Zaandam, 123
Zenith, 107, 108, 126
Zoncada, Nino, 29, 32, 36, 74
Zuiderdam, 156

A pool deck scene at dusk on Compagnie de Ponant's L'Austral.

Photographic credits

Jonathan Boonzaier: 177; Philip Dawson: 86, 90; Miles Cowsill/Ferry Publications Library: 83, 153, 161; Meyer Werft: 8, 9, 174, 175, 177; Ann Haynes/Ann Haynes collection: 24, 171; Kalle Id: 136; Trevor Jones: 48, 81; Allan Jordan: 92; Andrew Kilk: 64, 77, 85, 86, 112, 114, 115, 141, 144; Mick Lindsay/Mick Lindsay collection: 30, 36, 46, 64, 71, 73, 97, 99, 108, 110, 124, 172; Mike Louagie: Cover, 1, 45, 6, 8, 10, 11, 128, 129, 130, 133, 134, 147, 156, 159, 162, 166, 167, 168, 169, 174, 175, 176, 181, 182, 183, 199-200, 207, 208; Pjotr Mahhonin/Wikicommons 184; Chris Owen/Wikicommons 165; Bruce Peter/Bruce Peter collection: 3, 7, 13, 14, 15, 16, 18, 19, 20, 21, 22, 24, 25, 26, 27, 28, 29, 31, 32, 33, 34, 37, 38, 41, 42, 43, 44, 45, 46, 47, 48, 49, 50, 52, 54, 55, 56, 57, 58, 60, 61, 62, 63, 65, 66, 70, 71, 72, 73, 74, 75, 76, 77, 78, 79, 80, 81, 82, 83, 84, 90, 91, 92, 93, 94, 96, 98, 99, 100, 101, 103, 104, 105, 106, 107, 108, 109, 110, 111, 112, 114, 115, 116, 118, 119, 120, 122, 124, 125, 126, 127, 131, 132, 135, 137, 138, 141, 142, 143, 144, 145, 146, 149, 150, 151, 152, 153, 158, 160, 162, 163, 169, 173, 178, 179, 180; Regent Seven Seas Cruises: 184, 185, 186, 187; Royal Caribbean: 6, 7, 167; Ian Schiffman: 37, 52, 90, 92, 96, 99, 120, 122, 128, 143, 148; ShipPax: 178; Marko Stampehl: 176, 193; David Trevor-Jones 124, 137; Rich Turnwald: 103, 117, 139.